Essentials of the English Legal System

Visit the *Essentials of The English Legal System, second edition* Companion Website at **www.pearsoned.co.uk/wheeler** to find valuable **student** learning material including:

- Updates to the book
- Advice on how to use law resources
- Progress tests and answers for you to test your understanding of key areas
- Links to relevant sites on the web

PEARSON

Education

We work with leading authors to develop the strongest
educational materials in law, bringing cutting-edge thinking
and best learning practice to a global market.

Under a range of well-known imprints, including Longman,
we craft high quality print and electronic publications
which help readers to understand and apply their content,
whether studying or at work.

To find out more about the complete range of our
publishing, please visit us on the World Wide Web at:
www.pearsoned.co.uk

Essentials of the English Legal System

SECOND EDITION

John Wheeler

Senior Lecturer in Law
Roehampton University

PEARSON
Longman

Harlow, England • London • New York • Boston • San Francisco • Toronto
Sydney • Tokyo • Singapore • Hong Kong • Seoul • Taipei • New Delhi
Cape Town • Madrid • Mexico City • Amsterdam • Munich • Paris • Milan

Pearson Education Limited

Edinburgh Gate
Harlow
Essex CM20 2JE
England

And Associated Companies throughout the world

Visit us on the World Wide Web at:
www.pearsoned.co.uk

First published 2002
Second edition published 2006

ISBN 1 405 81167 6

British Library Cataloguing-in-Publication Data
A catalogue record for this book is available from the British Library

Library of Congress Cataloging-in-Publication Data
A catalog record for this book is available from the Library of Congress

10 9 8 7 6 5 4 3 2 1
10 09 08 07 06

Typeset in 10.5 point in New Baskerville by 3
Printed in Great Britain by Henry Ling Ltd., at the Dorset Press, Dorchester, Dorset

The publisher's policy is to use paper manufactured from sustainable forests.

In memory of Sheila

Contents

5   The law-making process 2: Primary legislation   67

6   The law-making process 3: Subordinate legislation   86

11 Criminal justice system 2   207

PART FOUR APPENDICES   361

Appendix 1 Evolution of the common law and equity   363

Appendix 2 Human Rights Act 1998, Schedule 1   375

Appendix 3 Allocation questionnaire   381

Supporting resources

Visit **www.pearsoned.co.uk/wheeler** to find valuable online resources

Companion Website for students
- Updates to the book
- Advice on how to use law resources
- Progress tests and answers for you to test your understanding of key areas
- Links to relevant sites on the web

For instructors
- Updates to the book
- PowerPoint slides that can be downloaded and used as OHTs
- Seminar activities

For more information please contact your local Pearson Education sales representative or visit **www.pearsoned.co.uk/wheeler**

Guided Tour

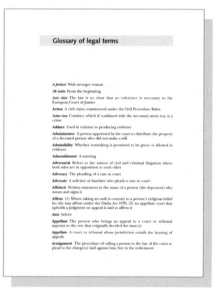

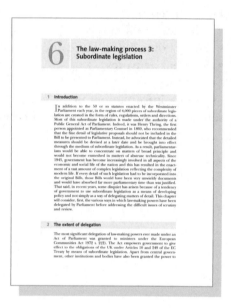

The glossary of legal terms at the start of the book can be referred to throughout your reading of the text to clarify unfamiliar terms.

The introduction to each chapter concisely describes the main themes and tensions explored, so you can assess the importance of the chapter at a specific point in your study.

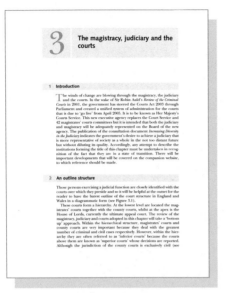

Real forms are included where relevant to help you to understand the actual processes of the legal system.

The summaries at the end of each chapter enable you to focus on what you should have learnt by the end of the chapter.

Each chapter ends with progress tests for you to test your understanding and track your progress. Answers to the tests are available on the companion website at www.pearsoned.co.uk/wheeler

Each chapter is supported by a further reading section, containing both article and book chapter references, and a list of useful websites, to direct your independent study to valuable printed and electronic resources. The web links are also available on the companion website at www.pearsoned.co.uk/wheeler, allowing you to link directly to relevant resources.

Preface to the second edition

Since the appearance of the first edition of this book, the pace of change has been relentless. At the time of submitting the manuscript for the second edition, it seemed that there would be an early general election. The election was delayed until May 2005 and the Constitutional Reform Bill received the Royal Assent on 24 March before the dissolution of Parliament. Although the ancient office of Lord Chancellor survives it is not in its traditional form. The judicial functions are transferred to the President of the Courts of England and Wales. The more recently created Cabinet position of Secretary of State for Constitutional Affairs will continue although the holder of that post will probably hold the ancient office of Lord Chancellor as well for the time being. The Lord Chancellor can now be appointed from either the House of Commons or the House of Lords. In the newly elected Parliament, there will almost certainly be legislation revamping the Tribunal system along the lines set out in the White Paper entitled *Transforming Public Services: Complaints, Redress and Tribunals*. All these developments will be covered on the companion website at the earliest opportunity.

As with the first edition, a number of people have helped me prepare this edition by reading the revised chapters and by providing constructive criticism. In particular I should like to thank my former colleague at Roehampton, Jane Offler, Bill McDowell and Eileen Thorogood. Although I have endeavoured to state the law as at 31 December 2004, I have taken the liberty of assuming that the provisions of the Criminal Justice Act 2003, referred to in the text, are operative on the basis that this is most likely to be the case by the time the book reaches the bookshops.

John Wheeler
New Malden, Surrey

Preface to the first edition

One of the problems that I have experienced in the year that it has taken to write this book has been ensuring that the content of the earlier chapters remains up to date. It has been necessary to revisit some completed chapters to include material that takes account of the most recent developments and excise the material that has become outdated. For example, Chapter 7 had to be revisited in order to include new material necessitated by the signing of the Treaty of Nice in February 2001 and revisited again to reflect the 'no' vote in the Irish referendum in June 2001. The creation of a companion website is intended to ensure that the text does not become dated too soon. Unfortunately, it has not been possible to incorporate the findings and recommendations of the report by Sir Andrew Leggatt on tribunals and the system of administrative justice as publication has been delayed. The same applies to the long awaited final report of Lord Justice Auld on the criminal courts which is likely to suggest far-reaching changes. I hope to be able to deal with these developments on the website in due course.

In writing the book, I have aimed to produce an accessible text that covers the topics forming an English legal system course of an LLB or similar undergraduate degree programme in reasonable depth. I hope that this book will provide the reader with a bridge to the more scholarly texts and articles that have been listed at the end of each chapter. These will enable the reader to develop his/her understanding of the various topics still further. They should also raise the reader's awarenes of the fact that not everything in law is as cut and dried as might at first appear and that there is scope for debate and controversy. It is this which makes law such a stimulating academic discipline.

A number of people have helped me in the course of writing the book by providing constructive criticism and suggestions. I should like to express my thanks to Pat Bond at Pearson Education, my colleague at Roehampton, Jane Offler, Dr Ann Brady, Jeff Kenner, Barry Sweeney and to one other who cannot be specifically acknowledged for his comments on Chapter 11. None of these is in any way responsible for any errors that might have crept into the text although it has been checked and double-checked. Special thanks are due to Eileen Thorogood and Mary Clare McNamara who did so much to improve the general readability of the text. I have endeavoured to state the law as at 30 June 2001.

John Wheeler
Roehampton

Acknowledgements

We are grateful to HMSO for permission to reproduce the following copyright material:

Figure 10.1 Metropolitan Police Service Bail Form 60B, © Crown copyright; Figure 13.1 The Court Service Claim Form from the County Court, © Crown copyright; Table 14.1 Employment Tribunal Statistics 2003–2004, from *ETS 2003–2004 Annual Report & Accounts*, DTI, www.ets.gov.uk/annualreport2004.pdf, © Crown copyright; Appendix 3 Allocation questionnaire, The Court Service website, © Crown copyright; extract from Halliday, J. (2003) *Quinquennial Review of the Law Commission*, Department of Constitutional Affairs, March 2003, www.dca.gov.uk, © Crown copyright; extract from Human Rights Act 1988 © Crown copyright.

Crown copyright material is reproduced with the permission of the Controller of HMSO and the Queen's Printer for Scotland.

Table of Cases

Table of Statutes

Table of Statutory Instruments

EU treaties and other international instruments

EU Secondary Legislation

Abbreviations

AC	Appeal Cases
ACAS	Advisory, Conciliation and Arbitration Service
ACI	Arbitration a Commercial Initiative
ADR	Alternative (Appropriate) dispute resolution
All ER	All England Reports
BVC	Bar Vocational Course
CBI	Confederation of British Industry
CEDR	Centre for Effective Dispute Resolution
CFI	Court of First Instance (Luxembourg)
Ch	Chancery Division of High Court
CIA	Chartered Institute of Arbitrators
CLS	Community Legal Service
CPE	Common Professional Examination
CPR	Civil Procedure Rules
CPS	Crown Prosecution Service
DPP	Director of Public Prosecutions
EAT	Employment Appeal Tribunal
ECHR	European Convention on Human Rights and Fundamental Freedoms
ECJ	European Court of Justice (Luxembourg)
ECSC	European Coal and Steel Community
EDM	Early day motion
EEC	European Economic Community (now the European Community)
ETS	Employment Tribunals Service
EU	European Union
ICC	International Chamber of Commerce
ICLREW	Incorporated Council for Law Reporting in England and Wales
ILO	International Labour Organisation
JSB	Judicial Studies Board
LPC	Legal Practice Course
LSC	Legal Services Commission
LSCC	Legal Services Complaints Commission
LSO	Legal Services Ombudsman
MEP	Member of the European Parliament
ODA	Overseas Development Administration
OSS	Office for the Supervision of Solicitors

PACE	Police and Criminal Evidence Act
PCC	Professional Conduct and Complaints Committee of the Bar
PDH	Plea and Directions Hearing
QB	Queen's Bench
TUC	Trades Union Congress

Glossary of legal terms

A fortiori With stronger reason

Ab initio From the beginning

Acte clair The law is so clear that no reference is necessary to the European Court of Justice

Action A civil claim commenced under the Civil Procedure Rules

Actus reus Conduct, which if combined with the necessary mens rea, is a crime

Adduce Used in relation to producing evidence

Administrator A person appointed by the court to distribute the property of a deceased person who did not make a will

Admissibility Whether something is permitted to be given or allowed in evidence

Admonishment A warning

Adversarial Refers to the nature of civil and criminal litigation where both sides are in opposition to each other

Advocacy The pleading of a case in court

Advocate A solicitor or barrister who pleads a case in court

Affidavit Written statement in the name of a person (the deponent) who swears and signs it

Affirm (1) Where taking an oath is contrary to a person's religious belief he/she may affirm under the Oaths Act 1878; (2) an appellate court that upholds a judgment on appeal is said to affirm it

Ante before

Appellant The person who brings an appeal to a court or tribunal superior to the one that originally decided the issue(s)

Appellate A court or tribunal whose jurisdiction entails the hearing of appeals

Arraignment The procedure of calling a person to the bar of the court to plead to the charge(s) laid against him/her in the indictment

Attorney General The principal legal adviser to the Crown who is appointed by letters patent – he/she is *ex officio* leader of the Bar and is a member of the government

Bail Effectively the release from custody of a person who has been arrested but where the release is conditional on complying with whatever conditions are imposed

Beneficiary A person for whose benefit a trust is created

Bona fide In good faith

Brief A document instructing a barrister to appear in court

Case law Law as contained in precedent – see *ratio decidendi*

Case stated A statement of a case prepared by a lower court for consideration by a higher court

Cause of action A recognised form of liability, for example a tort or breach of contract based on a set of facts

Caveats These may be notes of caution to be heeded

Chancery The term used to describe the office or court of the Chancellor

Chose in action Personal property that is intangible

Commissioner for oaths A person appointed by the Lord Chancellor to administer oaths or affirmations and take affidavits

Common law This term has a number of meanings but its primary meaning is in relation to rules developed in the old courts of common law. It is sometimes used to distinguish judge-made law from statute law

Conditional fee agreement An agreement between a solicitor and client whereby the solicitor takes the risk that if he/she does not win the case, no fee will be charged but an additional amount based on the normal fee will be recovered if the case is won

Contempt of court Failing to comply with an order of a superior court or an insult to the court or the judge(s)

Contentious proceedings In general, these are proceedings begun before a court or arbitrator in England and Wales

Contingency fee An agreement whereby a lawyer agrees to take a case on the basis that if the case is won the lawyer will receive a percentage of the damages

Contra Against, or to the contrary

Convention A form of treaty

Conyeyancing This is a process whereby the legal title to land is transferred from the seller to the purchaser

Coroner These are usually persons with medical qualifications who convene inquests to inquire into the circumstances surrounding the death of a person who has died in unusual or suspicious circumstances

Cur. adv. vult Indicating that the court took some time to formulate its judgment

Cross appeal This is where both parties to a case appeal

Custom Certain local customs have the force of law but they must have existed since 1189, be reasonable, certain and not contrary to any statute

Damages Financial compensation

Deed A document executed under seal and witnessed but which must also be delivered to the party in whose favour it is made

De minimis Insignificant or unimportant things

Director of Public Prosecutions Head of the Crown Prosecution Service but the office was originally created in 1879 for a person to carry on criminal proceedings under the supervision of the Attorney General

Disbar Expel a barrister from his/her Inn

Disbursements Payment of expenses usually incurred with litigation or some legal service

Divisional Court A court normally comprising two or three High Court judges

Empanelled Refers to the swearing in of jury

Enactment A general word denoting an Act of Parliament

Equity The rules and remedies developed in the Court of Chancery but it can be used in a general sense to mean fairness or natural justice

Et cetera Usually written etc. indicating and other thing of that kind

Ex gratia Literally, 'as a favour', but it is normally used in the context of payments made without legal liability to do so

Ex officio By virtue of office

Ex parte (often abbreviated ex p.) An application in legal proceedings made by an interested person who is not a party, or by one party in the absence of the other; or proceedings brought on behalf of one interested party

Exchequer Medieval court dealing with royal revenue but from 1550 it developed a common law jurisdiction

Executor/executrix A person appointed to carry out the directions of a deceased person contained in a will

Factual distinguishing Differentiating an earlier precedent on its facts from the case under consideration

Fiduciary duties Duties owed by a person placed in a position of trust and confidence

Fiscal To do with taxation

Frustration of contract Premature termination of a contract because performance has been rendered impossible or so different that it would be unreasonable to hold the parties bound

Garnisheee proceedings A procedure whereby a person's bank is ordered to pay over money to a court having deducted the amount from the person's account – they are now referred to as third party debt orders

Habeas corpus A court order for obtaining the release of a subject who has been imprisoned

Incorporated A legal process whereby a group of people are collectively recognised as being a separate legal person

Indemnity An undertaking to be responsible for the debts of another irrespective of whether the debtor is able to pay

Indictable offence An offence which, if committed by an adult, can only be tried in a Crown Court

Indictment The document containing the counts to which the accused must plead

Infra below

Injunction A court order requiring the person to whom it is addressed to refrain from doing some act (prohibitory) or to do an act (mandatory)

Inns of Court Voluntary unincorporated societies where persons used to study to become barristers

Inquest An inquiry held by a coroner

Insolvency The state of being unable to pay one's debts as and when they fall due

Interlocutory order An interim order pending the determination of the rights of the parties

Inter partes Between the parties

Ipse dixit An assertion unsupported by legal authority

Judicial Of judges

Judicial activism An allegation often made against the judges of the European Court of Justice that they seek to interpret EU law creatively rather than literally

Jurisdiction Literally, the legal authority to decide

Jurisprudence Can refer to legal theory but can also refer to the body of case law created by a particular court such as the European Court of Justice

Justiciable Capable of being decided by a court

Legacy A gift of personal property under a will

Legal person All natural persons are legal persons but so are entities known as corporations, the most numerous being companies

Legal title In effect, legal ownership

Letters patent Open letters containing public directions from the monarch bearing the Great Seal

Levy A form of tax

Litigant Someone who goes to law

Litigation Generally, resolving disputes through the courts

Lobby To petition for some cause

Locus standi The right to be heard before a court

Mandatory order An order addressed to a lower court or tribunal usually requiring it to rehear a case

Mens rea The necessary mental state required for the commission of certain crimes

Misfeasance Literally, wrongdoing

Mitigate Literally, to make less of

Monist Where international law and national law are part of the same legal order

Municipal A large unit of local government

Negligence A tort that enables a person who suffers loss or damage from the defendant's breach of duty of care to recover compensation provided the other conditions of liability are satisfied

Obiter dicta That part of the judgment that does not refer to the facts as established at trial

Ombudsman A Swedish word that refers to a person who deals with complaints from citizens against government departments or agencies

Per curiam By the court or in the opinion of the court

Per incuriam A decision of the court that is mistaken

Per se By itself

Personal representative An administrator or executor

Plaintiff The old term for a person who brings a legal action

Plenary session Literally, a session comprising all members of a legislature or a court hearing with all the judges of the court in attendance

Pluralism A form of society where the members of groups maintain their independence and traditions without encroachment by government

Post mortem After death

Precedent A decided case the ratio of which can be applied in future cases

Prerogative orders These are the quashing, mandatory and prohibiting orders that can be made by the Administrative Court

Prima facie On first impression

Privy Council (1) An appeal court that hears appeals from certain Commonwealth countries; (2) an advisory body to the monarch

Probate A certificate granted by a court indicating that the last will and testament of a deceased person has been proved

Proportionality Doing no more than is necessary to achieve an end or outcome

Protocol Part of a treaty usually found at the end

Pupillage A period of apprenticeship undertaken by barristers

Qua In the capacity of . . .

Quasi As if

Quorum The requisite number of persons who must be present before any business of an organisation may be transacted

Ratio decidendi The principle of law which is the basis of the decision that can be applied in subsequent cases; it is always linked to the facts of the earlier case

Re In the matter of . . .

Recognisances These are the obligations entered into to secure the performance of an act, usually the appearance of another in court to stand trial

Rectification An equitable remedy that puts right an error in a document

Remission Part of a person's prison sentence that is not served

Remit (1) To send a case back to the court that originally heard it; (2)

'statutory remit' meaning what an organisation or body was established to do

Repeal The nullifying of a statute or part of a statute

Res judicata The principle that a matter, having been adjudicated on by a competent court, may not be reopened subsequently or challenged

Rescission An equitable remedy that ends a contract

Respondent The party that responds to an appeal that is brought

Retrospective effect Having effect from a date earlier than the date of the measure itself

Sed But

Sine die Indefinitely

Specific performance An equitable remedy requiring the person to whom it is addressed to perform that which was promised in a contract

Standing order An order passed by the House of Commons intended to speed the progress of business

Statute This term is used to refer to an Act of Parliament

Statutory instrument A form of subordinate legislation

Subpoena A court order requiring a person to come before the court at a certain place and time subject to a penalty if he/she does not

Summons An order issued by magistrates requiring attendance at court

Sureties Persons who enter into recognisances to secure the appearance of another in court

Tenure A feudal land holding or can be used more generally to signify a period that an office is held

Tort A civil wrong that is neither a breach of contract nor a breach of trust

Tortious Conduct that involves committing a tort

Treaty A legally binding agreement between two states

Trustee A person who holds the legal title to some right or property not for his/her benefit but for the benefit of others

Ultra vires Literally, 'beyond the powers of ...' and an act which so designated has no legal effect

Vested rights Rights owned by a person in whom they are vested

Vicarious liability A substitution of liability whereby a person becomes liable (in certain circumstances) for the acts of another where there is a special relationship such as employer/employee

Vis à vis (French) opposite to, or face to face

Viz Abbreviation for *vide licet* meaning that is to say

Warrant of execution A court order entitling a bailiff to seize property

Wingers Persons who sit on a tribunal to assist the chairperson

Writ A written order or warrant – prior to the Civil Procedure Rules a writ was an order issued in the name of the sovereign to commence an action before a court

1 Introduction

The UK has two distinct legal systems in that Scotland, although it is an integral part of the UK, has its own system of law and legal institutions. English law, however, applies throughout the remainder of the UK. You have chosen to study the English legal system at a particularly exciting time because it is in the throes of a process of dynamic change. This book has been written specifically to explain how the various elements that combine to make up the legal system of England and Wales relate to each other and function at a time of unprecedented innovation. On 12 June 2003 the government announced that it intended to abolish the ancient office of Lord Chancellor with its diverse roles within the legal system and government on the retirement of Lord Irvine. The Lord Chancellor's Department (whose annual budget was over £3 bn) was promptly renamed the Department for Constitutional Affairs. By mid December 2004 the government had changed its mind and has decided to retain this ancient office albeit probably in a revised form. For the time being the functions of the Lord Chancellor are being discharged by the Secretary of State for Constitutional Affairs, Lord Falconer. In order to give effect to these and other proposals, such as the eventual scrapping of the House of Lords as the ultimate appeal court and its replacement with a new Supreme Court together with the creation of a completely independent Judicial Appointment Commission, the government introduced the Constitutional Reform Bill into Parliament. At the time of submission of the manuscript for the second edition, the Bill had reached its report stage in the House of Lords' chamber. The Bill will be referred to as and when appropriate in this text. As you will have seen from the Contents page, the book is divided into four parts.

■ Part One

The objective of Part One is to provide you with an insight into the legal profession and its regulation. The Courts and Legal Services Act 1990 brought to an end the monopoly that barristers enjoyed to appear as advocates in the superior courts. The government wished to introduce greater competition into the provision of legal services with a view to reducing costs by abolishing what it perceived as restrictive practices. A large number of solicitors have now acquired 'rights of audience' in the superior civil and criminal courts in order to represent their clients. The Access to Justice Act 1999 has since streamlined the procedure whereby the Law Society and other professional bodies are able to grant rights of audience to their members. These developments and others continue to impact on the organisation and structure of the legal profession. As a result of the Clementi Report published in December 2004 it seems that the profession's long-standing system of self-regulation may soon be brought to an end. Another objective of Part One is to examine the courts, the magistracy and judiciary. The 'winds of change' are blowing through the ranks of the judiciary as may be seen from the consultation document published by the Department for Constitutional Affairs in October 2004 entitled *Increasing Diversity in the Judiciary*. The Courts and Legal Services Act 1990 not only changed the rules relating to rights of audience in the superior courts, but also changed the rules governing the eligibility for judicial appointments so that solicitors could be appointed. Solicitors are now entering the lower ranks of the judiciary in increasing numbers and those who show flair are being promoted. Women are still under-represented among the ranks of the senior judiciary, as are members of ethnic minorities, but it is clear from the consultation document that the government intends to take steps to make the judiciary more representative of society as a whole whilst at the same time maintaining its high calibre and international reputation.

■ Part Two

Part Two focuses on the law-making processes that are either embedded in, or impact directly on, the English legal system. This entails an examination of the judicial contribution to the law-making process through the creation of case law and development of precedent. Although case law is an important source of law, legislation is the dominant form of law-making in the English legal system and so the legislative process comes under scrutiny. There is also a consideration of the concept and extent of Parliamentary sovereignty. European Union law has been firmly implanted in the English legal system by the European Communities Act 1972. Certain Treaty Articles and regulations form part of the law of England and Wales as a result of the concept of 'direct effect'. The concept of 'direct effect', devised by the Court of Justice in Luxembourg, means that the English and Welsh courts routinely apply directly applicable EU law in appropriate cases. When they encounter difficulties of interpretation, they continue to make applications to Luxembourg. As the process of European integration proceeds apace, government is required to respond to the directives that are adopted at the European level by implementing them, mainly through the medium of primary or subordinate legislation. The creation of the concept of state liability by the Court of Justice means that the UK government can be sued by its own citizens in their national courts over its failure to implement directives on time where these confer rights on them. Moreover, it is clear that the state itself can be held liable in damages for any 'serious breach' of EU law by those affected whether they are nationals or not. Part Two of the book concludes with an examination of the problems that can arise in interpreting legislation, whether of national or European origin.

Part Three

Part Three commences with a consideration of the funding of legal advice and representation. The Access to Justice Act 1999 created the Legal Services Commission to replace the Legal Aid Board. The LSC, which was inaugurated in April 2000, has overall responsibility for its sub-entities: the Community Legal Service and the Criminal Defence Service. The former was responsible for creating the Community Legal Service which has developed local 'partnerships' to coordinate legal services at a local level. The latter launched its Public Defender Service in May 2001 which employs lawyers to provide advice to those arrested by the police and representation for accused persons appearing in court. An investigation of the new arrangements for the provision of legal services paves the way for a survey of key aspects of the criminal justice system. The criminal justice system is a major sub-system of the English legal system. Widespread deviant behaviour obviously poses a serious threat to any civilised society. It is the role of the criminal justice system to deal effectively with this by ensuring that those who have engaged in criminal activity are apprehended, punished and, if possible, reformed and rehabilitated. There have been major developments in the criminal justice system, some of which have been implemented already but others are due for implementation in the near future. Chapters 10 and 11 have been completely written on the basis that all these changes are in force because by the time the book reaches the bookshelves this is likely to be the case. Further legislation impacting on the criminal justice system was highlighted in the Queen's speech in November 2004 and this will be covered on the companion website to this text in due course. Disputes between individuals and organisations need to be settled justly but it is advantageous to both sides if they can also be settled quickly and cheaply. Solicitors and barristers who engage in civil litigation on behalf of clients have been required to adjust to the new climate in which civil litigation is now conducted under the Civil Procedure Rules that were introduced in April 1999. The rules, made under the Civil Procedure Act 1997, were the government's response to Lord Woolf's report *Access to Justice* in which he heavily criticised the old culture of civil litigation which was renowned for its delay and expense. The new regime has resulted in a huge reduction in delays. This is directly attributable to the new system of judicial case management and cost penalties. It is not clear, however, whether the costs of litigation have been reduced significantly. Parties are now actively encouraged to settle their differences at an early stage through the medium of the Pre-action Protocol and this innovation seems to have produced a higher rate of early settlements. The rules also encourage parties in dispute to consider alternatives to litigation such as mediation and conciliation. Lawyers are now seeking to qualify as mediators in ever greater numbers under schemes operated by bodies such as the Centre for Dispute Resolution as they increasingly perceive mediation and conciliation as income-generating activities. Arbitration, a long-established system of dispute resolution, was completely revamped under the Arbitration Act 1996 to encourage parties in dispute to make greater use of it. In consequence, a number of new arbitration schemes have been launched by lawyers. It may be that in the near future there will actually be a decline in court-based dispute resolution as ADR becomes more widely known and accepted as a realistic alternative. Although most disputes concern private law rights and obligations, a significant number come within the province of 'public law' because they take the form of grievances with government and other public bodies. Historically, the judges have considered it to be part of their role to protect individuals and groups in society against the abuse of power by local and national government through the process of judicial review. In recent years, this jurisdiction has expanded beyond all expectations. The Administrative Court is now firmly established within the High Court structure to deal exclusively with public and administrative law cases as recommended by the Bowman Committee. Part Three concludes with a consideration of the need for ongoing law reform and focuses on the role of the Law Commission.

Part Four

This comprises two Appendices. Appendix 1 is really a 'freestanding' chapter on the historical development of the English legal system since the earliest beginnings. The material has been placed in this part of the book so that those who are not very interested in history can read the main text without having to wade through pages of history. However, it is helpful for readers to have an historical perspective, especially those who are intending to pursue a legal career. Appendix 2 comprises the text of Schedule 1 to the Human Rights Act 1998.

Human Rights Act 1998

The Human Rights Act 1998 is a recurring theme throughout the book. The Act has been sending tremors through the entire legal system since October 2000 when the rights available under the European Convention of Human Rights and Fundamental Freedoms became available in national law. The Act marks a fundamental shift from a legal system in which the civil and political rights of individuals were largely 'residual' to one where individuals now enjoy positive rights. Irrespective of whether it was enacted before or since October 2000, all legislation is now to be interpreted, in so far as it is possible to do so, in a way that is compatible with the Convention rights contained in Schedule 1 to the Act. Since it is unlawful for a public authority to act in a way that is incompatible with a Convention right (unless it is required to do so by primary legislation), there is now far greater scope for challenging the actions of government by way of claims for judicial review. The Act also continues to make a great impact in the sphere of criminal justice and there are references to Convention rights in Chapters 10 and 11. There is an obvious link between the fundamental rights recognised by the European Court of Justice as considered in Chapter 7 and the Convention rights considered in Chapter 8. Many commentators now speak of the Convention rights being 'incorporated' into national law: the use of the word 'incorporated' as a convenient form of 'shorthand' is acceptable but it must be remembered that the Convention is not part of UK law in the same way that EU law is part of UK law. The English and Welsh courts are obliged to suspend (and have suspended) any UK Act of Parliament (or part thereof) that conflicts with EU law. For example, the Anti-terrorism, Crime and Security Act 2001 has proved to be a very controversial piece of legislation because it permits foreign nationals to be held in indefinite detention without charge on the basis of a certificate issued by the Secretary of State for the Home Department under s. 21. Although the House of Lords in *A (FC) and others* v *Secretary of State for the Home Department* declared on 16 December 2004 that the legislation was 'incompatible' with the Convention rights contained in Schedule 1, this did not operate to suspend the operation of the Act which, at the time of writing, remains in force. Nor did it result in the immediate release of those detained.

The companion website

When considering the many changes that have occurred since the first edition of this book appeared in 2002, it seems on reflection that the companion website has to be regarded as an integral part of the book that will keep the reader abreast of future developments. This is a great innovation by Pearson Education. A new set of web pages should be in place by the end of September 2005 and it is hoped that the reader will refer to them at www.pearsoned.co.uk/wheeler. This companion website will contain: *student resources* comprising updates, indicative answers to progress tests, pdfs of the skills section and weblinks; and *lecturer resources* comprising PowerPoint slides and seminar activities. Feedback is always welcome: please e-mail your comments or observations to J.Wheeler@roehampton.ac.uk.

Part 1

The personnel of the law

2   The changing legal profession

1   Introduction

An efficient legal system can only exist if there is a body of highly trained professional men and women who are able to undertake a wide range of varied roles. The distinctive feature of the legal profession in England and Wales is its division into two branches each of which is represented by its own professional body: solicitors represented by the Law Society and the Bar Council representing barristers. Even today, anyone considering a legal career must still decide at the outset whether to qualify as a solicitor or as a barrister despite the fact that the rigid distinctions between the roles of these two branches of the profession are becoming increasingly blurred. In the past, those persons who wished to have the option of undertaking a wide variety of legal work and were not particularly attracted by advocacy in the higher courts would decide to train and qualify as solicitors by taking the examinations prescribed by the Law Society of England and Wales. The Law Society originated in 1845 and is the organisation which sets the educational and professional standards for solicitors. Those persons who were particularly attracted by a career in advocacy in the higher courts and who aspired to a judicial appointment opted to train and qualify as barristers. Young entrants to the legal profession nowadays who believe that they have what it takes to become successful advocates in the higher courts still choose the barristers' side of the profession by taking the qualifying examinations prescribed by the Council for Legal Education. This chapter focuses initially on solicitors before examining the emerging profession of legal executive. The profession of barrister will then be considered which is the longest established and, some would argue, the most prestigious. This chapter is also the most apt place to deal with the disciplinary framework for the profession including the offices of the Legal Services Ombudsman and Legal Services Commissioner.

2   Solicitors

The statistical report of the Law Society for 2003 indicates that there were 116,110 solicitors in England and Wales on the official Roll. Approximately

59 per cent of this total were men, whilst 41 per cent were women; but in terms of new entrants to the profession, women now outnumber men. The number of solicitors from ethnic minorities has grown over the years and in 2003 amounted to 17 per cent of the profession. In order to act in the capacity of a solicitor it is necessary to hold a current practising certificate issued by the Law Society, which has to be renewed annually. Although there were 116,110 names on the Roll, only 92,752 solicitors held practising certificates, 40 per cent of whom were women. However, of the 92,752 with practising certificates, only 72,545 were actually engaged in private practice offering legal services to businesses and individuals. A significant number were employed in the government legal service, the Crown Prosecution Service and by local authorities. Some were employed in the legal departments of large corporations.

In 2003 approximately 8.5 per cent of solicitors in private practice were 'sole practitioners' and 45 per cent of solicitors' firms were 'sole practices', which obviously limits the range of services that they can offer. Much of the fee income of these practices will typically be derived from conveyancing (transferring the ownership of land) and from probate work (taking charge of and then distributing the assets of recently deceased persons). A few offer specialist advocacy services in particular branches of the law. Most established solicitors, however, choose to form partnerships with other solicitors and become equity partners. Equity partners contribute to the capital of the firm and share in its annual profits. Recently qualified solicitors tend to work as salaried employees, often for larger partnerships, in the capacity of 'assistant solicitors' until such time as they are able to make the move to equity partner there or elsewhere. In some of the large international law firms headquartered in central London, some solicitors have the hybrid status of being 'salaried partners' as distinct from equity partners but most solicitors employed there are salaried employees.

Nowadays, the solicitors' branch of the profession is a highly differentiated one in which there were 9,198 firms of various sizes in 2003. The sole practitioner has already been referred to and survives despite a highly competitive market for legal services. Competitive and other pressures oblige most solicitors to work together in partnership firms usually comprising up to four partners who, between them, will offer a wider range of legal services to the residents and business community where their offices are located. Approximately 85 per cent of firms in 2003 had four or fewer partners. Some of these local firms specialise in legal aid work although such work is not very profitable. Nevertheless, such firms continue to attract staff and those members of the profession who wish to make a specific social commitment in the areas of immigration, family law and welfare law. Other local firms will be more profit orientated and tend to offer services such as advocacy, drafting of documents (contracts of various types and wills), the formation of partnerships and companies, conveyancing, probate services, as well as the provision of legal advice (but not to legally aided clients). They may also deal with the preparatory stages of higher level civil litigation entailing the commencement of proceedings (for which see Chapter 12) and the interviewing of witnesses. The next step up in scale is the larger partnership comprising upwards of 20 partners, which will have offices in more than one town or city. Such firms are likely to seek and attract the more lucrative commercial work in the larger commercial centres. The huge international law firms, at the far end of the spectrum, have offices in the City of London, New York, Paris and other major capital cities. In addition to having very impressive offices in which to accommodate their employees and partners, they also have vast revenues. The names of the top ten international law firms frequently appear in the serious press and in rank order they are as follows:

1 Clifford Chance
2 Skadden, Arps, Slate Meagher & Flom
3 Baker & McKenzie
4 Freshfields Bruckhaus Derringer
5 Linklaters
6 DLA, Piper Rudnick, Gray Cary
7 Jones & Day
8 Allen & Overy
9 Latham & Watkins
10 Sidley, Austin, Brown & Wood

As indicated, Clifford Chance is the largest international firm, which has fee income approaching £1bn. These firms tend to specialise in offering legal services to multinational corporations and are very often closely involved with their clients, advising on the legal aspects of mergers and acquisitions or assisting directors with the defence of hostile take-over bids. At this level there is competition between firms to recruit the best qualified graduates every year and these firms offer a challenging career to those young men and women seeking to enter the profession, arguably, at its most demanding level. Female solicitors in such firms, whether at partner level or not, are able to take career breaks and are increasingly able to work flexibly to fit their work commitments around their family commitments albeit, often, at some cost.

3 Qualifying as a solicitor

The quickest way to qualify as a solicitor is still to study law at a university. Provided the course covers the core subjects prescribed for the Common Professional Examination (CPE) or Postgraduate Diploma in Law and is approved by the Law Society the graduate can, on obtaining student membership of the Law Society, undertake the Legal Practice Course (LPC). Litigation and advocacy skills are now a compulsory part of the generic LPC. In 2000 eight international firms based in the City of London broke ranks and established a 'City LPC' and one has since had its plans approved to offer a 'firm specific LPC' in 2006. The Legal Services Commission (see Chapter 9) and the College of Law are collaborating on the devising of an LPC course specifically for those intending to become 'legal aid solicitors'.

Having passed all the examinations and assessments prescribed for the LPC it is then necessary to obtain a training contract with an established firm of solicitors or alternatively with certain approved agencies of central or local government or the Crown Prosecution Service. This is vital in the process of qualifying but every year there are about 3,000 more young people searching for training contracts than there are contracts available, although the number of contracts on offer continues to increase annually. Regrettably, this means that those who have been unable to secure a training contract, even though they have successfully completed the LPC, will not be able to qualify as solicitors.

All trainees must now undertake the Professional Skills Course during their training contract in which the advocacy skills module is a compulsory part. After two years have been spent as a trainee with an established firm of solicitors or some other agency approved by the Law Society, the former trainee must apply to have his/her name entered on the Roll of solicitors maintained by the Law Society. This confers the status of being an admitted solicitor. Only at this point does the former trainee become fully qualified. Even though he/she has attained the status of qualified solicitor, he/she must continue to attend seminars or courses for three years after qualifying as part of the Law Society's Continuing Education Scheme. For a solicitor working at least 32 hours a week, it will be necessary to complete 16 hours of continuing professional development (CPD) annually.

For someone who does not study law at university it is necessary to take a one-year preparatory course at a university or at some other approved centre before being eligible to enrol on the Legal Practice Course. This preparatory course can be taken as the CPE or as a Postgraduate Diploma in Law, referred to above, and some City firms offer sponsorship to highly qualified graduates. The core subjects are: law of obligations I (contract); law of obligations II (torts); foundations of the criminal law; foundations of equity and the law of trusts; foundations of the law of the EU; foundations of property law; and foundations of public law. Satisfactory completion of this course does not, however, guarantee a place on the Legal Practice Course, which is another hurdle to be surmounted involving even greater expense. Increasingly, a number of nurses, doctors and teachers who decide upon a mid-life career change are taking this route to qualification.

4   Courts and Legal Services Act 1990

Prior to 1990, those solicitors who wished to develop advocacy skills in the higher courts had to apply to have their names deleted from the Roll of Solicitors so that they could become barristers, but this is no longer necessary. The Courts and Legal Services Act 1990 made fundamental changes in the legal profession reflecting the desire of the government of the day to introduce greater competition into the provision of legal services. One of its key provisions put an end to the monopoly that barristers had long enjoyed in relation to advocacy in the superior courts because the Law Society was empowered to grant its members rights of audience under conditions specified in regulations made in 1992 and subsequently in 1998. By the end of July 1998 the Law Society had granted rights of audience to 651 solicitors in England and Wales to appear in the superior courts, and by January 2004 this total had reached nearly 2,000. A significant number of those who had been granted rights of audience in the higher courts in the early years were former barristers who had transferred to the solicitors' branch of the profession but nowadays more solicitors are being encouraged to apply. The Access to Justice Act 1999 s. 36 substituted a new s. 31 into the Courts and Legal Services Act 1990, which provides that:

> Every solicitor shall be deemed to have been granted by the Law Society (a) a right of audience before every court in relation to all proceedings (exercisable in accordance with the qualification regulations and rules of conduct of the Law Society approved for the purposes of s. 27 in relation to the right); and (b) a right to conduct litigation in relation to every court and all proceedings (exercisable in accordance with the qualification regulations and rules of conduct of the Law Society approved for the purposes of s. 28 in relation to the right).

The Council of the Law Society was empowered to make the Higher Courts Qualification Regulations 2000 (to replace its previous regulations). These came into effect from 1 October 2000. Regulation 2(3) makes it clear that no solicitor is entitled to exercise any right of audience (other than those that could be exercised before 7 December 1989) unless he/she holds a Higher Courts Advocacy Qualification granted under these or the earlier regulations entitling him/her to exercise that right of audience. The Law Society can grant one of three qualifications to solicitors who meet the necessary requirements as follows:

1 Higher Courts (All Proceedings) Qualification, which entitles the solicitor to exercise rights of audience in all proceedings in the higher civil and criminal courts.
2 Higher Courts (Civil Proceedings) Qualification, which entitles the solicitor to exercise rights of audience in all civil proceedings in the higher courts including judicial review in any court arising from any criminal cause.
3 Higher Courts (Criminal Proceedings) Qualification, which entitles the solicitor to exercise rights of audience in all criminal proceedings in the higher courts including judicial review proceedings in any court arising out of any criminal cause.

New entrants to the profession must satisfy the Law Society that they have successfully undertaken a training course that includes assessment in evidence, procedure and ethics applicable to the higher civil and/or criminal courts. They must also successfully undertake training and assess-ment in advocacy skills applicable to these higher courts. In addition, the Law Society requires evidence of one year's experience of litigation and advocacy and at least six months of this must have been gained after admission to the Roll. This will be evidenced by a portfolio that must be attested by another experienced solicitor who has been appointed as mentor. Any solicitor may opt to gain a Higher Courts Qualification at any stage in his/her career by this route, which is referred to as the Development Route. For solicitors who have already gained extensive experience of litigation there is an opportunity to gain a Higher Courts Qualification by the Accreditation Route or by the Exemption Route to which special requirements apply. All solicitor advocates are required by Regulation 13 to undertake at least five hours' continuing professional development a year relating to the provision of advocacy services in the higher courts. The Law Society anticipates that the number of solicitor advocates will continue to grow steadily in the years ahead.

5 Legal executives – an emerging profession

Not all of the staff working in a solicitor's practice are fully qualified solic-itors. This is quite obviously true of the reception and secretarial staff but there will also be other staff, apart from trainee solicitors, who are engaged in legal work under the supervision of a qualified solicitor. These people are highly likely to be members of the Institute of Legal Executives, a professional body formed in 1963, but not one enjoying the same status and prestige as the Law Society. The total membership is cur-rently over 22,000 including trainees but it is only fellows of the Institute who are permitted to call themselves 'legal executives'. The Institute pre-scribes a course of study that enables those who join it to become qualified members and, subsequently, fellows. Members are those who have passed the Level 3 (national qualification framework) Professional Diploma in Law and the Level 4 Professional Higher Diploma. In addition, members are normally under the age of 25 but they will have completed four years' qualifying employment in a solicitor's practice or some other form of approved supervised training. In order to become a fellow it is necessary to have completed the Level 3 and Level 4 Diplomas and be over the age of 25 with a total of five years' qualifying employment.

A number of legal executives specialise in conveyancing or in the drafting of wills or in the administration of the affairs of those deceased persons who have made wills. Fellows are now able to conclude compro-mise agreements arsing from the settlement of employment-related disputes. For many years some legal executives have been undertaking advocacy of a low-level and limited nature, mainly appearing before tri-bunals and before judges in chambers. The Courts and Legal Services Act 1990 expanded the opportunities for persons other than barristers to undertake advocacy. It is expressly provided in s. 27 that an 'authorised body' may grant rights of audience to their members and the Access to Justice Act 1999 s. 40(2) specifies that the Institute is an 'authorised body'. Only fellows of the Institute working under the supervision of solicitors are eligible to apply for the necessary training to be accorded rights of audience by the Institute's Rights of Audience Committee. Three separate certificates are available from the Committee for the three areas in which legal executives may function as advocates. These are:

(a) Civil Proceedings Certificate
(b) Matrimonial Proceedings Certificate
(c) Coroners Proceedings Certificate.

A candidate making an application for (a) or (b) above must have completed 36 hours of directed private study on the rules of evidence and pre-trial procedure, after which it is necessary to pass a three-hour written examination. In addition, it is necessary to satisfactorily complete the advocacy skills programme. This is in two parts, comprising 18 hours of study and the satisfactory completion of a two-hour test, after which it is necessary to undergo 18 hours of face-to-face training that incorporates an assessment of advocacy skills. Candidates wishing to obtain a Coroners Proceedings Certificate must undertake a programme of eight hours' tuition prior to taking 12 hours of examinations. All applications for rights of audience must be accompanied by evidence of some previous advocacy experience. The minimum necessary is 20 appearances a year during the preceding two years either before a judge in chambers or before tribunals, including appearances on contested matters.

The Civil Proceedings Certificate entitles the legal executive advocate to appear in the county court on all matters within the normal jurisdiction of a district judge or to appear in a magistrates' court in relation to all matters originating by complaint or application. The Certificate will also entitle the legal executive advocate to appear before any tribunal that is under the supervision of the Council on Tribunals.

The Family Proceedings Certificate enables him/her to appear as an advocate before magistrates in cases that come before the Family Proceedings Court and in certain family proceedings before a district judge in the county court. All advocacy certificates have to be renewed annually by the Institute's Rights of Audience Committee who will require evidence of at least eight hours of continuing professional development, sight of a logbook showing details of the advocacy experience gained and a statement from the employer of the rights of audience to be exercised during the next year. In March 2000 the Institute announced that the first six 'legal executive advocates' had qualified under the Courts and Legal Services Act 1990 and now there are over 20. Members of the Institute may also become Commissioners for Oaths and are therefore able to attest to swearing of legal documents that require this degree of formality.

Each year between 100 and 150 qualified members of the Institute opt to qualify as solicitors. Qualified members and fellows can be exempted from the CPE or Postgraduate Diploma in Law provided that they have completed the necessary papers in a four-year block within seven years of gaining their membership qualification. Fellows of the Institute will be exempted from the normal two-year training contract that trainee solicitors must undertake before being admitted as solicitors so that it has become an alternative mode of entry into the solicitors' branch of the profession for some. Fiona Bawdon, in an article entitled 'Second class status' published in the *New Law Journal* on 17 October 1997, suggested that former legal executives who took the initiative to qualify as solicitors met with discrimination from some solicitor colleagues. Sadly this seemed to be attributable to 'academic snobbery' on the part of graduate solicitors who tended to look down on non-graduates. However, since September 2002 qualified members and fellows of the Institute are able to achieve an LLB (Honours) degree as a result of collaboration between the Institute and the University of East London. Qualifying first as a legal executive is increasingly being viewed as an alternative method of qualifying as a solicitor without accumulating the vast amount of student debt that most young people are now required to incur in order to qualify, whilst at the same time gaining valuable experience.

6   Complaints against solicitors

The system for dealing with complaints against lawyers in England and Wales operates in two stages. In the first instance there is self-regulation by the profession and then a referral to the Legal Services Ombudsman (see **15**) if the complainant is dissatisfied with the way in which the complaint has been handled by the profession. The Solicitors' Costs Information and Client Care Code – drawn up by the Council of the Law Society – requires solicitors in private practice to operate a complaints handling procedure. The Code stipulates that every firm must:

(a) ensure that the client is informed of the name of the person in the practice to contact regarding any problem(s) with the service provided,

(b) have a written complaints procedure and ensure that complaints are handled in accordance with it, and

(c) ensure that the client is given a copy of the complaints procedure on request.

In August 2000, the Office for the Supervision of Solicitors distributed 40,000 copies of a guide to solicitors in private practice in England and Wales entitled 'Handling Complaints Effectively'. The guide gives advice on establishing a good in-house complaints procedure, including an appeals stage. Clients who have not been able to obtain satisfaction under the Code can then complain to the Office for the Supervision of Solicitors.

7 Office for the Supervision of Solicitors

In September 1996 the Law Society established the Office for the Supervision of Solicitors (OSS) to investigate complaints against solicitors. The OSS also assumed responsibility for the operation of the Solicitors' Compensation Fund which had been established to provide compensation to clients in appropriate cases. The OSS was under-resourced from the outset and was hard pressed to deal with the rising annual number of complaints against solicitors. Following a critical report prepared by the management consultants Ernst & Young, the Law Society increased the resources available to the OSS but this has not stemmed the tide of criticism levelled at the OSS. In the face of what the government perceived to be the inertia of the Law Society, the Secretary of State for Constitutional Affairs commissioned a review of legal services under Sir David Clementi. Sir David's main recommendations are contained in his report, *Review of the Regulatory Framework for Legal Services in England and Wales*, published in December 2004. These include the creation of a new regulator with significant powers under what has become known as 'model B+'. He advocates the separation of the representative and regulatory functions of both professional bodies. The regulation entrusted to both professional bodies in future would be subject to the oversight of the new regulator. Precisely how these recommendations will be implemented by government remains to be seen and will be covered on the companion website in the near future. The government will produce a White Paper in 2005 and this too will be covered on the companion website.

8 Professional discipline

Practising solicitors are regarded as officers of the Supreme Court subject to the direct discipline of the judges, but in practice it is the Law Society that is responsible for supervising its members in private practice and it has extensive powers to intervene in the functioning of any solicitor's practice. Solicitors who are considered to have been involved in some form of professional misconduct may be required to appear before the Solicitors' Disciplinary Tribunal, which was established under the Solicitors Act 1974. The tribunal is completely independent of the Law Society as its members are appointed by the Master of the Rolls (the senior judge of the civil division of the Court of Appeal) from among solicitors who have at least 10 years' post-qualifying experience. Laypersons are also appointed so that each tribunal panel comprises two solicitors and a layperson. At the close of its proceedings, a tribunal panel can make whatever order it sees fit. For example, it may remove the solicitor's name from the official Roll, suspend him/her from practising for a time, order a penalty not exceeding £5,000 and make an order for costs and expenses against him/her. The tribunal itself is obliged to make an annual report to the Lord Chancellor and this must be published for distribution to interested members of the public.

9   Barristers

The word 'barrister' seems to have entered the language around the middle of the fifteenth century to refer to members of the Inns of Court. From the fourteenth century onwards, young men who wished to undertake the programme of vocational training that would enable them to practise as advocates in the courts of common law, would enrol at these institutions. Today the 'Bar', as practising barristers are collectively known, is a thoroughly modern profession, albeit one with a distinguished tradition. Barristers practising as advocates are not permitted to form partnerships but must operate as self-employed, independent professionals. A cluster of barristers will usually join together to occupy a suite of offices that are referred to as 'chambers'. A set of chambers will usually be presided over by one or more senior barristers who have reached the rank of Queen's Counsel. Grouping together in a set of chambers enables the barristers to pool the costs of employing the essential support staff as well as share the other operating expenses. The day-to-day management of a set of chambers will be entrusted to one or more barristers' clerks. It is they who negotiate barristers' fees with firms of solicitors and those persons and organisations with 'direct access' and allocate the incoming briefs to members of the chambers.

According to the Bar Council, in 2003 there were 13,985 registered barristers but 2,737 were in salaried employment, some working for solicitors' firms. It is immediately apparent, therefore, that the barristers' side of the profession is far smaller than the solicitors' side. The majority, 11,248, were independent practising barristers acting as advocates in England and Wales. Of this total, 71 per cent were men, so it remains a largely male-dominated profession. However, just over 50 per cent of pupils in training in 2003 were female and 20 per cent of pupils were from ethnic minority backgrounds so there will be changes in the composition of the profession in the years ahead. There were 353 sets of chambers in 2003. Most of these chambers (208) were situated in and around the four Inns of Court in London and, of the total number of practising barristers, most were London based. There were 145 sets of chambers outside London in 2003. In recent years some well-established barristers have decided to set up their 'chambers' in their own homes because they prefer to work from home, taking advantage of the latest electronic information services and communications technology. A barrister may only do this if he/she has spent at least three years with an established set of chambers and has access to an adequate law library. According to the Annual Report of the Bar Council for 2003, there were 240 of these 'sole practitioners'.

10 Qualifying as a barrister

Anyone aspiring to become a barrister must be a graduate and must still apply to join one of the four Inns of Court (Inner Temple, Middle Temple, Gray's Inn and Lincoln's Inn). If the person concerned does not have a law degree, he/she must take the course leading to the CPE or Postgraduate Diploma in Law before enrolling on the Bar Vocational Course (BVC) on either a full-time or a part-time basis. Having become a student member of one of the Inns, it is necessary to attend the Inn on a certain number of occasions to dine there. This can be done whilst the student is taking the BVC at the Inns of Court Law School. For those who take the BVC outside London, officials of the Inns visit these provincial centres and dine with the entire student cohort.

On successful completion of the BVC the candidates are presently 'called to the bar' at a ceremony at the Inn that they elected to join but there are proposals to defer 'call' after 2008 until, at least, partial completion of pupillage. It is essential to secure 'pupillage' in a set of chambers if a newly qualified barrister wishes to practise as an advocate in the English and Welsh courts. Although there is an online system for pupillage applications, there are usually more young persons seeking pupillage than the number of pupillages available. Since 2002 all pupils have been entitled to an annual award from their chambers of at least £10,000 plus reasonable travelling expenses.

The period of pupillage lasts 12 months and is divided into two six-month periods; but not all chambers will offer a pupillage for the entire 12 months and so it may be necessary to change to another set at the half-way point. The first six-month period in chambers is likely to be spent becoming conversant with the legal paperwork under the general supervision of a 'pupil master'. In a set of chambers specialising in particular branches of the civil law, the pupil barrister may be set to work drafting documents and writing opinions, albeit under supervision. On satisfactory completion of this initial period, the pupil is issued with a practising certificate. If the pupil barrister intends to work at the 'employed Bar' rather than in private practice, the first six-month period of pupillage may be undertaken in the government legal service, Crown Prosecution Service or in local government under the supervision of an 'employed' barrister pupil master. In the second six-month period the pupil barrister may be given some briefs and may appear in court and thereby generate some income. A final certificate is issued at the end of the second six-month period. Once pupillage is over, unless the young barrister is offered a tenancy in the chambers where he/she has undertaken pupillage, it will be necessary for him/her to find a tenancy in another set of chambers in order to be able to practise.

Well over one thousand men and women complete the BVC each year but only half will obtain a pupillage, and of these only 60 per cent or so will ultimately obtain tenancies. Recently qualified barristers who do not succeed in establishing themselves in practice at the Bar can often look forward to very well paid career opportunities at the 'employed Bar' working in the government legal service or Crown Prosecution Service where their legal skills are very much in demand. Some barristers unable to obtain tenancies even choose to work as salaried employees for the large London-based international law firms and provide advocacy services to clients of these firms when required.

11   The work of barristers

Most people have seen films or television dramas in which actors have taken the parts of barristers either prosecuting or defending persons charged with criminal offences. Although a large number of practising barristers do specialise in criminal law, many others opt to perfect their advocacy skills in one or more of the branches of civil law or public law. These barristers are likely to spend as much time on legal paperwork as they do in court. The paperwork will involve them in drafting pleadings for the clients that they are to represent and in drafting opinions, at the request of solicitors, on difficult points of law prior to the commencement of any litigation. Whilst it is correct in principle that any barrister is supposed to be technically competent to perform advocacy for either side in criminal or civil cases, the reality is somewhat different. A degree of specialisation is necessary in order to keep abreast of the vast amount of reading that needs to be done to keep up to date. Indeed, entire sets of chambers are known within the profession to specialise in particular branches of the law and they will obviously seek to attract as tenants those possessing the relevant specialisms. The pace of change at the Bar is such that new entrants may now be expected to retrain and re-specialise two or even three times during their careers in order to generate sufficient income. Once it could be said that the Bar operated as a 'referral only' profession in that the public did not have direct access. Also, the Bar was said to operate a 'cab rank' principle in that a barrister who was not currently engaged on a case was obliged to accept as a client anyone referred to him/her within his/her area of expertise via a solicitor. This has begun to change as a result of modifications to the Bar Code of Conduct. There are certain organisations who were approved for direct access under the old BARdirect scheme (now referred to as licensed access) but nowadays members of the public are able to contact chambers without having to do so via a solicitor. Although they are not obliged to, barristers can accept 'direct access' clients and, where they decide to do so, the 'cab rank rule' does not apply. However, barristers accepting direct access instructions must observe a 'non-discrimination' rule. This stipulates that a barrister must not refuse a case on the following grounds:

(a) that the nature of the case is objectionable to him/her or to any section of the public; or

(b) that the conduct, opinions or beliefs of the prospective client are unacceptable to him/her or to any section of the public; or

(c)   on any ground relating to the source of any financial support which may properly be given to the prospective client for the proceedings in question (for example, on the ground that such support will be available as part of the Community Legal Service or Criminal Defence Service).

Accordingly, a barrister who is willing to act as an advocate on a direct access basis cannot refuse such a case simply because he/she considers that the case or the client is unpopular or because the client is legally aided. For a barrister to take on work on a direct access basis, it is necessary to:

(a)   have practised for a total of three years after completion of pupillage;
(b)   have attended a training course designated by the Bar Council; and
(c)   notify the Bar Council (and Indemnity Fund) of an intention to undertake work on a direct access basis.

Moreover, on every occasion that a barrister acts for a client he/she is obliged to send out a client care letter that makes it clear what the barrister can and cannot do for that client. Since barristers are not 'authorised litigators' as defined by the Courts and Legal Services Act 1990 they cannot conduct litigation in the way in which solicitors are able to do. Consequently, barristers are unable to issue proceedings, correspond with the other side, instruct expert witnesses and take witness statements other than a witness statement from the client. They are forbidden to:

(a)   receive or handle clients' money, or
(b)   undertake the general management of clients' affairs.

There are certain areas of work for which barristers may not accept direct access instructions and these areas are:

(a)   immigration or asylum work;
(b)   family or criminal proceedings other than for advice where proceedings have not been commenced (but not to attend interviews conducted by prosecuting or investigating authorities) or some appeals;
(c)   where the instructions come from intermediaries and are in connection with any family or criminal proceedings.

Some chambers are now providing indicative examples of the type of direct access work that they are willing to take on via their websites.

12   Career progression

Many practising barristers are ambitious and hope to achieve great distinction in their profession and perhaps eventually enter the ranks of the judiciary. Some even use the Bar as a 'launching pad' to a career in politics. After about ten years or so in successful practice a barrister can apply to become a Queen's Counsel (QC). This will only be done by those barristers who genuinely consider that they have achieved some distinction within the profession. Although the actual appointment is made by HM the Queen by letters patent, applications are now, as a result of an agreement with the Bar Council and the Law Society, to be vetted by an independently appointed selection board of nine persons. The chairperson and three other members of this board are to be distinguished non-lawyers. The other members are to include two barristers, two solicitors and a judge. In future, the board will interview each applicant whose written application appears to meet the criteria for appointment. Since September 1995, solicitors who practise as solicitor advocates have been eligible to apply to become QCs but few bother to avail themselves of the opportunity. However, this may change with the new, more transparent, system for making appointments. At present, only about 10 per cent of the independent Bar have the rank of QC and in the new proposals there is provision for revoking the title of poorly performing QCs by the selection panel.

Once a barrister has been appointed to the rank of QC, he/she will command higher fees for his/her advocacy and will often appear in court with a 'junior' (an ordinary barrister) who will assist with the more routine aspects of the case such as the drafting of pleadings. The QC will normally present the legal argument but the 'junior' may also address the court after the QC. As a mark of distinction, QCs have the privilege of being able to wear a silk gown (as well as full bottomed wigs) and for this reason are often referred to as 'silks'.

13   Barristers and professional negligence

In *Arthur J.S. Hall & Co.* v *Simons* [2000] the House of Lords reversed its long-standing decision in the case of *Rondel* v *Worsley* [1967] that barristers cannot be sued by their clients for professional negligence in the provision of advocacy services. All seven Law Lords ruled in favour of abolishing this long-standing immunity in civil litigation and a majority decided that it should no longer be applicable in criminal proceedings. In the course of his judgment Lord Steyn stated:

> There is no reason to fear a flood of negligence suits against barristers. The mere doing of [his/her] duty to the court by the advocate to the detriment of his client could never be called negligent.

The Courts and Legal Services Act 1990 s. 62 had extended the immunity that had been enjoyed by barristers to solicitor advocates and it is interesting to note that in *Arthur J.S. Hall & Co.* v *Simons* the appellants were in fact solicitors who had acted as advocates. The decision of the House of Lords to end the immunity for professional negligence therefore applies to both barristers and solicitor advocates.

14 Complaints against barristers

In 1997, a new system was established for dealing with complaints against barristers. The General Council of the Bar produces a leaflet entitled *How to Complain About a Barrister* detailing what is now an elaborate complaints system. This makes it clear that, although a barrister has an overriding duty to the court to ensure that justice is properly administered, he/she also has a duty to clients to act in their best interests. If a client considers that a formal complaint ought to be made against a barrister, a complaint form can be obtained from the Bar Council together with a set of guidance notes on how to complete the form. The complaints procedure is set in motion once the complaints department receives the completed form. It may take between two and six months to resolve the matter unless the complaint is deemed unjustified, but more serious complaints are likely to take longer to resolve. The complaint form is examined by the Complaints Commissioner – a non-lawyer who will decide on one of three possible courses of action:

(a) to dismiss the complaint because it is not justified;
(b) that the complaint may be resolved by conciliation between the client and the barrister;
(c) that the complaint should be investigated.

If the complaint is dismissed the client will be informed of this decision and of the reasons for it and it is then for the client to decide whether to refer the matter to the Legal Services Ombudsman. If the Commissioner takes the view that the complaint is suitable for conciliation because it does not amount to inadequate professional service or professional misconduct, the Commissioner will write to both parties suggesting that conciliation should take place. The letter to the barrister concerned will make it clear that he/she should initiate the conciliation process. On the other hand, if the Commissioner takes the view that the complaint should be investigated, the barrister concerned will be asked to comment on the allegation(s) made in the complaint form. A copy of the letter sent to the barrister will be sent to the instructing solicitors and to other relevant witnesses who will be asked to submit comments. On receipt of the barrister's response and submissions from other parties, the Commissioner will then re-examine the complaint. Having done so, he/she may decide to dismiss it, giving reasons for the decision to the complainant. If the Commissioner takes the view that the complaint should be taken further, the matter will be referred to the Professional Conduct and Complaints Committee of the Bar Council (known as the PCC).

The PCC comprises a number of barristers who are appointed by the chairperson of the Bar, two lay representatives and the Complaints Commissioner. On considering the complaint the PCC can adopt one of three possible courses of action:

(a) dismiss the complaint, if and only if the two lay representatives agree;
(b) decide that the barrister may have provided an inadequate professional service;

(c)   decide that the barrister may have engaged in unprofessional misconduct which may or may not amount to a breach of the Code of
Conduct.

If the complaint is dismissed the client will be informed of this decision
and of the reasons. It is then for the client to decide whether to refer the
matter to the Legal Services Ombudsman. Inadequate professional service
may range from serious rudeness to the client, delay in dealing with
papers, to poor or inadequate work on the case.

If the PCC takes the view that the barrister may have provided inadequate professional service but has not engaged in professional misconduct
the complaint will be passed to an adjudication panel that will be chaired
by the Complaints Commissioner. He/she will be assisted by two barristers
and a member of the Bar Council's panel of lay representatives. The adjudication itself will be conducted on the basis of documents and
correspondence received – neither the complainant nor the barrister concerned will appear in person although both will be notified of the date on
which the panel is to be convened. If some important matter is raised at
the hearing on which the complainant should be given the opportunity to
comment, the hearing will be adjourned. At the end of the hearing, if the
Panel is satisfied with the barrister's explanation, it can dismiss the complaint provided it gives reasons for its decision. If this should happen the
complainant must then decide whether to refer the matter to the Legal
Services Ombudsman. On the other hand, should the Adjudication Panel
decide that the barrister has provided inadequate professional service, it
may require the barrister to apologise to the client, refund or waive all or
part of his/her fee or to pay compensation of up to £5,000.

Where the PCC has decided that the barrister may have engaged in professional misconduct or may be in breach of the Code of Conduct it can
decide that the matter be dealt with in one of three ways:

(a)   refer the matter for an informal hearing;
(b)   refer the matter for consideration by a Summary Procedure Panel;
(c)   refer the matter to a disciplinary tribunal.

Informal hearings are conducted by a panel of four comprising a QC (as
chairperson), two barristers and a member of the Bar Council's panel of
lay representatives. Copies of the relevant papers will be sent to the parties
beforehand and the barrister concerned is required to appear before the
panel to provide it with an explanation of his/her conduct. At the end of
the process, if the panel is satisfied with the barrister's explanation it will
dismiss the complaint giving its reasons and it is then for the client to
decide whether to refer the matter to the Legal Services Ombudsman.
Alternatively, the panel may decide that the barrister has provided inadequate professional service or that the barrister's conduct amounts to
professional misconduct. In the event of the former, the sanctions available to the panel are the same as those that were available to the
adjudication panel considered earlier. If the finding is one of professional
misconduct the panel may 'admonish' the barrister or advise him/her

regarding his/her future conduct. Such a finding will go on to the barrister's personal record at the Bar Council and will be disclosed to the Lord Chancellor if he/she ever applies to become a QC or a judge.

The composition of a summary procedure panel is similar to that of the panel for informal hearings. It too may dismiss the complaint if the barrister provides a satisfactory explanation of his/her conduct. The principal difference between the two panels is that the summary procedure panel can impose a number of penalties ranging from 'advice' as to future conduct to suspension from practice for a period of up to three months for professional misconduct. An adverse outcome for the barrister will result in the panel's findings being entered on to his/her record with the same implications as above for his/her future career.

The most serious allegations of professional misconduct will be dealt with by a disciplinary tribunal that will be chaired by a judge. The judge will be assisted by three barristers and a lay representative. Disciplinary tribunals are usually conducted in public and both the complainant and the barrister concerned will be present. In 2003, of the 685 complaints received, only 53 were referred for Disciplinary Tribunal hearings. Although the tribunal may dismiss the complaint, this is less likely to occur than with the procedures already considered. Nevertheless, the tribunal could decide that the barrister's conduct amounts to inadequate professional service rather than professional misconduct. In the event of such a finding, the sanctions will be those that could be imposed under the summary procedure. A finding of professional misconduct will be entered on to the barrister's record; and in 2003 there were 38 such findings. A finding of professional misconduct entitles the tribunal to impose one or more of the following sanctions:

(a) advice as to future conduct, or
(b) admonishment, or
(c) reprimand, or
(d) repayment or reduction of fees, or
(e) a fine of up to £5,000 payable to the Bar Council, or
(f) suspension for any period the tribunal considers appropriate, or
(g) disbarment.

Disbarment is the most serious sanction because it means that the barrister can no longer practise as an advocate. In 2003 seven barristers were disbarred but ten were suspended from practising for some time. It should be noted that a barrister can appeal a decision made against him/her in the disciplinary process. However, appeal must be made within 28 days of the decision (21 days for decisions of a summary procedure panel or a disciplinary tribunal). An appeal against a finding of inadequate professional service by an adjudication panel or informal panel will go to an appeals panel established by the Bar Council, which may reverse the earlier decision or reduce or even increase the award. Appeals against a finding of professional misconduct by a summary panel or disciplinary tribunal are heard by Visitors of the Inns of Court and the appeal tribunal will be chaired by a High Court judge.

15 Legal Services Ombudsman

The Office of the Legal Services Ombudsman (LSO) was created by the Courts and Legal Services Act 1990 s. 21 and the office-holder is appointed by the Secretary of State for Constitutional Affairs exercising the powers of the Lord Chancellor. The role of the LSO is set out in s. 22 which states that he/she is to oversee the way that complaints against lawyers are dealt with chiefly by the General Council of the Bar and the Office for Supervision of Solicitors.

The majority of complaints against lawyers are dealt with to the reasonable satisfaction of the complainants by the agencies established by the professional bodies but, that said, the LSO does receive well over a thousand complaints annually from dissatisfied complainants. A dissatisfied complainant has three months from the date of the final decision of the agency concerned to refer the matter to the office of the LSO which is based in Manchester. There is a simple application form and a leaflet setting out the functions of the LSO. An investigating team will review the way in which the agency of the professional body has dealt with the complaint. Having considered an individual complaint, the LSO can recommend that the lawyer concerned or the professional body pay compensation to the complainant for loss, distress or inconvenience. It may even recommend that the complaint be reconsidered and that the lawyer concerned should be disciplined.

Although the addressee of a recommendation is required to notify the LSO of the proposed action to be taken, a weakness of the scheme has been that the LSO's recommendations are not legally binding even though the Courts and Legal Services Act 1990 does require that those who fail to comply with the recommendations of the LSO publicise their failure and the reasons for it in whatever fashion the LSO may specify. If the LSO takes the view that stronger action is required, the Access to Justice Act 1999 s. 49 now empowers the LSO to order the lawyer or the appropriate organisation to take action following an investigation with a view to making amends. The LSO has indicated her general satisfaction with the Bar Council's system of complaints handling but there will undoubtedly be changes following the Clementi Report in the near future.

16 Legal Services Complaints Commissioner

The Access to Justice Act 1999 s. 51 empowered the Lord Chancellor to appoint a Legal Services Complaints Commissioner (LSCC) for a term not exceeding three years but there is a possibility for reappointment for a further period. As with the LSO, the person appointed LSCC must not be a professional lawyer. The powers exercisable by the LSCC are more extensive than those currently exercised by the LSO in that the LSCC can impose penalties on the professional bodies should they fail to put in place adequate systems for the handling of complaints. The maximum amount of any penalty under s. 52(3) of the Access to Justice Act 1999 is whichever is the lesser of:

(a) £1,000,000; and

(b) 1 per cent of the amount which is specified as the total income from all sources of the professional body in that body's most recent audited accounts at the date on which the penalty is imposed.

In what may be seen as a mark of the government's frustration with the Law Society and its system of complaints handling, the current Legal Services Ombudsman was appointed as Legal Services Complaints Commissioner in October 2004 by the Secretary of State for Constitutional Affairs in exercise of his powers as Lord Chancellor.

17 Is there a case for a unified legal profession?

Over the years arguments have been put forward to the effect that a divided profession and its working practices result in great inefficiencies and inflated costs. Not only are there unnecessary delays, it has also been argued that the present structure reduces users' confidence in the system and makes access to justice too expensive for most individuals unless they have some form of legal insurance. The Bar is against fusion as such because of its long history and established traditions, but the Law Society is largely in favour. Although some savings might be made by the client in civil litigation, these may not be very great and there might be advantages to the client in some instances of retaining the services of both a solicitor and a barrister. In some cases, the self-employed barrister might be able to undertake the advocacy of a case in court at a substantially lower cost than a partner in a firm of solicitors because the overheads of some firms of solicitors are very high, especially those based in London. The high costs of running a large solicitors' practice must be charged to clients on an hourly basis and in many instances the total cost could be much higher than the fee charged by a barrister. Moreover, the barrister is likely to be more detached and objective in his/her approach to the case and may be in a better position to advise a client on the likely attitude of a judge to the claim being brought to court. If the government were to force fusion on the profession it is possible that the most successful barristers would be 'head-hunted' by the large London law firms and their services would only be available to those persons who were able to become clients of those firms. The small solicitors' practices, of which there are a large number, especially those outside London, would no longer be able to compete on equal terms with the larger London law firms. At present they all have 'equality of access' to the same specialist pool of advocates for their clients.

The debate over fusion continues but it is possible that fusion may occur in the future through further blurring of the distinctions between barristers and solicitors. In its *First Report on Legal Education and Training* the now defunct Lord Chancellor's Advisory Committee on Legal Education called for common vocational training for all would-be lawyers irrespective of whether they intend to practise as barristers or solicitors. If this were to be adopted, it might lead to a situation where all new entrants to the legal profession qualified initially as solicitors. Those solicitors who wished to specialise in advocacy in the superior courts might then join chambers and become members of a smaller but even more highly special- ised independent Bar to offer their services to the public at large and organisations.

Sir David Clementi, in his report which appeared in December 2004, has stopped short of recommending outright fusion but has proposed the creation of Legal Disciplinary Practices which would permit solicitors and barristers to work together. These practices would also permit non-lawyers to be involved in their management, which is highly controversial. How the government will respond to these proposals will be covered in the forthcoming White Paper.

■ Summary

The two principal branches of the legal profession continue to evolve. The very rigid distinctions between these two branches are becoming increas- ingly blurred although most high profile advocates are barristers and this is likely to be the case for some time to come. It is probable that an even greater number of young people will choose to enter the legal profession by training first as a legal executive, in order to obtain valuable practical experience and avoid the burden of undergraduate debt. The point has been reached that more women than men are qualifying annually as solicitors and barristers and it will be interesting to track the changes that will result from a change in the gender balance of the legal profession. There will be changes in the regulatory regime as a result of the Clementi Report although the Law Society and Bar Council will continue to be first line regulators.

WWW PROGRESS TEST

For suggested answers to the tests below, go to the companion website at www.pearsoned.co.uk/wheeler

1 How is the legal profession in England and Wales structured?
2 What services might a local firm of solicitors be expected to provide to the local business community?
3 If a non-graduate were to begin as a trainee legal executive, approxi- mately how long would it take him/her to become a fully qualified solicitor?
4 Why would a person determined on a legal career opt to qualify as a barrister?

5 Why do barristers (and some solicitors) apply to become Queen's Counsel?

6 What currently is the role of the Office for the Supervision of Solicitors? Should all complaints against solicitors be made to the OSS in the first instance?

7 How does the Bar Council's complaints system operate?

8 Why was the Office of Legal Services Ombudsman created?

9 If there is to be a new regulator for the legal profession will there still need to be a Legal Services Ombudsman?

10 Are the arguments against a fused legal profession convincing?

FURTHER READING

■ **Books**

Bailey, S. H., M.J. Gunn, D. Ormerod and J. Ching (2002) *The Modern English Legal System* (London: Sweet & Maxwell, chapters 3 and 4).

Cownie, F. and A. Bradney (2002) *The English Legal System in Context* (Oxford: Oxford University Press, chapter 8).

Slapper, G. and D. Kelly (2004) *The English Legal System* (London: Cavendish Publishing, chapter 11).

Ward, R. (2005) *Walker and Walker's English Legal System* (Oxford: Oxford University Press, chapter 12).

■ **Articles**

Christensen, C. and J. Worthington (2001) 'Complaint handling within chambers', *The New Law Journal* Vol. 151, No. 6968.

Drummond, H. (1996) 'Standards of advocacy revisited', *The New Law Journal* Vol. 146, No. 6742, p. 655.

Kerridge, R. and G. Davis (1999) 'Reform of the legal profession: an alternative way ahead', *Modern Law Review* Vol. 62, No. 6.

USEFUL WEBSITES

The Law Society website is located at www.lawsociety.org.uk and its annual report is a useful source of information on the solicitors' branch of the profession.

The official website of the Institute of Legal Executives is www.ilex.org.uk

The website for the Office for the Supervision of Solicitors can be accessed via the website for the Law Society, which is www.lawsociety.org.uk

Current information on the barristers' side of the profession can be obtained from www.barcouncil.org.uk and the Bar Council's Annual Report is a useful source of information about the changing Bar.

Information on the Inns of Court can be obtained from the following websites: www.graysinn.org.uk

www.lincolnsinn.org.uk
www.innertemple.org.uk
www.middletemple.org.uk.
Further information on the office of Legal Services Ombudsman can be
   obtained from the website www.oslo.org.

3

The magistracy, judiciary and the courts

1 Introduction

The winds of change are blowing through the magistracy, the judiciary and the courts. In the wake of Sir Robin Auld's *Review of the Criminal Courts* in 2001, the government has steered the Courts Act 2003 through Parliament and created a unified system of administration for the courts that is due to 'go live' from April 2005. It is to be known as Her Majesty's Courts Service. This new executive agency replaces the Court Service and 42 magistrates' courts committees but it is intended that both the judiciary and magistracy will be adequately represented on the Board of the new agency. The publication of the consultation document *Increasing Diversity in the Judiciary* indicates the government's desire to achieve a judiciary that is more representative of society as a whole in the not too distant future but without diluting its quality. Accordingly, any attempt to describe the institutions forming the title of this chapter must be undertaken in recognition of the fact that they are in a state of transition. There will be important developments that will be covered on the companion website, to which reference should be made.

2 An outline structure

Those persons exercising a judicial function are closely identified with the courts over which they preside and so it will be helpful at the outset for the reader to have the barest outline of the court structure in England and Wales in a diagrammatic form (see Figure 3.1).

These courts form a hierarchy. At the lowest level are located the magistrates' courts together with the county courts, whilst at the apex is the House of Lords, currently the ultimate appeal court. The review of the magistracy, judiciary and courts adopted in this chapter will take a 'bottom up' approach. Within the hierarchical structure, magistrates' courts and county courts are very important because they deal with the greatest number of criminal and civil cases respectively. However, within the hierarchy they are often referred to as 'inferior courts' because the courts above them are known as 'superior courts' whose decisions are reported. Although the jurisdiction of the county courts is exclusively civil (see

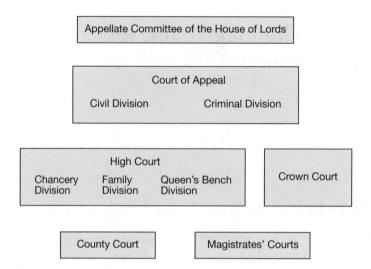

Figure 3.1 **Hierarchy of courts**

Chapter 12) there is no simple, neat division between civil courts on the one hand and criminal courts on the other, as will be seen.

3   Lord Chancellor/Secretary of State for Constitutional Affairs

Historically, the Lord Chancellor, in his capacity as head of the judiciary, has always played a key role in all judicial appointments including the appointment of magistrates. The prime minister of the day always chose a distinguished lawyer who was a member of his/her political party to fulfil this important office and become a member of his/her Cabinet. As indicated in Chapter 1, the powers of the Lord Chancellor are currently being exercised by the Secretary of State for Constitutional Affairs. Even though the government has decided to retain the ancient office of Lord Chancellor, it is clear that the Lord Chief Justice will now be the head of the judiciary. It is not entirely clear what the eventual division of powers will be between the Lord Chancellor and Secretary of State for Constitutional Affairs and whether the latter will be a member of the House of Commons. This will not be clarified until such time as the Constitutional Reform Bill, at the time of writing before Parliament, receives the Royal Assent and becomes the Constitutional Reform Act. When the Lord Chancellor Irvine set up a Commission for Judicial Appointments in 2001, in response to the Peach Report on judicial appointments, he did not hand over his powers to make appointments. In its present form, the Commission does not currently make recommendations for appointments. Nevertheless, the government does intend to create an independent Judicial Appointments Commission that will make recommendations for appointments to the senior judiciary and probably for appointments to some of the lower ranks. The relevant provisions form clauses 49 and 50 of the Constitutional Reform Bill but it is likely that the Lord Chancellor/Secretary of State for Constitutional Affairs will still have the final say in most appointments for the time being. Since 1994 there has been open competition for most judicial appointments below the level of the High Court.

4 Magistrates' courts and the magistracy

In the region of 97 per cent of all criminal cases begin and end in the magistrates' courts and so these courts are a vital part of the criminal justice system, which is discussed in more detail in Chapter 11. There are 435 magistrates' courts in England and Wales, 40 of which are located in the Greater London area. They are to be linked up with the other parts of the criminal justice system and the Crown Court by means of a sophisticated Information Technology system known as XHIBIT. Magistrates' courts are sometimes presided over by a professional judge (District Judge – Magistrates' Court) who sits alone without a jury but a District Judge may sometimes sit with a lay magistrate. District Judges of Magistrates' Courts are full-time members of the judiciary and deal with a wide range of cases but, in particular, are expected to hear the lengthier and more complex criminal cases coming before the magistrates' courts. According to Appendix G (Table 2) of the consultation document entitled *Increasing Diversity in the Judiciary*, the statistics for what may be viewed as the 'professional magistracy' in 2004 were as follows:

	District Judges Magistrates' Courts	Deputy District Judges Magistrates' Courts
Male	100	135
Female	24	38
Total	**124**	**173**
% Female	19.4	22

The Deputy District Judges are part-time appointees but both they and their full-time colleagues are appointed by the Crown (HM the Queen) on the recommendation of the Lord Chancellor/Secretary of State for Constitutional Affairs. Prior to their appointment they will have been practising barristers or solicitors having had at least seven years' practical experience of advocacy in magistrates' courts. The Courts Act 2003 s. 23 makes provision for the appointment from among the ranks of full-time District Judges of Magistrates' Courts, a Senior District Judge and a Deputy Senior District Judge.

Although there is a necessity for full-time and indeed part-time professional judges in magistrates' courts, the criminal justice system is largely dependent upon the approximately 28,700 part-time, lay magistrates who are required to sit for a minimum 26 half-days annually. It is they who hear the majority of the cases that come before the magistrates' courts of

England and Wales. These magistrates, or 'justices of the peace' as they are referred to in the Courts Act 2003 s. 9, do not possess professional legal qualifications but they receive 'on the job training'. They are chosen from among persons who are active in their local communities and who are interested in the functioning of the criminal justice system. Most adult persons of good character between the ages of 27–60 can apply to become magistrates but persons convicted of a serious criminal offence, bankrupts, serving members of the armed forces, and those working in the prison service or police service are not eligible for appointment. It is intended that the composition of the magistracy should, as far as possible, reflect the social and ethnic mix of the locality with a balance between gender and age but this is yet to be achieved in many areas of the country. Although in 2004 the gender balance was almost even, at 50.6 per cent male to 49.4 per cent female, the age range is skewed towards the higher end with 82 per cent over the age of 50 years. Currently the proportion of lay magistrates from ethnic minority backgrounds is just over 6 per cent as compared with 7.9 per cent for the population as a whole, although there are variations from area to area. The Department for Constitutional Affairs is taking steps through its National Recruitment Strategy to encourage suitable candidates from ethnic minorities to apply to the Regional Advisory Committees to be considered for appointment. The Lord Chancellor/Secretary of State for Constitutional Affairs also wishes to attract applications from younger persons. In the past, younger applicants may have been deterred from applying for financial reasons. Even though employers are obliged to release employees to undertake this vital function, they are not obliged to pay them. Therefore, the Courts Act 2003 s. 15 now empowers the Lord Chancellor/Secretary of State for Constitutional Affairs to pay allowances to magistrates and reimburse travelling expenses, which may encourage more self-employed persons and those younger people whose employers are not prepared to pay them when performing a public service during normal working hours to come forward.

All prospective candidates must pass two interviews in order to be recommended by an Advisory Committee to the Lord Chancellor/Secretary of State for Constitutional Affairs for appointment. Appointments in Lancashire, Merseyside and Greater Manchester are made by the Chancellor of the Duchy of Lancaster but this is currently under review and all appointments may be centralised in future. Suitability for appointment is measured against six key qualities, namely:

- good character;
- understanding communication;
- social awareness;
- maturity and sound temperament;
- sound judgment; and
- commitment and reliability.

On being appointed, all new magistrates must undergo an initial three-month training programme during which they acquire a working knowledge of the law of evidence and an understanding of the principles and purpose of sentencing including the new sentencing framework. A new scheme for the training of magistrates has been implemented nationally which focuses on the acquisition of 'competences'. All magistrates, whether newly appointed or not, are required to complete a Personal Development Log that is issued by the Magisterial Committee of the Judicial Studies Board. For its part, the Magistrates' Association has established a national scheme for the training of experienced magistrates as 'mentors' who will support all new magistrates in their personal development during their first two years on the Bench. All magistrates must use their Personal Development Logs as a basis for demonstrating that they have attained the necessary 'competences', which will be assessed through a system of appraisal by mentors. The system of training is currently under review and there may be some important changes in the near future since the Courts Act 2003 s. 19 makes provision for the making of rules for the training, development and appraisal of magistrates.

England and Wales are divided into 'local justice areas' and magistrates are appointed to act for one of the 42 criminal justice areas which are aligned with county and metropolitan police districts. London has six such areas. Magistrates are required to live in or within 15 miles of the particular area for which they sit. The areas are then subdivided into petty sessional divisions, each of which has its own magistrates' court. Even though magistrates are eligible to sit in any of the courts in their justice area, they are usually assigned to a bench for the division where they either live or work. In court they may sit as a panel of two but usually they sit as a panel of three comprising an experienced chairperson with two 'wingers'. They sit without a jury, but they are assisted by a legally qualified court clerk who advises on points of law and procedure. However, the court clerk does not participate in the decision making on guilt/innocence. Most of the offences that come to a magistrates' court are classed as 'summary offences' which are defined as such by Act of Parliament. There are other offences that can be tried 'either way', that is, summarily or on indictment at the Crown Court. Many accused persons charged with 'either way' offences opt for summary trial when they intend to plead 'guilty', often in the hope that they will receive a lighter sentence. Lay magistrates can currently impose fines of up to £5,000 at level 5 and custodial sentences within the sentencing framework of the Criminal Justice Act 2003 (for which see Chapter 11) of up to 12 months. Apart from trying most criminal cases they also deal with such matters as:

- applications for bail from persons charged with offences;
- the granting of search and arrest warrants;
- issuing licences for betting shops and casinos;
- hearing licensing appeals for the sale of alcohol by public houses and restaurants;
- administering oaths under the Courts and Legal Services Act 1990 s. 56 for the grant of probate or letters of administration;

- the recovery of civil debts such as unpaid income tax, national insurance contributions, utility bills and council tax; and
- applications for Anti-Social Behaviour Orders.

Lay magistrates with special training sit as Youth Courts dealing with juvenile crime and as Family Proceedings Courts dealing with matters such as the finalising of adoptions or access to children on the break-up of a relationship. When sitting as a Youth Court or Family Proceedings Court there must be at least one male and one female lay magistrate on the bench. Both lay magistrates and District Judges of Magistrates' Courts must retire at the age of 70 but many opt to do so at an earlier age.

5 County courts and district judges

Despite indications to the contrary, county courts are not only to be found in the counties of England and Wales. They are also to be found in the metropolitan areas including London, so that in 2004, there were in total 228 such courts. London hosts the Patents County Court where small and medium-size enterprises can litigate disputes concerning patents. Some courthouses in certain parts of the country (e.g. Preston) are 'combined' in that they share a building with the Crown Court but the courts themselves are separate. As stated previously, the jurisdiction of county courts is exclusively civil so that most of the cases heard tend to be contractual-type disputes (including mortgage repossessions, Consumer Credit Act claims and other forms of debt claim) together with personal injury (tort) claims not involving compensation in excess of £50,000. A large number of county courts have jurisdiction through specially nominated judges to make care orders under the Children Act 1989 on the application of local authorities. In fact, the majority of all family law cases are dealt with by county court judges, including over 90 per cent of all divorce petitions. Some county courts have special jurisdiction in insolvency matters and are therefore able to deal with the bankruptcy of individuals and the administration and/or liquidation of small companies. Most of the civil claims that are brought each year are disposed of in the county courts but there are financial limits to many aspects of the jurisdiction of county courts. Small claims involving £5,000 or less, which form about half of all the financial claims, are heard by District Judges or their deputies, as are most 'fast-track' claims up to £15,000. Circuit Judges assigned to county courts usually hear the more complex cases and those involving claims over £15,000.

District Judges are salaried, full-time appointees who are assisted by Deputy District Judges who serve in a part-time capacity and who are remunerated on a fee basis. Although both are appointed by HM the Queen, it is the Lord Chancellor/Secretary of State for Constitutional Affairs who is instrumental in making the appointment. Applicants usually respond to an advertisement in the legal press and in the first instance are likely to be appointed to the position of Deputy District Judge before being confirmed to a full-time appointment. Part-time fee paid service is usually a prerequisite for appointment to full-time office. All applicants must either be citizens of the United Kingdom; a citizen of Ireland; a citizen of a Commonwealth country; or hold dual nationality, one of which falls into one of these categories. Apart from the requirement to be of good character, it is necessary for those solicitors and barristers eligible to apply to have been practising advocates for seven years prior to appointment. There may be changes in the eligibility criteria in future to increase the pool of potential applicants. In 2004 the relevant statistics, according to Appendix G (Table 2) of the consultation document entitled *Increasing Diversity in the Judiciary*, were as follows:

	District Judges	Deputy District Judges
Male	350	603
Female	81	179
Total	**431**	**782**
% Female	18.8	22.9

There has not been a significant increase in the number of female appointees since 2000 and some careful thought may have to be given to changes in working practices if there is to be a significant increase in the number of female appointees in the years ahead. Ethnic minorities are even more under-represented among the appointees on this first rung of the judicial ladder, as are disabled lawyers.

6 The Crown Court and its judges

The Crown Court was brought into existence by the Courts Act 1971. However, it now derives its jurisdiction from the Supreme Court Act 1981 and is part of the Supreme Court of Judicature together with the High Court and Court of Appeal. In many respects, it is regarded as being on par with the High Court; yet, in certain matters, it is subject to the supervisory jurisdiction of the High Court. This is because certain decisions taken on appeals from magistrates' courts can be challenged in the High Court either by way of 'case stated' or by application for judicial review. As its name implies, it is a single, unitary court but its 100 or so courthouses are organised geographically into six circuits as follows:

1 Midland and Oxford;
2 North Eastern;
3 Northern;
4 Wales and Cheshire;
5 Western; and
6 South Eastern.

Each circuit is presided over by a Senior Presiding Judge who oversees the allocation of the case load. Within each circuit there are a number of courthouses which are ranked in order of importance as being:

(a) first tier centres; or
(b) second tier centres; or
(c) third tier centres.

Each centre has a Resident Judge who has to match his/her case list with suitably authorised judges that are available (as explained below). The most famous 'first tier' centre is the Central Criminal Court in London, which is known as the *Old Bailey*, where the most serious criminal trials take place. Despite the nickname, there is nothing quaint about the Central Criminal Court. In common with over half of the Crown Court courthouses in England and Wales, it has been brought into the twenty-first century with a very sophisticated IT infrastructure as part of a project known as LINK which makes it possible for evidence to be presented electronically and to be given via video link. Documents and e-mails can now be transmitted securely to other parts of the criminal justice system using XHIBIT. It is planned to extend these facilities to the remaining Crown Court courthouses in the near future.

Although the jurisdiction of the Crown Court is mainly criminal it does exercise a limited civil jurisdiction by way of hearing licensing appeals from and appeals against decisions not to grant firearm licences by the police. According to *Judicial Statistics 2003*, a total of 84,412 cases were committed or sent to the Crown Court for trial on indictment. According to *Practice Direction (Criminal Proceedings: Consolidation)* [2002], cases are classified into one of four Classes depending on the seriousness of the crime. Class 1 (which includes murder and attempted murder) is the most serious and Class 4 the least serious. There are effectively four ranks of judge that can preside over cases in the Crown Court. High Court judges who come on 'circuit' can preside over any case within the jurisdiction of the Crown Court but they are likely to spend their time hearing Class 1 and Class 2 cases at first tier centres and serious fraud cases which are in Class 3. There is a system of 'ticketing' by which some experienced Circuit Judges can be authorised to try certain Class 1 and Class 2 cases. These judges form the second rank. The majority of Circuit Judges try the cases in Classes 3 and 4 and they form the third rank. The fourth rank of Crown Court judges is made up of Recorders. Very experienced Recorders can try cases in Class 2 but mostly try cases in Classes 3 and 4 because of their limited availability. Persons convicted by a magistrates' court who pleaded 'not guilty' can appeal as of right against conviction to the Crown Court. For those who pleaded 'guilty' it is possible for them to appeal against sentence. Such appeals are heard by a Circuit Judge or Recorder sitting with at least two magistrates who were not involved in the case previously. In appeals against conviction, the evidence is re-heard but there is no jury. According to *Judicial Statistics 2003*, the total number of appeals heard in the Crown Court amounted to 11,858.

Circuit Judges are appointed by the Crown (HM the Queen) on the advice of the Lord Chancellor/Secretary of State for Constitutional Affairs. In order to be eligible for appointment to the rank of Circuit Judge, a candidate must satisfy the nationality requirement and must normally have exercised rights of audience in the Crown Court or County Court for at least 10 years as required by the Courts and Legal Services Act 1990 s. 71 or have held office as a Recorder for at least three years. The Supreme Court Act 1981 s. 8(1) allowed for the appointment of Deputy Circuit Judges to assist with the workload of the Crown Court but the qualification requirement is the same. Recorders are appointed to sit on a part-time basis in the Crown Court but they too must have the same minimum qualification for appointment as required for a Circuit Judge. Circuit Judges, Deputy Circuit Judges and Recorders should be addressed in court as 'Your Honour' but any Circuit Judge who is called upon to sit at the Central Criminal Courts (Old Bailey) should be addressed in the same way that High Court Judges are, namely either as 'My Lord' or 'My Lady'.

According to Appendix G (Table 2) of the consultation document entitled *Increasing Diversity in the Judiciary* the numbers of Circuit Judges, Deputy Circuit Judges, Recorders and Assistant Recorders in 2004 were as follows:

	Circuit Judges/ Deputy Circuit Judges	Recorders/ Assist. Recorders
Male	560	1,186
Female	63	180
Total	**623**	**1,366**
% Female	10.1	13.2

The Department for Constitutional Affairs re-launched its 'work shadowing scheme' whereby qualified solicitors and barristers who are interested in being appointed as Recorders or Deputy District Judges can spend up to five days observing the work of a District Judge or Circuit Judge.

7 The High Court and its judges

The High Court was a creation of the Judicature Act 1873 but it has undergone a number of modifications since then. Although it is divided into three main divisions – Chancery, Queen's Bench and Family – it also includes a number of specialist courts. These are the Commercial Court, the Admiralty Court (dealing mainly with collision and cargo claims), the Technology and Construction Court and the Administrative Court, which are linked to the Queen's Bench Division. The Patents Court and Companies Court are linked to the Chancery Division. Any division of the High Court can sit anywhere in England and Wales but many of the sittings take place in the gothic building, which dates from 1878, that houses the Royal Courts of Justice in the Strand, London. The Family Division, however, is located in a modern building in Holborn. The Lord Chancellor is notionally head of the Chancery Division but in practice it is presided over by a senior judge known as the Vice Chancellor. The Lord

Chief Justice is the head of, and presides over, the Queen's Bench Division whilst the head of the Family Division is simply known as the President.

The High Court is a 'court of first instance' where cases are normally argued before a single High Court Judge who usually sits without a jury. In 2004 there were 107 High Court Judges. Since only 17 of these judges were assigned to the Chancery Division, with another 18 or so to the Family Division, it is evident that the Queen's Bench Division is the largest division with the heaviest workload. As its name implies, the Family Division is concerned with the custody of children on the break-up of relationships as well as guardianship and maintenance matters. The jurisdiction of the Chancery Division is also exclusively civil. It hears cases concerning disputed wills (known as contentious probate actions) as well as disputes relating to trusts, trust property and mortgages in general. Important cases involving disputes in relation to intellectual property matters (copyright, patents and trade marks) are also routinely assigned to the Chancery Division. In addition, it has a significant jurisdiction in insolvency matters dealing with personal bankruptcies in cases beyond the financial jurisdiction of the county courts. As previously indicated, the Companies Court is linked to the Chancery Division. As its title suggests, it is a specialist court that is concerned with receivership, the administration and liquidation of companies and disqualification of company directors of failed companies.

Although most of the work of the Queen's Bench Division is done in London, it also functions through the district registries of the High Court which are located at many of the county courts throughout England and Wales. Its jurisdiction is very wide ranging and is both civil and appellate criminal. According to *Judicial Statistics 2003* almost 75 per cent of its judgments were high value tort claims (mainly for medical negligence and other types of personal injury) that could not be dealt with in the county courts. In just over 62 per cent of these cases, the compensation awarded exceeded £50,000. High value contract disputes (not allocated to the Chancery Division) and debt claims beyond the jurisdiction of the county courts will be heard in the Queen's Bench Division, including enforcement proceedings for large debts. The print and broadcast media report the outcome of all high value defamation cases that are tried in the Queen's Bench Division before a judge and jury, but that represents only a small part of its case load.

Apart from being a court of first instance, the High Court also functions as an appeal court through its 'Divisional Courts' in which two High Court Judges often sit to hear an appeal. At the time of writing no statistics were available for 2004, but in 2003 a total of 60 appeals were set down to be heard in the Divisional Court of the Family Division from orders made in magistrates' courts. In 2003 the Divisional Court of the Chancery Division heard 102 appeals. Of these, 48 per cent were bankruptcy appeals from county courts whilst the remainder dealt with other subject matter within the court's jurisdiction including tax appeals. The Divisional Court of Queen's Bench received a total of 5,949 applications for leave to apply for judicial review in 2003 before the Administrative Court, less than 25 per cent of which were granted. The topic of judicial review is dealt with extensively in Chapter 15. In addition, the Administrative Court received a further 831 appeals and applications other than by way of judicial review in 2003. The Divisional Court of Queen's Bench also received 119 appeals by way of 'case stated' in 2003, of which, 96 were appeals from magistrates' courts with 20 from the Crown Court and 3 from elsewhere.

A full-time appointment to the High Court bench is highly regarded and prestigious. Male appointees have knighthoods conferred upon them by HM the Queen but their female counterparts have to be satisfied with being created Dames of the British Empire. In court they are addressed as 'My Lord' or 'My Lady' as appropriate and in legal textbooks and Law Reports their surname is printed first, followed by a capital J (e.g. Green J). Few direct full-time appointments are made and most appointees will usually serve as Deputy High Court Judges for an initial period to assess their suitability. Both solicitors and barristers are eligible for appointment provided they have exercised a general right of audience in the High Court for 10 years or have held office as a Circuit Judge for at least two years. However, most High Court Judges are former barristers. In October 2000 Dr Lawrence Collins QC, a solicitor and highly respected legal scholar, was appointed to the Chancery Division of the High Court bench having sat as a Deputy High Court judge since 1997. Apart from the heads of the various divisions, there were 107 full-time High Court Judges but only 9 were female. In 2004 Linda Dobbs QC made legal history as the first female High Court Judge to be appointed from an ethnic minority background.

Apart from the judges, there is a group of people known as High Court Masters (and Assistant Masters) who carry out much of the routine business of the High Court that does not involve hearings in open court. These men and women are judicial officers who must be either barristers or solicitors. They must have been practising in the courts for at least seven years to be eligible for appointment and they are normally appointed to work for particular divisions within the High Court.

8 The Court of Appeal and the Lords Justices of Appeal

The courtrooms of the Court of Appeal and its offices are located within the Royal Courts of Justice in the Strand, London. As indicated on the diagram, Figure 3.1, the Court of Appeal has two divisions. The Civil Division is presided over by the Master of the Rolls whilst the Criminal Division is presided over by the Lord Chief Justice (and Vice President of the Criminal Division) but the Vice Chancellor and President of the Family Division may also sit as judges to hear appeals and do so for part of their time. According to Appendix G (Table 2) of the consultation document entitled *Increasing Diversity in the Judiciary* there were 37 Lord Justices of Appeal in 2004 – 35 men and 2 women. As with High Court Judges, the mode of address is 'My Lord' or 'My Lady' and in legal textbooks and Law

Reports their surname appears first, followed by the abbreviation LJ. For the most part, the Lord and Lady Justices of Appeal are appointed from among the ranks of exceptional High Court Judges. In the past this was done by the Crown on the advice of the prime minister of the day who always consulted with the Lord Chancellor. This is likely to change with the enactment of the Constitutional Reform Bill in 2005 and the creation of an independent Judicial Appointments Commission.

The judges of the Court of Appeal are kept very busy indeed but according to *Judicial Statistics 2003* the Civil Division has again been able to reduce its 'hear by dates' to a maximum of 10 months. In 2003 the Civil Division received 1,127 applications for leave to appeal, of which 1,075 were actually dealt with in one way or another including the 209 that were dismissed by consent and the 128 otherwise disposed of. More than half of these were appeals from three divisions of the High Court and specialist courts within the High Court. A significant number of appeals came directly from county courts (293), the Employment Appeal Tribunal (71) and the Immigration Appeal Tribunal (102). The Criminal Division, in comparison, dealt with far more applications for leave to appeal in the same year according to *Judicial Statistics 2003*. These numbered 7,451, of which 1,787 were against conviction in the Crown Court with 5,664 against the actual sentence imposed. Not all of these were considered by the end of the year but, of those that were considered, more applications were declined than were granted in both categories. The Criminal Division actually heard 2,906 appeals in 2003 – 542 against conviction and 2,364 against sentence. It allowed 178 appeals against conviction and 1,685 appeals against sentence.

9 The House of Lords ('Supreme Court') and its judges

The Appellate Jurisdiction Act 1876 reconstituted the Appellate Committee of the House of Lords as an appeal court above the Court of Appeal for Great Britain and Northern Ireland. The Act provides for the creation of a number of salaried life peers with the official title of Lords of Appeal in Ordinary, whose main function is to hear both civil and criminal appeals – usually from the Court of Appeal but occasionally from lower courts. In the past the Lord Chancellor sometimes sat as a judge but was normally too busy to do so. The present Lord Chancellor/Secretary of State for Constitutional Affairs has declined to sit as part of the Appellate Committee. More often than not, work of the court is conducted by the twelve Law Lords sitting either as a court of five or seven (even though the Act allows for the convening of a court of just three if the Lord Chancellor sits as a judge). Most recently, the judgment of the Appellate Committee in *A (FC) and others* v *Secretary of State for the Home Department* [2004] was delivered by nine Law Lords, including Baroness Hale who is the only female member of the Appellate Committee. A civil appeal to the House of Lords is possible only if either the Court of Appeal or the House of

Lords itself gives permission; and in criminal cases there is an additional requirement that the appeal has to focus on a point of law of general public importance. All petitions for leave to appeal in criminal cases must be in writing and are referred to an Appeal Committee of three Law Lords. However, before making a final decision on the application for leave to appeal the Committee may decide to hear argument from counsel. In the past, appointments to the House of Lords were made by the Queen on the advice of the prime minister who would always consult with the Lord Chancellor. In practice, virtually all appointments are made from the ranks of the Lords Justices of Appeal.

In 2003 (not an untypical year) the Appellate Committee received 237 petitions for leave to appeal. Most of these (202) were from decisions of the Court of Appeal – 180 from the Civil Division and 22 from the Criminal Division. A total of 26 petitions were from decisions of the High Court (many under the so-called 'leap frog' procedure whereby appeals bypass the Court of Appeal) and the remainder were from Northern Ireland. All appeals are normally heard by the Appellate Committee at the Palace of Westminster in a committee room. The judgments, usually referred to as 'opinions', are read out in the presence of the advocates in the House of Lords Chamber on a day specifically set aside for judicial business. During 2003 a total of 65 such judgments were delivered by the Law Lords. It is interesting to note that in the same period the Civil Division of the Court of Appeal alone heard over 700 appeals.

In December 2004 the Lord Chancellor/Secretary of State for Constitutional Affairs announced that the Middlesex Guildhall (almost opposite the Palace of Westminster) was the government's preferred location for the new 'Supreme Court' that will eventually replace the Appellate Committee of the House of Lords as the ultimate appeal court. Locating the new court outside the Palace of Westminster is intended to demonstrate a formal separation between the judiciary and legislature. Nevertheless, it is unlikely that the building will be ready until 2008 and the Constitutional Reform Bill is likely to receive the Royal Assent long before then. So it will be interesting to see whether the government will opt for an interim solution or whether the Appellate Committee of the House of Lords will remain in being until the new courthouse is ready. Clause 18 of the Constitutional Reform Bill envisages that many of the present Law Lords will be re-designated Judges of the Supreme Court but they will lose their right to sit and participate in the proceedings of the second chamber. Other and subsequent appointments will be made by the Crown on the advice of the Prime Minister on the basis of recommendations made to him by the Judicial Appointments Commission. The title 'Supreme Court' is not unproblematic because, as indicated above, there is already in being a Supreme Court of Judicature comprising the Crown Court, High Court and Court of Appeal. Consequently there may have to be some changes in nomenclature along the way. The new court will not be similar to the Supreme Court of the USA which can strike down any legislation it considers to be 'unconstitutional'. The Supreme Court at Westminster will be subordinate to the will of Parliament and it will not have jurisdiction to hear Scottish Appeals as the House of Lords does at present. However, it is envisaged that it will deal with devolution issues currently dealt with by the Judicial Committee of the Privy Council.

10 Judicial Committee of the Privy Council

Some of the Law Lords also sit from time to time as members of the Judicial Committee of the Privy Council assisted by other judges who are privy councillors that have held, or hold, high judicial office including former Lord Chancellors. The origins of the Judicial Committee of the Privy Council as an appellate court can be traced back several centuries but in its modern form it dates from the enactment of the Judicial Committee Act 1833 which established it as special committee of the Monarch's Privy Council to hear appeals from overseas territories of the Crown. With the dissolution of the British Empire and creation of the Commonwealth, the Judicial Committee of the Privy Council still functions as the final court of appeal for New Zealand and certain West Indian states such as Jamaica and Trinidad. Closer to home, it hears final appeals from the Channel Islands and Isle of Man as well as certain domestic tribunals such as the Professional Conduct Committee of the General Medical Council. It is usual for five judges to hear an appeal, with the exception of appeals from certain domestic tribunals which are heard by three judges. Permission to appeal is usually required. In 2003 the Judicial Committee of the Privy Council heard 59 appeals of which 47 were civil and 12 were criminal. In previous years most appeals came from New Zealand but in 2003 Trinidad and Tobago produced the largest number of appeals. The Judicial Committee of the Privy Council has been given the jurisdiction under the Government of Wales Act 1998, the Scotland Act 1998 and the Northern Ireland Act 1998 to decide issues relating to the competences of the executive authorities and legislative assemblies of Scotland and Northern Ireland established under these statutes. This jurisdiction will be transferred to the new Supreme Court in due course.

11 Judicial tenure

Since it is the task of the judiciary to uphold the rule of law, it is vital that senior judges, in particular, should not only be independent of government but also have security of tenure and so not be open to manipulation. According to the Supreme Court Act 1981 all full-time appointees at the level of the High Court and above hold office subject to their 'good behaviour' which means that they can only be removed by the Queen as a result of an address by both Houses of Parliament. However, one High Court Judge did retire in 1998 having been publicly criticised by the Court of Appeal over an inordinate delay in giving judgment in a case. Circuit Judges and District Judges, on the other hand, can be removed from office because of incompetence or misbehaviour, by the Lord Chancellor/Secretary of State for Constitutional Affairs alone. He can also remove and does remove lay magistrates if there is good cause. As previously indicated, the normal retirement age for judges and magistrates is now 70. Many judges retire before reaching this age because after 20 years' service a judge can retire on a pension equivalent to half salary. There are, nevertheless, a few serving judges over the age of 70 who were appointed before the retirement age was lowered.

12 The Judicial Studies Board

In 1979 a review was conducted by Lord Justice Bridge of the needs of the judiciary presiding over criminal cases for training and development. As a result, the Judicial Studies Board was established as an autonomous non-governmental agency to ensure that judicial independence was not compromised in the training process. Then in 1985 the remit of the Board was widened to cover the training needs of other members of the judiciary whose jurisdiction was in the various branches of the civil law and family law. The training of magistrates and chairpersons of administrative tribunals was also included. The Board now has five operational objectives as follows:

1 to provide high quality training to full and part-time judges in the exercise of their jurisdiction in civil, criminal and family law;
2 to advise the Lord Chancellor on the policy for, and content of, training for lay magistrates and on the efficiency and effectiveness with which Magistrates' Courts Committees deliver such training;
3 to advise the Lord Chancellor and government departments on the appropriate standards for, and content of, training for judicial officers of tribunals;
4 to advise the government on the training requirements of judges, magistrates and judicial officers of tribunals if proposed changes to the law, procedure and court organisation are to be effective and to provide and advise on the content of such training; and
5 to promote closer international cooperation over judicial training.

The Lord Chief Justice is the patron of the Board but it operates through a main Board whose Chairperson and members are appointed by the Lord Chancellor including the chairpersons of its six committees that are responsible for organising the provision of training. Apart from the chairpersons of its six committees, the main Board comprises other members of the judiciary, a lay magistrate, at least one academic, a QC and civil servants from the Department of Constitutional Affairs and the Home Office. Appointments to the individual committees are made by the committee chairperson having regard to the Nolan principles. A full-time Director of Studies is now appointed by the Board who must be a circuit judge whose remit is to oversee and coordinate the various training programmes including IT training. The pivotal role of the Director of Studies is under-lined by the fact that he/she attends all meetings of the Board and its six committees. The routine day-to-day work of the Judicial Studies Board is carried out by a full-time secretariat of about 30 civil servants who are supervised by the Secretary to the Board.

All part-time judges are required to attend an induction course organ-ised by the JSB before they are allowed to preside judicially and every full-time and part-time judge must attend a refresher seminar every three years in every major area of jurisdiction over which he/she presides. Many of the courses are planned and actually delivered by practising judges but the JSB does invite leading academics and practitioners to contribute to the courses that are offered. The range of courses provided and the names of those who have delivered them are set out in the Annual Report which can be downloaded from the JSB website.

The JSB has links with similar bodies in North America and Europe and each year it receives a number of visitations. The JSB also arranges study trips abroad for members of the judiciary from time to time.

■ Summary

Although there may be no neat division between criminal courts on the one hand and civil courts on the other when looking at the hierarchical structure, it is clear, nevertheless, that the criminal justice system revolves around the magistrates' courts, the Crown Court and Criminal Division of the Court of Appeal. The salient feature of the criminal justice system in England and Wales is the extent to which it depends largely on the services of non-professional judges in the form of lay mag-istrates. Those who practise law in the courts tend to specialise either in criminal law or civil law and, even though there is scope to change their areas of specialism, judicial appointments are often based on a bar-rister's/solicitor's area of specialism. Those who aspire to be appointed as full-time judges are appointed first to sit on a part-time, fee paid basis. Success as a part-time appointee opens up the possibility of a full-time appointment. Success as a full-time appointee opens up the prospect of promotion further up the court hierarchy. The publication by the gov-ernment of *Increasing Diversity in the Judiciary* is an important event in that it signals its desire to have a judiciary, in the not too distant future, that is more representative of the wider society in terms of gender balance and ethnicity.

WWW PROGRESS TEST

1 How are magistrates' courts in England and Wales configured and staffed?
2 How are lay magistrates (i) chosen, and (ii) trained?

3 What is the role of the court clerk in a court presided over by lay magistrates?

4 What are the qualifications for appointment to the 'professional' magistracy?

5 How are the county courts staffed?

6 How is the Crown Court organised and how is it staffed?

7 How is the High Court structured and what are the qualifications for appointment to the High Court bench?

8 How have the judges of the Court of Appeal been selected and appointed and is this likely to change?

9 How does the Court of Appeal stand in relationship to the House of Lords in the hierarchical structure?

10 What is the role of the Judicial Studies Board?

FURTHER READING

■ Books

Bailey, S.H., M.J. Gunn, D. Ormerod and J. Ching (2002) *The Modern English Legal System* (Oxford: Oxford University Press, chapter 4).

Cownie, F. and A. Bradney (2003) *The English Legal System in Context* (Oxford: Oxford University Press, chapter 9).

Department for Constitutional Affairs (2004) *Increasing Diversity in the Judiciary*.

Griffith, J.A.G. (1997) *The Politics of the Judiciary* (London: Fontana).

Slapper, G. and D. Kelly (2004) *The English Legal System* (London: Cavendish Publishing, chapter 6).

Ward, R. (2005) *English Legal System* (Oxford: Oxford University Press, chapter 12).

■ Articles

Frazer, C. (2000) 'Judicial Independence', *New Law Journal* Vol. 150, No. 6928.

USEFUL WEBSITES

The website www.dca.gov.uk is that of the Lord Chancellor/Secretary of State for Constitutional Affairs and contains much useful information on the judiciary and magistracy. This website also hosts the publication *Judicial Statistics* which gives a valuable insight into the work of the various courts.

The website of the Judicial Studies Board is www.jsboard.co.uk and the website of the Judicial Committee of the Privy Council is www.privy-council.org.uk. Additional information on the work of the Appellate Committee of the House of Lords can be located at www.parliament.uk.

The website of HM Court Service is www.courtservice.gov.uk.

Part 2

The law-making process

4 The law-making process 1: Case law, precedent and law reporting

1 Introduction

Over the centuries the judges have created a vast body of case law consisting of both civil and criminal precedents. Although it is quite important to have an understanding of the historical development of case law through common law and equity, this can be deferred until after the basic principles of law making by precedent have been grasped. Accordingly, the reader is advised to read Appendix 1 *after* reading this chapter, in order to deepen his/her knowledge and understanding. Given that it seems likely that there will be a comprehensive criminal code for England and Wales in the near future, as indicated in the White Paper *Justice for All*, it would be rather pointless now to study law-making by precedent through the criminal law. Once there is a comprehensive criminal code in place, criminal law will be largely a study of statutory interpretation. It has been decided, instead, to focus this chapter on law-making by precedent in the context of civil law through contract and tort. The initial case studies chosen have been taken from the law of contract as the study of this branch of the law comes quite early in a programme of legal studies. Law-making by precedent in the law of contract arises in the course of dispute settlement. From time to time disputes arise which the parties are unable or unwilling to settle amicably and so they bring them to a court for resolution. After a judge hears the evidence and decides the outcome (either in favour of the claimant or for the defendant), he/she will issue an order giving effect to his/her decision which will be entered in the court records. The judgment so entered is binding on the parties unless it is subsequently overturned on appeal – as lawyers would say, the matter is *res judicata* (settled) simply because the decision resolves the dispute. Normally the judgment formulated will be based on the application of one or more legal principles to the facts as established before the court. It is this aspect of the case that lawyers refer to as the *ratio decidendi* (or *ratio* pronounced 'rayshio') which is capable of becoming a precedent for the future should another dispute arise involving similar facts since the same ruling can be applied. In this way, much of the law of contract is 'judge made' in the form of precedents and to be knowledgeable about this branch of the law, a student must embark on a detailed study of precedents embedded in case law. This chapter commences with a study of the development of an important concept in the law of contract through case law so that the basic principles of law-making by precedent can be thoroughly understood before examining how precedent operates within the hierarchical configuration of the courts. Since the Human Rights Act 1998 has been in force the courts have been required to take account of their obligations under the Act and so it is necessary to consider the impact of this legislation on law-making by precedent. Since law-making by precedent is tied in with law reporting, something must be said about this activity; but the historical aspects of law reporting are dealt with in Appendix 1.

2 Case studies

These case studies focus on an important aspect of the law of contract, namely the precise nature of contractual obligations and the development of the modern concept of 'frustration of contract'. Until the second half of the nineteenth century it was widely accepted by the judiciary that contractual obligations were absolute. In other words, unforeseen subsequent events did not normally provide an excuse for non-performance. The entire notion of a contract as a legally binding agreement would be seriously undermined if it were possible for one of the parties, having freely entered into the contract, to abandon it simply because he/she regarded his/her obligations as too onerous in the light of some subsequent event. Exceptions to this general principle had long been acknowledged where performance of the contract had been rendered unlawful because of the application of a rule of law or, in the case of contracts for personal services, by the death or permanent incapacity of one of the parties. However, in all other instances, the judges were of the view that once a party had freely entered into a contract he/she must perform it or pay compensation (damages) to the other party who had suffered because of his/her failure to perform what had been agreed at the outset. This is well illustrated by the old case of *Paradine* v *Jane* (1647) where a lessee of a farm was still held liable for rent of a farm even though he had been dispossessed for two years by the Parliamentary army during the English civil war and was unable to cultivate his fields.

It was against this background that the dispute in the case of *Taylor* v *Caldwell* (1863) came before the Court of Queen's Bench for resolution. The case was brought by Taylor, who was an impresario. The defendant, Caldwell, owned a concert venue known as the Surrey Gardens and Music Hall and the two entered into a contract. It was agreed that Taylor could hire the venue to stage a series of four concerts in the summer months. Taylor agreed to pay Caldwell a substantial sum of money (by the standards of the time) just prior to each concert to use the venue. A few days before the first concert was to be given a fire broke out and the music hall was gutted by the blaze. The debris was strewn about the venue so that it could no longer be used as intended. Taylor took the view that Caldwell's obligation to provide the venue was absolute and he therefore sued, alleging breach of contract, claiming as damages all the expenses that he had incurred in publicising and organising the concerts. Caldwell's defence was that the fire was not his fault and that it was impossible to carry out the contract as envisaged because the music hall had been virtually destroyed. The judge had to decide whether the obligations arising under the contract were, as a matter of legal principle, at an end or whether Caldwell, the defendant, was obliged to pay the damages claimed by Taylor for breach of contract. Blackburn J, in giving his judgment after careful consideration, stated:

> In the present case, looking at the whole contract, we find that the parties contracted on the basis of the continued existence of the music hall at the time when the concerts were to be given, that being essential to their performance. We think, therefore, that, the music hall having ceased to exist without fault of either party, both parties are excused, [Taylor] from taking the gardens and paying the money and the defendant from performing their promise to give the use of the hall and gardens, and other things.

Blackburn J did not use the phrase 'frustration of contract'. Rather, he preferred to base his judgment on the existence of an 'implied term' that he took to be assumed by the parties to the effect that the contract would be ended if performance became impossible through destruction of the venue. Since there was no breach of contract, there could be no claim for damages. The precedent created in *Taylor* v *Caldwell* was then applied in the later case of *Appleby Bros* v *Myers* (1867) by Blackburn J. In that case Appleby Bros contracted to supply and erect certain machinery on the defendant's premises and to keep it in good repair for two years. The price agreed for the work and materials was to be paid by the defendant on completion. After part of the work had been completed and whilst other parts were in progress, a fire accidentally broke out which destroyed the premises and all the machinery. Although the subject matter of the contract was the machinery, Blackburn J had no hesitation in extending the principle developed in the earlier case to cover the destruction of the thing essential to its performance – the factory. The precedent in *Taylor* v *Caldwell* was then extended further in *Nickoll and Knight* v *Ashton* [1901] to a slightly different set of facts. In this case there was a contract for the sale of a cargo of cotton seed to be shipped from Alexandria to the United Kingdom during January 1900 by the steamship *Orlando*. After the contract had been made, the *Orlando*, which was then in the Baltic, became stranded. The vessel had been badly damaged and the sellers gave notice on 20 December to Nickoll and Knight (the buyers) that it would be impossible for the *Orlando* to load before March. On 28 December, the buyers informed the sellers that, as performance of the contract had been rendered impossible, they considered it cancelled. Somewhat surprisingly, this did not stop the buyers suing for damages for breach of contract and the case eventually reached the Court of Appeal. Two of the three judges in the Court of Appeal affirmed the judgment of the lower court and ruled that the precedent established in *Taylor* v *Caldwell* should be applied and, as a result, there could be no claim for breach of contract and damages. The precise legal basis for what is now referred to as the concept of 'frustration' was debated in legal and academic circles as there was some dissatisfaction with the so-called theory of the implied term. In *W.J. Tatem Ltd* v *Gamboa* (1938) Goddard J wrestled with the issue of the juristic basis of the concept. He had to adjudicate in a dispute in which the claimants were the owners of a ship, the *SS Moulton*, which they had chartered to the defendant, who was a representative of the Spanish Republican Government at the time of the Spanish Civil War. He rejected the theory of the implied term. He preferred to justify what is now recognised as the concept of frustration, on the basis that where a contract depends for its performance upon the continued existence of a certain state of facts, once those facts no longer obtain, the contract is frustrated. He found support for this line of reasoning in Lord Sumner's judgment in *Bank Line* v *Arthur Capel & Co.* [1919]. This approach was subsequently confirmed by Lord Radcliffe in *Davis Contractors Ltd* v *Fareham UDC* [1956] when he said:

> ... it would be simpler to say at the outset that frustration occurs whenever the law recognises that, without default of either party, a contractual obligation has become incapable of being performed because the circumstances in which performance is called for would render it a thing radically different from that which was undertaken by the contract.

3   *Ratio decidendi* and *obiter dicta*

As indicated above, a case may stand as authority for a proposition of law. However, not everything that a judge says in delivering his/her judgment will constitute the *ratio decidendi* of a case, which is the statement(s) of law based on the key facts. A judge may refer to a number of matters in the course of delivering his/her judgment that do not relate directly to the key or material facts as established in the case. Sometimes a judge may even hypothesise on the outcome if the facts were somewhat different than those established. However, it is only the material facts and the principles of law as applied to those facts which lead to the decision that constitutes the *ratio decidendi.* Everything else said by the judge in the course of delivering his/her judgment is referred to as *obiter dicta* (literally, things said by the way). *Obiter dicta* is not precedent and will not therefore be binding on another court.

Extracting the *ratio decidendi* of a case is likely to prove a relatively straightforward task where there is just one judgment to consider when the case is initially tried. If there is a subsequent appeal, the Lords Justices of Appeal may concur with the court of first instance, in which case extracting the *ratio decidendi* may again be relatively straightforward. However, the process becomes more complex if there is an appeal with the original judgment being overruled, unless there is a leading judgment in the Court of Appeal with which the other judges concur and add very little. This is because the three judges (occasionally five) in the Court of Appeal have the right to deliver independent judgments and, although they may agree on the outcome, they may adopt different lines of reasoning sometimes invoking different legal principles. There could even be a split decision of two to one (as there was in *Nickoll and Knight* v *Ashton*) even though it is the majority decision that will count. These difficulties may be compounded if there is a subsequent appeal to the House of Lords. Only rarely does the House of Lords issue a joint judgment as in *Heaton Transport* v *TGWU* [1973]. When the House of Lords overrules the decision of the Court of Appeal, extracting the *ratio* may be complex because appeals in the House of Lords are heard by five Law Lords each of whom may deliver a full judgment. Some students will be content to rely on the skill of the law reporter who will state what he/she considers to be the *ratio decidendi* at the end of the headnote. Students who wish to probe for themselves must make some attempt to extract the *ratio* and may take a ruler and make five columns on a sheet of A3 so that they can line up similar statements of legal principle made by each of the Law Lords alongside each other to ascertain whether common reasoning is used by the judges. It has to be admitted, nevertheless, that on occasion, extracting the *ratio* may prove to be an impossible task. This impossibility is well illustrated by the House of Lords' decision in the case of *Elder, Dempster & Co. Ltd* v *Paterson, Zochonis & Co. Ltd* [1924]. When considering this case in the later case of *Scruttons Ltd* v *Midland Silicones Ltd* [1962], Lord Reid, a highly respected Law Lord, said:

> It can hardly be denied that the *ratio decidendi* of the Elder, Dempster decision is very obscure ... when I look for such a principle I cannot find it and the extensive and able arguments of counsel ... have failed to discover it.

In the former case, the House of Lords had to decide whether a ship owner could claim the advantage of an exclusion clause in a bill of lading, even though the contract of carriage was between the shipper and the charterer of the vessel.

Clearly, isolating the *ratio decidendi* of a case is not the equivalent of isolating a chemical element in an experiment. It is a matter of summarising the relevant part of the judgment based on the facts but this can often be done at different levels of generalisation (or abstraction). For example, a very narrow formulation of the *ratio* in *Taylor* v *Caldwell* would have limited it to the destruction of entertainment venues, but Blackburn J evidently did not intend that it should be construed so narrowly. He obviously formulated his *ratio* on the basis that it should be capable of a wider application and applied it in *Appleby Bros* v *Myers* to cover a contract for the installation of equipment when the business premises were destroyed by fire. Since then, what has become known as the principle of frustration of contract has been applied to contracts where there was no destruction of the subject matter by fire, as in *Nickoll and Knight* v *Ashton* and in *Krell* v *Henry* [1903] (to be discussed later). Thus, there is a sense in which the understanding and application of the *ratio decidendi* of an earlier case can be affected by how it comes to be interpreted and applied by subsequent courts. This has been shown in relation to *W.J. Tatem Ltd* v *Gamboa* (1938) and in *Davis Contractors Ltd* v *Fareham UDC* [1956], although in the latter case the contract was not found to have been frustrated.

4   Influential *obiter*

Although what is deemed to be *obiter dicta* does not form part of the precedent this does not mean that it is of no value whatsoever. The dicta of judges in the Court of Appeal and House of Lords may be important for the subsequent evolution of case law. For example, the *obiter dicta* of Lord Denning MR delivered as part of his judgment in the Court of Appeal in *Central London Property Trust Ltd v High Trees House Ltd* [1947] signalled an important development in the law of contract in the area of contractual waiver. Moreover, the *obiter dicta* of the Law Lords in *Hedley Byrne Ltd* v *Heller & Partners Ltd* [1964] indicated that there would be an important development in the tort of negligence, although the bankers that were sued in that case were not liable in the tort of negligence by reason of a disclaimer of liability that had been given. Nevertheless, their Lordships stated that in future there should be liability under certain circumstances for negligent misstatements that cause financial loss. This is the way in which the law of negligence has subsequently developed through cases such as *Smith* v *Eric S. Bush* [1989] and *Morgan Crucible Co. Plc* v *Hill Samuel* [1991].

5   Precedent and the hierarchy of the courts

Since the latter part of the nineteenth century, there has existed a clear hierarchy of courts and the process of law-making by precedent operates through this hierarchical structure (see Figure 3.1). A precedent established in the High Court is not, strictly speaking, binding in the sense of having to be followed by another High Court judge who is called upon to decide a case with similar facts at a later date. That said, however, it will be strongly persuasive and will usually be followed on the basis that, as a matter of procedural justice, like cases should be treated alike. This predisposition to follow established precedent is often referred to by the Latin phrase *stare decisis*. You will recall that the ratio in *Taylor* v *Caldwell* was followed in *Appleby Bros* v *Myers* even though it was not a binding precedent. Divisional Courts of the High Court are bound by their previous decisions in both civil and criminal cases but they do not bind Crown Courts. Precedents established in the High Court are binding on all lower courts such as county courts and magistrates' courts in respect of their civil jurisdiction. Since decisions of county court judges are rarely reported, they bind only the parties to the litigation but no other court. All precedents established in the appellate courts are regarded as particularly authoritative if the judges agree on the outcome and have employed similar lines of reasoning. Thus precedents set by the House of Lords bind the Court of Appeal and all lower courts and tribunals, but since 1966 the House of Lords has been free to depart from its own precedents. The Practice Statement [1966] 1 WLR 1234 issued by Lord Gardiner, the then Lord Chancellor, on behalf of the Law Lords stated:

> Their Lordships regard the use of precedent as an indispensable foundation upon which to decide what is the law and its application to individual cases. It provides at least some degree of certainty upon which individuals can rely in the conduct of their affairs as well as a basis for orderly development of legal rules. Their Lordships nevertheless recognise that too rigid adherence to precedent may lead to injustice in a particular case and also unduly restrict the proper development of the law. They propose therefore to modify their present practice and, while treating former decisions of this House as normally binding, to depart from a previous decision when it appears right to do so. In this connection they will bear in mind the danger of disturbing retrospectively the basis on which contracts, settlements of property and fiscal arrangements have been entered into and also the special need for certainty as to the criminal law. This announcement is not intended to affect the use of precedent elsewhere than in this House.

The House of Lords first exercised its power to overrule one of its earlier precedents in *Conway* v *Rimmer* [1968] by overruling *Duncan* v *Cammell Laird & Co.* [1942]. In relation to the number of occasions on which the House of Lords has been asked by counsel to overrule one of its established precedents, it has exercised this freedom infrequently and with caution. The House did overrule its earlier precedent set in *Robert Addie & Sons (Collieries) Ltd* v *Dumbreck* [1929] in the later case of *British Railways Board* v *Herrington* [1972] ruling that an occupier of premises may incur liability in the tort of negligence to a trespasser. It is interesting to note, however, that in *R* v *Kansal (No. 2)* [2001] four of the five Law Lords upheld the earlier House of Lords precedent in *R* v *Lambert* [2001] even though three of the four Law Lords thought it had been wrongly decided. Both cases involved the application of the Human Rights Act 1998 and the Convention rights made available under it in UK law. They had to decide whether a person convicted before the implementation of the legislation could rely on the Convention rights in a post-implementation appeal. In deciding that this was not possible, they demonstrated their attachment to the principle of *stare decisis*.

Although the Court of Appeal (Civil Division) is bound by precedents established by the House of Lords, it is also bound by its own precedents on the principle of *stare decisis*. The exceptions to this state of affairs were set out by Lord Green MR in *Young* v *Bristol Aeroplane Co. Ltd* [1944] and may be summarised as follows:

(a) Where two previous precedents of the Court of Appeal on similar facts are shown to differ, one must be followed and the other rejected.

(b) Where a previous decision of the Court of Appeal is at variance with a later decision of the House of Lords, its previous decision cannot be followed even if it was not expressly overruled by the House of Lords.

(c) Where a previous decision of the Court of Appeal can be shown to be given *per incuriam* (literally, through want of care) it should not be followed, but this principle has been interpreted narrowly to apply to instances in which some binding authority or statutory provision has been overlooked by the court.

6   The *per incuriam* exception

The case of *Rakhit* v *Carty* [1990] provides a good example of (c) above. The claimant, who was a landlord, let a furnished flat to the defendant, Mrs Carty, for 364 days at a rent of £450 per month. Neither party was aware that a 'fair rent' of £550 per annum had been registered in respect of this flat in 1974 when the flat was unfurnished and was recorded as such in the rent register. When Mrs Carty's contractual tenancy came to an end she remained in occupation as a 'statutory tenant' and so the landlord commenced legal proceedings against her for possession. He argued that he reasonably required the flat as a residence for himself under the Rent Act 1977 Schedule 15, Case 9, and he claimed arrears of rent and expenses. The defendant resisted the claim for possession on the basis that it was not reasonable to make the order and that pursuant to Schedule 15 Part III greater hardship would be caused to her by granting the order than would be caused to the landlord by refusing to grant it. She also counterclaimed for arrears of rent on the basis that, where a fair rent was registered, the rent recoverable for any contractual period of a regulated tenancy was limited to the rent so registered. In a nutshell, she argued that there were no arrears of rent but that she had overpaid the rent for the flat and was entitled to a refund. The county court judge upheld the landlord's claim and dismissed Mrs Carty's counterclaim because he considered himself bound by earlier decisions of the Court of Appeal. Mrs Carty appealed contending, among other matters, that the Court of Appeal's earlier decisions had been given *per incuriam* because it had not considered the Rent Act 1977 s. 67(3). This subsection provided that if there was a change in the condition of the dwelling, terms of the tenancy or the quantity, quality or condition of any furniture provided so as to make the registered rent no longer a fair rent either party could apply for a re-registration. The Court of Appeal held that since its earlier decisions had not referred to s. 67(3), it was justified in treating them as having been given *per incuriam* because they had been given in ignorance of the subsection. Accordingly, Mrs Carty's appeal against the dismissal of her counterclaim was allowed but the Court of Appeal saw no basis for interfering with the county court judge's decision to make a possession order. Thus her appeal against the possession order failed. In giving the judgment of the Court of Appeal, Russell LJ cited part of the judgment of

Lord Donaldson MR in *Ricards* v *Ricards* [1989] when the latter referred to *Young* v *Bristol Aeroplane Co. Ltd* and some later cases. In that case Lord Donaldson MR stated:

> These decisions show that this court is justified in refusing to follow one of its own previous decisions not only where that decision is given in ignorance or forgetfulness of some inconsistent statutory provision or some authority binding on it, but also, in rare and exceptional cases, if it is satisfied that the decision involved a manifest slip or error. In previous cases the judges of this court have always refrained from defining this exceptional category and I have no intention of departing from that approach save to echo the words of Lord Greene MR ... and to say that they will be of the rarest occurrence.

Since the exceptions set out by Lord Greene MR in *Young* v *Bristol Aeroplane Co. Ltd*, a fourth exception has emerged from *Boys* v *Chaplin* [1968]. It is now clear that the Court of Appeal (Civil Division) is not bound by an interlocutory (interim) order made by two appeal court judges sitting as the Court of Appeal. The Criminal Division of the Court of Appeal is never bound by its previous decisions if it considers the law has been misapplied or misunderstood in an earlier case but it is bound by precedents established by the House of Lords.

7 Flexibility or rigidity?

Given the way in which law-making by precedent operates through the hierarchical structure of the civil courts, the reader might wonder whether the process places judges in the Court of Appeal and those lower down the hierarchy in something of a straitjacket. The judges do, in fact, have a degree of freedom and flexibility within certain limits. Even at the level of the High Court it is possible for a judge to 'distinguish' a precedent cited by an advocate that the judge has been invited to follow. Such a precedent will be direct authority only if the facts are alike. However, the judge may be able to 'distinguish' the present case on its facts by emphasising some important factual dissimilarity to the facts of the precedent cited by an advocate. Of course, this must be justifiable on the basis of the material or key facts as established in evidence in the case under review. If this cannot be done, a departure from existing precedent would require some other justification, such as a necessary limiting of the scope of the rule of law established by the earlier precedent. Factual distinguishing, if adopted, enables the judge to reach an independent decision and in the process a new precedent may be created.

An example of the process of 'factual distinguishing' may be given by considering its application within the doctrine of frustration of contract by comparing and contrasting two cases. The precedent of *Taylor* v *Caldwell* was applied in the case of *Krell* v *Henry* [1903]. Krell was the tenant of some rooms in Pall Mall, London, which overlooked the route that the coronation procession of Edward VII was destined to take. The litigation arose out of a contract that he made with the defendant, Henry. Under this contract Krell agreed, for a fee, to make the rooms available to the defendant on the days on which the coronation procession was scheduled to pass by so that he could view it from a vantage point. Unfortunately, after the contract had been made and just before the date set for the coronation pageant, the King became very ill and the event was cancelled. This did not inhibit Krell from suing to recover the agreed fee and the case eventually went on appeal to the Court of Appeal. All three judges ruled that the principle enunciated in *Taylor* v *Caldwell* should be applied and so there was no basis for Krell's claim since the contract had been discharged as a matter of law when the coronation pageant was cancelled. At about the same time, the Court of Appeal had to deal with the case of *Herne Bay Steam Boat Co.* v *Hutton* [1903]. The company owned and operated a steamboat and it made a contract with the defendant under which he could hire it to take a party of people to see the naval review by Edward VII of the British fleet of warships anchored off Spithead. After watching the review it was planned to spend the rest of the time cruising around the fleet that was at anchor. The naval review was officially postponed on 25 June because of the King's illness but the fleet remained at anchor off Spithead. Although the company telegraphed the defendant, no reply was received and he failed to arrive with his party of people on the due date. When he subsequently refused to pay the balance of the hire fee, the company then sued for breach of contract claiming damages. The Court of Appeal declined to apply the precedent of *Taylor* v *Caldwell* and distinguished it from the case under consideration on the basis that the naval review of the fleet by the King was not the sole basis of the contract as it would still have been possible for the defendant and his party to cruise around the fleet anchored off Spithead. Accordingly, there had been a breach of contract and the defendant was liable in damages.

There is always a danger that factual distinguishing may be taken too far in order to achieve a difference of outcome from an earlier precedent that a judge does not wish to follow. This can result in the making of some very fine distinctions of fact which merely serve to make the law on a particular subject unnecessarily complex. Factual distinguishing is not the only stratagem available to the judges, as indicated above. Another possibility would be to say that the rule or principle of law formulated in the earlier case cited by an advocate was formulated far too widely by the court and that this was unnecessary to achieve the desired result in that case. This is known as 'restrictive distinguishing'. It is a process by which the judge or judges reduce the scope of the earlier rule or principle so that it no longer extends to and encompasses the facts and circumstances of the case under consideration, thus paving the way for an independent decision and another distinct precedent.

In order to avoid following a precedent set in the High Court and cited by an advocate as authority to be followed, a judge can say that the previous case was wrongly decided and that therefore the *ratio* is 'faulty'. The previous precedent is then said to be 'disapproved', but this can only be done in practice if there is some consensus among legal commentators that the earlier decision was wrong and that it should no longer be followed. It is not something a judge would do without careful consideration and it is to be noted that one High Court judge cannot overrule another. Disapproving is a technique that can be used by the appellate courts although the Court of Appeal can never disapprove of a precedent set in the House of Lords.

Precedents set in the lower courts can, of course, be overruled by the appellate courts. The House of Lords can overrule a precedent set in the Court of Appeal, although the Court of Appeal cannot overrule a precedent established by the House of Lords. Once a precedent has been overruled it may no longer be cited as authority in any court. It is no longer good law.

8 Precedent and the Human Rights Act 1998

It is expressly provided in the Human Rights Act 1998 s. 6(1) that it is unlawful for a public authority (including a court or tribunal) to act in a way that is incompatible with a Convention right as contained in Schedule 1. Moreover, s. 2(1) states that a court or tribunal in determining a question that has arisen in connection with a Convention right must take account of any judgment, decision, declaration or advisory opinion of the European Court of Human Rights and any opinion of the Human Rights Commission in a report adopted under Article 31 of the Convention. The effect of all this is that all previous rulings of the European Court of Human Rights become jurisprudence that British courts must at least consider. The Act itself gives a claimant a cause of action against a public authority if his/her Convention rights are infringed. If an existing precedent, in the sphere of public law, can be shown to be at variance with a ruling of the European Court of Human Rights, it may have to be disregarded. At the time of writing, legal commentators are divided over whether the Human Rights Act 1998 has horizontal effect as between private legal persons (individuals and companies). The prevailing view seems to be that, in general, it does not give rise to any new causes of action as between private legal persons. However, where there is law already developed governing private relations, it must be developed in a way to achieve compatibility with Convention rights and on this basis actions may be brought against private legal persons. The courts are endeavouring to develop the law in relation to Article 8(1) which confers the right to respect for private and family life (although this right is qualified in Article 8(2)).

The High Court in exercise of its equitable jurisdiction (see Appendix 1) prior to the coming into force of the Human Rights Act 1998 recognised a 'breach of confidence' in particular circumstances as giving a cause of action for which relief by way of an injunction could be granted. Thus, in *Stephens* v *Avery and others* [1988] the claimant brought her action against three defendants, the first of whom she had communicated certain information in confidence and the second and third defendants had been responsible for publishing this confidential information in a Sunday newspaper. The defendants applied to have the claimant's claim struck out on the basis that it disclosed no reasonable cause of action. When this was refused, they appealed contending that the information pertaining to a person's extra-marital sexual activity was not protected by the law relating to confidential information and that the relationship between the claimant and first defendant did not give rise to a duty of confidence. The court held that information relating to sexual conduct could be subject to a legally enforceable duty of confidence if it would be unconscionable for the recipient (who had obtained the information on the express basis that it was to be confidential) to reveal it to another. The decision of the High Court Master to refuse to strike out the claim was upheld. In giving judgment in the High Court, Sir Nicholas Browne-Wilkinson (as he then was) cited a number of earlier precedents going back to 1916.

Since the coming into force of the Human Rights Act 1998 the courts have reviewed this case law in the light of Article 8 and indeed Article 10 (conferring a qualified right to freedom of expression). In *Douglas and others* v *Hello Ltd* [2001] the Court of Appeal had to adjudicate in an appeal by *Hello* magazine where a celebrity couple had sought and obtained an injunction from the High Court restraining the magazine from publishing unauthorised photographs of their wedding which had been conducted at a hotel with some 250 guests. The issues that arose for consideration were the application of the Human Rights Act 1998 s. 12 and whether this gave Article 10 (freedom of expression) priority over Article 8. In addition, it was questioned whether s. 12 was compatible with the Convention rights and whether English law protected a person from unwanted intrusions into their privacy in the absence of an obligation of confidence. Both Sedley LJ and Keene LJ expressed the view that a pre-existing confidential relationship between the parties was not an essential requirement for a breach of confidence action. There could be liability for breach of confidence owing to the nature of the subject matter or due to the defendant's activities. The Court of Appeal found no conflict between s. 12 of the Act and the Convention rights and was not prepared to accord Article 10(1) priority over Article 8(1). It did, however, lift the injunction because it considered that damages would be an adequate remedy. In the subsequent case on liability *Douglas* v *Hello (No. 3)* [2003], the High Court did award damages against *Hello* magazine on the basis that the magazine had unjustifiably intruded into the private lives of the couple without consent. Moreover, the rights granted to *OK* magazine were said to be analogous to a commercial property right, which had been infringed by *Hello*.

Although the Court of Appeal in *Douglas and others* v *Hello Ltd* had recognised a qualified right to privacy in English law, a differently constituted Court of Appeal had to consider how this was to be balanced against Article 10(1) and freedom of the press in *A* v *B* [2002]. In this case the first defendant, a national newspaper, appealed from the decision of Jack J in the High Court to grant an injunction restraining the first defendant from publishing two articles relating to the extra-marital affairs of a premier league football player with a young family. Since the issue turned on press freedom in an open society a single judgment was delivered by Lord Woolf CJ who set aside the injunction granted by the High Court. In doing so he indicated that, when dealing with applications for interim injunctions to restrain publication by the media of confidential information that is alleged to infringe the claimant's privacy, a court had to balance conflicting rights. This in turn frequently required a balancing of facts rather than a technical approach to the law. The weight to be attached to each relevant consideration might vary depending on the circumstances, with no clear movement in the direction of safeguarding privacy. If this should be the case, the court should refuse to grant interim injunctions. At present there is a lack of clarity surrounding the law on privacy and further developments in English law will be influenced by developments in the jurisprudence of the European Court of Human Rights in Strasbourg. It should also be noted that the Human Rights Act 1998 has been invoked to develop the tort of private nuisance. Damages were recovered by the claimant in *Marcic* v *Thames Water* [2001].

9 Reporting precedents

Law-making by precedent depends to a very large extent on the accurate reporting of the decisions of the superior courts. It is important that lawyers and judges (as well as law students) are able to refer to the more significant judgments that are delivered in these courts. Indeed, it is difficult to envisage how a system of binding precedent could operate without a reliable system of law reporting. Fortunately this is undertaken by a quasi-official body, the Incorporated Council for Law Reporting in England and Wales.

It now publishes four sets of reports annually, known as 'the Law Reports'. The Appeal Cases are decisions of the House of Lords but the set also contains reports of cases heard by the Law Lords sitting as the Judicial Committee of the Privy Council which hears civil and criminal appeals from certain Commonwealth countries. In addition, there is one set of reports for each division of the High Court, namely Queen's Bench, Chancery and Family Division. Decisions of the Court of Appeal do not appear in the Appeal Cases but in the reports for the three divisions of the High Court, the particular volume being determined by the court that heard the case at first instance. In Practice Direction [1999] 1 WLR 1027, the Court of Appeal (Civil Division) made it clear that if a case is published by the Incorporated Council for Law Reporting for England and Wales, this is the version that should be cited in court. The reasons are twofold. First, it is a requirement that the barrister or solicitor responsible for preparing the report must be in court when the judgment is handed down. Secondly, the judges themselves edit their judgments prior to publication and the advocates edit the summaries of their arguments that are to be included in the report. The Law Reports always appear in bound form many months after the calendar year to which they relate. Consequently, since 1953, the Incorporated Council has published the Weekly Law Reports in paperback parts to ensure that all the more important judgments are available to practitioners as quickly as possible. The judgments in these reports are not revised by the judges prior to publication but they are still of great value to lawyers, academics and law students. There is a website where it is possible to get summaries of recent decisions of the Court of Appeal and High Court. Recent judgments of the House of Lords are available at the UK Parliament website.

10   Other law reports

In addition to the law reports produced by the Incorporated Council, there are a number of highly regarded reports produced by commercial publishers. The best known series is the All England Law Reports now published by Butterworths – Lexis/Nexis which originally date from 1936. This excellent series contains judgments of the High Court, Court of Appeal and House of Lords in the same annual volumes. There are also a number of lesser known reports including Lloyd's Law Reports, Simon's Tax Cases and the Industrial Relations Law Reports.

■ Summary

Important branches of the civil law (e.g. contract and tort) are largely judge-made in that the law is to be found in the form of precedents embedded in case law. Consequently, anyone wishing to become familiar with these branches of the law must become familiar with the technique of law-making by precedent. In doing so, it is necessary to understand how precedent operates through the hierarchical structure of the civil courts. The study of case law also entails acquiring an understanding of the process of law reporting and the ability to locate the *ratio decidendi* of a case in a report. Despite indications to the contrary, this is not a static, nor a rigid, form of law-making because established precedents are reviewed from time to time. In the process they can be distinguished and even overruled. The fact that the House of Lords is free to depart from its established precedents also means that there is a possibility of change. The Human Rights Act 1998 has added a new dimension to this form of law-making and opens up the prospect of fresh developments as has been seen, in particular, in relation to the law on privacy.

WWW **PROGRESS TEST**

For suggested answers to the tests below, go to the companion website at
www.pearsoned.co.uk/wheeler

1 What do you consider to be the *ratio decidendi* of *Taylor* v *Caldwell*?
2 In what later cases was the *ratio* in *Taylor* v *Caldwell* applied?
3 What is the basis of the distinction between *ratio decidendi* and *obiter dicta*?
4 Are precedents created by High Court judges binding or persuasive?
5 What do you understand by the principle of *stare decisis*?
6 To what extent is the Court of Appeal bound by its previous decisions?
7 Does the House of Lords tend to follow its previous decisions and is it bound to do so?
8 What do you understand by the phrase 'factual distinguishing'?
9 What do you understand by the phrase 'restrictive distinguishing'?
10 To what extent, if at all, does the Human Rights Act 1998 affect the operation of law-making by precedent?

FURTHER READING

■ Books

Ingman, T. (2004) *The English Legal Process* (Oxford: Oxford University Press, chapters 9 and 10).

Slapper, G. and D. Kelly (2004) *The English Legal System* (London: Cavendish Publishing, pp. 44–56).

Twining, W. and D. Miers (1999) *How To Do Things With Rules* (Cambridge: Cambridge University Press, chapter 8).

Ward, R. (2005) *Walker and Walker's English Legal System* (Oxford: Oxford University Press, chapter 3).

Zander, M. (2004) *The Law Making Process* (Cambridge: Cambridge University Press).

■ Articles

Beyleveld, D. and S.D. Pattinson (2002) 'Horizontal Applicability and Horizontal Effect', *Law Quarterly Review* Vol. 118, October.

Harris, B.V. (2002) 'Final Appellate Courts Overruling their own "Wrong" Precedents: The Ongoing Search for Principle', *Law Quarterly Review* Vol. 118, July.

USEFUL WEBSITES

The website www.bailii.org for the British and Irish Legal Information
Institute (BAILII) contains a wealth of information on UK and Irish
legislation and case law.

The website of the Incorporated Council for Law Reporting in England
and Wales can be found at www.lawreports.co.uk.

HM Court Service publishes recent judgments of the Court of Appeal and
High Court on its website at www.courtservice.gov.uk.

5 The law-making process 2: Primary legislation

1 Introduction

The Westminster Parliament is the legislature of the United Kingdom and it also functions as a forum and focal point for political debate. It has evolved over hundreds of years and dates from the Provisions of Oxford in 1258. In the past three hundred years especially, Parliament has been called upon to enact numerous detailed schemes of law to facilitate the political, economic and social evolution of the UK. As a result, enacted law (or statute law or legislation as it is otherwise known) has long since become the predominant form of law-making in the UK. By comparison, the ongoing contribution of the judiciary to the law-making process through development of precedent occurs on a relatively modest scale. Moreover, law-making by precedent is also an unplanned process, depending, as it does, on the randomness of litigation. Thus, legislation should be viewed as a systematic approach to law-making, the complexity of which tends to reflect the sophistication of modern economic and social life. This chapter focuses on the legislative process but, before doing so, it will be necessary to consider some aspects of UK constitutional law. Having dealt with the legislative process, it will then be appropriate to examine the doctrine of parliamentary sovereignty before critiquing the quality of some statute law.

2 Constitutional settlements past and present

The United Kingdom is a relatively modern creation in the long history of the British Isles. It came into being in 1707 as a result of a treaty between England and Scotland, after which the Scottish parliament in Edinburgh was dissolved. Wales had operated within the same political and legal framework as England since 1536 and was automatically subsumed into the union in 1707. As a result of another Act of Union in 1800, the whole of the island of Ireland became part of the United Kingdom in 1801. Then in 1922, when the Irish Free State (later to be known as the Republic of Ireland) was created following an armed struggle for independence, only the six northern counties remained within the United Kingdom with England, Wales and Scotland. The Labour government that was elected in

1997 was committed to a radical programme of constitutional reform through devolution of political power to the regions. As a result, Scotland has been granted a system of devolved government by the Westminster Parliament with a new Scottish Parliament sitting in Edinburgh. The Edinburgh Parliament has the power to enact primary legislation for the whole of Scotland within the limits specified in the Scotland Act 1998. In this respect the Welsh Assembly is different because it does not have the power to enact primary legislation. Northern Ireland was granted a new system of devolved government in the Northern Ireland Act 1998 similar to that for Scotland but this has been suspended for the time being. The Westminster Parliament, nevertheless, retains the power to legislate for the entire UK on a wide range of matters including taxation, defence and foreign relations, as well as to incorporate EU directives. In an average year the UK Parliament produces in the region of 50 statutes, known as Acts of Parliament, on a very wide range of topics, most of which are outlined in the Queen's speech at the state opening in November.

3 Composition of the Westminster Parliament

In the constitutional law of the UK the Westminster Parliament comprises the House of Commons, the House of Lords and the Queen in Parliament. The House of Commons is the only elected element, comprising 659 members who represent the various parliamentary constituencies as defined by the Parliamentary Constituencies Act 1986. The House of Lords (which is to be distinguished from the present appeal court of the same name) is unelected and at present comprises 92 hereditary peers, 26 bishops of the Church of England and a large number of life peers, many of whom are former politicians. The number of hereditary peers with voting rights was reduced by the House of Lords Act 1999 as part of the Labour government's package of constitutional reforms. Life peers may be created under the Life Peerages Act 1958 and they now outnumber hereditary peers. The Stevenson Commission has been established to oversee the appointment of future life peers. Having taken up references and interviewed applicants, it will recommend the appointment of between eight and ten 'outstanding' persons each year as life peers. Just to complicate matters, the Law Lords who presently comprise the appellate court known as the House of Lords are life peers. As such, they currently have the right to sit and participate in proceedings of the House although they do not usually participate in party political debates. It is likely that they will lose this right when the government's constitutional reforms contained in the Constitutional Reform Bill are enacted.

The role of the monarch is largely ceremonial. It is mainly confined to summoning a newly elected Parliament, opening each annual session (during which the Queen's speech is delivered from the throne in the House of Lord's chamber) and dissolving Parliament prior to a general election being called. Although the Labour government plans to modernise the procedure of the House of Commons, it was reported in the *Financial Times* (30 March 1998) that the prime minister has insisted that the Queen's speech and all aspects of the ceremony surrounding it must be kept. The monarch must, in principle, assent to all new legislation before it can become law and so the reality surrounding the Royal Assent will be considered subsequently.

4 Proposals for new legislation

Some of the government's proposals for new legislation will have derived from specific manifesto pledges on which it was elected to office. For example, it was a manifesto commitment of the Labour Party in 1997 to devolve power from Westminster to the regions and make available the rights enshrined in the European Convention on Human Rights and Fundamental Freedoms in national law. These commitments were subsequently fulfilled through the enactment of the Human Rights Act 1998 and the devolution legislation mentioned above. Most of the proposals for new legislation, however, derive from within the various Whitehall departments as the civil service endeavours to implement the overall policy objectives of the government.

The government of the day is lobbied from time to time by a variety of pressure groups (for example, the CBI, TUC, Consumers' Association, National Union of Farmers, Child Poverty Action Group). In November 2004 the Voluntary Euthanasia Society was trying to put pressure on government to change the law on assisted suicide. If the government decides to take action in response to pressure group activity, then new legislation may be called for. In addition there are usually proposals for law reform from the Law Commission requiring implementation, and sometimes from a Royal Commission that the government may have established to investigate some particular urgent problem. Ordinary members of the Commons and members of the House of Lords are also lobbied to introduce Private Members' Bills by various interest groups who wish to see changes in the law. A Bill to legalise assisted suicide was introduced in the House of Lords in November 2004. In the case of members of the House of Commons, they are likely to be petitioned if they secure one of the slots by ballot that enables them to propose new legislation on one of the 13 occasions in each session allowed for considering such proposals. However, unless the government takes an interest in a private member's proposal, the MP will not receive assistance from the Office of Parliamentary Counsel with the drafting of the Bill. Moreover, unless the government allows sufficient parliamentary time, it is unlikely that the proposal will be enacted. A recent example of a successful Private Member's Bill is the so-called 'whistle blowing' legislation. Richard Shepherd, a Conservative MP, introduced a Private Member's Bill to protect people who exposed fraud, crime in general and malpractice in the workplace. The Bill received the support of Ian McCartney, a government minister, and it was subsequently enacted as the Public Interest Disclosure Act 1998. Frequently, government plans for new legislation will be preceded by a White Paper that sets out the government's standpoint on a range of issues within the particular area of policy. Sometimes a White Paper may be preceded by a Green Paper which sets out proposals for consideration and comment by the public at large.

5   Time pressures

There is always a shortage of parliamentary time. There is never a shortage of proposals for new legislation from within government and the civil service. Ministers, conscious of their place in history, are often anxious to have a monument to their time in office and have major pieces of legislation associated with them. By constitutional convention the maximum duration of a Parliament is five years, at the end of which there must be a general election. Within this timescale there will be annual sessions that usually commence in November in one year and run to the following October, interspersed with recesses for long vacations. Therefore, in an annual session, Parliament sits for only about 30 weeks (a week of four-and-a-half days). As a result, the government of the day tends to monopolise the parliamentary timetable because it wishes to ensure that all its proposed legislation for the session can be debated and enacted within the limited time available. For these reasons the government may on occasion resort to what the popular media refer to as 'guillotining' a Bill that is controversial, as it did for the Hunting Bill. This entails setting time limits for the various stages in the parliamentary process. The setting of such time limits by a Standing Committee of MPs prior to, or immediately after Second Reading is more properly known as 'programming', which is conducted under Standing Orders 82 and 83.

6   Establishing priorities for legislation

Except when there has been a change of government, approximately six weeks into the new session of Parliament (mid-December) the Cabinet Office will ask the various government departments to submit lists of proposed Bills required for the next session of Parliament. The departments will be asked to rank these proposals in order of importance and provide an indication when the instructions to the parliamentary draftspersons will be ready. These lists are then submitted to a special Cabinet committee known as the Future Legislation Committee whose members include the leaders of both Houses and the government's chief whip. In the following January, the Cabinet committee will draw up a provisional list of proposed Bills for discussion with the ministers of the departments that originally put forward the proposals. After discussions with the ministers concerned and the First Parliamentary Counsel from the Office of Parliamentary Counsel, a shortlist will be compiled for the next session of Parliament, to be submitted to the full Cabinet. All this may take five months. The order of priority is likely to be altered as a result of discussion in Cabinet, and the list that is finally agreed becomes the government's programme for the next session of Parliament. Since this planning process is forward-looking, the legislation that is mentioned in the Queen's speech at the state opening of Parliament will normally comprise the list that was agreed by the Cabinet during the previous session of Parliament unless a general election has intervened. Control of the government's current legislative programme, which is outlined in the Queen's speech, then passes to the Legislation Committee. It is this committee which also regulates the flow of instructions to the parliamentary draftspersons. However, there has to be some flexibility in the government's current programme to allow for the possibility of emergency legislation which can be slotted in if and when necessary.

7 Role of the drafters

The Bills that are destined to become Public General Acts of Parliament will be drafted by an elite corps of solicitors and barristers working in the Office of Parliamentary Counsel which is part of the Cabinet Office. They work in teams and are supervised by the First Parliamentary Counsel. The department was established in 1869 in Whitehall and now comprises a professional staff of about 60 lawyers with 20 support staff. Once a proposed Bill has been included in the government's current legislative programme, the First Parliamentary Counsel will sometimes receive detailed written instructions from the relevant Whitehall department, but often the policy brief will be partly oral and partly in writing. The First Parliamentary Counsel will usually assign a team comprising a senior drafter and one or two juniors to the task of producing an initial draft Bill. The persons so tasked will liaise with the senior legal civil servants and junior ministers in the relevant department as they prepare this first draft for their consideration. Following the production of the initial draft, there will often be a series of conferences that will give rise to successive redraftings for major pieces of legislation. It is often an iterative process that can take several months. Parliamentary Counsel do not function as passive scribes but are able to offer advice on the precise wording of the various provisions to be included in a Bill and on their likely effectiveness. They also have the responsibility for deciding when the Bill is in a final form such that it can be presented to Parliament. It is now government policy to publish the more important Bills in draft form for pre-legislative scrutiny by expert bodies and individuals. The drafters may then have to work on changes requested by government in response to the scrutiny exercise. The Bill, when ready, will usually be presented to Parliament by the Cabinet minister whose department has sponsored it. Just prior to this a copy will have been delivered by one of the parliamentary draftspersons to the Public Bill Office of the House where the Bill is to be introduced. Thereafter, the drafters will be on hand to assist with the framing of any amendments as the Bill proceeds through its various parliamentary stages.

Although some Bills can be quite short, comprising just a few pages, a Bill on a very important topic might run to 200 or even 300 pages of A4. It will be set out in a schematic fashion, divided into parts so that each part can be identified by an Arabic numeral. The rules of law contained therein will be set out in a very precise verbal form and will be identified by numbered clauses and sub-clauses that will subsequently be referred to as 'sections' and 'subsections' once the Bill becomes an Act of Parliament. The record for the longest piece of legislation is held by the Finance Act 2000, which runs to 613 pages and was worked on by three teams of drafters.

8   Process of enactment – the Commons

If a Bill is to be enacted it must normally have three readings in both Houses before being presented for the Royal Assent. If a Bill is not politically controversial and does not involve the expenditure of public money it can be introduced into the House of Lords before being passed to the House of Commons. The majority of government Bills that are destined to become Public General Acts are introduced in the House of Commons. Moreover, all Bills involving the raising of tax and expenditure of public funds must, by constitutional convention, be introduced into the House of Commons before being passed to the House of Lords. The so-called First Reading is something of a misnomer because it does not entail the recitation of the entire Bill in the Chamber. If a Bill originates in the House of Commons, Standing Order 57(2) requires that it must be 'read for the first time' without discussion, that a date for the Second Reading is fixed and that it shall be ordered to be printed. All these are taken together as a single formal stage in the overall process. The Clerk of the House of Commons reads out the short title of the Bill and the Speaker then calls on the minister or member presenting the Bill to name a day for the Second Reading. The Speaker reiterates this date, whereupon the short title is entered into the Journal of the House. The Bill is then ordered to be read a second time on the specified date and it is also ordered to be printed at public expense.

Once the draft of the Bill has been examined it is sent for printing in accordance with the order made by the House so that its contents are available to every MP (and every interested member of the public) prior to the Second Reading. The date for the Second Reading will normally be set two weeks after the date of the First Reading in the case of government Bills. It is an established convention that two weekends should pass between the introduction of a Bill and Second Reading. The Human Rights Act 1998 s. 19 provides that, before the Second Reading, the minister sponsoring the Bill must make a statement in writing to the effect that in his/her view the provisions of the Bill are compatible with the Convention rights set out in Schedule 1 to the Act. Alternatively, he/she must make a statement to the effect that, although he/she is unable to make such a statement, the government nevertheless wishes the House to proceed with the Bill. There is now a Joint Committee on Human Rights at Westminster that scrutinises Bills for their compatibility with the Convention rights but it is only advisory and has no legal powers.

9 Process of enactment – Second Reading

The Second Reading is the crucial stage through which all government and private members' Bills have to pass. The short title appears on the Notice Paper with the other orders of the day and the minister or member in charge of the Bill puts forward a motion 'That the Bill now be read a second time'. It is only at the Second Reading that there will be an opportunity to debate the general principles and merits (or otherwise) of the Bill. However, the debate does not extend to the details of the various clauses comprising the Bill. A Cabinet minister will usually open the debate if the Bill is a government Bill, outlining its principles and summarising the most important clauses. The relevant opposition spokesperson must then respond, and during the debate the views of backbench MPs of all parties will also be heard. At the end of the time allotted, a junior minister will wind up the debate by responding to the points raised.

It is not uncommon for the government to limit the amount of time available in the House of Commons for debate and for the other stages of the Bill due to the shortage of parliamentary time. Opponents of the Bill will often vote against the motion in the form of a question put by the Speaker for a Second Reading, but it is also possible for them to put forward a reasoned amendment to the question. There is usually a vote at the end of the Second Reading debate.

After the debate on the question is over, the question must be put to the House. To do this the Speaker rises from his/her chair and puts to the House: 'The question is, That ... [the Speaker puts the proposal].' He/she then says, 'As many as are of that opinion say, "aye", and as many as are of the contrary opinion say, "no". The Speaker does his/her best to judge the respective volumes of each response and expresses his/her opinion by saying: 'I think the ayes (or noes) have it.' If the House concurs with this decision, the question is said to be 'agreed to' or 'negatived' as the case may be. Nevertheless, his/her judgment is not final in the matter because those deemed to be in the minority can dispute the Speaker's decision by crying 'no' or 'aye'. If this should happen, the Speaker will then say 'Clear the lobby'. This is to arrange for a physical count of the members for and against by the official tellers. If there is a vote against the Bill at the end of the Second Reading stage it is 'lost', but this seldom happens to government Bills where the government of the day has a substantial majority of MPs. If a Bill should be 'lost' at the end of the Second Reading it will not be possible to introduce a fresh Bill with the same provisions in that session of Parliament.

As an alternative to a Second Reading on the floor of the House, Standing Order 90 provides that a public Bill can be referred to a Second Reading Committee. The Committee is convened in an upstairs committee room provided a motion to do this is put by a government minister at the commencement of public business on the day in question. It is necessary for him/her to give 10 days' notice of any such motion and it must be put to the House immediately. If at least 20 MPs signify their objection by standing up, the Speaker must declare that the motion is defeated. Under Standing Order 59, all Law Commission Bills are referred to a Second Reading Committee (see Chapter 16).

10   Process of enactment – Committee stage and beyond

If a public Bill survives its Second Reading in the House of Commons it must, unless it is exempted by the House, be considered in Committee. Unless the Bill is to be considered by a Committee of the Whole House in the chamber, a standing committee of between 16 and 50 MPs is empanelled to consider the Bill clause by clause, each of which must be approved. Although the committee is referred to as a standing committee, the MPs sit at tables facing each other in one of the upstairs committee rooms in the Palace of Westminster (Parliament Building). Some members of the House of Commons staff will be in attendance together with some staff of Hansard who will record the official version of the proceedings. It is quite normal for parliamentary counsel to be in attendance too with senior civil servants who will be on hand to give advice to ministers. The membership of the Committee itself is weighted to reflect the relative strength of the political parties in the House of Commons so that the government will always have an inbuilt majority, but the Speaker appoints the chairperson and that person is supposed to be impartial. Amendments to the Bill can be included at the Committee Stage but opposition amendments are unlikely to be included unless they are acceptable to the government. Whilst government MPs are able to call upon the services of parliamentary counsel to draft their amendments, opposition MPs are obliged to seek the assistance of the staff in the Public Bill Office to draft their amendments. At the conclusion of the committee stage, the Bill is 'reported' back to the House. It may be reprinted to take account of all the amendments that have been made at the Committee Stage. If an amendment is carried at the Committee Stage to be incorporated in a government Bill but the amendment is not acceptable to the government, the Bill can be withdrawn and the government can later present a fresh Bill which has the same effect as the original. This second Bill can then be put forward for the Royal Assent provided that it completes all its stages in both Houses. If a Bill has been selected for 'guillotining', it is possible, however, that there may not be enough time for a detailed clause by clause examination of the entire Bill and it is possible for the Bill to be 'approved' with many of its clauses and schedules undebated.

Further amendments can be incorporated into the Bill at the Report Stage and some debate may be allowed on these and amendments that were made during the Committee Stage. Although the Report Stage must be conducted on the floor of the House, it is usually of short duration. If the Bill was amended during the Report Stage it may be reprinted to take account of these amendments.

The Third Reading follows immediately after the Report Stage. There will be a short review of the content of the Bill and any further debate must normally be confined to its final content but no further amendments are permitted. If a vote did not take place at the end of the Second Reading, a vote may follow at the end of the Third Reading before the official copy of the Bill is endorsed by the Clerk of the House and passed to the House of Lords.

11 Process of enactment – the Lords

In the House of Lords the Bill will be introduced by a peer who is also a government minister. The procedure in the House of Lords is similar in many respects except that there is no standing committee – the Bill is considered by the entire House. Thus all members of the House of Lords can, in principle, put down amendments to the Bill during its Committee Stage. At the Third Reading there is no debate but only a formal motion that is put to the House to the effect that the Bill should be passed. It often happens that the Bill is amended in the House of Lords and, if so, it must go back to the House of Commons for further consideration. If the amendments are acceptable to the government, all will be well. If this should not be the case, a compromise of some kind may be reached but, if this proves impossible, the government can invoke the Parliament Acts 1911 and 1949 to ensure that its will prevails. If a Bill is enacted under the Parliament Acts the enacting formula is varied. It will state:

> Be it enacted by the Queen's most Excellent Majesty, by and with the advice and consent of the Commons in this present Parliament assembled in accordance with the provisions of the Parliament Act 1911 and by the authority of the same as follows.

By virtue of this legislation a Bill can only be delayed by the House of Lords for one year and, in the case of a Bill dealing with taxation or finance, it can only be delayed for a month no matter how much the House of Lords should object to its content. However, the Parliament Acts cannot be invoked in respect of Bills that have been introduced in the House of Lords. The most recent piece of legislation for which the government has had to invoke the Parliament Act 1911 s. 2 is the Hunting Act

2004. Prior to this, the legislation has only been invoked on three other occasions since 1945.

12 Royal Assent

It is necessary for a Bill to receive the Royal Assent in order for it to become an Act of Parliament. This is almost a formality because by constitutional convention the monarch's assent cannot be withheld. The last time that a reigning monarch pronounced the Royal Assent in person was in 1854, and since 1541 it has been possible for the Royal Assent to be given by Commissioners on behalf of the monarch. Bills are not assented to individually and nowadays, as a result of the Royal Assent Act 1967, there is a simplified procedure for giving the Assent. The Lord Chancellor, as speaker of the House of Lords, periodically submits a list of Bills requiring the Royal Assent to the monarch. The list is actually compiled by the Clerk to the Parliaments but an advance copy is sent to the Clerk of the Crown, an official of the Lord Chancellor's office, to ensure that he/she includes the relevant Bills in the letters patent that will be executed by the monarch. When the letters patent have been executed by the monarch, the Clerk of the Crown will read the short titles of those Bills requiring the Assent. He does so in the presence of the Lord Chancellor, in his capacity as Speaker of the House of Lords, the Speaker of the House of Commons and the Clerk of the Parliaments (sic) in the House of Lords. The Royal Assent is then pronounced in Norman French '*La Reyne le veult*' on behalf of the monarch by the Clerk of the Parliaments who is empowered to do so under the letters patent. Norman French was the language of government in the period after the Norman conquest in 1066. The assent is then notified to each House separately by its Speaker in English. Each Speaker merely states: 'I have to notify the House, in accordance with the Royal Assent Act 1967 that the Queen has signified her Royal Assent to the following Acts.' The short titles are then read out.

Although a copy of the Act is prepared for printing and general distribution, about six months after the Royal Assent has been given, two official copies of the Act are prepared on vellum, one of which is filed with the House of Lords' records and the other is held at the Public Records Office. The Royal Assent does sometimes operate to bring the Act into operation immediately but it is quite common for the commencement of all or part of an Act to be suspended, to be brought into effect at some future date.

Once a statute has been enacted it does not cease to be operative simply because of the passage of time unless this has been expressly stated in the Act. Thus a statute usually has to be expressly repealed by a subsequent statute.

13 Other forms of Public General Act

Legislation may be used occasionally in order to codify a body of case law on a particular topic. The aim is to simplify the law by converting all the established precedents into a single statute or code for the benefit of practitioners and others. Thereafter, it will be the sections of the Act and not the previous case law that will be referred to as the source of various legal rules. This was done in relation to the law on partnership by the Partnership Act 1890 and to the law on contracts of sale by the Sale of Goods Act 1893 which has been subsequently consolidated with other related statutes into the Sale of Goods Act 1979.

The enactment of a number of statutes on a given topic such as employment law (where later statutes amend the provisions of earlier ones) can make it difficult to ascertain the law on a particular point quickly. Therefore the process of 'consolidation' of statutes is a great help to practitioners and others. The consolidation process entails bringing together in a single statute all the existing statute law contained in several statutes. A good example of this is the Employment Rights Act 1996 which consolidated all the previous legislation relating to individual employment rights. There is a special expedited process for the enactment of consolidated statutes. The Bill must start in the House of Lords but it is then passed to the Joint Consolidation Committee with the comments of the draftsperson explaining those parts that are not a strict consolidation of the existing law. The Consolidation of Enactments (Procedure) Act 1949 makes it possible for corrections and minor improvements to be made in a consolidation statute. The Bill is considered on a clause by clause basis by the Committee with the draftsperson in attendance who is obliged to answer any questions posed by the Committee. When it has done its work the Committee will report to the Lords and Commons and, provided the report is favourable, the Bill can be passed in both Houses without delay. If there is any debate at all, it must be confined to alterations that have been made to the earlier legislation. These days most of the work on consolidation is undertaken by Parliamentary Counsel seconded to the Law Commission, whose work is considered in Chapter 16.

14 Private Acts of Parliament

Attention has so far focused on Public General Acts of Parliament which are so called because they impinge upon the general public, business and other organisations. From time to time, however, Parliament does enact Private Acts that deal with the particular concerns and interests of certain organisations and institutions including local authorities. There is a special procedure for enacting private Bills which varies depending on whether the measure is opposed or unopposed by outside interests. In the past, certain commercial enterprises have been incorporated by means of a Private Act of Parliament.

15   Citation

The old method of citing legislation was quite cumbersome. A statute was referred to by reference to the regnal year of the monarch in relation to the session of Parliament in which it was enacted, followed by a chapter number. As a result of the enactment of the Acts of Parliament Numbering and Citation Act 1962, all subsequent Acts are referred to by means of the short title and the calendar year of enactment.

16   Supremacy of statute law over case law

The supremacy of statute law over judge made law was finally established in the Revolution Settlement in 1688 when James II (1685–88) was deposed. The Bill of Rights 1689 proclaimed that thenceforward Parliament was superior to the monarch and the courts. Statute law is therefore a higher form of law than case law and statutes have sometimes been enacted to neutralise politically unacceptable judicial decisions. A good example of such a decision is provided from the area of trade union law. The House of Lords' judgment in *Taff Vale Railway Co. Ltd* v *ASRS* [1901] was effectively neutralised by the Trade Disputes Act 1906. Since 1689 the courts have accepted that they cannot normally question the validity of an Act of Parliament. Difficulties do occasionally arise because there may be an inconsistency between the wording of a provision in an earlier Act and the wording of a subsequent Act that has not expressly repealed the earlier legislation. The courts resolve this difficulty by invoking the doctrine of 'implied repeal' by which they assert that the later Act has impliedly repealed the earlier Act to the extent of the inconsistency.

The complete legislative supremacy of the Westminster Parliament is now difficult to reconcile with the fact of UK membership of the EU. It was much easier to declare the traditional doctrine of parliamentary sovereignty which asserts that there are no limits to the legislative power of Parliament in an era when the Westminster Parliament was at the hub of a vast colonial empire upon which the sun was reputed 'never to set'. Once the government of Edward Heath signed the Treaty of Accession to the Treaty of Rome in 1972 it committed the UK to participate indefinitely in the ongoing process of ever-closer European economic and political integration with the other member states. Membership of the EU requires that EU law in the form of Treaty provisions and regulations must override any inconsistent national law of every member state; otherwise the process of achieving closer economic and political integration would come to a standstill. Whilst it is true that EU law could only become part of the law of the UK as a result of the enactment of the European Communities Act 1972 and that this statute could be repealed in future, such a repeal is unlikely because of the highly adverse economic consequences. Thus, for as long as the European Communities Act 1972 is part of the statute law of the UK, the courts must accord precedence to EU law over national law.

17 Supremacy of EU law over national law

The supremacy of EU law over inconsistent national law was forcefully demonstrated in *Factortame Ltd and others* v *Secretary of State for Transport (No. 2)* [1991]. In order to understand the background to this very important case one needs to be aware that the EC Treaty guarantees the nationals of all member states certain rights. Article 43 guarantees the right to set up a business in any other member state, and Article 49 guarantees the right to provide services across borders. Moreover, Article 294 requires that member states must accord nationals of other member states the same rights as their own nationals with regard to the ownership of shares in companies. The claimants were companies formed and registered in England whose directors and shareholders were, for the most part, Spanish nationals. In 1970 the EEC (as it then was) established a common fisheries policy to conserve fish stocks and ensure equality of access for the vessels of member states to fishing grounds and exclude the fishing fleets of non-member states except on agreed terms. A special agreement was made by the Community with Spain in 1980 that gave Spanish vessels the right to fish for particular species in designated waters of the member states. Spain did not join the EEC until 1986 but when the UK joined in 1973 it had to comply with the rules of the common fisheries policy. European Regulation 170/83, operative across the European Community, set up a system of national quotas in 1983 for total allowable catches. Prior to that, Spain, by Royal decree, had conferred advantages by way of landing rights on those Spanish fishing companies that were registered with another state to enable them to fish in the fishing grounds of that state. The UK government took the view that the Spanish vessels that were registered on the British register in order to have access to the fishing grounds of the UK were exploiting the 1980 agreement between the EEC and Spain. In other words, they were Spanish vessels availing themselves of the British quota and there was considerable domestic political pressure to exclude foreign vessels from fishing under the British quota. Under the Merchant Shipping Act 1988, the Secretary of State was empowered to create a new register of British fishing vessels that would govern the ability of such vessels to fish under the British fishing quota.

The Merchant Shipping Act 1988 s. 14(2) provided that a vessel would qualify for registration if the company owning it was at least 75 per cent owned by British citizens. The claimants did not qualify because most of their directors and shareholders were Spanish nationals living in Spain and they sought to challenge Part II of the Act and Regulations made under it on the basis that they contravened Treaty provisions and thereby deprived them of their legal rights under EU law in relation to freedom of establishment and non-discrimination. Although the action was commenced in the High Court, the case was of such constitutional importance that it eventually reached the House of Lords and the Law Lords were asked to issue an interim injunction suspending the operation of the relevant part of the legislation. The House of Lords considered itself bound by the principle of common law that an injunction could not be issued against the Crown (effectively the government) and declined to do so but referred the matter to the European Court of Justice for a preliminary ruling (see *Factortame Ltd and others* v *Secretary of State for Transport* [1989]). The European Court of Justice ruled in Case C-213/89 *R* v *Secretary of State for Transport ex p. Factortame Ltd and others* [1990] that a national court was obliged to set aside a rule of national law that prevents it from granting interim relief where rights are claimed under EU law. Thereafter, the House of Lords issued an interim injunction against the Crown which prevented the minister from enforcing the relevant provision of the Merchant Shipping Act 1988 and the Regulations. In doing so the House of Lords created an important precedent and made constitutional history.

Thus parliamentarians are now only too well aware, if they were not at the time, that Parliament as an institution must not legislate in a way that is at variance with EU law whilst the UK continues to be a member state of the EU. Failure to observe this fundamental principle is likely to prove very expensive. In 1997, a Divisional Court of the Queen's Bench ruled that, following the decision of the European Court of Justice in joined Cases C-46/93 and C-48/93 *Brasserie du Pecheur SA* v *Germany* and *R* v *Secretary of State for Transport ex p. Factortame Ltd and others*, the UK was obliged to pay substantial compensation (but not exemplary damages) to the trawler companies owned by the Spanish nationals for a serious breach of EU law by the UK Parliament in approving the legislation. This was subsequently affirmed on appeal by both the Court of Appeal and House of Lords (see *R* v *Secretary of State for Transport ex p. Factortame Ltd and others* [1999]).

Conflicts between EU law and national law do not arise frequently. Thus, in general, the courts will not be sympathetic to any attempt by an individual or an organisation to challenge the validity of a UK Act of Parliament. In *British Railways Board* v *Pickin* [1974] an attempt to impugn the validity of a Private Act of Parliament by an individual was dismissed as an abuse of the legal process.

18   The effect of the Human Rights Act 1998 on UK law

When the government steered the Human Rights Act 1998 through Parliament, it declined to permit the courts to suspend the operation of an Act of Parliament should its provisions be found to contravene the Convention rights as embodied in Schedule 1 to the Act. The Human Rights Act 1998 s. 4(2) merely enables a court to make a declaration of 'incompatibility' and it is then the responsibility of Parliament (effectively the government of the day) thereafter to decide whether to repeal the relevant provision(s) or not. If Parliament should fail to do so, s. 3(2)(b) provides that the validity, continuing operation or enforcement of the legislation is not affected just because it happens to be incompatible with the Convention rights as contained in Schedule 1.

This is to be contrasted with the legal position *vis à vis* EU law. When the government rushed the Anti-terrorism, Crime and Security Act 2001 through Parliament in November 2001, it was only too well aware of the fact that the provisions in Part 4 would conflict with the Convention rights contained in Schedule 1. It was for this reason that it laid the Human Rights (Designated Derogation) Order 2001 (SI 2001 No. 3644) before Parliament on 12 November making it clear that the government was seeking a derogation.

19 The clarity of legislation

During the 1960s there was growing concern among a group of lawyers over the clarity of some of the legislation that was being drafted and enacted by Parliament. It was argued by some that it was a fundamental civil liberty that citizens who live under the rule of law should be entitled to know what the law is. Moreover, from a human rights perspective, it is essential the people should be able to predict when and how legal power can be used against them. Unfortunately, the reality often was that statute law was frequently unintelligible to the ordinary citizen. This was particularly worrying in the sphere of criminal law where ignorance of the law is no defence. It is just as important, however, in the sphere of the civil law that people should be able to arrange their affairs and plan for the future on the basis of being certain what the law is as it pertains to their lives and business dealings. In the context of the civil law, this lack of transparency and prolixity can be illustrated by considering an example afforded by the Misrepresentation Act 1967 s. 2(1) which states:

> Where a person has entered into a contract after a misrepresentation has been made to him by another party thereto and as a result thereof he has suffered loss, then, if the person making the misrepresentation would be liable to damages in respect thereof had the misrepresentation been made fraudulently, the person shall be so liable notwithstanding that the misrepresentation was not made fraudulently, unless he proves that he had reasonable grounds to believe and did believe up to the time that the contract was made that the facts represented were true.

If the reader has undertaken a careful study of the law of contract and, in particular, the evolution of the law relating to misrepresentation (which is not the easiest of concepts to grasp), very little difficulty would be experienced in grasping the meaning of this provision. In the past, the drafters in preparing legislation were often addressing themselves exclusively to lawyers and judges using a language that they would understand without much concern for other users.

20 Statute Law Society and the aftermath

In 1968, the Statute Law Society was established by a concerned group of lawyers who wished to see improvements in the quality of the legislation that was emanating from Parliament from the standpoint of users. The Society started to publish its own journal, the *Statute Law Review*. It was in this climate that the government set up the Renton Committee in 1973 on the Preparation of Legislation. The Committee took evidence and published its report in 1975 comprising some 40 conclusions and 81 recommendations which raised the general level of awareness regarding the shortcomings of the drafting process. It was well received by parliamentarians and by the serious press. It was also read by staff in the Office of Parliamentary Counsel. Although many of its recommendations have long since been accepted either wholly or in part, a number of issues still remain to be tackled. Yet another report appeared in 1992, namely the Report of the Commission on the Legislative Process sponsored by the Hansard Society. The Commission recommended that Bills should be examined before the Second Reading by a select committee that would receive recommendations on the precise wording from experts, representatives of those affected and from interested members of the public; and an increasing amount of legislation is now subject to pre-legislative screening. By way of an example, the Civil Contingencies Bill 2003, which subsequently became the Civil Contingencies Act 2004, was put out for public consultation for a period of some 18 months.

Readers interested in the ongoing debate concerning the clarity of drafting and the intelligibility of statute law may wish to refer to the *Statute Law Review* for January 1993. Mr Martin Cutts, who had long campaigned for the use of plain English in commerce and the law, produced a redraft of the Timeshare Act 1992 in plain English which he entitled the Clearer Timeshare Act 1993. His redraft was submitted to the Office of Parliamentary Counsel, and the draftsperson, Euan Sutherland, responded to Mr Cutt's redraft. Euan Sutherland's article appears in the *Statute Law Review* (Vol. 14 (1993) p.163) and it makes interesting reading. The commitment of the present First Parliamentary Counsel, Sir Geoffrey Bowman, to clearer drafting is evident from his evidence to the House of Lords Constitution Committee in June 2004 in which he said:

> Our attempt to produce legislation that works and is comprehensible and neat is largely a matter of professional pride. Certainly over the years I have striven to adapt my style so that it is modern and crisp, direct – some people would say rather stark, but I can live with that – and indeed this has been the desire of most members of the office. I think everybody has signed up to that.

Nevertheless, it has to be said that it is not always possible to draft legislation in simple, straightforward language such that it would be immediately intelligible to the average citizen, and there are a number of reasons for this. First, government frequently makes unrealistic demands on the draftspersons in terms of the time allotted for the drafting process.

It is sometimes a choice between a 'quick fix' and a more considered piece of work, with the former sometimes given priority. Secondly, a statute, unlike a White Paper, is a legal text that must be 'justiciable' in the courts. It is the need for precision that is often the main cause of complexity in drafting as the draftsperson seeks to anticipate possible misunderstandings and tries to deal with a variety of situations that may arise. Thirdly, the subject matter itself may not lend itself to a concise treatment in simple language. This is particularly true of aspects of finance and revenue law, although the Inland Revenue is currently engaged in a project to simplify tax law and make it more 'user friendly'.

In recent years some statutes have been singled out and praised for their clarity and precision. The Arbitration Act 1996 in particular has been praised as an example of outstanding drafting. Members of the legal profession and judiciary, together with others possessing special expertise, were consulted on the text of the Bill before it was presented to Parliament. In winding up the Second Reading debate in the House of Lords, Lord Fraser of Carmyllie stated:

> My Lords, I reflect somewhat ruefully that when I once had responsibility for the activities of some of the draftsmen, I can never recollect an occasion when drafting of a Bill was approved in such a magnificent form and which secured the approval of so many distinguished judges. Nevertheless, as the departmental Minister responsible for the Bill in your Lordships' House, I am delighted there has been such a universal degree of approval for the fashion in which the Bill has been drafted. I am particularly grateful to the noble and learned Lord, Lord Ackner. A number of people were rightly complimented on their contributions, but it was good of the noble and learned Lord to mention the way in which parliamentary counsel finally drew the Bill together in such an acceptable form. I have no doubt that those who have contributed to the drafting will be particularly flattered that my noble friend Lord Hacking should go so far as to compare it with the great statutes, with which we are all familiar, of the 19th century.

Even though great care was taken with its drafting, an error was subsequently discovered in the Act in the case of *Inco Europe Ltd and others* v *First Choice Distribution and others* [2000] (see Chapter 8 on the interpretation of legislation).

21 Statute law database

As yet there is no official computerised database of current legislation available to all citizens although work is underway on creating one. The nearest thing is the commercial database known as *Halsbury's Statutes* but this is a subscription service.

■ Summary

This chapter has examined the bicameral nature and composition of the Westminster Parliament. It has been seen that proposals for new legislation derive from a number of sources but that it is the government of the day that controls the parliamentary timetable to ensure that it can achieve the enactment of its legislation. The services of the Office of Parliamentary Counsel are therefore largely given over to the drafting of government legislation. The process of enactment has been considered because it is helpful to have an understanding of this. It is quite a lengthy procedure which is supposed to ensure that the legislation that emerges is workable in terms of the aims to be achieved. In this connection, the House of Lords performs a valuable function as a revising chamber. Owing to the complexity of some proposed legislation, a practice has developed of pre-legislative scrutiny of draft Bills by parliamentary committees before the Bills are formally introduced. Although primary legislation enacted by the Westminster Parliament is the highest form of national law, the concept of parliamentary sovereignty has been eroded by the enactment of the European Communities Act 1972. As a result it is necessary for the superior courts in England and Wales to suspend the operation of any Act of Parliament that can be shown to be at variance with some directly effective rule or principle of EU law.

WWW PROGRESS TEST

For suggested answers to the tests below, go to the companion website at www.pearsoned.co.uk/wheeler

1 What are the constituent elements of the Westminster Parliament?
2 How easy is it for a backbench MP to propose a new piece of legislation and what is the likelihood that he/she will see it enacted?
3 Who is actually responsible for drafting government Bills and who provides the brief?
4 Who introduces a government Bill to Parliament and must this always be done in the House of Commons?
5 How likely is it that amendments put forward by the opposition in the House of Commons will be incorporated into the Bill?
6 Suppose the House of Lords refuses to pass a Bill that has completed all its stages in the House of Commons, having been introduced there. Can the government still lawfully present the Bill for the Royal Assent?
7 Does the Queen assent to legislation in person? Can the Royal Assent be withheld by the monarch?
8 What do you understand by the phrase 'consolidated statute'?
9 Can the Human Rights Act 1998 be invoked successfully to challenge the validity of an Act of Parliament in the courts?
10 Can EU law be invoked successfully to challenge the validity of an Act of Parliament in the courts?

FURTHER READING

■ Books

Ingman, T. (2004) *The English Legal Process* (London: Oxford University Press, chapter 5).

Limon, Sir D. and W.R. Mckay (eds) (1997) *Erskine May's Treatise on the Law*, Privileges, Proceedings and Usage of Parliament (London: Butterworths).

Slapper, G. and D. Kelly (2004) *The English Legal System* (London: Cavendish Publishing, chapter 2).

Twining, W. and D. Miers (1999) *How To Do Things With Rules* (Cambridge: Cambridge University Press, chapter 9).

Zander, M. (2004) *The Law Making Process* (Cambridge: Cambridge University Press, chapters 1 and 2).

■ Articles

Feldman, D. (2004) 'The Impact of Human Rights on the UK Legislative Process' *Statute Law Review* Vol. 25, No. 2, pp. 91–115.

Hunt, B. (2004) 'Plain Language in Legislative Drafting: An Achievable Objective or Laudable Ideal?' *Statute Law Review* Vol. 24, No. 2, pp. 112–124.

USEFUL WEBSITES

The website of the Westminster Parliament is www.parliament.uk
and texts of recent Acts of Parliament may be accessed on www.hmso.gov.uk.
An easy website to access for alphabetical and chronological lists of Acts is www.infolaw.co.uk.
Bills introduced into Parliament can be found at www.parliament.the-stationery-office.co.uk/pa/pabills.htm.
The Plain English Campaign's arguments for clearer legal drafting can be viewed at www.plainenglish.co.uk/drafting.
The website of the Office of Parliamentary Counsel can be viewed at www.Parliamentary-counsel.gov.uk.

6 The law-making process 3: Subordinate legislation

1 Introduction

In addition to the 50 or so statutes enacted by the Westminster Parliament each year, in the region of 4,000 pieces of subordinate legislation are created in the form of rules, regulations, orders and directions. Most of this subordinate legislation is made under the authority of a Public General Act of Parliament. Indeed, it was Henry Thring, the first person appointed as Parliamentary Counsel in 1869, who recommended that the fine detail of legislative proposals should not be included in the Bill to be presented to Parliament. Instead, he advocated that the detailed measures should be devised at a later date and be brought into effect through the medium of subordinate legislation. As a result, parliamentarians would be able to concentrate on matters of broad principle and would not become enmeshed in matters of abstruse technicality. Since 1945, government has become increasingly involved in all aspects of the economic and social life of the nation and this has resulted in the enactment of a vast amount of complex legislation reflecting the complexity of modern life. If every detail of such legislation had to be incorporated into the original Bills, those Bills would have been very unwieldy documents and would have absorbed far more parliamentary time than was justified. That said, in recent years, some disquiet has arisen because of a tendency of government to use subordinate legislation as a means of developing policy and not simply as a way of delegating matters of detail. This chapter will consider, first, the various ways in which law-making powers have been delegated by Parliament before addressing the difficult issues of scrutiny and review.

2 The extent of delegation

The most significant delegation of law-making powers ever made under an Act of Parliament was granted to ministers under the European Communities Act 1972 s. 2(2). The Act empowers government to give effect to the obligations of the UK under Articles 10 and 249 of the EC Treaty by means of subordinate legislation. Apart from central government, other institutions and bodies have also been granted the power to make subordinate legislation. The Welsh Assembly has authority under the Government of Wales Act 1998 s. 44 to create subordinate legislation for those aspects of the government of Wales for which the Assembly has delegated powers. The Northern Ireland Assembly enjoys similar powers under the Northern Ireland Act 1998. Local authorities can make compulsory purchase orders to acquire land under the Acquisition of Land Act 1981, and district local authorities as well as the London boroughs can make bye-laws for their respective areas under a procedure set out in the Local Government Act 1972. Most of these bye-laws must first be sent in draft for approval by the Secretary of State for Environment, Transport and the Regions. Bye-laws can also be made by certain public corporations that have been empowered to do so by Act of Parliament, and they too are normally subject to approval by the relevant government minister. If there is an infringement of a bye-law, the body responsible for making the bye-law can have recourse to criminal proceedings to enforce it. In *Boddington* v *British Transport Police* [1998] the validity of a bye-law imposing a fine for smoking on a train was upheld by the House of Lords. In order to ensure efficient management of the civil courts, the Civil Procedure Rules Committee has the power under the Civil Procedure Act 1997 to make rules for the conduct of litigation and case management.

3 Statutory Instruments Act 1946

Most of the more important pieces of subordinate legislation take the form of statutory instruments. The Statutory Instruments Act 1946 s. 1(1) provides that statutory instruments can take the form of Orders in Council (orders approved by the monarch) as well as orders or regulations made by a government minister where the enabling Act so states. The Act re-enacted provisions of the Rules of Publication Act 1893, and so under s. 1(2) it was expressly provided that the rules of those rule-making authorities who had previously enjoyed delegated law-making powers would also be known as statutory instruments. The bye-laws of local authorities, however, are not statutory instruments nor are compulsory purchase orders made by them. Whether a statutory instrument is to take the form of an Order in Council or simply a regulation made by a minister is determined by the precise wording of the provision in the enabling Act under which delegation is authorised. The Statutory Instruments Act 1946 s. 2(1) provides that immediately after an instrument has been made it must be sent to the Queen's printer, numbered in accordance with the scheme devised by the Statutory Publications Office and put on sale. The Queen's printer is the Controller of HM Stationery Office. Statutory instruments dealing with purely local matters are exempted from the requirements of printing and sale.

4 Drafting of statutory instruments

Most routine statutory instruments are drafted within the various government departments by civil servants who are legally qualified either as solicitors or barristers. If a particular department does not have a legal section, the drafting can be done by the Treasury Solicitor's Department. Although care is needed, many statutory instruments are relatively straightforward because they just increase financial thresholds and levels of benefit or amounts of compensation payable to allow for the effect of inflation. As previously stated, it is also quite common to use statutory instruments to bring parts of Acts of Parliament that have received the Royal Assent into operation, and these are known as 'commencement orders'. These will simply mention the sections of the Act to be made operative. If, however, a statutory instrument is likely to assume special importance, perhaps because it transposes an EU directive or because it deals with complex subject matter, the department concerned may call on the expertise of a parliamentary draftsperson from the Office of Parliamentary Counsel. Where a statutory instrument amends primary legislation, assistance is also likely to be sought from the Office of Parliamentary Counsel who are concerned with maintaining the integrity and overall coherence of the general body of statute law.

5 Citation

It is usual to cite statutory instruments by giving the title first. After the title comes the year in which the instrument was made, followed by the number given to the instrument. Consider these examples: The Institute of Legal Executives Order 1998 (SI 1998 No. 1077), and Maternity and Parental Leave Etc. Regulations 1999 (SI 1999 No. 3312). The first was an Order in Council made under the authority of the Courts and Legal Services Act 1990 whereas the second was a ministerial order made under the Employment Rights Act 1996.

6 Parliamentary awareness

Not all statutory instruments must be drawn to the attention of Parliament. This is particularly true of those instruments that are of purely local concern but it may also apply to instruments of minor significance where the enabling Act does not require it. For those instruments that must be brought to the attention of Parliament, the enabling Act will specify that an instrument must be laid before Parliament either in draft or in final form. The official copies must be certified as facsimiles of the original document that is retained by the government department responsible for creating the instrument. An instrument cannot normally become operative until it is filed with the Office of Votes and Proceedings in the House of Commons but, in the event of some great urgency, the instrument may become operative immediately provided notification and a proper explanation is given at the time to the Lord Chancellor and the Speaker of the House of Commons. Usually an instrument that must be laid before Parliament will be filed with the Office of Votes and Proceedings at least 21 days before it comes into effect. A list of all statutory instruments received at Westminster is published weekly in the House of Commons for the benefit of members.

Most of the statutory instruments that are required to be laid before Parliament will be subject to the negative resolution procedure which means that unless there is an objection by either House the instruments will become law by default.

Nevertheless, any member of the Lords or Commons can move a 'prayer' (a motion) that an instrument be annulled or, if it was laid in draft, that it is not made in final form. The Statutory Instruments Act 1946 provides that this must happen within 40 business days of the date of the instrument being laid before Parliament. In the House of Commons such a motion takes the form of an Early Day Motion, which is usually submitted to the Table Office on a specially printed form. Normally there is very little prospect of this motion ever being debated unless it is put down by the official Opposition or another opposition party, usually in the name of its leader. Early Day Motions put down in the name of the official Opposition are more likely to be debated but not on the floor of the House. Standing Order 118(4) provides that where a motion has been put down that a statutory instrument be annulled, a minister may put a motion at the commencement of business that the instrument should be referred to a standing committee on delegated legislation. Only if 20 or more members rise immediately to object will this motion be defeated and if there is no such objection the instrument will be passed to a standing committee for consideration. This procedure was invoked for the Transnational Information and Consultation of Employees Regulations 1999 (SI 1999 No. 3323) which were made under the European Communities Act 1972 s. 2(2) to implement Directive 97/74 EC which extended to the UK the directive on establishing European works councils or information and consultation procedures for employees. The previous Conservative government had negotiated an 'opt out' from the Social Policy Protocol and Social Policy Agreement of the Treaty of European Union but this had been reversed shortly after the Labour Party had won the general election in 1997. The statutory instrument in question was made on 12 December 1999 and laid before Parliament on 14 December; subject to a negative resolution, it was due to come into force on 15 January 2000. It was hardly surprising therefore that the leader of the Opposition put down an early day motion, EDM 293, that the instrument and the regulations it contained should be annulled. The instrument was considered and debated by the Seventh Standing Committee on Delegated Legislation on 3 February for just over two hours and the Committee then voted 9:3 in favour of the measure. Such an outcome is hardly surprising bearing in mind that the composition of the standing committee reflects the relative strengths of the political parties in the House of Commons.

An alternative to the negative resolution procedure is the affirmative resolution procedure which can take one of three forms. An instrument can be made by the appropriate government department and take immediate effect with the proviso in the enabling Act that it will lapse if it is not approved by one or both Houses within a period of 28–40 days. This procedure is often used for instruments dealing with taxation but is used for other measures. The provisions contained within ss. 21–23 of the Anti-terrorism, Crime and Security Act 2001 need to be extended annually in this way. Another possibility is for the enabling Act to require the instrument to be laid in draft form before one or both Houses with the proviso that it is not to be made final and brought into effect unless one or both Houses present an address asking for this to be done. The third and simplest alternative is for the enabling Act to require the minister to lay the instrument in final form with the proviso that it will come into effect only after a resolution by one or both Houses has been passed.

Standing Order No. 118(3) of the House of Commons requires that all instruments that have to be approved by an affirmative resolution must be referred to a standing committee on delegated legislation unless the government agrees that they can be debated on the floor of the House. Following a debate in committee, which should not exceed 90 minutes, a motion to approve the instrument is put to the House. During the debate the instrument cannot be amended and must be withdrawn if a majority vote cannot eventually be secured in its favour. In the House of Lords the motion for an affirmative resolution cannot be put until a report is received from the Joint Committee on Statutory Instruments. The affirmative resolution procedure is often incorporated into primary legislation for the creation of subordinate legislation that is considered to need greater scrutiny by Parliament because of its importance, but this is not invariably the case. Moreover, subject matter that may have been considered as very important thirty or forty years ago may not be so regarded today, yet the creation of subordinate legislation may still be subject to the affirmative resolution procedure.

7 Deregulation orders

The Deregulation and Contracting Out Act 1994 permits a government minister by statutory instrument to amend or repeal provisions in other statutes enacted prior to the end of the 1993/94 session of Parliament if he/she considers they impose a burden on persons carrying out trade, business or other professions. These powers have been used quite extensively to date. Each House has established its own select committee to report on proposals and on the draft instruments to be made under the Act. Having consulted with the interested parties, if a minister takes the view that a deregulation order should be made, he/she is obliged to lay his/her proposal before Parliament in the form of an explanatory memo-randum describing:

(a) the burden to be relieved;
(b) the financial and other benefits of the proposed change;
(c) how any necessary protection is to be continued;
(d) details of the consultation process undertaken;
(e) the changes, if any, that he/she has made in view of the responses received from the consultation process.

The period of 60 days for Parliamentary consideration begins to run from the date that the proposals have been laid before Parliament but only normal business days are counted. The process is more than a mere formality because the House of Commons Deregulation Committee has to report that a draft order should be laid before the House on the basis of the terms contained in the memorandum. Alternatively, it may report that the proposal should be amended before a draft order is prepared and laid before Parliament or that the order-making power should not be used in this instance. The Committee has indeed recommended on a few occasions that the order-making power should not be used. The minister is required to take account of the report of the Deregulation Committee and the report of the Delegated Powers and Deregulation Committee of the House of Lords as well as representations received from interested parties within the 60-day period referred to above. At the expiration of the 60-day period the minister can prepare his/her draft order and lay it before Parliament with a statement that gives details of the reports made by the Committees of both Houses together with any other representations received, and describing any changes that have been made to the proposal in the light of them. Standing Order 141 requires that the draft order must be referred to the Deregulation Committee but at this stage the Committee cannot put forward any amendments to the order. Within 15 business days following the laying of the order before Parliament, the Committee must report its recommendation whether the draft order should be approved. Although the minister is not obliged to wait for the Committee's report before asking the House to approve the order, he/she will wait for the report to be compiled. If the Committee recommends approval of the draft order without a need for a division on the report, the motion to approve the draft must be put to the House straight away. If the approval of the draft order came about only after a division on the report, further debate on the motion can continue on the floor of the House but for no longer than 90 minutes. As soon as the time allowed for debate has elapsed, a motion to approve the draft must be put to the House. In the event that the Committee reports that the draft order should not be approved, the House must first consider a motion whether to disagree with the Committee's report. Such a debate must not exceed three hours and, should the House resolve to disagree with the report at the conclusion of the debate, the motion to approve the draft order must be put straight away. The procedure adopted in the House of Lords is similar but not identical.

8 Remedial orders

The Human Rights Act 1998 s. 10 has made it possible for a minister to amend primary legislation by statutory instrument where it has been declared by a superior court to be 'incompatible' with the Convention rights contained in Schedule 1 to the Act. The minister may also decide to amend other legislation in the light of the court's declaration other than the statute that contains the incompatible provision. Where a minister decides to exercise his/her power under s. 10 to make a 'remedial order' one of two procedures is available depending on the urgency of the matter. If there is no great urgency, the normal procedure as set out in Schedule 2 requires the minister to lay before Parliament the 'required information' comprising an explanation of the incompatibility which the proposed order seeks to remove, including details of the relevant declaration and a statement of the reasons for proceeding under s. 10. The minister also has to explain in his/her statement the reasons for making the draft order in the terms in which it has been drafted. The information and the draft order must be laid before Parliament for a period of 60 business days. If the minister receives representations from lobby groups and others during this period, a summary of these representations and any changes to the draft order arising from these representations must be incorporated into a statement to accompany the order in its final form which must also be laid before Parliament. At the end of a subsequent 60-day period the order must be approved by a resolution of each House.

If the matter should be urgent, the minister can use the emergency procedure set out in Schedule 2 para. 2(b) which enables him/her to make the order in final form before laying it before Parliament in draft. The order must state that the normal procedure is being bypassed because of the urgency of the matter. Nevertheless, the order must still be laid before Parliament after it has been made, together with the 'required information' specified above. As with the normal procedure, if the minister receives representations from lobby groups and others within 60 days of the making of the order, he/she must present to Parliament a statement containing a summary of these representations and any changes he/she considers it appropriate to make to the original order in the light of these representations. In any event, the original order must be replaced by a second remedial order at the end of the 60-day period, which must be laid before Parliament for a further 60 days. If a resolution approving the order has not been passed by each House at the end of a period of 120 business days beginning with the date on which the original order was made, it will cease to have legal effect. This does not, however, invalidate anything done whilst the order was in force. It is likely that the government will do its utmost to ensure that the necessary resolutions are passed in each House to validate the order. The first remedial order made under the Act was made following a finding of incompatibility in *R (on the application of H)* v *Mental Health Review Tribunal* [2002]. In that case s. 73 of the Mental Health Act 1983 was found to be incompatible with Article 5

because the burden of proof lay with the patient *against* continued detention. As a result of the change, it is for the hospital to prove the need for
continued detention.

9 Regulatory Reform Act 2001

This is the most recent piece of legislation to be enacted that makes it
possible to repeal, amend or insert new text into one or more Acts of
Parliament. Any minister of the Crown is empowered by s. 1 to make an
order to the purpose of reforming legislation which has the effect of
imposing burdens affecting persons in the carrying on of any activity with
a view to one or more of the following objects:

(a) the removal or reduction of any of those burdens,

(b) the re-enacting of provisions having the effect of imposing any of
     those burdens in cases where the burden is proportionate to the
     benefit which is expected to result from the re-enactment,

(c) the making of new provisions having the effect of imposing a burden
     which –

   (i) affects any person in the carrying on of the activity, but

   (ii) is proportionate to the benefit which is expected to result from
        its creation, and

(d) the removal of inconsistencies and anomalies.

   According to s. 4 any order made under s. 1 has to be made by statutory
instrument but a draft of the order must be laid before and approved by
each House. Details of the government's plans for the use of this legislation can be viewed at the website www.cabinet-office.gov.uk. It is
intended that, in future, the Law Commission should make use of this
method of amending primary legislation where appropriate. A Regulatory
Reform Order, namely the Regulatory Reform (Business Tenancies)
(England and Wales) Order 2003 (SI 2003 No. 3096) was made by Keith
Hill, a minister at the Office of the Deputy Prime Minister on 1 December
2003. It came into force on 1 June 2004 and implements most of the rec-
ommendations of the Law Commission contained in their 1992 paper
Business Tenancies: A Periodic Review of the Landlord and Tenant Act Part II
(Law Com No. 208). It repealed and amended certain provisions of Part
II of the Landlord and Tenant Act 1954.

10 Orders in Council

The procedure for giving effect to Orders in Council is a little different
from that governing the bringing into effect of ministerial orders and
regulations. Orders in Council are so called because they are approved at
a meeting of the Privy Council even though the authority for their creation derived from an Act of Parliament. There are in excess of 400

members of the Privy Council and so it never meets with the monarch in its entirety. By convention, all Cabinet ministers must be duly sworn as Privy Councillors and it is they who attend the meetings for the approval of Orders in Council. These meetings are usually held at Buckingham Palace or Windsor Castle. Once Orders in Council have been drafted, they are laid before Parliament and, if a challenge is made in either House, a motion will be passed that the Order is not submitted to HM the Queen. Those that are unchallenged will be listed for approval at a scheduled meeting of the Privy Council. At the meeting the Queen stands surrounded by her ministers who also stand in her presence. As the titles of the various Orders are read aloud by the Lord President, the Queen, who does not see the Orders in advance, merely utters the word 'agreed' at the end of the title of each Order. The Orders then become operative from the date specified in the instrument.

11   The case for scrutiny of statutory instruments

A number of modern statutes contain what are known as Henry VIII clauses, which are so called because the Statute of Proclamations 1539 conferred sweeping powers on the Tudor monarch to govern by Royal decree. It may be argued that the conferring of very wide-ranging powers on the government, exercisable through the creation of subordinate legislation, merits careful scrutiny. As indicated above, there are special parliamentary procedures for dealing with deregulation orders made under the Deregulation and Contracting Out Act 1994 and remedial orders under the Human Rights Act 1998. Nevertheless, there are a number of statutes that grant wide-ranging powers to ministers that are not subject to special procedures.

An example of such a statute is the International Transport Conventions Act 1983. Sections 8 and 9 permit the Act to be amended by means of statutory instrument. The Transport Act 1985 s. 46 confers even wider powers because it provides that Part II of the Act can be repealed by statutory instrument. Thus it is readily apparent that statutory instruments can be used by government to bring about important legislative changes without recourse to the normal parliamentary process for enacting primary legislation. A strong case can therefore be made for effective scrutiny by Parliament of these instruments as well as others that are complex or produce important changes in the working environments of citizens.

12   Joint Committee on Statutory Instruments

For the most part, the task of scrutiny is entrusted to the Joint Committee on Statutory Instruments comprising seven members from each House. The chairperson is always an opposition MP and, although there are 14 members, it can function with a quorum as low as two. It is assisted in its task by Counsel to the Speaker and Counsel to the Lord Chairman of Committees as well as by other members of the parliamentary staff. Under the Committee's terms of reference it is required to decide whether it ought to draw the attention of both Houses to a particular statutory instrument for any of the following nine reasons:

1 It imposes a tax or a charge on the citizen or upon the public revenue.
2 It is made under primary legislation which expressly excludes the instrument from being challenged in the courts.
3 It appears to have retrospective effect whereas the enabling Act does not provide for this.
4 There appears to be an unjustifiable delay in publishing the instrument or in laying it before Parliament.
5 The instrument has come into operation prior to being laid before Parliament and there seems to have been an unjustifiable delay in sending notification as required by the Statutory Instruments Act 1946 s. 4(1).
6 It appears doubtful that the instrument is drafted within the powers conferred by the enabling Act or it seems to make some unusual or unexpected use of the powers conferred by the enabling Act.
7 The form or purport of the instrument requires clarification.
8 The drafting of the instrument seems to be defective in some important respect.
9 The existence of any other substantial reason other than one which impinges on the merits of the instrument or the policy behind it.

The Committee is not permitted to consider the actual merits of any instrument nor the underlying policy. It meets only for a few hours one afternoon a week, usually when Parliament is in session, which means it sits no more than about 30 times in each session. The chairperson is not always in attendance and other members attend as and when they can. This hardly amounts to close scrutiny of subordinate legislation. Moreover, when the Committee does report, there is no requirement that its views and recommendations are acted upon. Even if it does decide to draw the attention of Parliament to one or more statutory instruments, it is obliged first to give the department concerned the opportunity to explain itself either orally or in writing. Because of the special arrangements for dealing with deregulation orders made under the Deregulation and Contracting Out Act 1994, the Joint Committee on Statutory Instruments does not spend time scrutinising them.

In the 1973/74 session an attempt was made to increase the time available for the scrutiny of certain types of statutory instrument. The government decided that in future those statutory instruments that required only an affirmative resolution of the House of Commons (mainly those dealing with taxation) could be referred to a standing committee comprising 17 MPs. The referral can only be made by a minister and the proposal can be defeated if 20 MPs in the chamber object. The consensus of opinion is that, although this procedure has been invoked, it has not been a particularly successful innovation.

Under the Government of Wales Act 1998 s. 58, a scrutiny committee has been established to examine subordinate legislation for the ministerial functions that have been transferred to the Welsh Assembly and similar arrangements exist under the Northern Ireland Act 1998.

There continues to be dissatisfaction with the existing system of scrutiny among parliamentarians at Westminster because instruments do not receive the measure of scrutiny appropriate to their importance. The Commons Procedure Committee has called for particularly complex or significant instruments to be passed under the affirmative resolution procedure to be presented to Parliament by the relevant department of government in an early draft form prior to submission of the final draft. It remains to be seen whether this will be done on any scale pending legislation overhauling the system of scrutiny.

13   The validity of subordinate legislation

Although by constitutional convention the courts cannot normally question the validity of primary legislation it is possible for them to consider the validity of subordinate legislation if it is challenged. In *Hoffman La Roche* v *Secretary of State for Trade* [1975] the House of Lords considered an application by the Secretary of State for an injunction restraining certain pharmaceutical companies from charging prices for drugs above those specified in a statutory instrument. Lords Diplock and Cross indicated that the courts have jurisdiction to declare an order in the form of a statutory instrument invalid even where it has been the subject of an affirmative resolution procedure in both Houses. A challenge can be either direct or indirect. An indirect challenge occurs when it is argued as a defence in the course of enforcement proceedings that the instrument is *ultra vires*, that is, beyond the scope of the powers that were delegated by the enabling Act. If this should prove to be so, the court can declare the instrument invalid either completely or in part. A direct challenge would occur if an individual or organisation set out to challenge the validity of an instrument in a claim for judicial review. The aim would be to obtain a declaratory judgment that the instrument is invalid. This procedure is considered in detail in Chapter 15.

Challenges may be mounted on the basis that the instrument is procedurally *ultra vires* because the specified procedures have not been followed. Although it is often difficult to be sure how a court will interpret the procedural requirements, if certain procedural requirements are specified as mandatory and these have not been followed, then non-compliance will almost certainly render the instrument invalid. If there is an element of discretion regarding a consultation process, a failure to consult will not usually affect the validity of the instrument. On the other hand, a challenge on substantive grounds relates to the precise content of the instrument concerned and the allegation would be that all, or part, of the instrument exceeds the powers that were originally delegated by Parliament.

An example of substantive *ultra vires* is provided by the case of *Hotel and Catering Industry Training Board* v *Automotive Proprietary Ltd* [1969]. The Industrial Training Act 1964 s. 1 authorised the minister to establish industrial training boards for persons employed 'in any activities of industry or commerce' and s. 4 empowered the boards to impose training levies on employers in the relevant industries. The Hotel and Catering Board was then established under the provisions of a statutory instrument, and Schedule 1 para. 1(a) of the instrument specified that the activities of the hotel and catering industry included the supply of food and drink, in the course of any business, to persons for immediate consumption. Paragraph 3(c) of the same Schedule defined 'business' as including the activities of any person or body of persons in the management or operation of a club. The Board then sought to impose a levy on a private members' club. The House of Lords affirmed the decision of the Court of Appeal to the effect that the words 'in any activities of industry or commerce' should be given their ordinary meaning. Thus the instrument was declared to be invalid to the extent that it extended to private members' clubs. A challenge based on an infringement of fundamental rights is provided by *R* v *Lord Chancellor ex p. Witham* [1997]. The Lord Chancellor made the Supreme Court Fees (Amendment) Order 1996 under powers conferred on him by the Supreme Court Act 1981. Article 6 of this order amended the Supreme Court Fees Order 1980 in that it provided for a minimum fee of £120 for issuing a writ for claims of £10,000 or less and for a fee of £500 for issuing a writ where no monetary limit was specified. Article 3 of the same order nullified provisions in the 1980 order which excused 'litigants in person', who were in receipt of income support, from the obligation to pay fees and permitted the Lord Chancellor to reduce or waive the fee in any particular case on grounds of undue financial hardship in exceptional circumstances. The applicant wanted to bring proceedings for defamation as a 'litigant in person' but he was unemployed, had no savings and was in receipt of income support of just under £60 a week. Since legal aid was not available for defamation actions he was effectively prevented from bringing his action and so he sought to challenge the validity of Article 3 of the order on the basis that it was *ultra vires* the Supreme Court Act 1981 s. 130. The basis of his argument was that it deprived him of his common law constitutional right of access to the courts. The Divisional Court of Queen's Bench held that the applicant's common law right could only be abrogated by specific statutory provision or by regulations made pursuant to legislation that specifically conferred the power to abrogate that right. There was no provision in the Supreme Court Act 1981 s. 130 that conferred such a power on the Lord Chancellor to prescribe a level of fees that would preclude persons from having access to the courts. Moreover Article 3 operated to bar many persons from seeking justice in the courts. Accordingly Article 3 was held to be *ultra vires* s. 130 and unlawful.

A court may declare that all or part of a statutory instrument is 'incompatible' with the Human Rights Act 1998 if it has not been possible to interpret it according to the Convention rights contained in Schedule 1 nd it may disapply it unless the primary legislation prevents the removal f the incompatibility. If the primary legislation does prevent the removal f the incompatibility, then the instrument will remain operative unless and until a minister changes the parent Act by remedial order as described above. Although a remedial order can have retrospective effect this will not benefit either of the parties to the original proceedings. A freestanding piece of subordinate legislation that is not made under the authority of primary legislation (a comparatively rare occurrence) may be declared invalid and be disapplied if it is incompatible with a Convention right.

■ Summary

As has been seen, subordinate legislation comes in a variety of forms but, for the most part, these are species of statutory instrument made under the authority of an Act of Parliament. It is essential to have a mechanism for bringing into operation parts of statutes that are not to become operative at the time that the Royal Assent is given. It is also necessary to have a quick and convenient way of up-rating social security benefits, compensation levels and statutory fees without taking up scarce parliamentary time. Commencement orders and orders adjusting monetary amounts are the simplest and usually the least controversial forms of subordinate legislation. By no means all subordinate legislation is of this type. Some can be quite detailed and complex. This is particularly true of some sets of regulations that are made under the European Communities Act 1972 to implement EU directives and there are sometimes complaints in the business press that the regulations are more detailed and go further than the directive. Although certain types of subordinate legislation are subject to an affirmative resolution procedure (and there are special procedures for remedial and deregulation orders), much more is subject only to the rather ineffective negative resolution procedure. There is insufficient time to scrutinise much of the legislation. This means that if delegated powers have been exceeded for reasons of expediency, it is left to those adversely affected to challenge an instrument in the courts, which is costly and time-consuming for those concerned.

WWW PROGRESS TEST

For suggested answers to the tests below, go to the companion website at www.pearsoned.co.uk/wheeler

1 Is subordinate legislation really necessary?
2 What are the principal forms of subordinate legislation?
3 Who is responsible for drafting subordinate legislation?
4 What do you understand by the negative resolution procedure?
5 What do you understand by the positive resolution procedure?

6 Does all subordinate legislation have to be brought to the attention of Parliament?

7 How does an Order in Council differ from other statutory instruments?

8 What is the role of the Joint Committee on Statutory Instruments? How effective is it?

9 How effective have standing committees in the House of Commons been in the scrutiny of statutory instruments?

10 How does the Human Rights Act 1998 affect statutory instruments?

FURTHER READING

■ Books

Ingman, T. (2004) *The English Legal Process* (Oxford: Oxford University Press, chapter 5).

Parpworth, N. (2001) *Constitutional and Administrative Law* (Oxford: Oxford University Press).

Slapper, G. and D. Kelly (2004) *The English Legal System* (London: Cavendish Publishing).

Twining, W. and D. Miers (1999) *How To Do Things With Rules* (London: Butterworths, chapter 9).

Zander, M. (2004) *The Law Making Process* (Cambridge: Cambridge University Press).

USEFUL WEBSITES

Copies of all new statutory instruments can be accessed on the website www.hmso.gov.uk.

Information on the scrutiny of subordinate legislation may be obtained from the Westminster Parliament website at www.parliament.uk.

7 The impact of EU law

1 Introduction

It is impossible to give a full account of the modern English legal system without dealing with the impact of EU law. When the Westminster Parliament enacted the European Communities Act 1972, European law became part of the law of the UK from 1 January 1973 and it therefore became embedded in the law of England and Wales. Although the European Communities Act 1972 has the same status as any other Act of Parliament and could, in theory, be repealed at some future date, this is about as unthinkable as the repealing of the Human Rights Act 1998. This chapter will first attempt to convey an appreciation of the nature of the EU by giving a very brief account of its evolution. There then follows a short description of the institutions of the EU focusing mainly on the law-making institutions prior to an examination of the sources of EU law and the procedure for enacting secondary legislation. As will be seen, the jurisprudence of the European Court of Justice (ECJ) has long been an important source of EU law and due consideration needs to be given to a few of the very important legal concepts devised by the Court. The chapter concludes with the issue of fundamental rights in EU law and their wider impact.

2 Background

The EU is quite a complex entity that was brought into being by the Treaty of European Union signed at Maastricht, in the Netherlands, in 1992. However, the process of economic integration began long before that date. In fact, it can be traced back as far as 1951 with the signing of the Treaty of Paris by six European states establishing the European Coal and Steel Community. The aim of the treaty was to create a single market in coal and steel. There then followed two further treaties signed in Rome in 1957 by the same six states. One of these created the European Economic Community (which later became the European Community) and the other created the European Atomic Energy Community (Euratom). The aim of the former was the creation of a single market for goods and services whilst the latter focused on the creation of a common market in the peaceful use of nuclear energy. The basic idea was to achieve, through market integration, greater economic and political integration in Europe, a process in which other states could participate, if they wished to do so, provided they were willing to embrace democratic values. The EU continues to evolve and in 2004 another 10 European states joined the existing 15 so that the EU currently has 25 member states, and other states including Turkey have applied to join. On 29 October 2004, the heads of state and governments of the 25 signed the text of a treaty that will operate as a constitution for the EU if, and when, it is ratified by the member states. This constitution fuses the existing treaties and Communities, affirms the primacy of EU law and will confer legal personality on the EU for the first time. Until the ratification process is complete, however, the EU will continue to be defined by the Treaty of European Union 1992 as a political entity rather than a legal entity. Article A of the Treaty of European Union declares that the Union is founded upon the three existing supranational organisations already mentioned, together with two distinct intergovernmental agreements. Some commentators have used the metaphor of an ancient Greek temple, the portico of which is supported by three pillars, to describe the structure of the Union. The central or first pillar comprises the three existing Communities: the ECSC, EC and Euratom. The second pillar is the intergovernmental agreement relating to the development of a common foreign and security policy, whilst the third pillar is the intergovernmental agreement governing cooperation in the spheres of police, judicial and criminal matters. In future the EU may come to be regarded as a type of 'federation' of states with its distinct political and legal institutions. Nevertheless, the EU is not a state in international law and will not be a state even when the ratification process for the new constitution is complete.

THE INSTITUTIONS

3 The EU institutions

The institutions of the EU are those created by the treaty establishing the European Union but references to EU law are, unless there is a clear indication to the contrary, to the Consolidated EC Treaty. Part Five of this Treaty names these institutions as being:

(a) the Council of the European Union,
(b) the European Commission,
(c) the European Parliament,
(d) the European Court of Justice,
(e) the Court of Auditors.

These institutions are vital to the functioning of the EU and, with the exception of the Court of Auditors, to the law-making processes and must be considered briefly in turn.

■ The Council of the European Union

At the outset, it is important to differentiate between the European Council and the Council of the European Union. The European Council comprises the heads of states and President of the Commission. It usually meets at least twice a year to establish broad political guidelines. Its meetings are held in the territory of the member state holding the presidency of the Council at that time. The Council of the European Union, on the other hand, meets several times a month at the Council building in Brussels and is both a legislative and a decision-making body. It has greater political legitimacy than the Commission because its members are all ministers of democratically elected governments who must be authorised to commit their respective states in the decision-making process. They are accustomed to acting in the interests of their national governments and so the decision-making at the highest level in the EU tends to reflect the interests of the governments of the member states. General Council meetings are attended by the respective foreign ministers of the member states but specialist meetings are attended by the appropriate government ministers in relation to the business under discussion. So, if the Council is discussing agriculture, it will be constituted by the ministers for agriculture of the various member states. The powers of the Council are set out in Article 202 in the following terms:

> To ensure that the objectives set out in this Treaty are attained, the Council shall in accordance with the provisions of the Treaty:
> (a) ensure co-ordination of the general economic policies of the Member States;
> (b) have powers to take decisions;
> (c) confer on the Commission, in the acts which the Council adopts, powers for the implementation of the rules which the Council lays down.

The presidency of the Council is held by each member state in turn at six-monthly intervals and meetings are usually convened at the request of the president but they can be convened at the request of the Commission or any member state. The office of president has become increasingly important in recent years and a member state will use its occupancy of the office to promote issues that it deems of importance.

Since the Council of Ministers is not a fixed grouping, it is vital that there should be a body to ensure that there is continuity in its work. This is achieved through an entity known as COREPER (an acronym after its French title). The legal basis for the existence of COREPER is found in Article 4 of the Merger Treaty 1965 which provides that a Committee consisting of the permanent representatives of the member states shall be responsible for preparing the work of the Council and for carrying out the tasks assigned to it by the Council. COREPER also serves an important function as a permanent liaison body for the exchange of information between national governments and the Community institutions. It is in fact subdivided into two equal committees, namely COREPER I and COREPER II. The former is composed of deputy permanent representatives (deputy ambassadors) and the latter by the permanent representatives (ambassadors). The Council also has its own full-time secretariat based at the Council building in Brussels which has an important role in coordinating the work of the Council.

■ The European Commission

The Commission is a unique institution that has administrative, executive, quasi-judicial, as well as some delegated legislative functions. It has been likened to a national civil service but this analogy should not be taken too far. Its central concern is to facilitate the ongoing process of European integration. Its base of operation is in Brussels and its officials function under the political control of a College of Commissioners. The College currently comprises 25 Commissioners. The Commissioners are nominated by the governments of the member states. The governments of the member states have been required to reach a unanimous decision on the person they wish to nominate as President of the Commission. The governments then, by common accord, nominate those they wish to serve as Commissioners but these persons must be acceptable to the nominated president too. The European Parliament must then approve the appointment of the President and the members of the Commission as a whole in a single vote. Once this has been done, each Commissioner is formally appointed by his/her own government. The Council acting by a qualified majority vote will nominate the person it intends to appoint as President of the Commission and the nomination must then be approved by the European Parliament. Thereafter, the Council acting by qualified majority and by common accord with the nominee for President will nominate a list of other persons that it intends to appoint as Commissioners in accordance with the proposals made by each member state. Once the approval of the European Parliament is obtained, the President and other Commissioners will be appointed by the Council by qualified majority vote (see page 113).

Under the EC Treaty, Commissioners are required to act in the general interests of the Community and be completely independent of their national governments in the performance of their duties. The normal term of office is five years but this may be extended. Until now the members of the Commission have been allocated their different portfolios (areas of responsibility and interest) by the President on the basis of preliminary informal discussions even though the final allocation must be ratified by the Commission as a whole. Under the new Article 217 the Commission must work under the political guidance of its President who will decide its internal organisation in order to ensure that it acts consistently and effectively. The President will be able to reallocate portfolios during the Commission's term of office and he/she may require a member of the Commission to resign provided that the approval of the rest of the Commission is obtained. The Commission meets in private and all decisions are taken on the basis of simple majority vote. These decisions are of the Commission as a whole, for which there is collective responsibility.

Every Commissioner has his/her own personal staff of approximately six officials which is known as his/her 'cabinet'. The Commission also has a permanent secretariat of some 21,000 full-time officials that support the work undertaken by the various Commissioners. These are organised into 25 directorates-general (see the Europa website at www.europa.eu.int for details). Each directorate-general is under the overall supervision of its own director-general. Since every directorate-general comprises a number of separate directorates, each directorate is supervised by a director who reports to the director-general. In addition to the directorates-general, there are a number of service units such as the Legal Service and Statistical Office that provide services across the Commission. It is the Commission that is mainly responsible for producing the draft texts that form the basis of the secondary legislation enacted by the institutions of the EU.

The European Parliament

The European Parliament has been directly elected ever since 1979. Its function is to represent the peoples of the EU and it acts as co-legislator with the Council in most policy areas. Unfortunately, its proceedings are under-reported in the British media but the www.europa.eu.int website is an excellent source of up-to-date information. The committee work of the Parliament is carried out at the Parliament building in Luxembourg but the actual decision-taking is reserved for the monthly meetings that are held at Strasbourg. All 732 MEPs sit in groupings corresponding to their political alignments when the Parliament meets in full plenary session each month at Strasbourg, the largest grouping being Christian Democrat. Germany, as the largest member state, has the largest number of MEPs at 99, whilst France, Italy and the UK each have 78. Spain has 54 and the Netherlands has 27. Other member states each have 24 or fewer MEPs, with Luxembourg electing a mere 6. Although the European Parliament must approve the Community budget, it cannot enact legislation by itself and it has no tax-raising powers; yet its involvement in the law-making process has increased steadily since the mid-1980s.

The European Court of Justice

The European Court of Justice (ECJ) comprises 25 judges – one from each member state – and is based in Luxembourg. It is assisted by eight advocates-general but they are not members of the Court as such. They provide reasoned submissions to the Court on every case that it hears. The Court is not bound by these submissions and will sometimes decide the outcome of a particular case contrary to the submissions of the advocate-general. These submissions of the advocate-general are, nevertheless, useful in considering the issues that the Court has had to grapple with in the course of its deliberations because the Court only produces a single judgment – there are no dissenting judgments. The 25 judges are grouped together in 'chambers' of three or five, and most cases brought before the Court are heard by a 'chamber' of three or five judges rather than by the entire Court. Nevertheless, when a member state or an institution makes a formal request, the Court must sit in plenary session with 13 judges present. The Court is the supreme authority on all matters relating to Community law and its jurisdiction and powers are set out in Articles 220 to 245. It draws upon the legal principles and traditions of all member states in the formulation of its own procedures and principles. It is therefore heavily influenced by the Continental civil law model which is quite distinct from the English tradition. The working language of the Court is French and so all documents must be translated into French, and it delivers all its judgments in French which must then be translated. Since September 1989, the ECJ has been assisted by a Court of First Instance. Its jurisdiction was mainly confined to cases involving competition law excluding Article 234 references. It judicially reviews all Commission decisions in the sphere of competition law and deals with employment law disputes between the staff of the EU and its institutions. Under the Treaty of European Union, the Court of First Instance (CFI) was given jurisdiction to hear all action brought by parties other than member states or Community institutions including anti-dumping cases.

■ The Court of Auditors

The Court of Auditors is not a court as such but an institution whose function is to oversee the financial management of the EU and, in particular, to assist the Parliament and the Council with the implementation of the Budget.

THE EUROPEAN COMMUNITY

4 The Community and the Union

The most significant supranational organisation comprising the EU is the European Community. The European Community (EC), unlike the EU, is a legal entity and the bulk of EU law is, in fact, the law of the EC. The general aims of the EC, as distinct from the ECSC and Euratom, are set out in Article 2 of the Consolidated version of the EC Treaty which declares:

> The Community shall have as its task, by establishing a common market and an economic and monetary union and by implementing common policies or activities referred to in Articles 3 and 4, to promote throughout the Community a harmonious and balanced development of economic activities, a high level of employment and of social protection, equality between men and women, sustainable and non-inflationary growth, a high degree of competitiveness and convergence of economic performance, a high level of protection and improvement of the quality of the environment, the raising

of the standard of living and quality of life, and economic and social cohesion and solidarity among member states.

This is highly aspirational language and it is readily apparent that the aims of the EC, as a constituent element of the EU, extend far beyond the economic sphere to include social and environmental protection. These general aims are to be achieved through the means set out in Articles 3 and 4. The nature of the European Community and its relationship with its member states was declared soon after its inception by the ECJ in Case 26/62 *NV Algemene Transporten-Expeditie Onderneming Van Gend en Loos* v *Nederlandse Administratie der Belastingen* [1963], long before the UK joined, when it declared:

> the Community constitutes a new legal order of international law for the benefit of which the states have limited their sovereign rights, albeit within limited fields, and the subjects of which comprise not only Member States but also their nationals. Independently of the legislation of Member States, Community law therefore not only imposes obligations on individuals but is also intended to confer upon them rights which become part of their legal heritage. These rights arise not only where they are expressly granted by the Treaty, but also by reason of obligations which the Treaty imposes in a clearly defined way upon individuals as well as upon the Member States and upon the institutions of the Community.

In Case 294/83 *Les Vert-Parti Ecologiste* v *Parliament* [1986] the ECJ asserted that the EC 'is a Community based on the rule of law'. Accordingly, all actions and measures taken by the institutions are subject to judicial review. The principal sources of EU law operative in the UK are:

(a)   the EC Treaty and subsequent treaties amending this treaty;
(b)   the secondary legislation created by the institutions; and
(c)   the case law (jurisprudence) of the European Court of Justice.

These will be considered shortly, in turn. The fact that EU law has any impact on UK law at all is attributable to the fact that the Westminster Parliament enacted the European Communities Act 1972 soon after the government of the day had signed the Treaty of Accession. This was essential because the UK is a 'dualist' state for the purposes of international law rather than a 'monist' state. Thus, international treaties do not immediately become part of the law of the UK. If a treaty is to become part of UK law it must be specifically incorporated by Act of Parliament. The crucial provision of the European Communities Act 1972 is s. 2(1) which provides:

> All such rights, powers, liabilities, obligations and restrictions from time to time created or arising by or under the Treaties, and all such remedies and procedures from time to time provided for by or under the Treaties, as in accordance with the Treaties are without further enactment to be given legal effect or used in the United Kingdom shall be recognised and available in law, and be enforced, allowed and followed accordingly; and the expression 'enforceable Community right' and similar expressions shall be read as referring to one to which this subsection applies.

The legal effect of this somewhat convoluted provision is to make what is now referred to as EU law, part of the law of the UK. Not only is EU part of UK law, it is superior to it should there be a conflict of legal rules. This was forcibly demonstrated in Chapter 5 when the *Factortame* litigation was discussed in relation to parliamentary sovereignty.

SOURCES OF EU LAW

5 The EC Treaty

It was obvious that the EC Treaty imposed obligations on the member states that signed it, but, as indicated in the judgment of the ECJ in Case 26/62 *NV Algemene Transporten-Expeditie Onderneming Van Gend en Loos* v *Nederlandse Administratie der Belastingen* above, it is clear that the Treaty can also confer rights and obligations on private legal persons. In this case the ECJ devised the important doctrine of 'direct effect' whereby certain Treaty provisions could be operative in the national legal system of all member states without having to be individually enacted. The Court's initial motives for invoking this concept were to give momentum to the process of economic integration and directly to engage private legal persons and the national courts of the member states in implementing EC law within their jurisdictions. It is significant that this concept was not explicitly stated in the EC Treaty and it is an early example of what commentators have referred to as 'judicial activism' on the part of the ECJ. The Treaty provision in question (now Article 25) prohibited the creation of new customs duties and charges having equivalent effect and a Dutch company sought to enforce this Treaty provision against the Dutch government in respect of chemicals that it had imported from Germany. The advocate-general in his submissions to the ECJ argued that the Treaty only imposed obligations on member states – it did not create rights that other legal persons could enforce. The ECJ rejected the advocate-general's submissions. The Court subsequently set out the criteria that must be satisfied before a Treaty provision can have direct effect, the elements of which are as follows:

(a) the right in question must be clear, precise and it must be unconditional,

(b) it must not require implementing measures by a member state or an EC institution, and

(c) it must not leave scope for the exercise of discretion by a member state or an EC institution.

Thus, not all EC Treaty Articles have 'direct effect' but the ECJ has ruled in many subsequent cases that a considerable number do operate in this way, especially those dealing with free movement of goods and persons. The concept of direct effect has important practical applications in this regard. Imagine the plight of a British exporter who wishes to sell his products to a German importer but the goods are refused entry by the German authorities. Article 28 provides that qualitative restrictions on imports and all measures having equivalent effect are prohibited between member states. There would be little point in the British exporter suing the German authorities in the British courts because they have no jurisdiction in Germany. It is vital that the exporter can sue the German authorities in the German courts and this is what direct effect makes possible. The German judiciary, being fully conversant with the EC Treaty, can make the appropriate order against the relevant government agency in Germany that has blocked the entry of the goods contrary to Article 28. Similarly, it is vitally important that a German national who has exercised his/her rights to free movement under Article 39 and who encounters discrimination in employment in England should be able to sue in the English courts relying on the protection afforded by Article 39 if this should prove necessary.

The prohibition against discrimination in relation to 'pay' on the basis of gender was declared to have direct effect by the ECJ in Case 43/75 *Defrenne* v *SABENA* [1976] and so women have the right to insist on equal pay for work of equal value throughout the EU. The main provisions on competition law, namely Articles 81 and 82, also have direct effect so that action can be taken in national courts where infringements arise. In relation to Treaty Articles, the doctrine of direct effect operates both vertically and horizontally. This means that a Treaty Article can be enforced against the government of the state or some agency of the state (vertically) as well as against another private legal person (horizontally) such as a company. However, the doctrine of direct effect does not apply to any part of the intergovernmental agreement on a common foreign and security policy nor to the agreement on police and judicial cooperation in criminal matters.

■ Supremacy of EC law

Not long after the ECJ devised the doctrine of direct effect, it ruled in Case 6/64 *Costa* v *ENEL* [1964] that EC law took precedence over national law. It declared:

> The integration into the law of each Member State of provisions which derive from the Community, and more generally the terms and the spirit of the Treaty, make it impossible for the State, as a corollary, to accord precedence to a unilateral and subsequent measure over a legal system accepted by them on a basis of reciprocity. Such a measure cannot therefore be inconsistent with that legal system. The executive force of Community law cannot vary from one state to another in deference to subsequent domestic laws, without jeopardising the attainment of the objectives of the Treaty set out in Article 5(2) and giving rise to the discrimination prohibited by Article 7.
> . . .
> The precedence of Community law is confirmed by Article 189 [now Article 249], whereby a regulation 'shall be binding' and 'directly applicable in all

Member States'. This provision, which is subject to no reservation, would be quite meaningless if a State could unilaterally nullify its effects by means of a legislative measure which could prevail over Community law.

Then in Case 11/70 *Internationale Handelsgesellschaft GmbH* v *Einfur-und Vorratstelle für Getreide und Futtermittel* [1970] the ECJ declared:

> [The] validity of a Community measure or its effect within a Member State cannot be affected by allegations that it runs counter to either fundamental rights as formulated by the constitution of the State or the principles of a national constitutional structure.

The principle of the supremacy of Community law over inconsistent national law was even more clearly set out in Case 106/77 *Amministrazione delle Finanze dello Stato* v *Simmenthal* [1978] because the case dealt with legislation enacted prior to the coming into force of the Treaty as well as subsequent legislation. The ECJ declared:

> Furthermore, in accordance with the principle of the precedence of Community law, the relationship between the provisions of the Treaty and directly applicable measures of the institutions on the one hand and the national law of the Member States on the other is such that those provisions and measures not only by their entry into force render automatically inapplicable any conflicting provision of current national law but – in so far as they are an integral part of, and take precedence in, the legal order applicable in the territory of each of the Member States – also preclude the valid adoption of new national legislative measures to the extent to which they would be incompatible with Community provisions.

Clearly, if national law could override EC law, the ongoing process of integration would become stalled and the concept of direct effect would be rendered futile. The concepts of direct effect and supremacy (or primacy) are now regarded as the defining and essential characteristics of EC and EU law.

6 Secondary legislation

At the inception of the European Community, it was realised that the Treaty would be incapable of providing a complete code of law for the evolving needs of the Community. Thus express provision was made in the Treaty for the creation of new legislation by the institutions as and when necessary. Due consideration must therefore be given to the role of the Commission in proposing new legislation and to the involvement of the Council and the European Parliament in formally adopting it. There is no general legislative power that is conferred on the Community institutions by the EC Treaty. Instead, individual Treaty Articles confer the power to create legislation in particular areas and the same Treaty Articles also prescribe the legislative process to be adopted. Thus every piece of secondary legislation must have a legal base in the Treaty and this must actually be stated in the text of the instrument that is to be adopted. The Commission usually initiates the legislative process but the Council does not have to wait for a Commission proposal. It may ask the Commission to undertake a study and submit appropriate proposals to achieve any of the objectives set out in the EC Treaty. The European Parliament now has a similar power under Article 192 if a majority of its members so request, but the Commission in both cases retains the discretion regarding the content and the timing of any proposals it makes to the Council. The officials within the Commission draft a 'source text' in French which is then transposed into the other official languages by lawyer-linguists within the Commission.

The law-making powers of the institutions are set out in Article 249 which provides that:

> In order to carry out their task and in accordance with the provisions of this Treaty, the European Parliament acting jointly with the Council, the Council and the Commission shall make Regulations and issue Directives, take Decisions, make Recommendations or deliver Opinions.

■ Secondary legislation and subsidiarity

In the negotiations leading to the signing of the Treaty of European Union, some member states were concerned that power to initiate legislation that had long been exercised by national parliaments was being assumed by the Commission and that legislative decision-making was becoming over-centralised in Brussels. Thus the subsidiarity provision was inserted into the EC Treaty. The concept of subsidiarity requires that decision-making should take place at the lowest possible level to the people affected by the decision. The subsidiarity provision became Article 5 which is as follows:

> The Community shall act within the limits of the powers conferred upon it by this Treaty and of the objectives assigned to it therein. In areas which do not fall within its exclusive competence, the Community shall take action in accordance with the principle of subsidiarity, only if and in so far as the objectives of the proposed action cannot be sufficiently achieved by the Member States and can therefore, by reason of the scale or effects of the proposed action, be better achieved by the Community.
>
> Any action by the Community shall not go beyond what is necessary to achieve the objectives of this Treaty.

The Community has reserved exclusive competence for itself to make law in those areas where it has legislated already. These areas include free movement of goods, persons and capital together with freedom to provide services and freedom of establishment. Thus, there is no scope for member states to enact their own legislation in these areas unless it is to implement legislation that has been adopted by the Council. Nevertheless, there are areas where the Community has not yet claimed exclusive competence, for example, social policy, consumer protection, and environment. If new legislative action is proposed in these areas to achieve some objective or purpose it is then that the principle of subsidiarity comes into play. It is necessary for the Commission to consider initially whether the action would be better taken at national level or whether the matter demands action at Community level for the sake of overall effectiveness. In bringing forward a legislative proposal at Community level, the Commission must provide an explanatory memorandum justifying the necessity of Community action to satisfy the subsidiarity principle. Article 253 states:

> Regulations, directives and decisions adopted jointly by the European Parliament and the Council, and such acts adopted by the Council or the Commission, shall state the reasons on which they are based and shall refer to any proposals or opinions which were required to be obtained pursuant to this Treaty.

In a Protocol to the Treaty of Amsterdam 1997 it is expressly stipulated that the Commission must provide copies of legislative proposals in 'good time' so that national parliaments have an opportunity to consider them. National parliaments will, of course, wish to pass on their comments to the Commission having given due consideration to a proposal.

Although the legislative process is usually initiated by the Commission, the Council is empowered to legislate in a few areas without having received a proposal from the Commission and without even consulting with the European Parliament. Nevertheless, the Parliament has become increasingly involved in the legislative process since 1979 mainly through the devising of new legislative procedures with successive revisions of the Treaty after intergovernmental conferences. There are four distinct procedures that require consideration: (1) the consultation procedure; (2) the co-decision procedure; (3) the cooperation procedure; and (4) the assent procedure.

■ Consultation procedure

The consultation procedure is so called because of the requirement imposed on the Council to consult with the Parliament. In the past it was the most frequently used of the four procedures. A proposal, usually in the form of a draft regulation or directive, is put forward by the Commission. The requirement for consultation must be strictly complied with and the proposal will normally be considered by a committee of the Parliament. Failure to consult the Parliament amounts to the infringement of an essential procedural requirement and the measure can be annulled in proceedings before the Court of Justice as in Case 138/79 *Roquette Frères* v *Council* [1980] where the ECJ annulled a regulation. If the original proposal is subsequently amended by either the Council or the Commission there must normally be a further round of consultation with the Parliament. Although the Parliament must be consulted, it is the Council of Ministers that takes the final decision and it is not bound by the views of the Parliament. As a result of the Treaty of Amsterdam, the Council is now required to consult the European Parliament in respect of measures to be adopted under Title VI of the EC Treaty concerning police and cooperation in judicial and criminal matters.

■ Co-decision procedure

The co-decision procedure was created under the Treaty of European Union 1992 in response to demands from the Parliament for a much greater say in the legislative process. It is now contained in Article 251 of the Treaty having been modified slightly by the Treaty of Amsterdam 1997. It has now become by far the most important legislative procedure. Nevertheless, co-decision has not been extended to all legislative measures which already require qualified majority voting in the Council such as agricultural policy and trade policy.

The Commission is required to submit its draft regulation or directive to the Parliament and the Council. The Council must seek the opinion of the Parliament but need not adopt a 'common position' thereafter. If the Parliament does not put forward any amendments the Council can adopt the measure by a qualified majority vote and it may do the same if the amendments proposed by the Parliament are acceptable to it and are incorporated. If the Parliament does suggest amendments that are controversial, the Council must adopt a common position and communicate it to the Parliament together with the reasons which led it to adopt the common position. The Commission must also inform the Parliament of its own position. There is then a 'window' of three months within which the Parliament may approve the common position so that the Council can adopt the measure by qualified majority vote. If the Parliament does not respond within the three months, the Council can also adopt the measure at the expiry of this time. If the Parliament rejects the common position by majority vote, the measure cannot be adopted by the Council. On the other hand, if the Parliament puts forward amendments to the common position by majority vote, the amended text must be forwarded to the Council and to the Commission. The Commission must then deliver an opinion on the amendments. The Council can, acting by qualified majority, approve all the amendments and adopt the measure provided that these amendments are acceptable to the Commission. If not, the amendments can only be incorporated into the draft legislation if the Council can muster a unanimous vote. Nevertheless, the Parliament can still exercise a veto if it disapproves of the proposed measure.

■ Cooperation procedure

The cooperation procedure was introduced under the Single European Act 1986 in order to give the Parliament a little more input into the legislative process than it had under the consultation procedure. This procedure is now set out in Article 252 but the entire procedure has now been marginalised under the Treaty of Amsterdam 1997. It has been retained only for the monetary policy provisions of the EC Treaty.

■ Assent procedure

The assent procedure was introduced by the Single European Act 1986 and is used to approve (or not, as the case may be) applications for membership from states wishing to join the European Union. It also applies to measures conferring tasks on the European Central Bank in relation to supervision of financial institutions apart from insurance companies; the amendment of certain Articles of the Statute on European System of Central Banks; defining the tasks, objectives and organisation of the structural funds; and proposals on procedures for elections to the European Parliament.

■ Voting in the Council

Most legislation must pass a vote in Council. Article 205(1) provides that, unless otherwise stipulated in the Treaty, the voting in Council is to be by simple majority, but in most instances the Treaty does specify that the voting must be either by unanimous vote or by qualified majority. Measures of a constitutional nature usually require a unanimous vote but abstentions by member states will not prevent the adoption of an Act by the Council where unanimous voting is required. Unanimous voting is still required for proposals relating to: taxation, culture, coordination of social security schemes, foreign and security policy together with police and judicial cooperation in criminal matters.

Qualified majority voting was first introduced under the Single European Act 1986 as it was essential to ensure the completion of the legislative programme for the single market by the end of December 1992. It was extended to cover many other areas under the Treaty of European Union 1992. Decisions taken on the basis of a qualified majority vote are binding on all member states, not just those who voted in favour. It is a system of weighted voting detailed in Article 205 whereby member states have a certain number of votes to cast according to their size and population. The maximum number of votes allocated to all member states is currently 321 and a qualified majority is achieved if two conditions are met, namely:

(a) if there is a majority (but in some cases a two-thirds majority); and
(b) a minimum of 232 votes are cast in favour amounting to 72.3 per cent of the total.

A total of 90 votes will constitute a 'blocking minority'. In addition, a member state may ask for confirmation that the votes cast in favour represent at least 62 per cent of the total population (450 m) of the Union. If this is found *not* to be the case, the decision will not be adopted.

Careful consideration is given to all legislative proposals by the Council's own working parties and COREPER before the Council meets in formal session. Thus many votes can be taken in the Council without much discussion beforehand. The Council does, from time to time, confer delegated law-making powers on the Commission which the latter must be careful to exercise within the scope of the authority that has been granted. If the Commission should exceed the scope of the authority that has been granted in the way that it drafts the instrument, its validity may be challenged before the ECJ by way of judicial review.

■ Application of secondary legislation

The status of the different forms of secondary legislation is further elaborated upon in Article 249 which provides that a regulation shall have general application and shall be binding in its entirety and directly applicable in all member states. Thus, the provisions that make up a regulation are directly applicable and are capable of having direct effect both vertically and horizontally where the criteria for direct effect are satisfied. No action is necessary on the part of the UK government as a member state to give effect to a regulation. It becomes operative in legal systems of the UK from the date specified in the *Official Journal* or, if no date is specified, 20 days after its publication. Although derogation (i.e. withdrawal by a particular member state) may be provided for, all regulations are presumed valid until declared otherwise by the ECJ.

Directives must be notified to all member states and normally indicate a time limit for their implementation. These directives are to be binding upon member states as to the result to be achieved, but it is for the national authorities to choose the form and methods for implementation. As indicated previously, a directive may be implemented in the UK by means of primary legislation (for example, the Data Protection Act 1998) or by means of subordinate legislation. A general power to create subordinate legislation to implement directives is contained in the European Communities Act 1972 s. 2(2). If a directive is not implemented, or not properly implemented within the time limit specified, the member state in question will be in breach of Article 10 and the Commission can invoke enforcement proceedings under Article 226. A decision of the Council or Commission shall be binding in its entirety upon those to whom it is addressed and may have direct effect. Decisions of the Council and Commission become effective on their notification to the relevant addressees but their validity can be challenged by the parties before the ECJ. Recommendations and opinions have no binding force but they do have an influential role in EC policy-making as a form of soft law. For example, the Commission Recommendation 92/131/EEC on the Protection of the Dignity of Women and Men at Work has proved to be influential with employment tribunals in the UK when dealing with claims of sexual harassment.

7 Jurisprudence of the ECJ

The jurisprudence of the ECJ derives from its extensive jurisdiction which is firmly rooted in particular Treaty provisions. It has jurisdiction to hear infringement proceedings brought by the Commission under Article 226 against member states in which the Commission alleges that a member state has failed to comply with its obligations under Article 10, the text of which is as follows:

> Member States shall take all appropriate measures, whether general or particular, to ensure fulfilment of the obligations arising out of this Treaty or resulting from action taken by the institutions of the Community. They shall facilitate the achievement of the Community's tasks.
>
> They shall abstain from any measure which could jeopardise the attainment of the objectives of this Treaty.

Article 226 contains a lengthy procedure, comprising a number of stages, which is aimed at gaining compliance without the necessity of a hearing before the ECJ. Only if the Commission has been unable to secure compliance will the ECJ be required to adjudicate over a member state's alleged failure to comply. Over the years, the Commission has been obliged to institute infringement proceedings against most of the member states. The UK has been brought before the Court on many occasions but so have a number of other member states. Infringement actions may also be brought before the Court by another member state under Article 227. There is only one reported instance of this, however, in Case C-141/78 *France* v *UK* [1979] where the ECJ ruled that UK measures on mesh sizes for fishing net did not conform with EC law. Although most infringement actions are decided in favour of the Commission, some are decided in favour of the member states concerned. The judgment of the ECJ in infringement actions is only declaratory and the Court has no powers to enforce its judgments by levying penalties. Nowadays, as a result of an amendment to the EC Treaty, Article 228(2) provides that proceedings can now be brought by the Commission after the initial hearing under Article 226 for payment of a lump sum or penalty payment by the member state for non-compliance with the judgment of the Court. This is subject to the proviso that the timescale set by the Commission for compliance must have elapsed. This power was exercised in Case C-387/97 *Commission* v *Hellenic Republic* when Greece failed to fulfil it obligations under Directives 75/442/EEC and 78/319/EEC in relation to its failure to draw up plans for the disposal of toxic waste. Having failed to comply with the judgment arising from the infringement action within the time limit that had been set, the ECJ imposed a penalty payment, in this case of €20,000 for each day that Greece failed to comply with the judgment.

Under Article 230, the ECJ is able to review all acts of the Council, the Commission, the European Parliament and the European Central Bank other than recommendations or opinions. The grounds for challenging a measure are limited to lack of legal competence, infringement of an essential procedural requirement, infringement of the Treaty or any rule of law relating to its application or misuse of powers. The member states, together with the Council and Commission, are 'privileged applicants' in proceedings under Article 230 so that they are automatically entitled to bring an action before the ECJ. In order to protect their particular interests, the European Parliament, the Court of Auditors and the European Central Bank are also permitted to instigate actions for annulment. Private legal persons, on the other hand, are 'non-privileged applicants'. They must show either that a decision is addressed to them or that it is of direct and individual concern in order to challenge it. This latter requirement was established by the ECJ in Case 25/62 *Plaumann & Co. v Commission* [1963]. If an action under Article 230 is held to be well founded, the ECJ will declare the measure to be void. In Case C-295/90 *European Parliament v Council* [1992], Directive 90/366, dealing with the right of residence of students, was annulled because it was adopted under Article 235 (now Article 308 EC) rather than Article 6(2) (now Article 12(2)). The UK government sought to use Article 230 in Case C-84/94 *UK v Council* [1996] to challenge the legal base of Directive 93/104 on the regulation of working time but did not succeed. Article 232 complements Article 230 to ensure that the European Parliament, the Council and Commission do act on the powers conferred on them when there is a clear legal duty to act under the Treaty. Thus, the ECJ will hear applications from member states, the institutions and other interested parties over a failure to act when there is a clear obligation to do so.

Under Articles 235 and 288(2) the ECJ has jurisdiction to hear disputes relating to the non-contractual liability of the institutions of the EU where private legal persons have suffered loss. The ECJ may award damages to compensate persons who have suffered loss as a direct result of action taken by an institution. In Case 5/71 *Zuckerfabrik Schoppenstedt v Council* [1971] the ECJ formulated a test for determining liability for acts where the institutions are involved in economic policy choices, which was restated in Cases 83, 94/76; 4, 15, 40/77 *Bayerische HNL Vermehrungsbetriebe GmbH & Co. KG v Council and Commission* [1978] when the Court declared:

> the Community does not incur liability on account of a legislative measure which involves choices of economic policy unless a sufficiently serious breach of a superior rule of law for the protection of the individual has occurred.

The concept of a superior rule of law has not been restrictively interpreted and applies to some of the general principles of law adopted by the ECJ to be considered later. However, in the above case the 'sufficiently serious' requirement was expressed in terms of the Community institution having 'manifestly and gravely' disregarded the limits on the exercise of its powers. The requirement tends to make the recovery of compensation quite difficult where this adversely affects individual interests because it operates to protect the institutions when exercising legislative power.

A relatively recent aspect of the jurisdiction of the ECJ relates to the hearing of appeals on points of law from the Court of First Instance. According to Article 51 of the Statute of the Court, an appeal may be based on lack of competence of the CFI, a breach of procedure that adversely affects the interests of the appellant or the infringement of Community law by the CFI.

Jurisdiction under Article 234

Important though these aspects of the Court's jurisdiction are, it is its jurisdiction under what is now Article 234 (formerly Article 177) that has been the main means by which the ECJ has been able to develop its jurisprudence. In order to ensure the uniform application of European law in all member states, the ECJ is empowered by the Treaty to give preliminary rulings on matters of interpretation referred to it by national courts and tribunals concerning EU law. Once they have been given, such preliminary rulings are binding on the national courts and Article 234 has been of great importance for the development of some of the key concepts that now stand as part of EU law. References have already been made to Case 26/62 *NV Algemene Transporten-Expeditie Onderneming Van Gend en Loos* v *Nederlandse Administratie der Belastingen* in which the ECJ devised the doctrine of direct effect and to Case 6/64 *Costa* v *ENEL* in which it pronounced the supremacy of EC law over inconsistent national law. Given the reluctance on the part of member states to take legal action against each other under Article 227, one can only applaud the wisdom and foresight of the ECJ in devising the doctrine of direct effect whereby private legal persons can enforce treaty provisions through national courts. It should be noted that the jurisdiction of the ECJ is not confined to the EC Treaty and extends to all EU legislation.

Expansion of the doctrine of direct effect

As was stated earlier, the ECJ ruled that certain Treaty Articles were capable of having direct effect if they satisfied the stipulated criteria. It then sought to expand the scope of the doctrine through its case law when the opportunity presented itself. In Case 9/70 *Grad* v *Finanzamt Traunstein* [1970] a Munich tax tribunal asked for a preliminary ruling on whether an Article of a decision in conjunction with an Article in a directive produced direct effect between member states and those under their jurisdiction. The tribunal was also asking whether the provisions referred to created rights for individuals that national courts had to protect. The ECJ stated:

> However, although it is true that by virtue of Article [249], Regulations are directly applicable and therefore by virtue of their nature capable of producing direct effects, it does not follow from this that other categories of legal measures mentioned in that Article can never produce similar effects. In particular, the provision according to which decisions are binding in their entirety on those to whom they are addressed enables the question to be put whether the obligation created by the decision can only be invoked by the community institutions against the addressee or whether such a right may possibly be exercised by all those who have an interest in the fulfilment of this obligation. It would be incompatible with the binding effect attributed to decisions by Article [249] to exclude in principle the possibility that persons affected may invoke the obligation imposed by a decision. Particularly in cases where, for example, the Community authorities by

means of a decision have imposed an obligation on a Member State or all the Member States to act in a certain way, the effectiveness (*l'effet utile*) of such a measure would be weakened if the nationals of that State could not invoke it in the courts and the national courts could not take it into consideration as part of Community law.

Subsequently, in Case 41/74 *Van Duyn* v *Home Office* [1974] the ECJ had to decide whether Directive 64/221 would be invoked against the UK government when it had not transposed it into its national law. The directive defined the 'public policy' exceptions whereby a member state could refuse entry to a national from another member state who was otherwise guaranteed free movement under Article 48 (now Article 39 EC). A Dutch national was refused permission to enter the UK to take up employment with an organisation known as the Church of Scientology because the UK government considered this organisation to be socially undesirable. When this was challenged in the High Court, it applied for a preliminary ruling under Article 177 (now Article 234) to the ECJ. Having confirmed that Article 48 had direct effect, the ECJ virtually repeated its ruling in *Grad* v *Finanzamt Traunstein* and added:

> In particular, where the Community authorities have, by Directive, imposed on Member States the obligation to pursue a particular course of conduct, the useful effect of such an act would be weakened if individuals were prevented from relying on it before their national courts and if the latter were prevented from taking it into consideration as an element of Community Law.

The elements of the criteria for the 'direct effect' of a Treaty Article apply to a directive but there is the additional requirement which is that the time limit specified for implementation of the directive must have expired. If the directive has been defectively implemented, an individual may also invoke it before the national court provided, of course, that the date for implementation has passed. Initially the ECJ relied on the principle of effectiveness to justify its ruling that directives could have direct effect, but in Case 148/78 *Pubblico Ministero* v *Ratti* [1979] it also justified its ruling on the principle that a member state should not be able to rely on its own default in not implementing a directive as a defence. In these early cases the ECJ was dealing with the direct effect of a directive as against the government of the state (vertical direct effect). However, the ECJ subsequently expanded the boundaries of its concept of 'the state' in Case 152/84 *Marshall* v *Southampton and South West Hampshire Area Health Authority (Teaching)* [1986]. Helen Marshall was a dietician who worked for the health authority for some 14 years but she was dismissed in 1980 because she had passed the normal retirement age for women under the authority's employment policy. Female employees were supposed to retire at the age of 60 but male employees could work on to the age of 65. Under the existing national legislation, women became eligible to receive the state pension at the age of 60 but men did not become eligible until the age of 65. This did not impose any obligation on women under national law to retire at the age of 60 because payment of the state pension could be deferred to the date of actual retirement. Helen Marshall, who was in good health, did not wish to retire before the age of 65 because she wished to go on making contributions to the NHS pension fund. On this basis, when she did retire at 65 she would be able to draw an enhanced pension. When she was obliged to retire she felt that she had been discriminated against because of her sex – if she were a man there would have been no problem about her working to age 65. At that time the Sex Discrimination Act 1975 exempted all arrangements relating to retirement from the ambit of the legislation and consequently she could not challenge the area health authority's retirement policy as sex discrimination under national law. She therefore based her case on Directive 76/207 – the equal treatment directive – which required that national governments should amend their national law to ensure that men and women received equality of treatment in employment. Her case eventually worked its way from an industrial tribunal to the Court of Appeal which referred the question to the ECJ, asking whether she could rely on the provisions of the directive notwithstanding the apparent inconsistencies between it and the Sex Discrimination Act 1975.

The ECJ ruled that the directive could have direct effect since the date for implementing it had passed. If the Court had permitted the directive to be enforced against a private legal person this would be what lawyers refer to as horizontal direct effect; but on a strict interpretation of what is now Article 249, the ECJ would not permit this. Thus, it was fortunate that Helen Marshall worked in the public sector (for the NHS). Had she worked in the private sector (e.g. for a Nuffield Hospital) she would not have been able to rely on the directive at that time to contest the legality of her employer's decision to retire her before the age of 65. The Sex Discrimination Act 1975 was amended as a result of this ruling by the Court of Justice when the Westminster Parliament enacted the Sex Discrimination (Amendment) Act 1986. In giving its judgment in *Marshall v Southampton and South West Hampshire Area Health Authority (Teaching)*, the ECJ stated:

> With regard to the argument that a Directive may not be relied upon against an individual, it must be emphasised that according to Article 189 of the EEC Treaty [now 249 EC], the binding nature of a Directive, which constitutes the basis for the possibility of relying on the Directive before the national court, exists only in relation to 'each Member State to which it is addressed'. It follows that a Directive may not of itself impose obligations on an individual and that a provision of a Directive may not be relied upon as such against such a person. It must therefore be examined whether, in this case, the respondent must be regarded as having acted as an individual.
>
> In that respect it must be pointed out that where a person involved in legal proceedings is able to rely on a Directive as against the State he may do so regardless of the capacity in which the latter is acting, whether employer or public authority. In either case it is necessary to prevent the State from taking advantage of its own failure to comply with Community Law.

In Case 222/84 *Johnston* v *Chief Constable of the Royal Ulster Constabulary* [1986] the ECJ ruled that the police could be regarded as part of the state, and in Case C-188/89 *Foster* v *British Gas* [1990] it indicated in paragraph 20 of its judgment that the concept of the state could extend to:

> a body, whatever its legal form, which has been made responsible, pursuant to a measure adopted by the State for providing a public service under the control of the State and has for that purpose special powers beyond those which result from the normal rules applicable in relations between individuals, is included in any event among the bodies against which the provisions of a Directive capable of having direct effect may be relied upon.

Weatherill and Beaumont (*EU Law*, 3rd edition) have suggested that the ECJ in an earlier part of its judgment has created the possibility that directives may be invoked by individuals against a legal entity that is not itself under state control. The final part of paragraph 18 of the Court's judgment can be interpreted in this way. Support for this view is provided by paragraph 47 of the judgment of the Court in Joined Cases C-253/96 and C-258/96 *Kampelmann* v *Landschaftsverband Westfalen-Lippe* [1997] in which employees were allowed to rely on Article 2(2)(c) of Directive 91/533 as against their employer, a municipally owned utility company. In the event, the House of Lords interpreted the guidelines provided by the ECJ in *Foster* v *British Gas* and held that the provisions of Directive 76/207 could be invoked against British Gas which at the relevant time was a nationalised industry under state control even though it had been subsequently privatised. Following this ruling, Blackburne J in *Griffin* v *South West Water Services Ltd* [1995] decided that a privatised water company was an emanation of the state on the basis that it was under the control of the state. Then the Court of Appeal in *NUT and others* v *Governing Body of St Mary's Church of England (Aided) Junior School* [1997] held that, although the governors of a voluntary aided school were not under the direct control of the state, once the school obtained voluntary aided status it became part of the state education system. At that point the governors became a public body responsible for providing a public service, subject to statutory powers exercisable by the local education authority. It could therefore be regarded as an emanation of the state and the teachers could rely on the provisions of Directive 77/187 against the governing body. It does now seem that a directive may be enforced against entities that are not directly connected to state.

In Case 14/83 *Von Colson and Kamann* v *Land Nordrhein-Westfalen* [1984] and Case 79/83 *Harz* v *Deutsche Tradax* [1984] the ECJ had stated that all national authorities, including courts, had an obligation to interpret their national law in such a way that the aims of a directive were achieved. This principle was subsequently restated by the ECJ in Case C-106/89 *Marleasing SA* v *La Comercial Internacional de Alimentacion SA* [1990] but the ECJ added the rider that the obligation arose only where it was possible to do so. Nevertheless, this could result in a national court imposing liability on private legal persons in some instances which would be tantamount to giving horizontal direct effect to directives. Having expanded the scope of the doctrine of direct effect by expanding the concept of the state, it was predictable that the ECJ would eventually be asked to go one step further and rule that a directive could have horizontal direct effect. This was implicit in the reference that was made in Case C-91/92 *Faccini Dori* v *Recreb Srl* [1994]. The case was not without merit in that Ms Dori had made a contract at Milan station for the purchase of an English language correspondence course. Had Italy implemented Directive 85/577 which was intended to harmonise national law in respect of contracts negotiated away from business premises to provide a 'cooling-off period', she would have been able to withdraw from the contract during this period. She sought to rely on the directive as a defence to a claim brought by the other contracting party to enforce the contract and the Italian court applied for a preliminary ruling under Article 177 (now Article 234). The ECJ refused to ignore the very clear wording of Article 249 and stated that a directive could not impose obligations on private legal persons. Persons in Ms Dori's situation are no longer without a remedy because they can now sue the government of the state concerned and obtain reparation for its failure to implement a directive.

■ State liability

In the period prior to the completion of the single market, the ECJ was particularly concerned over the non-implementation or defective implementation of directives by some member states despite their obligations under what are now Articles 10 and 249. Non-implementation meant that Community law was not uniform across the Community and, if it were to happen on a wide enough scale, it could seriously retard the process of integration. The problem was highlighted by Cases 6 and 9/90 *Francovich and Bonifaci* v *Italian State* [1991]. In 1980, the Council had adopted Directive 80/987 on the protection of employees in the event of the insolvency of their employer. The directive provided that member states must ensure that an institution was established to guarantee payment of employees' outstanding claims for pay and redundancy compensation. Italy had failed to implement this directive by the date set and the Commission had already brought a successful infringement action against Italy in 1987 in Case 22/87 *Commission* v *Italy* [1989]. Despite a clear ruling against the Italian state, the Italian government had still not implemented the directive at the time this case was brought by Francovich and Bonifaci. The Court held that the Italian state was in breach of its obligations under Article 5 [now Article 10] of the Treaty. Although the ECJ stated that the directive in question was not sufficiently precise to give rise to direct effect, the Court went on to rule that a state had a duty to compensate individuals for loss suffered as a result of its failure to implement the directive by the specified deadline. However, the ECJ made it clear that this obligation on the part of member states would only arise when the following criteria were met:

(a) the directive conferred rights on individuals,
(b) the content of those rights could be identified from the terms of the directive,

(c)   there is causation (a clear link) between the member state's failure to implement and the loss/damage suffered by the individual.

The ECJ then went on to declare that it was a matter for each member state to designate the competent courts and to establish detailed procedural rules for the necessary legal proceedings aimed at safeguarding the rights that individuals derive from Community law. It then added that the rules for reparation in national law must not be less favourable than those relating to similar domestic claims and not be framed in such a way as to make it virtually impossible or excessively difficult to obtain reparation. Where individuals are able to claim against their own national governments for failure to implement directives, the distinction between horizontal and vertical direct effect is no longer of importance because the individuals concerned will be claiming against the state and not against a private employer or some other private legal person. Moreover, numerous claims for compensation against the government of a member state may have the desired result of inducing them to be more conscientious in future about implementing directives within the timescale permitted.

In the later Joined Cases C-46/93 and 48/93 *Brasserie du Pecheur SA* v *Germany* and *R* v *Secretary of State for Transport ex p. Factortame Ltd and others* [1996] the ECJ extended the scope for reparation against member states beyond the failure to implement directives to other breaches of EC law. Factortame Ltd and others sought compensation following the ruling that the UK was in breach of EC law and the Divisional Court of the High Court made a preliminary reference to establish whether the UK was liable to compensate the company and, if it was, what consideration should be taken into account in the assessment of claims for damages. The company's claim was joined with a similar reference made by a German court in respect of a claim by a French company against the German government for the infringement of a Treaty provision on the free movement of goods. The ECJ ruled that EC law conferred a right to reparation under three conditions:

(a)   the rule of law infringed must be intended to confer rights on individuals,

(b)   the breach must be sufficiently serious,

(c)   there must be a direct causal link between the breach of the obligation resting on the state and the damage sustained by the injured parties.

There was no difficulty with the first element of the criteria because both Articles 6 and 52 (*Factortame Ltd*) and Article 30 (*Brasserie du Pecheur*) had long ago been declared to have direct effect. In relation to the second element, the ECJ endeavoured to provide guidance when it stated in paragraphs 56 and 57:

> The factors which a competent court may take into consideration include the clarity and precision of the rule breached, the measure of discretion left by that rule to the national or Community authorities, whether the infringe-

ment and the damage caused was intentional or involuntary, whether any error of law excusable or inexcusable, the fact that the position taken by a Community institution may have contributed towards the omission, and the adoption or retention of national measures or practices contrary to Community Law.

On any view, a breach of Community Law will be sufficiently serious if it has persisted despite a judgment finding the infringement in question to be established or a preliminary ruling or settled case law of the Court on the matter from which it is clear that the conduct in question constituted an infringement.

In relation to the third element of the above criteria, the ECJ stated in paragraph 58 that it was for national courts to decide whether there was a direct causal link between the breach of the obligation by the state and the damage suffered. Thus national courts must not only decide whether there has been a sufficiently serious breach, they must also decide the issue of the causal link within which they must consider the application of a duty to mitigate loss through the prompt taking of legal action and the application of any contributory negligence. National rules on the limitation of actions also apply to such claims. The caveats provided by the ECJ are that national remedies must be effective and non-discriminatory in that Community rights must not receive less favourable treatment than similar national claims. From a UK perspective, this was novel because there was no existing principle of law of state liability for legislative acts.

The principle of state liability has been developed further through a series of subsequent cases:

(a) Case C-392/93 *HM Treasury* v *British Telecommunications Plc* [1996]
(b) Case C-5/94 *R* v *Ministry of Agriculture, Fisheries and Food ex p. Hedley Lomas* [1996]
(c) Joined Cases C-178/94, C-179/94, C-188/94, C-189/94 and C-190/94 *Dillenkofer and others* v *Germany* [1996]
(d) Joined Cases C-283/94, C-291 and C-292/94 *Denkavit International BV* v *Bundesamt für Finanzen* [1996].

However, there continues to be a degree of uncertainty over the nature of the breach necessary to give rise to liability. The ECJ has attempted to align the liability of member states to that of the non-contractual liability of EU institutions under Article 288(2) although the two are not strictly comparable in practice. Consequently, where a member state acts in an area where it has wide discretion, the ECJ is likely to take a less strict approach to the question of liability. The government and/or national authorities will only be liable if they have manifestly and gravely disregarded the limits of their discretion. If the member state has either no discretion in implementing EU law or no discretion to act in a way that is at variance with EU law, the infringement may be sufficient to establish the existence of a sufficiently serious breach. This is particularly so where there is a clear and inexcusable violation of a precise obligation.

The UK government was able to avoid the imposition of liability in *HM Treasury* v *British Telecommunications Plc* on the basis of the very clear guidance provided by the ECJ to the national court. The ECJ was firmly of the view that the provision of the directive in question lacked clarity and that the UK was acting in an area of wide discretion. Moreover the Commission had not objected to the text of the UK regulations implementing Directive 90/531, a copy of which was sent to it. On the other hand, in *R* v *Ministry of Agriculture, Fisheries and Food ex p. Hedley Lomas*, the ECJ took the view that the UK had little or no discretion in the granting of a licence and was not called upon to make legislative choices. On this basis there could be liability for breaching Article 34 (now Article 29) on free movement of goods. In *Dillenkofer and others* v *Germany*, liability could be imposed for the failure to transpose Directive 90/314 conferring consumer protection in the sphere of holiday travel by the specified deadline even though there had been no prior infringement action against Germany. On the other hand, in *Denkavit International BV* v *Bundesamt für Finanzen*, the ECJ applied the criteria set out in paragraph 56 of its judgment in *Brasserie du Pecheur SA* and held that the breach was not sufficiently serious because of the uncertainty surrounding Article 3(2) of Directive 90/435 on an aspect of company taxation. Other member states, having discussed the directive with the Council, had adopted the same faulty interpretation of the directive as Germany.

FUNDAMENTAL RIGHTS IN EU LAW

8 Fundamental human rights

The European Convention on Human Rights and Fundamental Freedoms (hereafter ECHR) was drafted in 1950 by the Council of Europe. The Council of Europe was established in 1949 as a political forum to foster political cooperation at the European level in the aftermath of the Second World War. It therefore predated the establishment of any of the European Communities referred to at the beginning of the chapter and is quite distinct from them. The Council of Europe drafted the ECHR in the form of a treaty to safeguard against the possibility of a political group similar to the Nazi party ever securing power in Western Europe again. It was signed by those European countries (including the UK) that were members of the Council of Europe at the time and other European states have since acceded. The ECHR comprises a number of civil and political rights and was inspired by the International Covenant on Civil and Political Rights which forms part of the UN Universal Declaration of Human Rights but, unlike the UN declaration, it has its own enforcement mechanisms centred on the European Court of Human Rights at Strasbourg. The Convention was not incorporated into the original EEC Treaty in 1957 probably because, in the beginning, the aims of the Community were purely economic and it was not envisaged that the individual rights of private legal persons were likely to be infringed. When the implications of the Court's declaration of the supremacy of Community law over inconsistent national law had been completely absorbed, it began to be appreciated that Community law might override constitutional guarantees of fundamental rights. This was the basis of the application to the ECJ in Case 11/70 *Internationale Handelsgesellschaft GmbH* v *Einfur-und Vorratsstelle für Getreide und Futtermittel* [1970] in which the ECJ declared in paragraph 3 of its judgment that 'respect for fundamental rights forms an integral part of the general principles of Community law protected by the Court of Justice'. However, this was qualified in the next sentence, in which the Court stated:

> The protection of such rights, whilst inspired by the constitutional traditions common to the Member States, must be ensured within the framework of the structure and objectives of the Community.

Having considered the grounds for the alleged infringement, the ECJ decided that there had been no infringement of the right claimed. This was because the restriction on the freedom to trade in the form of a deposit payable for the export of maize meal was not disproportionate to the general interest that the deposit system sought to achieve. However, when the case returned to the German Constitutional Court, a contrary conclusion was reached. In Case 4/73 *Nold* v *Commission* [1974] the ECJ enlarged on its earlier declaration, stating:

> ... fundamental rights form an integral part of the general principles of law, the observance of which it ensures.
>
> In safeguarding these rights, the Court is bound to draw inspiration from constitutional traditions common to the Member States, and it cannot therefore uphold measures which are incompatible with fundamental rights recognised and protected by the Constitutions of those States.
>
> Similarly, international treaties for the protection of human rights on which the Member States have collaborated or which they are signatories, can supply guidelines which should be followed within the framework of Community Law.

This indirect reference to the ECHR was made explicit in Case 222/84 *Johnston* v *Chief Constable of the RUC* [1986]. On numerous occasions, private legal persons have attempted to challenge the validity of Community legislation on the basis that it infringed fundamental human rights. In most instances the ECJ has decided on the facts that the legislation does not breach any fundamental human right as it interprets that right. A notable exception arose in Case 63/83 *R* v *Kent Kirk* [1985] where a Danish fisherman was able to avoid criminal liability for fishing in UK territorial waters by successfully pleading that UK legislation retroactively validated by a Community measure violated Article 7 of the Convention.

The ECJ has since developed its case law in Case 249/86 *Commission* v *Germany* [1989] to the point where member states are required to respect fundamental human rights when implementing Community law. This case concerned a violation of Article 7 of ECHR by Germany in implementing Article 10 of Regulation 1612/68 on free movement of persons. The

German authorities had refused to renew the residence permits of certain migrant workers and threatened to expel them to their country of origin. They had complained to the Commission over the implementation of Regulation 1612/68 by the German authorities. Nevertheless, the ECJ has stated in its Opinion 2/94 that the EC does not have the legal competence to accede to the Convention and that an amendment to the Treaty would be necessary if this was to be achieved. If this were to happen, it would mean that the ECJ would not have the final say on the application of fundamental human rights in the EU because it would have to defer to the European Court of Human Rights. Nevertheless, Article 6(2) of the Consolidated version of the Treaty of European Union states that the EU shall respect the fundamental rights guaranteed by the European Convention as they result from the constitutional traditions common to the member states and general principles of Community law.

9 General principles of EU law

The ECJ was only too well aware that the EC Treaty did not specifically safeguard fundamental human rights. It therefore gradually formulated a number of general principles of law which form part of its case law by drawing on legal principles operative on the various member states. In this way it was able to 'square the circle'. It could maintain the supremacy of Community law over inconsistent national law but refute any allegation that it had judicially incorporated the ECHR into Community law. At the same time, by drawing on the ECHR as a source of inspiration, it was able to assert that there was a consensus among the member states regarding the foundations of the general legal principles of Community law, or EU law as they should now be known. These principles are:

(a) proportionality;
(b) equality;
(c) legal certainty; and
(d) procedural justice.

10 Proportionality

The principle of proportionality is a borrowing from German administrative law and is applicable within a number of areas of EU law including the guaranteed rights in relation to free movement and freedom of establishment as well as the Common Agricultural Policy. It is used to test the legality of action taken in the context of EU law by the institutions as well as by member states. The application of the principle requires a balancing of means and ends so that the precise means chosen to achieve a particular end or outcome should be no more than is necessary to do so. Some weight or value must, of course, be assigned to the particular end to make a balancing process possible. A good example of the operation of this principle is provided by Case 114/76 *Bela-Muhle Josef Bergmann KG* v *Grows-Farm GmbH & Co. KG* [1977]. The Council adopted Regulation 563/76 on the compulsory purchase of skimmed milk powder. The intervention agencies had accumulated very large stocks of skimmed milk powder and these were still increasing. The Regulation aimed to reduce these stocks. The protein contained in the milk powder was to be used in processed animal feed. A provision in the Regulation made the grant of aid provided for certain vegetable protein products together with the free circulation in the Community of certain imported animal feed products subject to the obligation to purchase specified quantities of the treated milk powder. The purchase price imposed for the purchase of the treated milk powder was almost three times more expensive than the alternative feed made from soya. The defendant contested the validity of the Regulation on the basis that it conflicted with the objective of the Common Agricultural Policy and the principle of proportionality. The ECJ ruled that the compulsory purchase price imposed a disproportionate burden on importers and users of animal feed which could not be justified in terms of the objectives of the Common Agricultural Policy and declared the regulation devoid of legal effect. Proportionality was also used to test the legality of a member state's action in Case 120/78 *Cassis de Dijon*.

11 Equality

The principle of equality is expressed in Article 12 in terms of a prohibition on discrimination based on nationality, in Articles 39, 43 and 49–50 in relation to free movement and in Article 141 (formerly Article 119) with regard to equality of treatment as between men and women in relation to pay. In the context of the Common Agricultural Policy, Article 34(2) provides that there shall be no discrimination as between producers and consumers. In EU law the principle of equality, however, has a much wider application. The first stage in deciding whether a breach of the principle has taken place where two persons are similarly situated is to identify the difference in treatment. Having done so, the next stage is to decide whether the difference is justified in the particular circumstances or whether it is not permissible.

12 Legal certainty

Legal certainty requires that the law should, as far as possible, be available to whom it applies so that they can order their affairs and make necessary plans. In the context of this overarching principle there are three related principles: legitimate expectations, non-retroactivity and vested rights. The principle of legitimate expectations may be invoked to prevent an EU institution from going back on an undertaking that has been given. In order to invoke this principle, a private legal person must be able to show three things:

(a) the legitimate expectation was properly raised by the action of an institution – normally the Council or Commission,

(b) that reliance was placed on this action, and

(c) loss has been or would be suffered.

The ECJ has permitted the principle of legitimate expectations to be invoked to challenge the validity of a legislative act or decision. Infringement of the principle may also provide the basis for a claim for compensation under Article 288(2). The principle of non-retroactivity is a presumption and not an absolute rule. It is simply a presumption against the retrospective effect of legislative acts and decisions. In Case 88/76 *Exportation des Sucres* v *Commission* [1977], the ECJ ruled that the application of this principle prevented a regulation from taking effect before it was published in the *Official Journal.* However, in Case 98/78 *Racke* v *Hauptzollamt Mainz* [1979] the ECJ upheld the validity of two retrospective measures, stating that:

> Although in general the principle of legal certainty precludes a Community measure from taking effect from a point in time before its publication, it may exceptionally be otherwise where the purpose to be achieved so demands and where the legitimate expectations of those concerned are duly respected.

The principle that criminal legal provisions may not have retroactive effect is one that is common to the legal systems of all member states. Thus, in *R* v *Kent Kirk* the ECJ ruled that the retroactive nature of Regulation 170/83 could not be regarded as validating a national measure imposing criminal penalties. The retroactive application of a measure may be accepted by the Court in a non-criminal context where an important Community objective is being pursued and where legitimate expectations are properly respected. The principle of vested rights is linked to the principle of non-retroactivity in that rights acquired by private legal persons may be extinguished only if there are compelling reasons.

13 Procedural justice

The principle of procedural justice is a borrowing from English, Irish and Scots law and is nothing more than the application of the principles of natural justice. In Case 17/74 *Transocean Marine Paint Association* v *Commission* [1974] the Association had obtained from the Commission an exemption in respect of Article 85(3) (now Article 81(3)), for an agreement which was binding on its members, some of whom were within the EEC but others were not. When the Association applied to renew the agreement, the Commission imposed a condition relating to the provision of new information and the Association argued that it had not been given the opportunity to make its objection concerning this condition to the

Commission before a final decision was made. In giving its judgment the ECJ stated in paragraph 15:

> It is clear [that the relevant regulation implementing Regulation 17/62] applies the general rule that a person whose interests are perceptibly affected by a decision taken by a public authority must be given the opportunity to make his point of view known. This rule requires that an undertaking be clearly informed, in good time, of the essence of conditions to which the Commission intends to subject an exemption and it must have the opportunity to submit its observations to the Commission. This is especially so in the case of conditions which, as in this case, impose considerable obligations having far-reaching effects.

Another aspect to the principle of procedural justice is the requirement to give reasons for any decision that is taken so that it may be reviewed to ensure that it has not been formulated on an arbitrary basis.

Although these general principles of law have been derived from the legal systems of the member states, their adoption by the ECJ has resulted in their becoming somewhat detached and independent of specific principles within the constitutional and legal systems of the member states which originally inspired them.

The commitment to fundamental human rights has since been strengthened by Article 6 (paragraphs 1 and 2) of the Consolidated Text of the Treaty of European Union, as indicated previously, which provides that:

> The Union is founded on the principles of liberty, democracy, respect for human rights and fundamental freedoms, and the rule of law, principles which are common to the Member States. The Union shall respect fundamental rights, as guaranteed by the European Convention for the Protection of Human Rights and Fundamental Freedoms signed in Rome on 4 November, 1950 and as they result from the constitutional traditions common to the Member States, as general principles of Community Law.

Since Article 6 has not been incorporated into the EC Treaty, it is only binding on the member states. The Treaty of Amsterdam 1997, nevertheless, makes this Article justiciable before the ECJ. Thus a private legal person cannot bring a case to the European Court of Human Rights alleging that there has been an infringement of the Convention by an EU institution.

A European Charter of Fundamental Rights was finalised in October 2000 and was adopted by a proclamation of the Council, Parliament and the Commission at the European Council meeting in December 2000. The authors of the Charter intended that people in the EU should be better informed about their rights, and it has been incorporated into the new Constitution. This Charter is a fusion of the rights taken from the ECHR, decisions of the ECJ, together with other EU charters including the EU Charter on the Fundamental Rights of Workers. It also contains some totally new rights relating to the protection of personal data and rights in the sphere of bioethics. Although it was decided that this charter should not be legally binding, EU citizens can refer to it when challenging any decision taken by the institutions and by member states when implementing EU law. The ECJ has not yet cited it in any of its judgments.

Since the ECHR has not been incorporated into EU law as such (nor UK law in the sense that can override the law enacted by Parliament), a more detailed discussion of fundamental human rights as set out in the Convention has been deferred to Chapter 8 which deals with the interpretation of UK and EU law.

14   A note on citizenship of the EU

The Treaty of European Union established the concept of EU citizenship and Article 17 provides that everyone who holds the nationality of a member state is a citizen of the EU. This gives rise to certain rights in that every EU citizen is able to move and reside freely within the territory of any member state subject to the limitations specified in the EC Treaty. Having exercised this right, every EU citizen has the right to vote and stand as a candidate in municipal elections and elections to the European Parliament where he/she resides, under the same conditions as a national of that state (Article 19). Under Article 20 there is a right to the protection from diplomatic missions of other member states in countries where the citizen's own state is not represented. In addition, Article 21 provides that every EU citizen has the right to petition the European Parliament in accordance with Article 194 and to address complaints of maladministration to the Ombudsman under Article 195.

■ Summary

It is common knowledge that the people of the UK will make two important decisions in relation to the EU: (a) whether to ratify the new European Constitution and (b) whether to join the single currency. Important though these decisions will undoubtedly be, the fact remains that, whatever the outcome, the UK will still be a member state of the EU. This means that it will remain committed to the ongoing process of economic integration (with a degree of political integration) within Europe that it agreed to be part of when the government signed the treaty of accession in 1972. Until ratification is complete the EU will continue to be defined in terms of the Treaty of European Union and the existing structure of the EU has thus been examined in this chapter. The gradual integration of the European economy is given momentum by the law-making that occurs at the European level and so the role of the institutions in the law-making process has been explained. The Court of Justice has had an important role to play in the process of economic integration in the way in which it has developed its jurisprudence as the opportunities under, what is now, Article 234 have presented themselves. The concepts of direct effect, supremacy and state liability in particular represent an attempt by the Court of Justice to make the application of EU law more effective in all member states including the UK. The Court has dealt with the gap in the treaties in relation to fundamental human rights by devising its own general principles of law from the constitutional principles of the member states.

WWW PROGRESS TEST

For suggested answers to the tests below, go to the companion website at www.pearsoned.co.uk/wheeler

1 By what means did European Community law become part of the law of the UK?
2 What is meant by the 'primacy' of EU law and how crucial is this to the process of economic integration?
3 Which institution is responsible for drafting regulations and directives?
4 Which institutions are involved in enacting secondary legislation?
5 Which of the legislative processes confers least power on the European Parliament?
6 What powers does the European Parliament exercise over the European Commission?
7 Why is it necessary to have a Court of Justice? What is the jurisdiction of the Court of Justice?
8 Why should national courts wish to make references to the ECJ under Article 234?
9 What is the jurisdiction of the Court of First Instance and which aspect of its work do you consider is the most important for the maintenance of the single market?
10 Why is it important that Treaty Articles and the provisions of some secondary legislation should be accorded 'direct effect'?
11 What is the essential difference between a regulation and a directive?
12 Distinguish between vertical direct effect and horizontal direct effect?
13 What criteria must be met before a directive can have vertical direct effect?
14 Under what circumstances can a member state be held liable to compensate an individual over the failure to implement a directive?

FURTHER READING

■ Books

Craig, P. and G. de Burca (2002) EU *Law: Text and materials* (Oxford: Oxford University Press).

Steiner, J., L. Woods and C. Twigg-Flesner (2003) *Textbook on EC Law* (Oxford: Oxford University Press).

Weatherill, S. and P. Beaumont (1999) *EU Law* (Harmondsworth: Penguin).

■ **Articles**

Anagnostaras, G. (2001) 'The allocation of responsibility in state liability actions for breach of Community law: a modern Gordian knot?', *European Law Review* Vol. 26, No. 2.

Steiner, J. (1998) 'The limits of state liability for breach of European community law', *European Public Law* Vol. 4, No. 1.

Wilson, C. and Downes, T. (1999) 'Making sense of rights. Community rights in EC law', *European Law Review* Vol. 24, No. 2.

USEFUL WEBSITES

For general information on the EU visit www.europa.eu.int.
For the Court of Justice visit www.curia.eu.int.

8 Interpretation of UK and EU legislation

1 Introduction

It is not only lawyers and judges that find themselves in situations where they have to interpret primary and subordinate legislation. Tax inspectors must interpret tax legislation when making tax assessments and civil servants working at the Benefits Agency must interpret social security legislation in order to assess benefit entitlements. In addition, there is a vast array of legislation that impacts directly on business in areas such as health and safety, environmental protection, consumer protection and employment. Managers must become conversant with this legislation in so far as it pertains to their responsibilities so that they can ensure compliance by their respective organisations. It comes as a surprise to many people to learn that there is no Act of Parliament that lays down a clear set of principles that must be followed by anyone engaged in the task of statutory interpretation. Moreover, a leading practitioners' text on the subject entitled *Maxwell – On the Interpretation of Statutes* does not provide anything by way of a coherent body of principles for guidance. The Preface to *Maxwell* states:

> . . . it is, I trust, not taking too cynical a view of statutory interpretation in general, and this work in particular, to express the hope that counsel putting forward diverse interpretations of some statutory provision will each be able to find in *Maxwell* dicta and illustrations in support of his case.

This chapter will consider, first, the interpretation of national law before moving on to consider the impact of the Human Rights Act 1998. There will then be a consideration of the principles underlying the interpretation of EU law.

2 The normal rule

How should the numerous statutory provisions enacted by the Westminster Parliament be interpreted by managers and others? In view of the fact that a relatively small number of provisions ever give rise to disputed meanings, the only reasonable answer and one that has overwhelming judicial support is that the words used must be interpreted according to their normal grammatical meaning in context. For example, the Arbitration Act 1996 s. 26(1) states that: 'The authority of an arbitrator is personal and ceases on his death.' The meaning of this provision is straightforward. It is clear that if an arbitrator dies in the course of the proceedings, it will be necessary for a new arbitrator to be appointed if the arbitration is to continue. Where the words comprising the provision are clear and unambiguous, giving them their normal grammatical meaning will be consonant with the purpose behind the legislation because the draftsperson will have drafted the legislation with its readers and users in mind. Where technical terms are used these should be given their technical meaning and the draftsperson may have helped by including an 'interpretation' section in the Act that defines technical or special terms that have been used. Nevertheless, statutory provisions do vary in their degree of complexity and by no means all are as straightforward as the Arbitration Act 1996 s. 26(1). The Misrepresentation Act 1967 s. 2(1) has been previously cited as an example of complexity but consider the Sale of Goods Act 1979 s. 11(3):

> Whether a stipulation in a contract of sale is a condition, the breach of which may give rise to a right to treat the contract as repudiated, or a warranty, the breach of which may give rise to a claim for damages but not to a right to reject the goods and treat the contract as repudiated, depends in each case on the construction of the contract; and a stipulation may be a condition, though called a warranty in the contract.

A certain amount of legal learning has to be brought to bear in order to interpret this provision. It is not immediately clear how a condition is to be differentiated from a warranty and it might be necessary to have recourse to a solicitor unless the reader has made a detailed study of the law of contract.

In the English legal system, judges are frequently called upon to provide authoritative interpretations of statutory provisions where the meaning is disputed because the words used are ambiguous or obscure. Sitting as a court, one or more judges may have to decide whether an infringement of the criminal law has occurred under conditions of doubt. In the context of the civil law, where the wording of a provision is ambiguous or is obscure and forms the basis of a dispute between two or more parties, it will be necessary for the court to arrive at an authoritative interpretation to resolve the dispute.

3   Case study

Giving statutory words their normal grammatical meaning and, if technical terms are used, their normal technical meaning, will often produce a satisfactory outcome. Occasionally though, this approach may produce an unsatisfactory result that is arguably at odds with the purpose of the legislation or it may produce a manifestly unjust outcome. In such situations the court is likely to consider other possible meanings; but this has not always happened in the past, as is well illustrated by the case of *Carrington and others* v *Therm-A-Stor Ltd* [1983]. The Court of Appeal had to consider certain provisions which have since been re-enacted (without changes) in ss. 152 and 153 of the Trade Union and Labour Relations (Consolidation) Act 1992. Section 153 states that:

> Where the reason or principal reason for ... dismissal of an employee was that he was redundant but it is shown that the reason ... why he was selected for dismissal was one of those specified in section 152(1), the dismissal shall be regarded as unfair ...

Section 152(1)(a) states:

> ... the dismissal of an employee shall be regarded as unfair if the reason for it ... was that the employee was, or proposed to become a member of an independent trade union ...

The dispute arose when the management of the company dismissed 20 of its employees because virtually all of the employees at the company's newly opened factory had either joined or had applied for membership of the TGWU or were actively considering doing so. The senior management was antipathetic to the activities of trade unions and, when the district secretary of the union applied for 'official recognition' of the TGWU for the purpose of collective bargaining, the management instructed supervisors to select 20 employees for dismissal on the ostensible basis they were redundant (i.e. surplus to requirements). Obviously the senior management wished to signal its disapproval with a view to inducing its workforce to abandon any trade union involvement. Most of those dismissed were in fact trade unionists. When they presented a petition to a tribunal claiming that they had been dismissed contrary to their statutory right *not to be unfairly dismissed* because of their trade union membership, the tribunal rejected their claim because the supervisors, in selecting the employees for dismissal, did not, at the time of dismissal, take into account actual or proposed trade union membership. They dismissed the employees on a random basis. The Employment Appeal Tribunal reversed the tribunal's decision but the company then appealed to the Court of Appeal which restored the original decision of the tribunal. The leading judgment in the Court of appeal was given by Sir John Donaldson MR. He stated:

> As I read this section it is concerned solely with the dismissal of an employee and provides that it shall be regarded as unfair if the reason was that the employee had done or proposed to do one or more specified things. The reason why each of the employees was dismissed had nothing to do with anything which the employee concerned had personally done or proposed to do. The section therefore has no application.

Sir John Donaldson MR then went on to state that the reason why the dismissals had occurred was attributable to the response of management to the union's plea for official recognition. As you can see, this was not a contingency *specifically* provided for in the legislation cited and therefore the men were not protected by the statutory provisions even though they were trade unionists and, but for their joining the TGWU, their dismissals would probably not have happened. Counsel representing the dismissed men argued that what is now s. 153 of the Trade Union and Labour Relations (Consolidation) Act 1992 should be interpreted to mean that the men were collectively dismissed for their trade union membership – a more purposive approach to the interpretation of the legislation. However, in his judgment Sir John Donaldson went on to say:

> ... it is the duty of the court to give effect to the intention of Parliament. However, the concept that 'parliament must have intended a particular result' is not without its dangers. If regard is had solely to the apparent mischief and the need for a remedy, it is only too easy for a judge to persuade himself that parliament must have intended to provide a remedy which he would himself have decreed if he had legislative power. In fact, parliament may not have taken the same view of what is a mischief, [it] may have decided as a matter of policy not to legislate for a legal remedy or [it] may simply have failed to realise that the situation could ever arise.

By way of comment it may be said that the notion of 'the intention of Parliament' is a form of self-entrapment resulting in self-deception because Parliament comprises over a thousand individuals. Moreover, it may be considered that this very narrow, rather literal approach has little to commend it because it resulted in an unjust outcome for the men involved. They could not be reinstated in their jobs (a possible remedy) nor were they entitled to any compensation. It is possible that a similar case might be decided differently today. Although the Human Rights Act 1998 does not impose obligations on private legal persons, it is difficult to reconcile such a narrow interpretation of the provisions in question with the spirit of the Convention rights as contained in the Act, which are to be considered later. One of the fundamental rights guaranteed is 'freedom of association' which translates into the right to be a member of a trade union. However, the provisions in question were very clearly drafted in terms of individual employee rights. Lord Millett, a Lord of Appeal in Ordinary, writing in the *Statute Law Review 1999* Vol. 20, stated recently:

> ... we are all purposive constructionists now; but there are limits to what even purposive construction can achieve. The language of the statute is sometimes just too plain or too closely articulated to give any room for manoeuvre.

It could be that the High Court might regard itself as bound by the ruling in *Carrington and others* v *Therm-A-Stor Ltd*, as might the Court of Appeal itself. A future court could make a declaration of 'incompatibility' but this would not produce a difference of interpretation nor outcome unless and until Parliament alters the wording of the provisions. A case with facts similar to those of *Carrington and others* v *Therm-A-Stor Ltd* is unlikely to arise whilst the statutory recognition provisions favouring trade unions contained in the Employment Relations Act 1999 are in force but an incoming Conservative government might repeal these provisions.

If the meaning of a particular statutory provision is not readily apparent to a court and it wishes to consider possible alternative interpretations it can have recourse to the recognised intrinsic and extrinsic aids to construction.

4 Intrinsic aids

Judge(s) who are in doubt over the precise meaning of a provision can read the whole of the statute including the long and short titles, cross-headings and Schedules. Unfortunately the short title (e.g. The Employment Rights Act 1996) is just descriptive and is rarely of much assistance; but the long title which appears at the beginning of the enactment may be read sometimes to resolve ambiguity because it sets out the purpose of the legislation. Modern statutes rarely have preambles that commence with the word 'whereas' but when the statute does have a preamble the judge(s) can refer to it for assistance. The Schedules that appear on the end of an Act of Parliament may also be examined in cases of uncertainty and punctuation may be relied upon in some instances to resolve ambiguity. Although the marginal notes that appear in a modern statute are not discussed in the passage of a Bill through Parliament, they may sometimes be used as an aid to interpretation. The explanatory notes that accompany many modern complex statutes are very helpful to those who must apply or otherwise use the legislation but, strictly speaking, they do not form part of the legislation as enacted by Parliament and so cannot properly be regarded as 'intrinsic aids' to interpretation. In addition to these intrinsic aids mentioned, there are three well-established conventions of English usage that may be invoked by the judge(s) which can be stated as follows:

(a) General words such as 'or other' appearing at the end of a list of more particular words to save giving further examples take their meaning from the preceding list of particular words. This is often referred to as the *ejusdem generis* rule (meaning, of the same kind) and operates to confine the scope of the general words. In this context, see for example the case *DPP* v *Jordan* [1977].

(b) Words can be 'coloured' by their context. This is sometimes referred to as the *noscitur a sociis* rule and means simply that the meaning of a word can depend on the context in which it is used and should not be taken out of context. An example of this may be seen in the case *Pengelly* v *Bell Punch Co. Ltd* [1964].

(c) Express mention of one member of a class by implication excludes other members of the same class. This is sometimes referred to in Latin as *expressio unius exclusio alterius* which normally operates to confine the scope of a statutory provision. For an example of this see *Johnson* v *Moreton* [1980].

Such conventions may be invoked from time to time to deal with minor difficulties in the interpretation of legislative texts and were resorted to when a more literal approach to interpretation was in favour.

5 Extrinsic aids

A court can have recourse to a number of extrinsic aids. Their order of appearance should not be taken as an indication of an order of precedence. They may be listed as follows:

(a) authoritative evidence of the general historical climate at the time when the Act was passed;

(b) practitioners' textbooks and dictionaries but dictionaries must be used with care because they tend to reflect changes in usage over time;

(c) related statutes dealing with the same subject matter can be referred to provided they were enacted prior to the statute under consideration;

(d) statutory instruments made under the statute in question;

(e) reports of the Law Commission or a Royal Commission may be referred to in order to identify some defect or deficiency in the pre-existing state of the common law where legislation has been enacted to deal with it;

(f) if a statute incorporates an international treaty, the treaty itself and the historical background may be referred to as an aid to interpretation.

In relation to (e) above, the Court of Appeal in *Yaxley* v *Golls* [1999] stated that, where a statute has been enacted as a result of recommendations of a Law Commission report, it was both appropriate and permissible to consider the recommendations of that report in order to identify both the 'mischief' the Act was meant to cure and the public policy underpinning it. With regard to (f) above, in *Mandla* v *Dowell Lee* [1983] the International Convention on the Elimination of All Forms of Discrimination was referred to in the House of Lords to support an interpretation of the word 'ethnic' so that it could be applied to a Sikh.

The use of one or more of these intrinsic and extrinsic aids may resolve the ambiguity or obscurity, but, if not, it will be necessary to consider the purpose behind the legislation in so far as it has a single or dominant purpose. For example, the Civil Procedure Rules made under the authority of the Civil Procedure Act 1997 have not been drafted with the same precision as the old Rules of the Supreme Court that they have replaced. Nevertheless, the requirement that the courts give effect to the overriding objective of the CPR (to deal with cases justly) means that the courts must give these rules a purposive interpretation. However, in the case of multi-purpose statutes such as the Trade Union and Labour Relations (Consolidation) Act 1992 or Companies Act 1985, it will only be possible to consider the purpose behind particular parts of these legislative texts.

6 Search for the underlying purpose

Where the words used are ambiguous or altogether obscure it will be impossible to declare a single ordinary grammatical meaning and it is therefore necessary to consider a permissible secondary meaning that accords with the purpose behind the statutory provision. In the past it has not been possible for courts to refer to the parliamentary history of legislation as the Bill was being debated in Parliament. This has often prevented the courts from adopting a purposive approach. Referring to the parliamentary history entails reading Hansard (an edited version of the proceedings in both chambers of the legislature) and committee reports with a view to ascertaining the underlying reasons behind the legislation. In *Pepper (HM Inspector of Taxes)* v *Hart* [1993], the House of Lords finally abrogated this self-denying ordinance and indicated that courts could refer to Hansard where a statutory provision is ambiguous or otherwise obscure.

The appeal to the House of Lords in this case was made by the Inspector of Taxes who wished to tax a number of teachers and the bursar of an independent school under the Finance Act 1976 s. 61(1) on the basis that they had received a 'benefit in kind' in respect of having the full fees waived for their children who were attending the school. Although the school was not full, the 20 per cent of normal fees paid by the teachers did cover the additional cost to the school of educating their children. According to the Finance Act 1976 s. 63, the parents in question should be taxed on the 'cash equivalent' of the benefit which was 'an amount equal to the cost of the benefit'. This cost was 'the amount of any expense incurred in or in connection with its provision'. Whilst the Inspector of Taxes argued that they should pay an amount in tax related to the full fees normally payable, the parents argued that their tax liability should be linked to the additional cost to the school of educating their children which was met by the fees actually paid. Since the fees paid covered the costs incurred, it was argued that 'the cash equivalent of the benefit' was zero as was their tax liability in this regard. Six of the seven Law Lords considered that the Finance Act 1976 s. 63 was ambiguous in that the 'expense incurred in or in connection with' could be interpreted either as being the additional cost to the school of providing the benefit to the parents in question or a proportion of the total cost incurred in providing education at the school for all children. By referring to the parliamentary history of the Bill it was apparent that the Financial Secretary to the Treasury during the Committee stage of the Bill had made it clear that ss. 61 and 63 should be interpreted on the basis that in-house benefits, particularly concessionary education for the children of teachers, should be assessed on the additional cost to the employer and not on the proportion of the total cost of providing education at the school for all children. Thus the parents had no tax liability to meet on this benefit because on the interpretation adopted it was equivalent to zero.

Six of the seven Law Lords ruled that parliamentary materials could be referred to where:

(a)   the legislation was ambiguous or obscure or the literal meaning led
       to absurdity,
(b)   the material relied upon consisted of statements by a minister or
       other promoter of the Bill which led to the enactment of the legis-
       lation together, if necessary, with such other parliamentary material
       as was necessary to understand such statements and their effect, and
(c)   the statements relied on were clear.

This approach was subsequently taken by the House of Lords in
Warwickshire C.C. v *Johnson* [1993] where the manager of a high street elec-
trical appliance store was charged with an offence under the Consumer
Protection Act 1987 s. 20(1). This involved the giving of a misleading indication of price. The issue to be resolved by the House of Lords was
whether the manager, as distinct from the company of which he was an
employee, could be prosecuted for the offence. Section 20(2) stated:

> . . . a person shall be guilty of an offence if (a) in the course of any business
> of his, he has given an indication to any consumers which, after it was given,
> has become misleading as mentioned in subsection (1) above . . .

In giving the leading judgment in the House of Lords, Lord Roskill
referred to the official record of the proceedings on the Bill in Lord's
chamber in which it was noted that there was no intention to prosecute
employees for misleading price indications so that the words 'any business
of his' were interpreted to refer to the employer, not an employee.
    The material which may be relied upon is specified in a Supreme Court
Practice Note of 20 December 1994 reported in [1995] 1 All ER 234 as parliamentary proceedings recorded in the official reports of either House of
Parliament as they appear in Hansard. Other reports (e.g. in newspapers)
of parliamentary proceedings may not be relied upon. According to the
Note any party intending to refer to any extract from Hansard in support
of any such argument as is permitted by the decisions in *Pepper (Inspector
of Taxes)* v *Hart* and the earlier case of *Pickstone* v *Freemans Plc* [1982] must,
unless the judge otherwise directs, serve upon all other parties and the
court copies of any such extract together with a brief summary of the argument intended to be based upon such an extract. Subsequently, in *McKay*
v *Northern Ireland Public Service Alliance* [1995] it was indicated that White
Papers may be referred to in order to identify any 'mischief' that a statute
was enacted to cure where this can be demonstrated to be the case. In the
context of the criminal law, in *R* v *Mullen* [2000] the Court of Appeal
(Criminal Division) had to consider the Criminal Appeal Act 1968 s. 2(1)
as amended by the Criminal Appeal Act 1995. By referring to Hansard, the
court was able to ascertain that the new form of the Criminal Appeal Act
1968 s. 2(1) was intended to restate the existing practice of the Court of
Appeal. On this basis, the court was able to rely on 'abuse of process' as a
ground for quashing the conviction in question. It described the conduct
of the British authorities in procuring the deportation of the accused from
Zimbabwe as an affront to the public conscience.
    There have, however, been some indications of unease by the Law
Lords with the way in which advocates have reacted to the decision in

Pepper v *Hart* and the relaxation of the exclusionary rule. In the later case of *R* v *Secretary of State for the Environment, Transport and the Regions ex p. Spath Holme Ltd* [2001] the Law Lords took a strict view of the scope of *Pepper* v *Hart*. In that case Lord Bingham stated:

1 Unless the first of the conditions [established in the case] is strictly insisted upon, the real risk exists, feared by Lord Mackay, that the legal advisers to parties engaged in disputes on statutory construction will be required to comb through Hansard in practically every case (see pp. 614G, 616A). This would clearly defeat the intention of Lord Bridge of Harwich that such cases should be rare (p. 617A), and the submission of counsel that such cases should be exceptional (p. 597E).

2 It is one thing to rely on a statement by a responsible minister or promoter as to the meaning or effect of a provision in a bill thereafter accepted without amendment. It is quite another to rely on a statement made by anyone else, or even by a minister or promoter in the course of what may be lengthy and contentious parliamentary exchanges, particularly if the measure undergoes substantial amendment in the course of its passage through Parliament.

3 Unless parliamentary statements are indeed clear and unequivocal (or, as Lord Reid put it in *R* v *Warner* [1969] 2 AC 256 at 279E, such as 'would almost certainly settle the matter immediately one way or the other'), the court is likely to be drawn into comparing one statement with another, appraising the meaning and effect of what was said and considering what was left unsaid and why. In the course of such an exercise the court would come uncomfortably close to questioning the proceedings in Parliament contrary to article 9 of the Bill of Rights 1689 and might even violate that important constitutional prohibition.

It seems clear, therefore, that the House of Lords intends that Hansard should only be referred to in exceptional circumstances.

7 Adding words to the text

Judges may add to the words of a statute in order to prevent a provision from having a result that is clearly contrary to the underlying intention of the legislation. This may be illustrated in relation to a series of cases which have focused on the interpretation of the Race Relations Act 1976 s. 1(1)(a) and s. 4(2)(c). The former provides:

A person discriminates against another in any circumstances relevant for the purpose of any provision of this Act if
(a) on racial grounds he treats that other person less favourably than he treats or would treat other persons;

and the latter:

It is unlawful for a person, in the case of a person employed by him at an establishment in Great Britain, to discriminate against that employee –
(c) by dismissing him, or subjecting him to any other detriment.

The overriding objective of this statute is to make it unlawful for a person to engage in racial discrimination in the employment sphere and elsewhere. In *Zarczynska* v *Levy* [1979] the complainant was dismissed for serving a black customer contrary to her employer's express instructions. She had not been employed long enough to be able to make a claim for unfair dismissal under the relevant legislation so she was obliged to bring her claim under the Race Relations Act 1976. The tribunal that initially heard the complaint adopted a literal interpretation of the Act and decided that there was no racial discrimination because she was not dismissed because of *her own colour*. The Employment Appeal Tribunal declined to take such a narrow literal interpretation of the statutory provisions and decided that racial discrimination could include treating a person less favourably on the grounds of *another's colour*. In the later case of *Showboat Entertainment Centre Ltd* v *Owens* [1984] a white employee was dismissed for refusing to carry out an instruction from the employer to exclude young blacks from an entertainment centre. Although such an instruction was unlawful under the Race Relations Act 1976 s. 30 only the Commission for Racial Equality is empowered to take enforcement action of that section. Following its decision in *Zarczynska* v *Levy*, the Employment Appeal Tribunal decided that Parliament could not have intended to leave an employee without a remedy in such a situation – the phrase 'on racial grounds' in s. 1(1)(a) was interpreted as including discrimination on the grounds of another's race, colour etc. A similar approach was taken in *Weathersfield Ltd* v *Sargent* [1998] when a receptionist felt impelled to resign because she could not bring herself to comply with instructions from her employer to discriminate against black customers. This was deemed unlawful discrimination on the grounds of customers' race which had caused the necessary 'detriment' in the form of constructive dismissal.

Apart from being able to add some words to a statute, the House of Lords has recently restated the right of the judiciary to correct drafting errors in *Inco Europe Ltd and others* v *First Choice Distribution and others* [2000]. Lord Nicholls in giving judgment, with which all four of the other Law Lords concurred, said:

> ... the courts exercise considerable caution before adding or omitting or substituting words. Before interpreting a statute in this way the court must be abundantly sure of three matters: (1) the intended purpose of the statute or provision in question; (2) that by inadvertence the draftsman and Parliament failed to give effect to that purpose in the provision in question; and (3) the substance of the provision Parliament would have made, although not necessarily the precise words Parliament would have used, had the error in the Bill been noticed.

He stated that the third condition was of crucial importance otherwise any attempt to determine the meaning of the statutory provision in question would cross the boundary line between construction (interpretation) and judicial legislation which would not be permissible. In the particular circumstances of the case, Lord Nicholls ruled that the three conditions were fulfilled and the House of Lords then proceeded to correct a drafting error in the Arbitration Act 1996 Schedule 3 paragraph 37(2). He also indicated that, even where the above criteria are satisfied, a court may on occasion feel unable to alter the precise wording of the statute, especially one in the sphere of the criminal law where a strict interpretation is more usual. Once a court does give an authoritative pronouncement of the meaning of a statutory provision it takes the form of a precedent and, if the pronouncement is made in the House of Lords, it will be binding on all lower courts. Nevertheless, some existing precedents will require reconsideration in the light of the Human Rights Act 1998 and the jurisprudence of the European Court of Human Rights, although the Act does not oblige national courts to follow this jurisprudence.

8   Human Rights Act 1998

It is common to hear legal commentators and others say that the European Convention on Human Rights and Fundamental Freedoms has been incorporated into UK law. There is a sense in which this is correct, but there is also a sense in which it is *not*. The way in which the Act makes the Convention rights applicable and available in national law is one in which the courts cannot strike down or suspend an Act of Parliament simply because it is at variance with the Convention or some part of it. The obvious contrast is with EU law, where the courts of England and Wales are obliged to suspend the operation of any part of an Act of Parliament that conflicts with some principle of EU law that has direct effect. Whilst Parliament is at liberty to enact law that conflicts with the Convention rights, it is not at liberty to enact law that conflicts with EU law.

In the main, the Human Rights Act 1998 imposes human rights obligations on public authorities although it has been seen in Chapter 4 that the Convention has been invoked in cases where private legal persons have taken legal action to protect their privacy. Persons who consider that their Convention rights have been infringed by a 'public authority' can rely on the rights embodied in the Human Rights Act 1998 Schedule 1 as a defence in criminal or other public law proceedings or as a basis for an appeal. Alternatively, they may seek judicial review. The term 'public authority' against whom these rights may be enforced includes government departments, executive agencies, police, immigration officers, quangos and local authorities, as well as courts and tribunals. It is expressly provided that Parliament is not a public authority for the purposes of the Act but the Appeal Committee of the House of Lords is a public authority. The basic idea is that a victim or potential victim can invoke the Convention rights to prevent the misuse of power. It is likely that a public company which is exercising a public function, for example a company operating a remand centre or prison, could be subject to the provisions of the Act. Moreover, employees of the bodies indicated above should be able to enforce a number of Convention rights against their employers if their employers can be regarded as emanations of the state and if the employees concerned can establish that they are victims as required by s. 7(1). The term 'victim' is defined by s. 7(7).

Article 1 of the Convention requires that member states must ensure that everyone within their jurisdiction can enjoy the rights and freedoms contained within it. The UK has fulfilled this requirement by simply enacting the Human Rights Act 1998. The rights and freedoms set out in Schedule 1 are set out in full in Appendix 2 but are merely outlined below to facilitate discussion in the context of statutory interpretation:

Article 2	The right to life
Article 3	A prohibition of torture, inhuman or degrading treatment or punishment
Article 4	A prohibition of slavery or forced labour
Article 5	The right to liberty and security
Article 6	The right to a fair trial
Article 7	The right not to be punished unless it is sanctioned by law, and prohibition against the retroactive application of the criminal law
Article 8	The right to respect for private life and family life, the home and correspondence
Article 9	The right to freedom of thought, conscience and religion
Article 10	The right to freedom of expression including the right to receive information
Article 11	The right to freedom of assembly and freedom of association including the right to form and join a trade union
Article 12	The right to marry and found a family
Article 13	The requirement of an effective remedy for victims. This has not been specifically incorporated into Schedule 1 as such
Article 14	The prohibition of discrimination in relation to the enjoyment of the rights and freedoms guaranteed by the Convention.

Section 1(2) of the Act provides that the above Articles have effect subject to any designated derogation (opt out) or reservation as defined in ss. 14 and 15 as well as Schedule 3. Article 13 of the Convention is given effect through s. 7 of the Act, whereby Convention rights can be raised and argued before national courts by a victim, and s. 8, whereby the judges may grant whatever relief or remedy they consider 'just and appropriate'. Articles 2, 3, 4(1) and 7 as contained in Schedule 1 are absolute and cannot be qualified in any circumstances but Articles 4(2) and 4(3) and 5 are capable of derogation but they are not to be otherwise balanced against the wider public interest. In relation to Article 6, the Privy Council held in *Brown* v *Scott (Procurator Fiscal) and another* [2001] that, although the overall fairness of a criminal trial could not be compromised, the constituent rights within Article 6 were not in themselves absolute. Thus the right against self-incrimination could be qualified. Again, in *McIntosh* v *Lord Advocate and another* [2001] the Privy Council ruled that Article 6(2) was not an absolute right but could be qualified by a legitimate community interest. Articles 8, 9, 10 and 11 are qualified rights and can be balanced against the wider public interest as specified. In addition to the above Articles, there are rights under Protocols to the Convention that the UK has ratified. Under the First Protocol, Articles 1–3, there is the right to peaceful enjoyment of one's possessions, the right to education and a right to free elections. Under the Sixth Protocol, Articles 1–2, there is a prohibition on the death penalty in the absence of war.

As indicated already, the Convention operates primarily, albeit not exclusively, in the sphere of public law. According to s. 6(1) it is unlawful for a public authority to act in a way that is at variance with the rights designated as Convention rights. However, this is immediately qualified by s. 6(2) which provides that s. 6(1) does not apply if, as a result of one or more provisions of primary legislation, the authority could not have acted differently. There is a similar provision in the case of subordinate legislation which cannot be given effect in a way that is compatible with the Convention rights. On a literal interpretation, those through whom a public authority acts (its employees and agents) do not incur personal liability under s. 6(1). Thus the liability of a public authority under the Act is incurred directly and not vicariously. Section 6(1) forms the basis of the so-called 'interpretative obligation' which is supplemented by ss. 2 and 3. Section 3(1) of the Act requires that all primary and secondary legislation is to be read and given effect in a way that is compatible with the Convention *in so far as it is possible to do so*. It does not matter whether the legislation in question was passed before or after the Act and the general stipulation regarding interpretation applies to any agency administering the legislation and not just the courts. The House of Lords held in *R* v *A* [2001] that the Youth Justice and Criminal Evidence Act 1999 s. 41 should be interpreted so that it is compatible with Article 6(1) even though a literal interpretation would indicate that complainants must be protected from questioning in court concerning their prior sexual behaviour when they allege rape. In that case the House of Lords held that the accused's Convention right to a fair trial might be violated if relevant evidence of the type which the accused sought to adduce was excluded by the court. Section 2 of the Act requires all courts and tribunals that are called upon to decide a question that involves the application of a Convention right to take account of the jurisprudence of the European Court of Human Rights, the opinions of the European Commission of Human Rights (now defunct) and the decisions of the Committee of Ministers. This requirement does not, however, oblige the national courts to follow this jurisprudence.

It should be possible for a court to interpret the national legislation in question according to the particular Convention right(s) in issue where a minister has made a statement of compatibility prior to the second reading of the Bill under s. 19. Such a statement is not definitive, however, as the minister has merely given an honest opinion albeit with the benefit of legal advice. The difficulties are more likely to arise with older legislation. If the wording of a provision is quite clearly at variance with the right(s) in Schedule 1 then the provision must be interpreted according to its wording. Although s. 4 enables the court to make a declaration of 'incompatibility', according to s. 4(6) this does not affect the validity of the provision which must continue to be applied unless and until it is changed by Parliament. Nor will it affect the outcome of the case. Section 5(2) provides that the appropriate minister is entitled to be joined as a party to the proceedings if a court is contemplating making a declaration of incompatibility under s. 4(2) so that he/she can put the government's case. If the proceedings are criminal, where government has been made a party to the proceedings, it may appeal to the House of Lords against a declaration of 'incompatibility'. In *Wilson* v *First County Trust Ltd* [2001] the Court of Appeal made a declaration of incompatibility in relation to the Consumer Credit Act 1974 s. 127(3) on the basis that it was not compatible with the rights guaranteed under Article 6(1) of the Convention and Article 1 of the First Protocol as set out in the Human Rights Act 1998. The House of Lords in *R (on the application of Alconbury Developments Ltd)* v *Secretary of State for the Environment, Transport and the Regions* [2001] overturned a declaration of incompatibility made by the Divisional Court of Queen's Bench in relation to the minister's refusal to grant planning permission. The House of Lords took the view that the exercise by the minister of his powers under various statutes was not incompatible with Article 6(1).

Nevertheless, the House of Lords has made declarations of incompatibility in a number of cases such as *R (on the application of Anderson)* v *Secretary of State for the Home Department* [2002] and *Bellinger* v *Bellinger* [2003]. In both cases their Lordships considered it was impossible to interpret the statutes in question in a way that was compliant with the Convention rights in Schedule 1 to the Act. Yet in *Re S* and *Re W* [2002] the House of Lords rejected the 'adjustments' made by the Court of Appeal to the Children Act 1989 in an endeavour to make the legislation compliant. Although the legislation was acknowledged to be defective, the House of Lords declared that this did not make it incompatible with Article 8 of the Convention rights.

The Convention itself is a 'living text' and the European Court of Human Rights does not therefore follow a system of binding precedent as the English Courts do and which was explained in Chapter 4. In interpreting the Convention, the European Court of Human Rights follows the Vienna Convention on the Law of Treaties 1969. Accordingly, divergences might occur between the interpretation of the Convention by the European Court of Human Rights in Strasbourg and the application of Convention rights by courts in the UK.

9 European Law

It is clear from the ruling of the European Court of Justice in Case 26/62 *NV Algemene Transporten–Expeditie Onderneming Van Gend en Loos* v *Nederlandse Administratie der Belastingen* that national courts must apply all directly effective EU law. It is vital to the functioning of the EU that all EU legal provisions are interpreted uniformly so that there are no significant variations in the application of the law between the various member states. The authors of the EC Treaty were aware of the potential problem and what is now Article 234 (formerly Article 177) is intended to harmonise the way in which member states ultimately apply EU law. It provides:

> The Court of Justice shall have jurisdiction to give preliminary rulings concerning:
> (a) the interpretation of this Treaty;
> (b) the validity and interpretation of acts of the institutions of the Community and of the European Central Bank;
> (c) the interpretation of the statutes of bodies established by an act of the Council, where those statutes so provide.
> Where such a question is raised before any court or tribunal of a Member State, that court or tribunal may, if it considers that a decision on the question is necessary to enable it to give judgment, request the Court of Justice to give a ruling thereon.
> Where any such question is raised in a case pending before a court or tribunal of a Member State against whose decisions there is no judicial remedy under national law, that court or tribunal shall bring the matter before the Court of Justice.

It is clear that the ECJ may give authoritative interpretations of EU law whether in the form of Treaty provisions or legislative acts of the institutions as set out in Article 249 EC. Yet, the national court is to be the sole judge of whether a preliminary reference under Article 234 EC is required and the ECJ will not review the exercise of this discretion. According to the second paragraph of Article 234 EC, courts and tribunals whose decisions give rise to a remedy in national law have discretion in deciding whether or not to request a preliminary ruling on points of EU law they are called upon to apply. Bingham J (as he then was), in *Commissioners of Customs and Excise* v *Samex Ap S* [1983] highlighted the advantages of seeking a ruling from the ECJ when trying to interpret the 'guidelines' that had been laid down by Lord Denning MR in the earlier case of *H.P. Bulmer Ltd* v *J. Bollinger SA* [1974]. He said:

> Sitting as a judge in a national court, asked to decide questions of Community law, I am very conscious of the advantages enjoyed by the Court of Justice. It has a panoramic view of the Community and its institutions, a detailed knowledge of the Treaties and of much subordinate legislation made under them, and an intimate familiarity with the functioning of the Community market which no national judge denied the collective experience of the Court of Justice could hope to achieve. Where questions of administrative intention and practice arise the Court of Justice can receive submissions from the Community institutions, as also where relations between the Community and non-Member States are in issue. Where the interests of Member States are affected they can intervene to make their views known ... Where comparison falls to be made between Community texts in different languages, all texts being equally authentic, the multinational Court of Justice is equipped to carry out the task in a way which no national judge, whatever his linguistic skills, could rival. The interpretation of Community instruments involves very often not the process familiar to

common lawyers of laboriously extracting the meaning from words used but the more creative process of applying flesh to a spare and loosely constructed skeleton. The choice between alternative submissions may turn not on purely legal considerations, but on a broader view of what the orderly development of the Community requires. These are matters which the Court of Justice is very much better placed to assess and determine than a national court.

Bingham J then referred the issues of EU law in question to the ECJ for a preliminary ruling. An application under Article 234 can be made by both civil and criminal courts and, in the case of the latter, a reference is likely to be made because a provision of EU law has been raised as a defence in criminal proceedings. However, the mere fact that a party asserts that the resolution of the case necessitates the interpretation of EU law does not of itself mean that a court or tribunal is compelled to consider that a question has been raised within Article 234. This is a matter for the national court to determine. It is clear, nevertheless, from the third paragraph of Article 234, that where a matter of EU law is raised in a case pending before a national court or tribunal against whose decision there is no remedy in national law, that court or tribunal is supposed to refer the question(s) to the ECJ. This does not mean that only the House of Lords is obliged to make a reference because the ECJ in Case 6/64 *Costa* v *ENEL* [1964] ECR 585 was prepared to accept a reference from a *guidice conciliatore* in Milan. This was because the sum of money involved being so small, the magistrate had final jurisdiction in the particular case. Thus paragraph 3 applies to any court or tribunal from whose decision there is no appeal, such as the National Insurance Commissioners. Balcombe LJ set out the approach that would be taken by the Court of Appeal in *Chiron Corporation* v *Murex Diagnostics Ltd* [1995] when he said:

> Except in those cases ... where the Court of Appeal is the court of last resort, the Court of Appeal is not obliged to make a reference to the ECJ . .. If the Court of Appeal does not make a reference to the ECJ, and gives its final judgment on the appeal, then the House of Lords becomes the court of last resort. If either the Court of Appeal or the House of Lords grants leave to appeal, then there is no problem. If the Court of Appeal refuses leave to appeal, and the House of Lords is presented with an application for leave to appeal, before it refuses leave it should consider whether an issue of Community law arises which is necessary for its decision (whether to grant or refuse leave) and is not *acte clair*. If it considers that a reference is requisite, it will take such action as it may consider appropriate in the particular case.

The above statement would have been influenced by the ruling of the ECJ in Case 283/81 *CILFIT* v *Ministro della Sanità* [1982]. In that case the ECJ ruled that even courts of final resort are not obliged to request a preliminary reference where the answer to the question(s) on EU law cannot affect the outcome of the case. The question(s) raised must be central to the disposal of the case. Even where the questions of EU law are essential to disposing of the case, the ECJ ruled that courts of final resort are under no obligation to refer if:

(a) the point has already been decided in a previous ruling by the ECJ, irrespective of the form of the proceedings and even if the questions raised were not completely identical;

or

(b) the correct application of EU law is so obvious as to leave no scope for any reasonable doubt as to the manner in which the question raised is to be resolved.

In relation to (a) above, since the ECJ is not absolutely bound by its previous decisions, a UK court is free to refer a point of law if it wishes the ECJ to reconsider its earlier ruling. The ECJ may, of course, merely restate its earlier ruling but it may not. Previous rulings therefore have some value as 'precedents' and there is now a considerable body of such case law to guide national courts. Before a UK court can take upon itself the responsibility under (b) above it must be convinced that the matter is equally obvious to the courts of other member states and to the ECJ. The Court made it clear in Case 283/81 *CILFIT* v *Ministro della Sanità* [1982] that if a national court were to assume responsibility for interpreting EU law it should bear in mind the specific characteristics of EU law, the particular difficulties to which its interpretation gives rise and the risk of divergences in judicial decisions within the EU. Bearing in mind what was said in *Commissioners of Customs and Excise* v *Samex Ap S* it might seem that UK courts would have to be very confident indeed to assume responsibility for interpreting a provision of EU law in the absence of an earlier ruling by the ECJ. However, UK courts make fewer references under Article 234 EC than some smaller member states.

The national proceedings must be suspended pending the outcome of the reference under Article 234 which will normally be couched in terms of a set of general questions of law. In responding, the ECJ cannot rule on the facts of the case nor on the validity of national law as such. Its ruling will focus on the interpretation of EU law only and it is then for the UK court to apply the ruling to the case under consideration. As was indicated in Chapter 7, the Article 234 procedure has been responsible for the extensive development of the jurisprudence of the ECJ.

The ECJ has been far more flexible in its approach to the interpretation of EU legislation than UK courts are in relation to national legislation. The ECJ is not always over-concerned with the precise wording of a provision. Under conditions of doubt it will usually look to the aims of the Community as set in Article 2 of the EC Treaty and consider the general context and purpose of the legislation. The treaties in particular are drafted in quite general terms. The ECJ has therefore felt the need to engage in a certain amount of 'judicial activism' in order to fill gaps in the Treaty, drawing its inspiration from the general aims of the Community and from the general principles of law that it has adopted from the legal systems of various member states. This has already been considered in

Chapter 7 in relation to the doctrine of direct effect, supremacy and state liability.

10   Case study

The approach of the ECJ to the specific problem of interpretation may be examined by looking at its jurisprudence in the area of gender discrimination as a case study. Having ruled in Case 43/75 *Defrenne* v *SABENA* [1976] that Article 119 (now Article 141) had direct effect it has been concerned to eradicate differences between men and women in relation to 'pay'. The original wording of Article 119 (now Article 141) was as follows:

> Each Member State shall ... ensure and subsequently maintain the application of the principle that men and women should receive equal pay for equal work. For the purpose of this Article, 'pay' means the ordinary basic or minimum wage or salary and any other consideration, whether in cash or in kind, which the worker receives, directly or indirectly, in respect of his employment from his employer.
>   Equal pay without discrimination based on sex means:
> (a) that pay for the same work at piece rates shall be calculated on the basis of the same unit of measurement;
> (b) that pay for work at the same rates shall be the same for the same type of job.

Although the concept of 'pay' was quite widely defined in Article 119, the Court was prepared to give it an even wider meaning. In case 69/80 *Worringham* v *Lloyds Bank* [1981] a female employee contested the legality of supplementary payments made by the employer to male members of staff under the age of 25 for the purpose of compensating them for having to make contributions to the employer's occupational pension scheme. The ECJ ruled that these payments were 'pay' and since they had not been made to female staff there had been an infringement of Article 119. In Case 12/81 *Garland* v *British Rail Engineering* [1982] the ECJ ruled that the term 'pay' could extend to special travel facilities granted to ex-employees after retirement even though they were not based on a contractual entitlement. In Case 170/84 *Bilka-Kaufhaus GmbH* v *Weber von Hartz* [1986] the company operated a non-contributory pension scheme but part-time employees were only eligible to join after they had worked for the company for at least 15 years. This restriction was not imposed on full-time employees but, as most of the part-time employees were women, the complainant alleged that the scheme was discriminatory. Since the pension scheme was contractual, the ECJ ruled that it came within Article 119 so the difference in treatment, as it affected part-timers, was contrary to Article 119. In Case 171/88 *Rinner-Kuhn* v *FWW* [1989] the ECJ ruled that German legislation excluding part-time workers (most of whom were women) from an entitlement to sick pay was contrary to Article 119 unless objectively justified (a matter for the national court) because the continued payment of wages to workers during sickness came within Article

119. In Case C-262/88 *Barber* v *Guardian Royal Exchange Assurance Group* [1990] the ECJ not only ruled that differential retirement ages for men and women under an occupational pension scheme that operated to the disadvantage of men by way of them having to wait for pension benefits was unlawful, it also ruled that redundancy payments constituted 'pay' within the meaning of Article 119.

11 Transposed legislation

Interpreting subordinate legislation drafted to incorporate a directive according to the ordinary grammatical meaning of the words used will often be unsatisfactory, especially where this does not accord with the way in which Community law is developing. The extensive preamble to a directive may be particularly useful as an aid to interpretation of such subordinate legislation where there is uncertainty but in some cases the UK courts must follow the relevant case law of the ECJ. The House of Lords has usually adopted a purposive approach to the interpretation of subordinate legislation that has been enacted to incorporate a directive. In *Litster* v *Forth Dry Dock and Engineering Co. Ltd* [1989] their Lordships gave a purposive interpretation to Regulation 5(3) of the Transfer of Undertakings (Protection of Employment) Regulations 1981 which were made to implement Directive 77/187/EEC. The Directive made it possible for the automatic transfer of the contracts of employment of workers when a business is transferred to a new owner with all their existing rights and obligations preserved. It also protects workers from dismissal by the seller or new owner of the business unless the dismissals are permitted by the limited exceptions specified in the Directive. Their Lordships added the words '*or would have been so employed if he had not been unfairly dismissed in the circumstances described in Regulation 8(1)*' to the relevant statutory instrument. They did this so that the employees of an insolvent company who were dismissed because a business is sold to a new purchaser would have their employment transferred automatically to the new purchaser. Their Lordships' aim was to defeat the then widespread practice in the UK of dismissing employees prior to the transfer of the business leaving the new buyer to take on as many (or as few) of the workers as were needed on whatever terms that were thought suitable at the time. These would usually be much inferior to those previously enjoyed. Thus their Lordships actually read words into the statutory instrument so that it would be in conformity with the developing case law of the ECJ.

As has been mentioned previously, the ECJ has ruled in Case C-106/89 *Marleasing SA* v *La Commercial Internacional de Alimentacion SA* [1990] that national courts should interpret their national legislation whenever possible in such a way as to ensure that the objectives of European Community law are achieved. The emphasis is on the phrase 'whenever possible' and, of course, there are significant parts of national law that are untouched and therefore unaffected by EU law. Nevertheless, the obligation imposed on national courts by the ECJ is particularly relevant to the interpretation of subordinate legislation made to incorporate an EU directive. Subsequently, in *R* v *Secretary of State for Employment ex p. Seymour-Smith and Perez* [2000] the House of Lords indicated that a directive could be used as an aid to construction once it had been implemented.

■ Summary

There is as yet no grand, universally accepted, theory of statutory interpretation and there may never be one. For the most part, judges approach the task of interpreting contested legislative texts in a pragmatic fashion, having had the opportunity to reflect on argument from counsel. There is nowadays a predisposition to opt for an interpretation that accords with the purpose behind the text in so far as this can be ascertained and one which will render a fair outcome, if this is possible. Although all national legislation must now be interpreted in the light of the Human Rights Act 1998 in so far as it is possible to do so, it has been seen that this has not always proved to be possible. Historically, the ECJ has worked at the task of interpretation with a different mindset and has even been accused by some commentators of creating 'judicial legislation'. However, there are now signs that the era of audacious interpretations of treaty Articles is at an end but there may yet be one or two surprises in store.

WWW PROGRESS TEST

For suggested answers to the tests below, go to the companion website at www.pearsoned.co.uk/wheeler

1 Are the meanings of statutory provisions always self evident? What sense can you make of the Misrepresentation Act 1967 s. 2(1) and the Sale of Goods Act 1979 s. 11(3)?
2 Could an interpretation that focuses merely on the ordinary meaning of the words used in an Act of Parliament be regarded as a purposive approach?
3 Do you see anything wrong with the way in which the Court of Appeal interpreted the provisions from what is now the Trade Union and Labour Relations (Consolidation) Act 1992 in *Carrington* v *Therm-A-Stor*?
4 Why did the Employment Appeal Tribunal adopt a purposive approach in *Zarczynska* v *Levy*?
5 Identify the main 'intrinsic aids' to interpretation.
6 What do you understand by the term 'extrinsic aids' to interpretation? Give examples.
7 What obligation is imposed on UK courts by the Human Rights Act 1998 with regard to the interpretation of legislation?

8 If the Act had been in operation at the time that the Court of Appeal considered *Carrington* v *Therm-A-Stor*, do you think that it might have affected the outcome?

9 If the provisions of a UK statute are clearly contrary to the Human Rights Act 1998 do the UK courts have the power to disapply it?

10 How does the ECJ approach the task of interpreting EU law in general?

11 If a court or tribunal in the UK is unsure about the interpretation of some provision in an EU legal text, what can and should it do?

12 When is a court or tribunal in the UK bound to refer a question of the interpretation under Article 234?

FURTHER READING

■ **Books**

Adams, J.N. and R. Brownsword (2003) *Understanding Law* (London: Fontana).

Bell, J. and G. Engle (1995) *Cross on Statutory Interpretation* (London: Butterworths).

Craig, P. and G. de Burca (2002) *EU Law – text, cases and materials* (Oxford: Oxford University Press, chapter 10).

Langan, P. St J. (1980) Maxwell – *on the Interpretation of Statutes* (Bombay: Tripathi).

Twining, W. and D. Miers (1999) *How To Do Things With Rules* (London: Butterworths, chapter 10).

Zander, M. (2004) *The Law Making Process* (Cambridge: Cambridge University Press, chapter 3).

■ **Articles**

Arden, Rt Hon Lady Justice (2004) 'The Interpretation of UK Domestic Legislation in the Light of the European Convention on Human Rights Jurisprudence' *Statute Law Review* pp. 165–179.

Bennion, F. (2000) 'What interpretation is "possible" under section 3(1) of the Human Rights Act 1998?' *Public Law* Spring.

Millett, Lord (2000) 'Construing Statutes' *Statute Law Review* Vol. 20, No. 2.

Morris, D. (2000) 'The Human Rights Act 1998: too many loose ends?' *Statute Law Review* Vol. 21, No. 2.

Wade, Sir W. (2000) 'Horizons of horizontality' *The Law Quarterly Review*, Vol. 116, April.

USEFUL WEBSITES

Information on the European Convention on Human Rights and Fundamental Freedoms and on the European Court of Human Rights can be found at www.echr.coe.int.

Part 3

Law in action

9 Resourcing legal services

1 Introduction

Since the 1950s, successive governments have made funding available from general taxation to assist persons of limited financial means to ensure that they have been able to obtain legal advice. Funding has also been made available from the public purse to enable such persons to bring and defend civil claims and to defend themselves if charged with criminal offences. Over the years, public spending on what became known as 'legal aid' grew massively and governments tried, without much success, to control this expenditure. Shortly after taking office in 1997, the Labour government, in the person of the Lord Chancellor, appointed Sir Peter Middleton to conduct a review of civil legal aid in the context of an overall review of the civil justice system and then, in 1998, the government produced its White Paper entitled *Modernising Justice*. In the section dealing with civil legal aid, the government stated that it did not believe that the existing system was capable of meeting its objectives and priorities. The White Paper concluded as follows:

(a) Legal aid is too heavily biased towards expensive, court-based solutions to people's problems. The scheme is open-ended, thus it is impossible to target resources on priority areas, or the most efficient and effective way of dealing with a particular problem. Legal aid is spent almost entirely on lawyers' services. In practice, it is lawyers who determine where and how the money is spent.

(b) Legal aid is sometimes criticised for backing cases of insufficient merit and for allowing people to pursue cases unreasonably, forcing their opponents to agree unfair settlements.

(c) The scheme provides few effective means or incentives for improving value for money. Any lawyer can take a legal aid case and, as a result, there is little control over quality and no scope for competition to keep prices down. Lawyers' fees are calculated after the event, based on the amount of work done, so there is little incentive to work more efficiently. In recent years, higher spending has supported fewer cases. The number of full civil legal aid cases started each year has fallen by 31 per cent from 419,861 in 1992–93 to 319,432 in 1997–98.

(d) It is not possible to control expenditure effectively. The few means of control available, for example, cutting financial eligibility are crude and inflexible. Spending on all forms of civil and family legal aid has risen rapidly from £586 million in 1992–93 to £793 million in 1997–98. This level of growth in expenditure – 35 per cent compared to general inflation of 13 per cent – cannot be sustained in future.

In Chapter 6 of the White Paper, the government articulated its dissatisfaction with the way in which legal aid was operating within the criminal justice system as well as with its spiralling costs. As a result, the White Paper contained proposals for the abolition of the existing legal aid scheme in both the spheres of civil and criminal justice and its replacement with an entirely new system. These proposals and others contained in the White Paper ultimately found expression in a Bill that was presented to Parliament which was enacted as the Access to Justice Act 1999. A completely new entity in the form of the Legal Services Commission (LSC) was created by s. 1(1) to replace the Legal Aid Board from April 2000. It functions as an executive non-departmental body but the Department for Constitutional Affairs agrees the Commission's performance framework because the Secretary of State is responsible to Parliament for the activities and performance of the Commission. The LSC has its headquarters at Gray's Inn Road, London and it also operates from 13 regional offices throughout England and Wales. According to s. 1(2) of the Act, the Commission has important functions relating to its two sub-entities:

(a) the Community Legal Service, and
(b) the Criminal Defence Service.

The former is concerned with the provision of advice and legal services in the sphere of the civil law whilst the latter, as is clearly indicated by its title, is concerned exclusively with the provision of legal services to those being investigated and those charged by the police with criminal offences. The powers of the Legal Services Commission are set out in general terms in s. 3, but this chapter will focus mainly on the role of its two subordinate bodies before examining other forms of resource provision for legal services.

2   The Community Legal Service

The Access to Justice Act 1999 s. 4(1) required that the Legal Services Commission establish, maintain and develop a Community Legal Service thereby fulfilling a commitment that appeared in the Labour Party manifesto for the 1997 election. The work of this Community Legal Service is funded through a Community Legal Service Fund established by the Legal Services Commission in accordance with the Access to Justice Act 1999 s. 5(1). In the annual public expenditure planning process, the Lord Chancellor/Secretary of State for Constitutional Affairs sets an annual budget for the Community Legal Service. This takes account of the anticipated contributions and payments to be made by those who have recourse to the fund but the bulk of the funding for the Service comes via the

Department for Constitutional Affairs from the money voted by
Parliament when it approves the annual Finance Act. Although s. 5(3) of
the Act requires the Lord Chancellor/Secretary of State for Constitutional
Affairs to take account of the assessment of need made by the Legal
Services Commission in accordance with s. 4(6), it is the Lord
Chancellor/Secretary of State who determines how much will be paid into
the Community Legal Service Fund. The amount for 2000/01 was £749m
and this has increased annually, so that by 2003/04 the allocation had
reached £813m. Under s. 5(6) the Lord Chancellor/Secretary of State has
power to direct the Legal Services Commission to allocate parts of the
fund to provide particular types of service to ensure that resources are
allocated according to the government's priorities. The responsibilities of
the Community Legal Service are set out in the Access to Justice Act 1999
s. 4(2) and are as follows:

(a)   the provision of general information about the law and legal system
        and the availability of legal services;
(b)   the provision of help by the giving of advice as to how the law applies
        in particular circumstances;
(c)   the provision of help in preventing or settling or otherwise resolving
        disputes about legal rights and duties;
(d)   the provision of help in enforcing decisions by which such disputes
        are resolved; and
(e)   the provision of help in relation to legal proceedings not relating to
        disputes.

The development of the Community Legal Service has entailed the formation and development of Community Legal Services Partnerships
within every local government area. Despite the use of the term 'partnerships' they are not partnerships, as legally defined, but rather schemes for
local cooperation established between the funding bodies and the various
service providers. The funding bodies are mainly the regional offices of
the Legal Services Commission and local authorities but there may also be
local private funding bodies in the form of charities. The providing
bodies, such as the local Law Society (representing solicitors), Citizens'
Advice Bureaux (CAB) and Law Centres work with the funding bodies.
The aim is to plan and coordinate financing of local advice and legal services to ensure that, as far as possible, they meet local needs. Having
identified local needs for legal services and having assessed the extent to
which they are met by the existing provision, the participants in the
Community Legal Service partnership are then able to devise a strategy. It
was hoped that this would result in a closer match between local provision
and local need. It was intended that these local plans and strategies would
be kept under review so that it would be possible to incorporate future
developments in the provision of legal services. It was intended that at
least 90 per cent of the population of England and Wales would be served
by Community Legal Service Partnerships by 2002. These local partnerships are supported by the Community Legal Service website and the
Community Legal Service Directory. The former is said to receive over

50,000 'hits' each week. The Directory, which is in 13 parts, covers the various Community Legal Service Regions in England and Wales and gives details of organisations and other providers of legal services. An electronic version of the Directory is provided on the website where users can search to locate service providers who can deal with their queries. The website is updated regularly to ensure that the information contained therein is as accurate as possible. Apart from providing online legal information and advice, the website also contains information about Community Legal Service projects together with details of research so that there can be a debate about the functioning of aspects of the service. Links are provided to the websites of individual Community Legal Service Partnerships. The information is available in minority ethnic languages and the site has been constructed so that it can be used by persons with disabilities.

Service providers, who may be firms of solicitors, specialist or general advice agencies or law centres, who wish to participate in a local Community Legal Service Partnership must demonstrate that they meet the required standard for the service or services that they offer. In this scheme there are three categories, namely:

1 Information services,
2 General help, and
3 Specialist help.

The Community Legal Service Quality Task Force has devised a 'Quality Mark' accreditation system bearing the CLS logo for the three main cat-egories of service on offer. Service providers that meet the requirements set will display the appropriate CLS logo so that users can have confidence that the service provided meets the minimum standard laid down. Within the information service there are two tiers: self-help information and assisted information. The former requires that service providers are merely able to supply leaflets, provide access to directories and to the website. At this level, the amount of interaction with users is minimal. This service is available from information points in local council offices. Those providing assisted information at the second level must ensure that staff are on hand to help users with accessing and interpreting information as well as being capable of ascertaining when further information or advice is needed. They must also be able to identify the most appropriate source of information and advice. This service is available at Community Information Service outlets and main public libraries. There are also two tiers of general help. Service providers at the first level (normally Citizens' Advice Bureaux) must be capable of diagnosing a problem and, if it is a legal one, be able to explain the available options and give out appro-priate information. In addition, they must be capable of identifying any further action that needs to be taken by users and be able to give assist-ance with the completion of simple forms and with the drafting of letters. The second level comprises general help with casework which requires that service providers apply for this standard in the designated categories such as welfare benefits, housing, employment, immigration and nation-ality. Casework entails negotiation with third parties either face to face or on the telephone or by letter on behalf of a client and low-level advocacy before certain tribunals. Those providing the third category, 'specialist help', such as firms of solicitors, law centres and specialist advice agencies, will provide legal advice and assistance including representation for clients with more complex problems. Only those solicitors' firms, specialist advice agencies and law centres who have been accredited by the Community Legal Service are able to display the CLS Specialist Help logo. They must also have contracts with the Legal Services Commission. It is these service providers who are the only ones able to undertake publicly funded civil legal work in those areas of law for which they have been approved by a process of audit (to ensure that they meet the quality standards).

Operating within the context of each Community Legal Service Partnership, the Legal Services Commission Funding Code establishes six levels of service in civil matters, namely:

1 Legal Help
2 Help at Court
3 Approved Family Help
4 Family Mediation
5 Legal Representation
6 Support Funding.

The first and most basic level of service covers work that was previously done under the old legal aid 'green form' scheme by way of advice and assistance with any civil legal problem. Help at Court merely extends to providing a person to speak on the client's behalf in certain court hearings but without the person in question acting as an advocate for the entire proceedings. In this way it is intended that the cost to the Community Legal Service Fund can be kept to a minimum. Approved Family Help includes the services covered by Legal Help and comes in two forms: help with family mediation and general family help where no mediation is in progress. In the latter form, it includes representation in proceedings where this is necessary to obtain disclosure of information from another party. The Legal Services Commission provides funding for the mediation of a family dispute, for those couples who qualify financially, with a view to reaching a mutually acceptable solution. The fifth level of service is available in two forms, namely investigative help to ascertain the strength of a claim, and then full representation which may be granted to assist with the bringing or defending of a claim in court. It is possible for the first to be granted and yet, even if the claim is a strong one, full representation may be refused if it is considered that the case could be funded under a conditional fee agreement (to be discussed later). Support funding is the partial funding by the Community Legal Service Fund of very expensive cases. The aim is to assist with the cost of an investigation in order to establish the strength of a claim with a view to then financing the case itself on a conditional fee basis or alternatively as litigation support. This latter form of assistance would extend to partial funding of a very expensive case under a conditional fee agreement so that the cost is borne partly by the lawyers concerned and partly by the Community Legal Service Fund because the lawyers are unwilling to take the case entirely on the basis of conditional fee arrangement. Applications for litigation support must be submitted to the Legal Services Commission Special Cases Unit with a costed plan and it may only be approved where the costs of the case (excluding disbursements) are likely to exceed £15,000. In addition to these six levels of service prescribed by the Funding Code, the Lord Chancellor/Secretary of State may offer other services by making a specific order or direction. On 14 July 2004 the Community Legal Service Direct project was launched by the LSC which offers a national helpline operated through 12 organisations (contracted firms of solicitors and Citizens' Advice Bureaux) to provide information and advice. It is thought that this service will assist persons with mobility problems and those living in remote areas.

Financial assistance from the Community Legal Service is only available to individuals and, by virtue of Schedule 2 to the Access to Justice Act 1999, some forms of claim and service are excluded. These are as follows:

(a) claims in respect of personal injury or death (with the exception of clinical negligence claims) and claims for damage to property,
(b) the transfer of the legal title to houses/flats, known as conveyancing,
(c) boundary disputes affecting land,
(d) the making of wills,
(e) matters relating to the law of trusts,
(f) defamation claims and claims for malicious falsehood,
(g) matters relating to partnership and company law, and
(h) matters arising out of the operation of a business.

In March 2004 the CAB and the Law Society submitted evidence to the Constitutional Affairs Committee of the House of Commons. The CAB drew attention to the fact that the provision of the Community Legal Service (CLS) in some parts of the country was patchy. The Law Society produced figures to show that the number of civil CLS contracts in branches of law such as housing, debt, family and welfare law had actually declined between 2000 and 2003 which is cause for concern, given the government's commitment to tackling social exclusion.

3   Eligibility for assistance

Financial assistance from the Community Legal Service Fund is available where there is perceived to be genuine need. This means that persons whose income and capital do not exceed the thresholds currently in operation will not be asked to pay any contribution out of income or capital towards the cost of the services provided. Different thresholds are set for the various levels of service and they are set out in the booklet entitled *A Practical Guide to Community Legal Service Funding* which is available from the Legal Services Commission and the offices of solicitors and law centres. Persons whose income and capital do exceed the thresholds set, so that they are not entitled to an entirely free service, may still be eligible for some financial assistance on a graduated scale provided that their income and capital do not exceed the upper limits that have been set. However, this will be contingent upon their paying a contribution before receiving support from the Community Legal Service Fund. Solicitors and workers in advice agencies who are participants in the Community Legal Service scheme have the latest information to hand enabling them to undertake assessments of applicants' means. An assessment has to be made of both income and capital. This is done to ascertain whether financial support can be granted with or without contributions from individuals pursuing claims before mental health review tribunals, immigration adjudicators, the immigration appeal tribunal and in a limited range of family cases in magistrates' courts. Most other cases are assessed by assessment officers at the regional offices of the Legal Services Commission but for complex cases there is a Special Investigations Unit. If the matter has been dealt with by one of the regional offices of the Legal Services Commission and it has been decided that the case satisfies the merits criteria and the applicant qualifies on financial grounds, the LSC will issue a certificate where no contribution is required. Those persons in receipt of income support or income-based jobseeker's allowance are automatically eligible for the granting of a certificate. If a contribution is required, an 'offer' of a certificate is sent and, if the applicant accepts it, the contribution from savings has to be paid immediately whereas any contribution from income is paid by monthly instalments. The first contribution from income must be paid when the offer is accepted. Usually, solicitors must report to the LSC when they have reached a certain stage in their work for a client or have spent a predetermined amount.

Where Community Legal Service funding is made available and the person aided is successful, the solicitor (and barrister, if one was engaged) will expect to be paid his/her taxed costs. The amount that the applicant pays depends on whether:

(a) the other side is ordered to pay the costs of the action and does so, and

(b) the applicant is awarded any money or property by the court or under an agreement with the other side.

If the other side pays the applicant's costs in full, the applicant can expect to completely recover the amount of any contribution that was paid. If the other side does not pay the applicant's costs in full, the regional office of the Legal Services Commission must deduct from any money ordered to be paid by the court or agreed with the other side as much as may be necessary to cover the costs. This deduction is referred to as the 'statutory charge'. It will attach to property received by or preserved by the applicant in the case whether as a result of a court order or as a result of a settlement or compromise of the case. It does not attach to maintenance payments or to the first £2,500 recovered in divorce and family proceedings. There is a leaflet entitled *Paying Back the Legal Services Commission* –

The Statutory Charge which gives further details of when the statutory charge has to be paid. If the applicant should lose the case the most that he/she will be required to pay towards the solicitor's costs (and the barrister's fee, if applicable) will be the amount, if any, that was payable under the certificate that was granted. Well in excess of 300,000 certificates are granted annually to enable individuals to take or defend court proceedings. Occasionally, the other party to the proceedings (or some third party) will contact the LSC alleging that the case does not really merit subsidised assistance and therefore should not be allowed to proceed on that basis. Alternatively, an allegation might take the form that the person aided is not financially eligible, perhaps because he/she has not disclosed all his/her assets or income. The LSC will usually send a copy of an objection in relation to the merits of the case to the solicitor acting for the aided person with a request for comments on the allegation(s) raised. An allegation relating to the aided person's means will be referred to an assessment unit for investigation. The LSC can and does from time to time revoke a certificate but, if it does so, the person affected can ask for a review of the decision by an independent funding review committee, the members of which are unconnected with the LSC. As a result of such a review, a certificate could be reinstated but, if it is not, the person concerned will normally be obliged to refund all the money paid by the LSC.

4   The review of the Community Legal Service

An independent review of the Community Legal Service was carried out by Matrix Research and Consultancy in 2003/04 and the full Report can be viewed on the Department for Constitutional Affairs website. It was critical and identified five key areas for 'development'. First, it drew attention to a lack of overall accountability, with no executive responsible for driving forward the process of change. Secondly, the Report highlighted the lack of an 'evidence base' to demonstrate that the CLS delivers effective and cost-effective advice provision. Thirdly, the Report identified a number of problems with the way in which services within the CLS were funded and managed. It pointed to the fact that the civil legal aid budget was being eroded by the increasing demands of the criminal legal service provision. Fourthly, the Report indicated that there was a need to simplify the Quality Mark and develop quality assurance processes that place greater emphasis on the quality of advice provided. Fifthly, the Report highlighted a mis-match between needs analysis at the local level and its translation into funding, which would require a reform of Community Legal Service Partnerships with new ways of commissioning local services together with initiatives to improve access and referral. By way of response, the Department for Constitutional Affairs published a Framework Document in conjunction with the Legal Services Commission that purports to determine the relationship between the Department and the LSC over the next three years. In May 2004 the LSC stated that it had responded to some of the recommendations in the Report already by establishing a research centre and revising the accreditation process for the Quality Mark. The CLS also intends to introduce a 'lighter touch' regime for audits of service providers. It will be interesting to monitor progress over the next few years as well as the implementation of the EU Legal Aid Directive 2002/8/EC which came into operation on 30 November 2004. This will necessitate amendment of the LSC regulations in the near future because current financial eligibility thresholds do not apply to applicants who are financially eligible to receive legal aid in their member state of residence.

5 The Criminal Defence Service

The Access to Justice Act 1999 s. 12(1) required the Legal Services Commission to establish, maintain and develop the Criminal Defence Service. It operates from offices at six locations in England and Wales that are wholly separate from the existing regional offices of the Legal Services Commission. Its aim is to ensure that individuals who are subject to criminal investigations or criminal proceedings have access to the necessary advice, assistance and representation that the interests of justice require. Criminal proceedings are not simply confined to criminal trials because the definition contained in s. 12(2) extends to appeals and sentencing hearings, extradition hearings, binding-over proceedings, appeals on behalf of a convicted person who has died and to proceedings for contempt in the face of the court. A person who needs advice at the police station can call upon the duty solicitor or any solicitor in the area who has a contract for criminal work with the Legal Services Commission to provide advice free of charge. Contracts are only awarded to those firms of solicitors who are able to demonstrate to the Legal Services Commission that their members and staff who provide services under the scheme meet the standards set. Not only must they have the requisite legal knowledge but they must also be able demonstrate that they possess the skills and experience to advise suspects and conduct criminal cases. Those firms of solicitors who secure contracts from the Legal Services Commission are expected to compete with one another for the available work to ensure that best value is obtained for the services provided. Once a suspect is charged, that solicitor's firm will continue to represent him/her for the duration of the case unless the Criminal Defence Service agrees that there is a valid reason for a change. The Criminal Defence Service employs its own 'salaried defenders' so that persons charged with criminal offences requiring financial assistance with the cost of representation may choose between solicitors in private practice whose firms have contracts with the Legal Services Commission or lawyers employed by the Criminal Defence Service in its Public Defender Service. In accordance with the Access to Justice Act 1999 s. 16, the Commission has drawn up a

Code of Conduct to be observed by its salaried defenders as they carry out their duties. The government hopes that the service will fill gaps in the provision in parts of the country where there are just a few solicitors' firms and barristers' chambers participating in the scheme. A pilot project is due to begin in April 2005 whereby persons detained in a police station either in Liverpool or Boston, Lincolnshire will be able to obtain initial legal advice over the telephone concerning non-indictable crime from the Criminal Defence Service.

The Criminal Defence Service Bill currently before Parliament aims to transfer responsibility for the power to grant representation from magistrates' courts to the LSC although court staff would operate as 'agents' of the LSC under a service agreement. The Bill also reintroduces a means test for eligibility based on gross income. If gross income exceeds £27,500 an applicant will not normally be eligible for legal aid. Furthermore, as drafted, the Bill seeks power to include 'contribution orders' in certain high-cost cases. There will be more commentary on this legislation in due course on the companion website.

6 Eligibility for financial assistance

Where an individual has been charged with an offence at a police station and appears before magistrates either on bail or in custody, there is no means test to be satisfied before assistance is granted for representation. The same applies to persons appearing before a youth court and to the early administrative hearings under the Crime and Disorder Act 1998 s. 50 – no contribution whatever is payable towards the cost of representation. However, this does not apply to persons charged with indictable offences (those triable by jury at the Crown Court) or any other offence for which an individual is 'sent' to the Crown Court for trial under the Crime and Disorder Act 1998 s. 51. Such persons will continue to be subject to a means test but this will only be conducted if the person is convicted. If it emerges during the trial that the defendant has substantial assets, the judge can make an order when passing sentence regarding the contribution required towards the costs of representation. In other cases, the judges will ask the Criminal Defence Service to investigate the defendant's means and they will then make an order as to the amount of the contribution at a later date.

7 Conditional fee agreements – the background

The upper limits for financial assistance set by the Legal Aid Board, the forerunner of the Legal Services Commission, to meet the cost of commencing a civil action, were quite low. This has meant that many people on modest incomes have frequently been deterred from pursuing valid claims by the costs of litigation – not just their own costs but also the risk of having to pay the costs of the other party if the claim is unsuccessful. It has long been possible in the USA for civil claimants to enter into an agreement with a lawyer, the essence of which is that the lawyer will take the case on a 'no win, no fee' basis. If, however, the lawyer wins the case for his/her client, the lawyer will be entitled, under the terms of the agreement, to receive a percentage of the damages recovered or another specified sum. This obviously compensates lawyers for taking on those cases where the client loses. Awards of damages in the USA tend to be much higher than in the UK, perhaps because juries and judges are aware of the widespread use of contingency fee agreements. Consequently, lawyers in the USA often receive very large payments under these agreements.

Having restricted eligibility for legal aid in its Legal Aid Act 1988 as part of a general strategy to control public expenditure, the Conservative government sought other ways of widening access to justice. In its Courts and Legal Services Act 1990 s. 58 it therefore made it lawful, in principle, for certain types of litigation to be conducted under a variant of the contingency fee agreement, known as a 'conditional fee agreement'. The hallmark of such an agreement is that the fee uplift is not based on the level of damages awarded but on the lawyer's actual fee for the work done. These agreements were considered to be less open to exploitation by the unscrupulous than the simple contingency fee agreement. In 1995, the Lord Chancellor made a statutory instrument under the Courts and Legal Services Act 1990 which permitted conditional fee agreements to be entered into for personal injury claims, insolvency cases and cases before the European Commission of Human Rights.

As part of its agenda for modernising the civil justice system, the Blair government sought to broaden the coverage of conditional fee agreements but found itself constrained by the wording of the Courts and Legal Services Act 1990. It had been responsible for the Conditional Fee Agreements Order 1998 (SI 1998 No. 1860) which extended the range of proceedings in which conditional fee agreements were permissible. Then, in the Access to Justice Act 1999 s. 26, the original s. 58 of the Courts and Legal Services Act 1990 was replaced with two new sections. The new s. 58(1) requires that all conditional fee agreements must conform to s. 58(3) if they are to be legally enforceable and this has been reinforced by the Conditional Fee Agreements Regulations 2000 (SI 2000 No. 692). A new s. 58A(1) extends the coverage of conditional fee agreements by providing that only criminal proceedings (with the exception of those under the Environmental Protection Act 1990 s. 82) and family proceedings as set out in s. 58A(2) cannot be conducted under a valid conditional fee agreement and this is reiterated in the Conditional Fee Agreements Order 2000 (SI 2000 No. 823). Consequently, persons wishing to pursue civil claims (with the exception of family proceedings) who do not qualify for assistance from the Community Legal Service Fund, are able to negotiate conditional fee agreements for most civil claims with solicitors offering this service. As from April 2000, conditional fee agreements replaced subsidised legal assistance from the public purse for most personal injury cases. Moreover, the Access to Justice Act 1999 makes it lawful for the LSC to refuse subsidised legal assistance where a conditional fee agreement would be appropriate and both solicitors and barristers are able under their rules of professional conduct to enter into conditional fee agreements with clients. Solicitors are subject to controls on the advertising that they can put out when offering to conduct litigation under conditional fee agreements. In recognition of the fact that there is a potential conflict of interests, the Law Society's *Guide to the Professional Conduct of Solicitors 1999*, Principle 12.09 indicates that, in deciding whether a conditional fee agreement would be appropriate in the circumstances of a particular case, a solicitor should be careful to ensure that his/her own financial interests are not placed above the general interests of the client. Disciplinary action can be taken against a solicitor who overcharges a client. It is likely that there will be some reform of the existing regulatory framework governing conditional fee agreements in 2005 following the Department of Constitutional Affairs' consultation exercise in 2004 and any changes will be dealt with on the companion website in due course.

8 Conditional fee agreements – the mechanics

Under a conditional fee agreement, the client will usually be required to take out an insurance policy to cover the eventuality of an unsuccessful claim and the associated risk of having to pay the costs of the other side. This is normally referred to as 'after the event' insurance (as distinct from 'before the event' insurance) because it is arranged after a claim has arisen. Those firms of solicitors who have partners or employed solicitors who are members of the Law Society's Personal Injury Panel are able to offer an insurance policy to clients making moderate personal injury claims with a modest premium in the region of £100 (or less). However, insurance to cover the risk of having to pay the costs of the other side in a high-value medical negligence claim could be nearly ten times this amount, although the premium would be payable in instalments as the claim proceeds. Unless it is agreed to the contrary, the client will be responsible for paying expenses other than his/her own solicitor's fee until the outcome of the case is known. Some insurance products may cover essential disbursements (fees payable for expert witnesses, medical and police reports) in the event of an unsuccessful outcome. If the solicitor wins the case for the client he/she is able to charge a 'success fee' which may not exceed 100 per cent of the firm's costs – this means that the solicitor could recover a maximum of double his/her normal fee from the defendant or defendant's insurer.

A worked example will help to clarify the basic principles of a conditional fee agreement. Suppose that a solicitors' firm has won a case for a client on a conditional fee basis and the client was awarded and recovered £7,500 in damages. It should be assumed that the solicitor represented the client throughout and so there is no barrister's fee. If the costs incurred by the firm in pursuing the case were £8,000 but, of this, £6,000 was recovered from the other side after the process known as 'taxation of costs', there would be a shortfall of £2,000 to be paid by the client to his/her solicitor. A claim could not be made under the insurance policy because the client was successful. If a 'success fee' of 100 per cent were allowed, this would normally be calculated on the firm's costs and would entitle the firm to recover an additional £8,000, but if the cap of 25 per cent applied this would only entitle the firm to recover £1,875 (£7,500 × 0.25) as a success fee. The Access to Justice Act 1999 s. 58A(6) provides that the success fee and the insurance premium can be recovered from the party who has lost the action and so the successful claimant will receive the damages awarded less the £2,000 shortfall referred to above, the amount being £5,500. This sum will be supplemented by the amount of the insurance premium that is recovered. The award of damages will not, however, be reduced any further because the success fee is payable by the unsuccessful defendant in the action, who must find an additional £1,875 in addition to the costs and damages awarded. The claimant is obliged to notify the court and the defendant at the start of the claim of the existence of a conditional fee agreement although there is no necessity at this stage to disclose the amount of the success fee agreed. It is also necessary for the claimant to inform the defendant about the existence of the insurance policy. An unsuccessful defendant can challenge the amount of the success fee on the basis that it is unreasonable when the court assesses the costs at the end of the litigation and the amount of the insurance premium can be challenged too. If the defendant's challenge of the fee uplift is successful, the solicitor will not be able to recover the resulting shortfall in the success fee unless he/she applies to the court justifying the higher level of uplift. At the time of writing it is not altogether clear whether the solicitor is precluded from recovering this sum from the client. Conditional fee agreements have become a normal way of pursuing civil claims where a remedy other than damages is being sought now that the success fee, and indeed the insurance premium, can be recovered from the unsuccessful defendant. In practice, the amount of the success fee will always vary with the degree of risk associated with pursuing the claim, but it will be unusual for the percentage to be set at 100 per cent.

In June 2004 fixed success fees were introduced for claims arising from road traffic accidents and from October 2004 they were brought in for claims arising from accidents at work. As a result, an unsuccessful defendant's insurer will pay the claimant's solicitors their normal costs plus a success fee of 25 per cent of those costs if they achieve a settlement prior to a hearing in court. The overwhelming majority of such claims are settled without a hearing in court. However, an unsuccessful defendant's insurer will have to pay a success fee of up to 100 per cent in those riskier cases that actually go to trial, where judgment is given against the defendant.

Conditional fee agreements have not proved to be popular with members of the Bar. Barristers often object on the basis of a 'conflict of interests'. The case of *King* v *Telegraph Group Ltd* [2004] has highlighted how conditional fee agreements can give rise to very large claims against newspapers and could result in an interference with freedom of speech and expression in a free society, as guaranteed by the European Convention on Human Rights, Article 10. The Fleet Street Lawyers' Association is known to be lobbying for changes in the regulatory framework so that newspapers are not faced with huge cost claims in litigation funded by conditional fee agreements.

9   Contingency fee agreements

Although contingency fee agreements are not permitted in contentious proceedings to finance litigation under the Solicitors' Practice Rules 1990, they may be used as a means of financing non-contentious work. Non-contentious business is defined by the Solicitors Act 1974 s. 87(1) as any business done as a solicitor which is not contentious business which in general terms means work that does not involve proceedings begun before a court in England and Wales or an arbitrator. This would extend to all tribunal work (with the exception of the Lands Tribunal and Employment Appeals Tribunal) and for work undertaken in relation to Criminal Injuries Compensation Authority claims and to planning or public inquiries.

10   Pro *bono publico*

The phrase *pro bono publico* translates as 'for the public good' and has long been used to describe work done by lawyers free of charge mainly, although not exclusively, in the sphere of litigation for those unable to obtain funding under the state scheme. Solicitors interested in promoting *pro bono* work have formed a special Pro Bono Group. The Bar, too, has its own *pro bono* unit which has been specifically set up to offer free legal advice and representation in deserving cases where financial assistance from the state has not been available or where the person concerned simply cannot afford the full cost of these services. Unlike the situation that obtains in the USA, where the American Bar Association has a clear recommendation in its code of conduct to the effect that lawyers should perform in the region of 40 hours of free work each year, the professional bodies in the UK have not gone that far. For the time being they have left it to individual solicitors and barristers to decide how much, if any, free work they undertake. However, pressure is growing for solicitors' firms to draw up *pro bono* policies where they are prepared to consider direct approaches from members of the public. Such policy statements need to reflect the size of the firm and its areas of expertise. Ideally they should make it clear that *pro bono* work is not treated differently from other paid work in that the procedures followed and standards observed are the same. Members of some firms of solicitors undertake *pro bono* work with

Citizens' Advice Bureaux and neighbourhood law centres and may wish to make it clear in their publicity material that they will not deal with requests for help directly from the public. On 2 June 2000 the Law Centres' Federation and the Solicitors' *Pro Bono* Group launched a new initiative to be known as Law Works which is aimed at improving legal services in the major cities by matching volunteers with front-line agencies and by organising training in social welfare law for volunteer lawyers from the large commercial firms. In an attempt to stimulate interest in *pro bono* work among young lawyers the College of Law announced in March 2000 that it was offering a *pro bono* service whereby supervised *pro bono* 'clinics' would be integrated into the teaching programme and law students would be able to obtain credit for the work that they do. More recently, in 2004, the Law Society sponsored a national *Pro Bono* Week during which a specially decorated '*pro bono* bus' travelled from Bournemouth to Northumbria to encourage involvement by way of volunteering to assist in *pro bono* schemes. Although such initiatives are welcome, they can never be a substitute for state provision.

■ Summary

State funding of legal advice and representation remains a politically sensitive subject. The creation of the Legal Services Commission has certainly not resulted in a reduction in state spending on legal advice and representation, even though as a percentage of total public spending it remains small at around 0.4 per cent. Total spending has increased from £1.5bn in 1997 to around £2bn in 2004 but groups such as Legal Action consider this to be inadequate. There may now be better targeting of resources and better quality controls than before, but there continue to be areas of unmet need at a time when fewer young lawyers in training wish to specialise in legal aid work and the number of solicitors' firms with civil contracts with the LSC declines. It will be interesting to chart the work of the Legal Services Commission as it seeks to grapple with the problems in the years ahead. The introduction of conditional fee agreements has undoubtedly helped those who would not have qualified for legal aid to pursue valid claims and obtain compensation. They are clearly 'here to stay'. However, as indicated, conditional fee agreements are not without their problems and some reforms to the regulatory framework are needed and will, hopefully, address these problems. *Pro bono* initiatives are welcome but are unlikely to solve the considerable problem of unmet need which must be addressed by Community Legal Service Partnerships and *pro bono* can only be an element in the overall package.

WWW PROGRESS TEST

For suggested answers to the tests below, go to the companion website at www.pearsoned.co.uk/wheeler

1 What are the responsibilities of the Community Legal Service as set out in the Access to Justice Act 1999 s. 4(2)?
2 What is the main idea behind Community Legal Service Partnerships?
3 What are the six levels of service established under the Legal Services Funding Code?
4 What are the salient features of the Criminal Defence Service?
5 What is the difference between a contingency fee agreement and a conditional fee agreement?
6 Are there circumstances in which a solicitor is able to work under a contingency fee agreement?

FURTHER READING

■ Books

Sime, S. (2003) *A Practical Approach to Civil Procedure* (Oxford: Oxford University Press, chapter 4).

Society for Advanced Legal Studies (2001) *The Ethics of Conditional Fee Agreements* (Research Paper, London: Society for Advanced Legal Studies).

Underwood, K. (1999) *No Win No Fee – No Worries* (Welwyn Garden City: CLT Professional Publishing).

■ Articles

Bawdon, F. (2001) 'Conditional fee agreements', *New Law Journal* Vol. 151, No. 6972.

Moorhead, R. and A. Sherr (2001) 'Midnight in the Garden of the CFA People', *New Law Journal* Vol. 151, No. 6972.

Wignall, G. (2001) 'CFA and the Bar', *New Law Journal* Vol. 151, No. 6972.

USEFUL WEBSITES

The Legal Services Commission can be located at www.legalservices.gov.uk and the Community Legal Service at www.clsdirect.org.uk.

The magazine *Legal Aid Review* is available at the Legal Aid Practitioners Group website www.lapg.co.uk and *Legal Action*, another good source of information on legal aid, is available on www.lag.org.uk.

Information on conditional fee agreements can be obtained from the Law Society website, whilst information on *pro bono* schemes can be obtained from www.probonouk.net.

10 Criminal justice system 1

1 Introduction

It is an unfortunate fact but all societies are blighted, to a greater or lesser extent, by criminality. Moreover, certain forms of criminal activity do not stop at national frontiers and, regrettably, the internet has for some time provided opportunities for criminals in cyberspace. Anyone wishing to gain an insight into the incidence of the various forms of criminal activity occurring in the UK in the twenty-first century need only visit the Home Office web page. The criminal justice system may be viewed as a countervailing force combating the different forms of criminal activity which might otherwise undermine the prevailing economic and social order. If the system is to continue to be effective, it must continually evolve. Such an evolution is necessary just to keep pace with technological advances but it is also essential if the system is to benefit from the insights and recommendations of social scientists and official Commissions/Committees. The latter conduct research into criminal activity, as well as into the working of parts of the system itself. The system must also respond to threats posed by new forms of criminality as they arise. Anyone studying the criminal justice system has to be aware that there is a political dimension to be considered. What the broadcast and print media refer to as 'law and order' is always a 'live' political issue as there continues to be widespread public concern about the extent of crime and, indeed some would say, an irrational fear of crime. Ministers at the Home Office are only too well aware of this and are continually working on initiatives in order to demonstrate to the electorate that they are responding to its concerns. The official opposition party in Parliament will also formulate policy initiatives to incorporate into its manifesto on which it will campaign for political office. If elected, it will seek to implement these policies because, as the incoming government, it will assume that it has a 'mandate' to institute change and effect reform. Thus the criminal justice system has to be viewed very much as a 'work in progress'.

In terms of its constituent parts, the modern criminal justice system in England and Wales may be viewed as comprising the police, the Crown Prosecution Service, the courts, the probation and the prison service. As can be readily appreciated, it is a vast area of study and could comprise a degree programme in its own right. Consequently, a book of this size can only hope to provide an insight into aspects of the first three constituent elements of this system. This chapter will focus on police powers to stop, detain, search and arrest suspects, once the outline of the existing legislative structure of the system has been laid out. Due consideration will then be given to the rights of suspects in police detention. After that, it will be appropriate to deal with the charging of suspects and with the decision to prosecute and the alternatives to prosecution available to the police and CPS.

2 The legislative framework – some background

An understanding of the functioning of the criminal justice system in the twenty-first century will be facilitated if the reader has a little background information. A Royal Commission on Criminal Procedure (the Philips Commission) was established in 1978 at a time of widespread dissatisfaction with the functioning of the existing system, particularly among members of the non-white community. The Commission's remit was to review the entire process from initial investigation into criminal activity to the point of trial. The Conservative government of the time responded to the Commission's report when it was published in 1981 by steering the Police and Criminal Evidence Act 1984 (hereafter PACE) through Parliament. This landmark legislation was intended to change the way in which policing was conducted in England and Wales. As a result, most routine police work is still conducted in the context of the PACE 1984 and its Codes of Practice. These PACE Codes are brought into effect by statutory instrument made by the Home Secretary under s. 67(1) after they have been laid before Parliament in draft. The Prosecution of Offences Act 1985 inaugurated the Crown Prosecution Service so that the police would no longer be chiefly responsible for prosecuting those charged with criminal offences. Although PACE 1984 was a landmark piece of legislation, it did not address all the problems within the system nor ally all the concerns about its functioning. The media continued to draw attention to errors and malpractice on the part of serving officers in the police and in the prison service, as well as to miscarriages of justice. Following 1984, legislation impacting on the criminal justice system was enacted in every year from 1986 to 2001, except 1989 and 1992. The appointment of Sir William MacPherson in 1997 to enquire into the flawed investigation by the Metropolitan Police of the murder of the black teenager Stephen Lawrence (following a high-profile campaign by his parents) served to heighten concerns in official circles when the report was published in 1999. This was because it drew attention to racist attitudes of some serving officers in the Metropolitan Police. In 1999 John Halliday was asked to conduct a review of sentencing and his report entitled *Making Punishments Work* was published in 2001. Also, in December 1999 the government had asked Lord Justice Auld to conduct an exhaustive review of the functioning of the criminal courts. When his report was published in 2001, the government subsequently published its reform proposals in a White Paper entitled *Justice for All*. This White Paper was based on the proposals contained in the two reports referred to above. Five months later the government published another White Paper entitled *Policing a New Century: A Blueprint for Reform*, which was partly a response to the MacPherson Report although it did contain a significant number of other important innovations and initiatives.

3   Recent additions to the framework

Since the publication of *Justice for All* and *Policing for a New Century: A Blueprint for Reform*, the government has steered three crucially important pieces of legislation through Parliament. They are as follows:

Proceeds of Crime Act 2002,
Police Reform Act 2002, and
Criminal Justice Act 2003.

The Proceeds of Crime Act 2002 will be discussed in the next chapter. As is indicated by its title, the Police Reform Act 2002 is intended to make further far-reaching changes to the way in which policing is conducted and to give the Secretary of State greater powers over the police. The Criminal Justice Act 2003 institutes a number of important reforms and, in doing so, amends certain provisions of PACE 1984. It should be noted that on 1 August 2004 a revised set of PACE Codes governing police powers and conduct came into operation following a review of an earlier edition of the Codes by the Cabinet Office and Home Office. The latest Codes, of course, take account of the Police Reform Act 2002 and Criminal Justice Act 2003. If all this were not enough, the government has promised a comprehensive criminal code and so further legislation (probably in the form of a consolidating statute) can be expected in the not too distant future. For the time being, the student of the criminal justice system must become conversant with the vast raft of legislation, some of it enacted prior to1984, together with the more recent statutes. It may seem a daunting prospect.

4   Stop and search under PACE

Although the majority of offences that the police investigate are reported to them, it is evident that, if the police are to prevent crime and apprehend suspects, they must be endowed with adequate powers by the state in order to be pro-active. The PACE 1984 (and other earlier and subsequent legislation) confers on the police extensive powers of stop and search. There is also power to seize property, detain and arrest suspects. Thus, under s. 1 (as amended) a constable, whether in uniform or in plain clothes, may stop and search any person or vehicle for stolen or prohibited items. This is subject to the proviso that he/she has reasonable grounds for suspecting (as explained in Code A paras 2.3–2.5) that he/she will find stolen or prohibited items. Concerns have been voiced about the disproportionate use of the powers of stop and search against ethnic minorities, and so Code A para. 1.1 states:

> Powers to stop and search must be used fairly, responsibly, with respect for people being searched and without unlawful discrimination. The Race Relations (Amendment) Act 2000 makes it unlawful for police officers to discriminate on the grounds of race, colour, ethnic origin, nationality or national origins when using their powers.

In addition, para. 1.4 makes it quite clear that:

> The primary purpose of stop and search powers is to enable officers to allay or confirm suspicions about individuals without exercising their powers of arrest. Officers may be required to justify the use or authorisation of such powers, in relation both to individual searches and the overall pattern of their activity in this regard, to the supervisory officers or in court. Any misuse of the powers is likely to be harmful to policing and lead to mistrust of the police. Officers must also be able to explain their actions to the members of the public searched. The misuse of these powers can lead to disciplinary action.

In relation to the disciplinary action referred to above, it should be noted that the Police Reform Act 2002 s. 9 has created the Independent Police Complaints Commission to which complaints can be made in addition to the existing regime under the Police Act 1996. A constable who is about to conduct the search is required by s. 2(3) to inform the suspect of his/her name, the name of the police station where he/she is based, the precise legal search power that is being exercised, the purpose of the search and grounds for suspicion. A failure to do so will render the search unlawful and the illegality cannot be rectified because the search was reasonable in the circumstances or because the suspect consented to being searched. The powers to stop and search (and seize stolen or prohibited items) are to be exercised in public places where the public in general, or some section of the public, has access. They may not be exercised in a house/apartment but they can be exercised in a garden or yard provided the person to be searched does not reside in the house/apartment and is not there with the permission of the person who does reside there. Similar considerations apply to searches of vehicles. It should be noted that, in exercising their powers of stop and search, PACE s. 117 allows the police to use reasonable force. The search under PACE s. 1 must be carried out at or near the place where the person (or vehicle) was first detained and, in the case of searches of individuals, Code A para. 3.5 makes it clear that there is no power to remove any clothing in public other than an outer coat, jacket or gloves but an officer can place his/her hand inside the pockets of outer clothing. Any search under PACE s. 1 involving more than the removal of outer garments must be conducted by an officer of the same sex and all intimate searches must usually be conducted at a police station. Anyone who is searched is entitled to a copy of the record of the search.

Code A specifies very detailed recording requirements for officers carrying out searches and 'supervising officers' are required to monitor the use of stop and search powers by subordinates so that they can be completely satisfied that these powers are being used in accordance with the Code. In para. 5.4 there is provision for the stop and search records to be scrutinised by representatives of the community; however, the Code does not specify who these are. Most stops and searches are in fact made under PACE 1984 s. 1 but, of these, just over 10 per cent result in an arrest being made. Annual statistics are produced by the Home Office and can be viewed on its website.

5   Other statutory powers of stop and search

The Misuse of Drugs Act 1971 s. 23(2) empowers a police constable to stop and search persons for certain illegal drugs (referred to as controlled drugs) but he/she must have objective reasons for doing so. If the outcome is positive, the constable may then seize and retain anything found in the course of the search which appears to him/her to be evidence of an offence under the Act. A similar power exists in relation to the search for firearms under the Firearms Act 1968 s. 47.

If in any part of England and Wales there is unrest and likelihood of serious violence, the Criminal Justice and Public Order Act 1994 s. 60 enables a police officer of the rank of inspector or above (where no superintendent is available) who *reasonably believes* that serious violence may occur in his/her police area to give a written authorisation under s. 60(1) to prevent this. Such a reasonable belief on the part of the authorising officer must have an objective basis. Where such a belief exists, the officer is empowered to give an authorisation under s. 60(1) for a period not exceeding 24 hours so that police constables can stop and search pedestrians, drivers and their passengers anywhere for offensive weapons or dangerous instruments. It is clear from s. 60(4) that a constable need not have grounds for suspicion – it is sufficient that those stopped and searched are within the geographical area. Should a constable discover an offensive weapon, he/she is empowered by s. 60(6) to seize it. There is also power under s. 60AA whereby a constable can require a person to remove (in the presence of an officer of the same sex) any item which he/she reasonably believes is being worn to disguise identity, which can then be seized. Special powers are conferred by the Terrorism Act 2000 on officers of the rank of assistant chief constable or above, who can give authority for the exercise of powers of stop and search under s. 44 of the Act. Thus a police constable can stop and search vehicles, drivers and passengers anywhere within the locality authorised under s. 44(1), and under s. 44(2) pedestrians can be stopped and searched. This is subject to the proviso that the constable reasonably suspects those persons stopped to be terrorists and the power is exercised in order to discover whether they have in their possession anything which may constitute evidence that they are terrorists. In addition to outer clothing, a constable conducting the search may require the person concerned to remove (in public) headgear and footwear. A constable is empowered by s. 43(4) to seize and retain anything which he/she discovers in the course of a search of a person which he/she reasonably suspects may constitute evidence that the person is a terrorist. The power to stop and search a person is extended by s. 116(2) to include a vehicle.

Apart from the statutory powers of stop and search considered above (including a statutory power to conduct road checks under PACE s. 4(1)) the police are permitted under a common law power to set up road checks to prevent a breach of the peace. Provided a police officer honestly and reasonably forms the opinion that there is a real risk of a breach of the peace, he/she may take reasonable preventative steps. As indicated earlier, a stop and search may or may not lead to an arrest.

6 Search of premises

Police may wish to enter premises and conduct a search because they are reliably informed (and therefore have reasonable grounds to believe) that a serious crime has been committed. Equally, they may wish to enter premises and conduct a search because they are reliably informed that there are illegal drugs or stolen property on the premises. However, Article 8 of the Schedule to the Human Rights Act 1998 confers the right to respect for private and family life, which is extended by Article 1 of the First Protocol which deals with the peaceful enjoyment by a person of his/her possessions. Although these are not absolute rights, infringements require lawful justification. Thus, PACE 1984 s. 17 empowers the police to enter and search premises (using force if absolutely necessary) without a search warrant if certain conditions are met. It is readily understandable that the police should be able to do so in order to arrest someone for an arrestable offence or for a public order offence or to recapture someone who is unlawfully 'at large'. They are also empowered to enter and search without a separate search warrant when executing a warrant for arrest or a warrant of commitment. These powers of entry and search can only be exercised by a constable who has reasonable grounds for believing that the person whom he/she is seeking is on the premises. Moreover, it is clearly specified in s. 17(4) that the power of search is limited to the extent that is reasonably required for the purpose for which the power of entry is exercised. At other times, if the police cannot obtain the permission of the owner or tenant of the premises to search, they should apply to a justice of the peace (magistrate) for a warrant. If granted, this will authorise entry and a search of the premises for stolen property, illegal drugs, firearms or evidence. PACE 1984 s. 8(1) confers on magistrates a power to issue a search warrant for a search of premises (including vehicles, vessels and aircraft). This is subject to the proviso that the magistrate has reasonable grounds for believing that (a) a serious arrestable offence has been committed and (b) there is material on the premises specified which is likely to be of substantial value to the investigation of the offence and is likely to be admissible at a subsequent trial. Although an application for a search warrant can be made by any police officer, it should be endorsed by a senior police officer on duty if no inspector is available. Moreover, Code B makes it clear that the application must be in writing specifying the statute under which it is being made, the premises to be searched, the object of the search (in terms of the items sought) and the grounds for the application. It must also state that there are no reasonable grounds to believe the material sought includes items subject to legal privilege (lawyer–client communications, or excluded material (as defined by s. 11(1)) or special procedure material (journalistic material except excluded material and other material coming under s. 14). It should be noted, however, that a magistrate is not barred from issuing a warrant because there may be special procedure material or excluded material on the premises. The issue of the warrant would only be barred if the material falls into these categories and is, or forms part of, the subject matter of such an application.

Under PACE 1984 s. 16(2) a search warrant may authorise persons other than police officers to accompany a constable who is to execute the warrant. In practice, it is often necessary for someone who is an expert in computers or in accountancy and finance to assist a constable in searching premises where certain types of records are likely to be discovered. A new subsection, (2A), has been added by the Criminal Justice Act 2003 to s. 16(2), whereby the person accompanying a constable has the same powers as the constable whom he/she is accompanying in relation to the execution of the warrant. Thus the 'expert' is empowered to seize anything to which the warrant refers. In relation to the search of premises, in general, Code B para. 1.4 makes it clear that for every search an 'officer in charge' has to be appointed and that in all cases the police should exercise their powers courteously and with respect for persons and property. A violation of Article 8 is most likely to arise, as in *McLeod* v *UK* [1998], where the police seek entry to premises in exercise of common law powers without the authority of a warrant.

7 Search of premises under the Terrorism Act 2000

Under the Terrorism Act 2000 Schedule 5 para 1(1) a magistrate is empowered on the application of a constable to grant a warrant to enter and search premises (and anyone found thereon). This extends to a power to seize material that would be of substantial value in a terrorism investigation. In order to be able to exercise this power, the magistrate must be satisfied that three conditions are fulfilled:

(a)   the warrant is sought for a terrorism investigation;

(b) there are reasonable grounds for believing there is material on the premises likely to be of substantial value in an investigation not comprising special procedure or excluded material; and

(c) the issue of the warrant is likely to be necessary in the circumstances of the case.

8 Helping police with inquiries

It is not always necessary to arrest someone to obtain further information about a crime because the police can invite a person, with his/her agreement, to come to the police station so that he/she can be questioned more conveniently. Such a person has not been formally arrested but is just 'helping the police with their inquiries'. It is undoubtedly the case that some persons in this situation frequently feel pressurised to attend. They may believe that if they do not go voluntarily, they will be arrested. Code C para. 3.21 indicates that they should be cautioned if they are to be questioned for the purpose of obtaining evidence even though they are told that they are not under arrest and are informed that they are not required to remain with the police officer. Any person who remains at the police station is entitled to free legal advice from the duty solicitor and is entitled to communicate with anyone outside the police station. Moreover, PACE s. 29 makes it clear that a person is free to leave a police station at any time unless placed under arrest. The premises of a person helping police with their inquiries can be searched with his/her consent provided the constable informs the person that he/she is not obliged to consent. Of course, it is possible for someone who starts out helping police with their inquiries to be arrested if there is sufficient evidence against him/her but they must be cautioned on arrest before any questions about an offence are asked. The caution must comply with Code C para. 10.5 as follows:

> You do not have to say anything. But it may harm your defence if you do not mention when questioned something which you later rely on in Court. Anything you do say may be given in evidence.

9 The alternative to arrest and charge

The Criminal Justice Act 2003 s. 30(4) specifically retains the power of any person who is not a public prosecutor (as defined) to 'lay an information' for the purposes of obtaining the issue of a summons under the Magistrates' Courts Act 1980 s. 1. This will be done at the court office, usually in front of a clerk to the justices. A summons can then be served on the accused by the relevant magistrates' court requiring him/her to attend court on a particular day to answer the allegation in the summons. The police are included within the definition of 'public prosecutor' and so they will now use the 'new method' described in s. 29 instead, which does not require an arrest. According to the Magistrates' Court Act 1981 s. 127(1) a magistrates' court may not try a defendant for a summary offence unless the 'information' was laid within six months of the time when the offence was allegedly committed.

10   New method of instituting criminal proceedings

The Criminal Justice Act 2003 s. 29(1) has created a new method of instituting criminal proceedings available to any public prosecutor as defined in s. 29(5). The person to be prosecuted is issued with a written charge together with a 'requisition' for him/her to appear before a magistrates' court to answer the charge. The written charge has to be served on the person named in the charge and copied to the court. Rules of court can be made under s. 30(1) specifically in relation to the form, content, recording, authentication and services of such written charges and/or requisition. The data can be entered into a computer at a police station which is linked to a computer at the magistrates' court so that details appear immediately on the magistrates' court computer.

11   Arrest without warrant by police under PACE

Arrest is not defined in PACE – it is a common law concept. In *R* v *Brosch* [1988] the Court of Appeal confirmed that PACE follows the common law as set out in *Alderson* v *Booth* [1969]. Any arrest must entail a loss of liberty because the person is prevented from being able to proceed on his/her way, even if just for a short time. Thus, unless there is a lawful basis for it, an arrest will usually amount to the tort of false imprisonment rendering the arresting officer liable to be sued. Moreover, arrest without lawful authority will probably amount to an infringement of a person's Convention rights under the Human Rights Act 1998 (Article 5) because the police have an obligation to act in conformity with the Act and an action for damages is possible under s. 8. At common law, the police have long had the power to arrest without a warrant any persons they reasonably suspect are about to cause, or have caused, a breach of the peace. However, police powers of arrest without a warrant derive nowadays from statute. The most commonly cited are contained in PACE 1984 ss. 24–26, as amended, which preserve the common law powers of arrest for breach of the peace mentioned above. There are three categories of offence where a constable can arrest without a warrant, the first of these being referred to as 'arrestable offences'. These offences are (a) those carrying a fixed penalty; (b) those for which a person of 21 previously unconvicted could be sentenced to five years' imprisonment or more; and (c) those listed in the new Schedule 1A inserted into PACE 1984 by the Police Reform Act 2002. A constable may arrest anyone whom he/she reasonably expects to be guilty of having committed an arrestable offence (whether such an offence has actually been committed or not) and anyone whom he/she reasonably expects to be about to commit an arrestable offence. In addition, these powers extend to conspiracies and to attempts to commit arrestable offences. A narrower power to arrest without a warrant for less serious offences is conferred by s. 25 on a constable who has reasonable grounds to suspect an offence has been attempted or committed provided he/she can satisfy any one of a number of 'general arrest conditions' set out in that section (often the inability to verify the name and address of the suspect). Here, the power is discretionary and does not extend to situations where no crime has actually been committed; nor does it extend to persons who are merely suspected of being about to commit an offence. It should also be noted that the power of arrest does not extend to those whose involvement is only at the level of conspiracy or inciting, aiding and abetting. Comprising the third category are various statutory powers of arrest without a warrant, contained in statutes enacted prior to 1984, that are specified in Schedule 2 to PACE 1984.

Many powers of arrest are premised on the arresting officer having 'reasonable cause' to believe that the suspect has committed, is committing or is about to commit an offence and so there must be some objective basis in fact for such a belief. It is to be determined according to what a constable knew at the time. It could be formed as a result of a radio message received or even a result of an anonymous telephone call provided the person arrested fits the description given but it cannot simply be justified on instructions received from a superior. Failure to make inquiries before making an arrest could show that there were insufficient grounds for the arrest but an officer need not wait until he/she has sufficient evidence that would render a conviction more likely than not. Furthermore, it is clear from the decision in *Davies* v *DPP* [1994] that the arrest is not lawful unless and until the person arrested is informed of the fact and the grounds for the arrest. The grounds for the arrest can be, and often are, given in colloquial language ('You're nicked for ...') but an arrest will be invalid where the reason(s) given indicate an offence for which there is no power of arrest and it is clear that no other reasons were in the mind of the arresting officer at the time. It is lawful, however, for a police officer to arrest someone on a lesser 'holding charge' other than at a police station provided there are reasonable grounds for suspecting that the person committed the offence and it is one for which the suspect can be lawfully arrested. The phrase 'holding charge' is appropriate where the arresting officer has a clear intention to investigate a more serious offence after making the arrest. Once the officer reaches the point at which he/she has reasonable grounds to suspect that the person has committed the more serious offence, the suspect must be arrested for that offence.

12   Other statutory powers to arrest without a warrant

The Public Order Act 1986 s. 4(1) confers specific powers of arrest on a constable who reasonably suspects a person or persons of committing an offence. There are two offences: (a) threatening, abusive or insulting words or behaviour, or (b) distributing to another person any writing, sign or other visible representation which is threatening, abusive or insulting with intent to cause a person to believe that immediate unlawful violence will be used against him/her or another person or to provoke the immediate use of unlawful violence. Under s. 5(4) an arrest without warrant may be made in relation to harassment, causing alarm or distress by disorderly behaviour. Nevertheless, s. 5(4) requires that the constable must first warn the offender to stop the offensive conduct and may only arrest if the person engages in further offensive conduct. Although the constable must reasonably believe the offensive conduct constitutes an offence under the Act, the initial conduct and subsequent conduct need not be precisely the same. The Act also confers powers to arrest without warrant under ss. 12(4)–(6), 13(10), 14(4) and 18(3).

Under s. 12 a constable in uniform has the power to arrest without a warrant those persons failing to comply with conditions imposed on public processions and similar powers extend to those persons organising/participating in a prohibited public procession. Moreover, a constable, whether in uniform or not, may arrest a person without a warrant whom he/she suspects of using language with the intent of stirring up racial hatred.

The Criminal Justice and Public Order Act 1994 gives the police power to remove trespassers from land. Thus, a constable who reasonably suspects that a person is committing an offence under s. 61 may arrest that person without a warrant. Moreover, s. 62 enables a constable to seize and remove any vehicle which a person failed to remove having been required to do so. The legislation was also drafted to combat unlicensed 'raves' and so police constables were given the power under s. 65(6) to arrest without warrant any person that he/she has stopped and who has declined to turn back. As might be expected, the Terrorism Act 2000 ss. 40 and 41 empower a constable to arrest persons without a warrant whom he/she reasonably suspects of being a terrorist or who have been involved in acts of terrorism. A caution, in accordance with Code C, para. 10.5, may be given prior to arrest in all cases but it should be given on making the arrest unless this is impracticable because of the suspect's violent behaviour. It is important to note that arrest is not automatically followed by a charge at a police station.

13   Powers of arrest by ordinary civilians

As is generally known, people are arrested every day for theft in shops by private security staff. The legal authority to make such an arrest derives from PACE 1984 s. 24(4) which provides that:

> Any person may arrest without warrant –
> (a) anyone who is in the act of committing an arrestable offence;
> (b) anyone whom he/she has reasonable grounds for suspecting is committing such an offence.

Moreover, according to s. 24(5):

> Where an arrestable offence has been committed, any person may arrest without a warrant –
> (a) anyone guilty of the offence;
> (b) anyone whom he/she has reasonable grounds for suspecting to be guilty of the offence.

The power does *not* extend to situations where a person is reasonably expected to be about to commit an arrestable offence. Where someone is arrested in a shop or similar premises, although that person may be detained for a short time at the scene to decide whether to proceed further with the matter, the person making the arrest is normally obliged to ensure that the person arrested is properly taken into custody. It is clear from the wording of the Act that the power to arrest without a warrant is not limited to shop theft but extends to any arrestable offence. So any member of the public could effect an arrest if he/she sees someone committing an arrestable offence. The Police Reform Act 2002 s. 38 empowers chief police officers to designate trained civilians under their direction and control to undertake specified functions. There are four categories of these trained civilians: (i) community support officers; (ii) investigating officers; (iii) detention officers; and (iv) escort officers. Of these, community support officers (CSOs) have the highest public profile because their function is to deal with minor criminality and anti-social behaviour. The CSO does not have a specific power of arrest but can detain someone for a limited period pending the arrival of a constable. An investigating officer dealing with financial and IT crime does have a limited statutory power of arrest at a police station conferred by s. 38 of and Schedule 4 to the Act.

14   The use of force

The Criminal Law Act 1967 s. 3 applies to all arrests and to action in the prevention of crime whether by police or civilians. It is clear that force cannot be used either by the police or civilians where the suspect does not resist arrest nor attempt to escape. If the suspect does offer resistance, it is a different matter. Then, only such force as is reasonable in the circumstances can be used to restrain the suspect. Handcuffs should only be used where they are necessary to prevent escape or to prevent a breach of the peace. In an era when police are often armed, it should be noted that lethal force *cannot* be used just because this seems to be the only way to prevent a suspect from escaping.

15 Events following arrest without a warrant

A constable who arrests a person other than at a police station is empowered by PACE s. 32(3) to search the person if he/she has reason to believe that the suspect may be a danger to himself/herself or others. Moreover, the constable may seize and retain any object likely to cause injury to the person arrested or another. Under s. 32 (2) and (5) a constable may also search for anything which the person arrested might use to escape from lawful custody. A search is also justified for items which might constitute evidence of the offence where the constable has reasonable cause to believe the person arrested is in possession of such items. Although a constable may search the suspect's mouth, where the search takes place in public, it can only extend to the suspect's outer clothing. If, prior to the arrest, the person was on premises, then a constable is permitted by s. 32(2)(b) to enter and search the premises and any vehicles present. It should be noted that such searches must be conducted in compliance with Code B. In the event that a constable comes to believe that there are no longer any grounds for detaining the person whom he/she has arrested then under s. 30(7), as amended, he/she must release that person although the fact of the arrest needs to be recorded in a pocket book or on a form specially provided.

A constable (but not an ordinary civilian) can defer taking an arrested person to a designated police station in order to check out an alibi or with a view to searching his/her lodgings. As a result of the amendment to PACE s. 30 made by the Criminal Justice Act 2003 s. 4 it is now possible for a constable to grant immediate bail to a suspect following their arrest without the necessity of taking the suspect to a police station. This permits the police a degree of flexibility in their operations so that there is a degree of discretion in deciding when and where an arrested person should attend a police station for interview. No other condition, other than attendance, can be attached as a condition of bail under this provision but the person bailed must be given a written notice setting out the offence for which the arrest was made and also the grounds on which the arrest was made. There is now power under s. 30D for a constable to arrest, without a warrant, anyone failing to answer to bail under these new arrangements.

16 Arrest under warrant

The Magistrates' Courts Act 1980 s. 1 empowers a justice of the peace to issue a warrant for the arrest of a named person or persons on the

Metropolitan Police Service

| Logo | | |

Bailing of Persons to Police Station   Form 60B

Bail from Custody   [   ]   Re-bail | X | Not in Custody

Custody Record No.

Station Code
Other Refs.

Name of person bailed ……...

Address …………………………………………………………………..…

…………………………………………………………………………

I understand that I have been granted bail in accordance with the Bail Act 1976 and the provisions of Section 34(5)/37(7) Police and Criminal Evidence Act 1984 and that I must surrender

to custody at ……………………………..………………….. Police Station

on …….…...day the …………………… day of …………………….……. 200

I have been informed that unless I surrender to custody as shown above I may be liable to a fine or imprisonment or both.

Signature of person bailed …………………..………………………..

Signature of appropriate adult/interpreter …………………………….……

Signature of custody officer …………………………………………..

Date …………………… Time ………………….. a.m./ p.m.

Name and divisional number of custody officer ………………………………
(BLOCK CAPITALS)

Surety
I acknowledge my obligation to pay the Court the sum specified by my signature if the accused fails to surrender to custody as shown.

Name ……………………………………………….. £……………....…

Address
……………………………………………………………………………

Officer in case ……………………….. Rank ……………………………...
Div./ Branch ……………………….. Telephone …………………………

Figure 10.1 **Bail Form**
Source: © Crown copyright

strength of written information. The Criminal Justice Act 2003 s. 31 has removed the requirement to substantiate this information on oath. Once the warrant has been issued, the warrant can be executed by a constable anywhere in England and Wales. The warrant may, or may not, be endorsed for bail. If the warrant is 'backed for bail' the accused can be subsequently released on his/her own recognisance, which is a formal undertaking to surrender to custody on a specified date (see **Figure 10.1**). If the magistrates require one or more sureties to guarantee the appearance of the accused, the warrant will usually specify the amounts for which sureties are to be given. After making the arrest, the police must then release the offender if the sureties have entered into recognisances (formal financial undertakings) according to the endorsement on the warrant. Thereafter, the accused is obliged to appear before a magistrates' court at the time and place stated in the recognisance. It should be noted, however, that the power of a magistrates' court to issue an arrest warrant for a person who has attained the age of 17 is restricted by s. 1(4) in that the offence must either be triable on indictment or be punishable with a term of imprisonment or the person's address must be insufficiently established for a summons to be served upon him/her. Magistrates may also issue a warrant under s. 13 for the arrest of a suspect who has failed to answer a summons to attend court issued by magistrates. This is subject to the proviso that the offence to which the warrant relates is punishable with imprisonment or where the court proposes to impose a driving disqualification on him/her following conviction.

It should be noted that a warrant issued in the Republic of Ireland can be endorsed for execution by a magistrate in England and Wales under certain conditions as specified in the Backing of Warrants (Republic of Ireland) Act 1965. Moreover, there is a scheme under the Criminal Justice and Public Order Act 1994 s. 136 whereby warrants issued by magistrates in Scotland and Northern Ireland can be executed in England and Wales and vice versa.

The Extradition Act 2003 was enacted mainly to give effect to the decision of the Council of the EU contained in the Framework Decision of 13 June 2002. This obliges all member states of the EU to introduce the measures agreed upon in the Council into their national legal systems. It makes the European arrest warrant a reality so that persons suspected of criminal activity in one Member State can be extradited (subject to certain legal safeguards) under warrant to another member state. It is not a radical departure from the existing law on extradition but a further step in European cross-border judicial cooperation. It introduces the concept of 'mandatory extradition' for offences punishable by a maximum of three years' imprisonment.

17   Detention in police custody

PACE 1984 s. 34(1) states that only an arrested person can be kept in police detention and, even then, it can only be in accordance with the provisions of Part IV of the Act. Once a person is arrested, and assuming that 'street bail' is not to be granted, it is necessary for the suspect to be brought to a police station so that the decision can be made whether to charge the person with the offence for which he/she has been arrested. The key decision-maker is the 'custody officer', who should usually be a member of the uniform branch and must normally hold, at least, the rank of sergeant. The requirement for some seniority is understandable, given that the role of custody officer can, at times, be quite onerous. PACE 1984 s. 39 makes it clear that the custody officer is the person responsible for ensuring the integrity of the system of detention. The onus is therefore on the custody officer to ensure that all detainees are treated in accordance with PACE and its Codes of Practice. PACE s. 36(5) states that none of the functions of the custody officer can normally be performed by an officer engaged in the investigation of the offence for which the suspect has been arrested.

Although the decision in *DPP* v *L* [1999] makes it clear that the custody officer is entitled to assume that the arrest was lawful, the custody officer, nevertheless, must decide whether there is sufficient evidence to charge the suspect for the offence for which he/she has been arrested. He/she may not be able to do this quickly and so s. 37(1) empowers the custody officer to detain a suspect at a police station to enable him/her to make this decision. The suspect must be informed of the grounds for detention but he/she cannot be questioned by the custody officer about the offence.

A 'custody record' has to be made out for every suspect who is arrested and brought to a police station. This normally has to be done in the suspect's presence and a copy must travel with the suspect if he/she is subsequently transferred to another police station. According to Code C para. 3.4 the custody officer should note on the custody record any comments made by the suspect regarding the arresting officer's account of events although he/she should not invite such comment. However, the requirement relating to the making of a written record can be dispensed with if the suspect, at the relevant time, is incapable of understanding what is said or is violent or is likely to become violent or urgently needs medical attention.

There has been an amendment to PACE s. 54(1) so that the custody officer does not have to record everything a detained person has on his/her person on entering into police custody. The custody officer is, nevertheless, under a duty to ascertain what the suspect has with him/her on arrival but this record does not have to form part of the custody record. This process is necessary to discover whether the suspect has on him/her any property acquired for an unlawful or harmful purpose whilst in custody. Anything coming into either category can be seized and retained but, generally, a suspect is entitled to retain personal clothing and items of personal property (at their own risk) unless the custody officer reasonably believes that an item may be used to cause injury/damage or that it constitutes evidence relating to the offence. It is by no means the case that all suspects are routinely searched but the custody officer can, if he/she thinks it is necessary in the performance of his/her official duties, order that the suspect be searched. If a suspect is likely to be detained for a short time only and is not placed in a cell, the custody officer may decide that a search is quite unnecessary. If the custody officer does decide under s. 54(6) that a search is necessary, it is for him/her to decide how extensive such a search is to be.

18   Searches of a suspect

A search that involves more than the removal of outer clothing (including shoes and socks) is a strip search. This form of search may only take place if the custody officer thinks it necessary to remove an item which the suspect would not be allowed to keep and the officer reasonably considers the suspect might have concealed. Annex A para. 10 of Code C states that strips searches are not to be routinely carried out where there is no reason to consider that such items are concealed. Where they are justified, they must be carried out by an officer of the same sex as the suspect in an area where he/she cannot be seen by anyone who does not need to be present. Other than the suspect, there must normally be at least two other officers of the same sex as the suspect present. Persons who are searched in this way should not normally be asked to remove all their clothes at the same time and no physical contact should be made with body orifices (other than the mouth) by those carrying out the search.

In certain circumstances, a person who has been arrested and held in police detention can be subjected to an intimate search but it cannot be ordered for the purpose of securing evidence. The case of *R* v *Hughes* (1993) clarifies that, to qualify as an intimate search, there must be some intrusion into a body orifice. An intimate search may only be authorised under PACE s. 55(1) by an officer of the rank of inspector or above who has reasonable grounds for believing that:

(a)   the person may have concealed on themselves:
    (i)   anything which they could and might use to cause physical injury to themselves or others at the station; or
    (ii)   a Class A drug which they intend to supply to another or export; and
(b)   an intimate search is the only means of removing those items.

According to Code C Annexe A para. 2A the reasons why an intimate search is deemed necessary must be explained to the suspect before the search takes place. Intimate searches are comparatively rare events but, even so, they must normally be conducted by a registered medical practitioner or registered nurse. Only as a last resort can an intimate search be conducted by a police officer but never of a suspect of the opposite sex. Although intimate searches can be carried out by the personnel indicated at either a police station or medical premises in respect of (i) above, intimate searches for Class A drugs must only take place by the personnel indicated on medical premises. There are special provisions in Code C Annexe A para. 5 relating to the intimate searches of juveniles and/or mentally ill or incapacitated persons. In the event that an intimate search is ordered, this fact, together with the details and outcome, has to be entered into the custody record, which must indicate those parts of the body that were searched.

19 Notification of rights and entitlements

A suspect who is brought to a police station following his/her arrest is likely to be questioned, albeit not by the custody officer. Nevertheless, the custody officer is required by Code C para. 3.2 to give the detainee a written notice setting out his/her rights, namely:

(i)   the right to have someone informed of their arrest;
(ii)   the right to consult privately with a solicitor and that free independent legal advice is available; and
(iii) the right to consult the PACE Codes of Practice.

The same notice must also give the arrangements for obtaining legal advice, as well as inform the detainee of the right to have a copy of the custody record together with the text of the normal police caution. Code C para. 3.5 states that the custody officer is also required to ask the suspect whether he/she wishes to receive legal advice and/or someone to be informed of their detention. The suspect is then to be asked to sign the custody record confirming their decision in respect of these matters and any refusal to sign is to be recorded. In addition, a notice of entitlements is to be given which lists the basic entitlements whilst detained at a police station – these include food and drink, access to toilets, together with visits and contacts with outside parties. It also falls to the custody officer to determine whether the suspect might need medical attention.

20 Special categories of suspect

If the arrested suspect is a juvenile (a person, according to Code C, under the age of 17), the custody officer must, if practicable, ascertain the identity of a person responsible for the juvenile's welfare and inform that person that the juvenile has been arrested and the reason why he/she is being detained. Not only must the custody officer ascertain the identity of this 'appropriate adult', it is necessary that he/she be asked to come to the police station. It is important to note that a solicitor who is attending the police station on the suspect's behalf is not deemed to be an 'appropriate adult' for this purpose. In most instances, the appropriate adult is likely to be a parent (but not if the juvenile is estranged from the parent) or legal guardian. If the juvenile is 'in care' of a local authority or voluntary organisation, the appropriate adult would be a social worker. Similar considerations apply when the police are dealing with a suspect who is suffering from a mental illness or is mentally vulnerable. If there is to be a strip search, the appropriate adult must be in attendance. In the case of a juvenile who has been arrested, the custody officer who decides that it is necessary to detain the young person must ensure that he/she is moved to secure local authority custody unless the custody officer is prepared to issue a certificate stating that it is impracticable to do so.

21 Detention without charge

Although persons who are arrested by the police and taken to a police station are usually dealt with promptly, in some instances it is necessary to hold some suspects for a period whilst deciding whether to charge them or release them. Unless a suspect has been arrested for a serious arrestable offence, for which a prolonged period of detention has been authorised, a suspect cannot normally be held in police custody without charge for more than 24 hours. Even within this 24-hour period, eight hours must be allowed for sleeping. If it is necessary for a suspect to be kept in police detention for more than six hours, a constable must normally take the suspect to a designated police station, as defined by s. 35 (one having adequate facilities), where he/she can be detained. Once the 24-hour period has elapsed, if the suspect has not been charged he/she must, according to s. 41(7), be released either on police bail or without bail. Furthermore, the person released may not be re-arrested without a warrant for that offence unless new evidence has been uncovered that would justify re-arrest. The rules relating to the precise calculation of the 24-hour period are complex because of the need to allow for a number of eventualities, including attendance at hospital; but, for a suspect who is arrested in the same police area in which he/she is to be dealt with, the 'clock begins to tick' from the moment he/she is brought to the police station.

22 Police interviewing

It is the custody officer who must decide whether to deliver up a suspect to officers investigating the offence for which he/she was arrested. The interviewing of suspects by police is obviously a vital part of police work in the accumulation of evidence but it is a process that is highly regulated because of the possibility of oppression and abuse. In part, this regulation derives from common law sources but far more important these days are the PACE Codes of Practice, namely Codes C, E and F. Code C para. 11.1A is quite specific and defines an interview as:

... the questioning of a person regarding their involvement or suspected involvement in a criminal offence or offence, under which paragraph 10.1 must be carried out under caution. Whenever a person is interviewed they must be informed of the nature of the offence, or further offence. Procedures under the Road Traffic Act 1988, section 7 or the Transport and Works Act 1992, section 31 do not constitute interviewing for the purpose of this Code.

Paragraph 11.1 makes it clear that, following a decision to arrest a suspect, they must not be interviewed about the relevant offence except at a police station or other authorised place of detention unless the consequent delay would be likely to lead to:

- interference with, or harm to, evidence connected with an offence;
- interference with, or physical harm to, other people;
- serious loss of, or damage to, property;
- alerting other people suspected of committing an offence but not yet arrested for it; or
- hindering the recovery of property obtained in consequence of the commission of an offence.

Although these are clear exceptions to the general principle, the text of para. 11.1 further states that:

Interviewing in these circumstances shall cease once the relevant risk has been averted or the necessary questions have been put in order to attempt to avert that risk.

A suspect who has requested legal advice may not normally be interviewed without a solicitor being present unless the denial of access can be justified by the provisions of s. 58 but even this must be authorised by a superintendent.

An accurate record must be made of each interview. Interviews are often recorded and where there is tape recording, Code E (or Code F for Video Recording) must be complied with by those officers interviewing. In any event, para. 11.7 of Code C states:

(a) An accurate record must be made of each interview, whether or not the interview takes place at a police station.

(b) The record must state the place of the interview, the time it begins and ends, any interview breaks and, subject to paragraph 2.6A, the names of all those present; and must be made on the forms provided for this purpose or in the interviewer's pocket book or in accordance with the Codes E or F.

(c) Any written record must be made and completed during the interview, unless this would not be practicable or would interfere with the conduct of the interview, and must constitute either a verbatim record of what has been said or, failing this, an account of the interview which adequately and accurately summarises it.

However, para. 11.8 seems to equivocate because it states that, if a written record is not made during the interview, it must be made as soon as practicable after its completion. Nevertheless, para. 11.9 stipulates that written interview records must be timed and signed by the officer responsible. There are very strict rules in paras 11.15–11.17 of Code C relating to the questioning of juveniles, mentally disordered and mentally impaired persons who should only be interviewed in the presence of an appropriate adult.

23   Review of detention

Although most police interviews are quite short, some are conducted over a lengthy period by adjournment during which the suspect is detained in police custody, albeit without being charged. This is particularly likely to happen where the suspect remains silent and refuses to answer police questions. The interviewing officer must not only remind the suspect of his/her right to legal advice at the commencement of the interview but also at each recommencement of the interview.

Where someone is held in police custody without being charged, then, in accordance with s. 40, there has to be a review of detention by an officer of at least the rank of inspector (the reviewing officer) who has not been directly involved in the investigation. The first review should be no later than six hours after detention was first authorised by the custody officer. A second review must occur no later than nine hours after the first review and subsequent reviews must be at intervals not exceeding nine hours. A review may, nevertheless, be postponed if it would disrupt questioning then in progress and would prejudice the investigation. It may also be postponed if the review officer is not available at the time but a postponed review should be carried out as soon as possible thereafter. As a result of the insertion of ss. 40A and 45A into PACE 1984 reviews can now be conducted by video link and by telephone. In the case of the latter, there are provisos, namely that it is not possible for the reviewing officer to be present at the police station where the suspect is being held *and* it is not a review under s. 45A that is authorised to be conducted using video conferencing facilities.

The review is intended to provide an opportunity for a decision to be made by the reviewing officer as to whether the suspect should be charged with the offence for which he/she has been arrested. Alternatively, the reviewing officer must consider whether to order the release of the suspect on bail or without bail. It should be noted that the suspect and/or his/her solicitor may communicate with the reviewing officer orally or in writing regarding the decision to be made on each occasion.

24   Extended detention

As previously stated, the normal time limit for detention without charge is 24 hours but it may be very difficult to complete robbery investigations in particular within this timescale. The 24-hour period may be extended to a further 36 hours provided that three conditions, as specified in s. 42(1), are satisfied:

(a) a police officer of the rank of superintendent or above responsible for the police station concerned has reasonable grounds for believing that such detention is necessary to secure or preserve evidence relating to the offence or to obtain such evidence by questioning the suspect;

(b) that the offence for which the suspect is under arrest is a serious arrestable offence; and

(c) that the investigation is being conducted diligently and expeditiously (in relation to the complexity of the case).

The term 'serious arrestable offence' is defined in PACE 1984 in s. 116 and Schedule 5. Basically, there are three groups of offence, the first of which includes both common law and statutory offences (e.g. murder, manslaughter, rape, kidnapping). The second group comprises those set out in Schedule 5 Part II whilst the third group comprises drug trafficking offences defined in the Proceeds of Crime Act 2002 Schedule 2 para. 1 and offences under ss. 327 – 329 of the Act. Some offences under the Terrorism Act 2000 are also regarded as serious arrestable offences. An authorisation by a high-ranking police officer to extend detention without charge to up to 36 hours is subject to very strict time limits. No authorisation can be made more than 24 hours *after* the commencement of detention. This rules out the possibility of retrospective authorisation of detention without charge for longer than 24 hours once this initial period has elapsed. However, a further extension may be applied for and granted provided that the total period does not extend beyond 36 hours but no order to extend can be made before the second review of detention. Whenever a period of extended detention is authorised, the suspect must be informed of the grounds for the decision, which must be noted on the custody record together with the duration. The suspect and/or his solicitor is entitled to make representations orally or in writing to the reviewing officer, although, as in cases of normal detention, the officer can refuse to receive oral representation from the suspect if he/she thinks the suspect's general state and behaviour render the suspect unfit. As previously indicated, any person held in police custody without charge has the right (with some exceptions) to contact family or a friend and a solicitor. Where extended detention has been authorised and the suspect has not previously exercised any of these rights, the authorising officer must comply with s. 42(9) and:

(i) inform the suspect of his/her right(s)

(ii) decide whether he/she should be permitted to exercise a right;

(iii) record the decision on the custody record; and

(iv) in the case of a refusal, record the grounds for the decision in the custody record.

At the expiration of this extended period of detention, if the suspect has not been charged, he/she must be released either on bail or without bail unless further detention has been authorised by a magistrates' court. A person then released may not be re-arrested for the same offence without a warrant unless new evidence is discovered that would justify re-arrest. This does not preclude an arrest without warrant for failing to answer bail, which is possible under s. 46A.

If the police wish to detain a suspect for longer than 36 hours in total, an application must be made to a magistrates' court under s. 43 before the expiry of the 36-hour period. Very precise requirements are set out in s. 43 for such an application. An application may be made on oath by a constable but the application cannot be heard unless the suspect is actually brought before the court for the hearing. The suspect is also entitled to be legally represented. The police are required to prove further detention is necessary. If, after hearing the application, the court is satisfied that a period of further detention without charge is justified, it can issue a warrant for further detention for a period up to 24 hours. In principle, this could mean a suspect being held without charge for a total of 96 hours. If the application for a warrant is refused, the police must either charge the suspect or release him/her on bail or without bail. It should be noted that, under the exceptional circumstances envisaged by the provisions of the Terrorism Act 2000, a police officer of at least the rank of superintendent may apply to a judicial authority (as defined) for a warrant of further detention until a maximum period of seven days is reached, beginning with the time of arrest.

Whilst in police custody, suspects may be fingerprinted. PACE 1984 s. 61, as amended by the Criminal Justice Act 2003, empowers the police to take fingerprints electronically without consent from any person detained having been arrested for a recordable offence although the reason for doing so must be given to the suspect as soon as practicable. This is to ensure that persons giving a false name and address on being arrested can be identified against the national fingerprint database as well as to discover whether the suspect has been involved in other crimes.

25   The right to remain silent

The right to remain silent whilst in police detention remains but it was significantly undermined by the Criminal Justice and Public Order Act 1994 ss. 34–37 because the courts may draw inferences from a suspect's failure to mention facts in an interview that he/she later seeks to rely upon as a defence. In *Condron* v *UK* [2000] two men were accused of drug dealing. Their solicitor believed that they were unfit to answer police questions even though there was medical evidence to the contrary – both men refused to answer questions. They had been cautioned by the police and confirmed that they understood the implications of the warning regarding the inference that might be drawn by the jury arising from their exercise of their right to remain silent. The trial judge, when summing up, omitted to remind the jury that they could draw an adverse inference from the accuseds' silence only if that silence could be sensibly attributed to there being either no answer or none that would stand up to cross-examination in court. Having stated that the jury was not properly directed, the European Court of Human Rights ruled that the Court of Appeal could not adopt the role of the jury or second guess the outcome of jury deliberations if there was a misdirection by the trial judge. The Court went on to state: 'any other conclusion would be at variance with the fundamental importance of the right to silence, a right which, as observed earlier, lies at the heart of the notion of a fair procedure guaranteed by Article 6 of the Convention'.

26 The charging of suspects

Staff from the Crown Prosecution Service are now allocated to police stations in the capacity of 'duty prosecutors' on a full-time basis. These duty prosecutors are available for consultation by police officers and provide legal advice and guidance as and when required. This can be particularly helpful to investigating officers who may seek guidance on lines of inquiry and/or evidential requirements. In many instances this will not be necessary because, on arrival at the police station, a suspect may admit a particular offence for which he/she has been arrested and for which there is evidence. Alternatively, there may be compelling video evidence available so that protracted interviewing to gather evidence is unnecessary. Research indicates that the police obtain confessions in approximately 60 per cent of cases either prior to or during an interview. A point will normally be arrived at in questioning when the officer in charge of the investigation believes that there is sufficient evidence to provide a realistic prospect of conviction for the offence. At this point he/she must inform the custody officer that this stage has been reached.

Although the arresting/investigating officers may propose a particular charge, the decision to charge as well as the precise charge will be made by the duty prosecutors(s) although there will be some conferring between prosecutor(s) and the police. The police may only determine the charge in relatively minor offences under the Road Traffic Acts and for certain offences where the person arrested admits to the charge on which they were arrested on arrival at the police station. There is often, however, a difference between the notion of 'sufficient evidence to charge' as contained in PACE and evidence required for a realistic prospect of conviction. In deciding the appropriate charge, Crown Prosecutors need to consider the Guidance Notes issued by the DPP to police officers and prosecutors under PACE 1984 s. 37A. This makes it clear that the selection of charge(s) should seek to reflect the seriousness and extent of the offending. It is further provided in para. 10 that:

> Where appropriate a schedule of other admitted offences may be listed on a (form) MG 18 for the charged person to ask the court to take into consideration.

The duty prosecutor is then required to apply the so-called 'threshold test' which requires an overall assessment of whether in all the circumstances of the case there is reasonable suspicion against the suspect of having committed an offence. It is also necessary to decide whether, at that stage, it is in the public interest to proceed. A number of factors have to be taken into account including the following:

- the evidence available at the time and the likelihood and nature of further evidence being obtained;
- the reasonableness for believing that evidence will become available, the time that it will take and the steps being taken to gather it;
- the impact of the expected evidence on the case and the charges that the totality of the evidence will support; and
- whether there is a realistic prospect of a successful prosecution.

Of course, if there is insufficient evidence and no prospect of obtaining further evidence, the suspect should be released without charge. A suspect may, however, in some instances be released on pre-charge bail (where he/she is suitable for bail) by the custody officer who concludes that there is sufficient evidence for the suspect to be charged under s. 37(7)(a) whilst the Crown Prosecutor decides the actual charge because it is not readily apparent what the precise charge should be.

27 The act of charging

The protocol for charging detained persons is set out in Code C Part 16. When the suspect is charged he/she must be given a written notice giving particulars of the offence. As far as possible the particulars of the charge shall be stated in simple terms but it must also be legally precise. The notice must begin:

> You are charged with the offence(s) shown below ...

The suspect must also be cautioned as follows:

> You do not have to say anything. But it may harm your defence if you do not mention now something which you later rely on in court. Anything you do say may be given in evidence.

If the suspect is a juvenile, mentally disordered or otherwise mentally vulnerable, the notice is to be given to the appropriate adult.

The general rule is that questioning must end after a suspect has been charged with an offence. However, there are three exceptions to this rule, namely:

1 where a police officer wants to bring to the notice of the accused a written statement made by another person or the contents of an interview with another person;
2 where it is necessary to put questions to the accused in order to prevent or minimise harm or loss to some other person or the public at large or

where it is in the interests of justice that he/she should have an opportunity to comment on information concerning the offence which has been uncovered since the charging stage; and

3 where the Director of the Serious Fraud Office requires the production and explanation of certain documents under the Criminal Justice Act 1987 s. 2.

If there is to be an interview following a charge, the accused must be cautioned again. PACE 1984 s. 63 empowers the police to take a sample of urine (for the presence of Class A drugs) or non-intimate samples of DNA and other samples from persons held in custody prior to being charged on the authority of an inspector to prove or disprove an offence. Once a person has been charged with a recordable offence, such non-intimate samples may be taken without such authorisation, if needed. Indeed, persons under the age of 18 may be detained after charging to obtain a sample to be taken to test for a Class A drug. The person concerned must have reached the age of 14 and an appropriate adult must be present, if the accused is under 17 years of age.

28   Alternatives to charging suspects

The police may release a suspect without charge even though he/she was arrested for an offence. If a suspect was not arrested but warned instead that he/she might be prosecuted, the police may send him/her a notice that no summons will be issued. In such cases the police may give the suspect an informal warning with regard to his/her future behaviour. In addition to such informal warnings given for lesser offences, the police have discretion to issue a 'conditional caution' to an adult offender under the Criminal Justice Act 2003 s. 22. The Guidance Notes to Police Officers and Crown Prosecutors 2004 stipulate that, even in such situations, an investigating officer may wish to consult with a Crown Prosecutor before making a final decision. For a conditional caution to be given, s. 23 makes it clear that five requirements must be satisfied, namely:

1 the police have evidence that the offender has committed an offence;
2 the police (or prosecutor) have decided that there is sufficient evidence to charge the offender with the offence and a conditional caution is appropriate;
3 the offender *has admitted* that he/she committed the offence;
4 having explained the effect of the caution to the offender, the police warn him/her that failure to comply with the conditions attached may result in prosecution;
5 the offender is prepared to sign a document containing details of the offence, his admission, his consent to being cautioned and assent to the conditions attached; and
6 the offender must be of previous good character.

Cautions do not count as convictions but the Criminal Justice Act 2003 s. 24 makes it clear that if the offender fails, without reasonable excuse, to comply with any of the conditions that criminal proceedings may be instituted against him/her for the offence in question. The conditions may require, for example, attendance on a drug/alcohol rehabilitation programme or some reparation to be made in the near future. In the event that a person who has been given a caution should be convicted of another offence in the future, the caution could be cited at the sentencing stage (although it would not appear on the same form as the list of previous convictions). A conditional caution must be given by a police officer trained and authorised to do so and must normally be given at a police station. The Code of Practice on Conditional Cautioning, available on the Home Office website, may be consulted for further details of the scheme.

It is important to note that a caution does not preclude a private prosecution being undertaken but a defendant may be able to apply for a court order asking that the prosecution should be stayed. In *Hayter* v *L and another* [1998] the defendants were arrested for offences under the Public Order Act and the Offences against the Person Act 1861 when they attacked another young man. As the defendants were aged 16 at the time and were of previous good character, they received a formal caution from the police having received legal advice. The victim's father, who was a solicitor, laid informations before magistrates but the defendants then contended that for the magistrates to hear these informations preferred by the father would be an abuse of the process of the court. A youth court concluded that the private prosecution brought by the victim's father was an abuse of process and ordered that the proceedings be stayed. The victim's father then appealed to the Divisional Court of Queen's Bench by way of case stated. In giving judgment the court held that it was not an abuse of process to prosecute a defendant after he/she had been cautioned by the police unless the particular circumstances of the case disclosed an abuse. On this basis, the court ruled that there was no proper basis for the magistrates to have ordered a stay of proceedings.

29 Reprimands

The Crime and Disorder Act 1988 ss. 65 and 66 introduced a procedure for the reprimanding and warning of children and young persons who have committed offences. These apply where:

(a) a constable has sufficient evidence for there to be a reasonable prospect of the child or young person being convicted of an offence;

(b) the offender admits the offence and has not been convicted of any offence; and

(c) the constable is satisfied that it would not be in the public interest for the offender to be prosecuted.

A constable may reprimand an offender who has not previously been reprimanded or warned. Alternatively, the constable may take the graver step of warning an offender who has not been warned previously. If the offence has been committed more than two years after a previous warning and is not so serious as to require a charge to be brought, the constable may issue a further warning. All reprimands and warnings must be given in a police station. Where an offender is aged under 17, a reprimand must be given in the presence of an appropriate adult. A person who receives a warning will be referred to a youth offending team and arrangements will be made for him/her to participate in a rehabilitation programme. Failure on the part of the offender to participate in the rehabilitation scheme may be cited in criminal proceedings in the same circumstances as may a reprimand or warning.

30   Crown Prosecution Service deciding whether to prosecute

No matter how serious the offence, a prosecution should not go ahead if it does not pass the evidential test as set out in para. 4.1 of the Code for Crown Prosecutors. The Crown Prosecutor must be satisfied that there is enough evidence for there to be a realistic prospect of conviction against the defendant. According to para. 5.2, this is an objective test meaning that a jury or bench of magistrates properly directed, in accordance with the law, is more likely than not to convict the defendant of the charge alleged. In deciding whether the evidence is reliable and can be used, Crown Prosecutors should consider the matters set out in para. 5.3(b)–(c). Paragraph 5.4 states that Crown Prosecutors should not ignore evidence because they are not sure that it can be used or is reliable. They should look at such evidence closely when deciding whether there is a realistic prospect of conviction.

If there is enough evidence to justify a prosecution, Crown Prosecutors must then consider whether a prosecution would be in the public interest. The Code for Crown Prosecutors in para. 6.4 sets out the factors that indicate that proceedings may be required whilst para. 6.5 sets out the factors tending against a prosecution. Paragraph 6.6 of the Code states that Crown Prosecutors should not add up the number of factors on each side. Rather, they should carry out an evaluation exercise to form an overview of the case. They should have regard to the interests of the victim (or the victim's family) but it does not follow that a prosecution must be stopped merely because the victim (or the victim's family) so desires. Crown Prosecutors must also consider the interests of young offenders when deciding whether it is in the public interest to prosecute but should not avoid a prosecution merely because of the age of the person concerned. Paragraph 6.9 makes it clear that it is the seriousness of the offence and/or the youth's past behaviour that is important in deciding whether to prosecute or not to prosecute.

31 The decision not to prosecute and judicial review

A decision not to prosecute may be subject to judicial review. Even though the DPP is not obliged to give reasons for a decision not to prosecute, failure to provide a sufficient explanation in certain circumstances may give rise to a claim for judicial review. In *DPP ex p. Manning* [2000] the applicant's brother had died of asphyxia whilst under restraint following an intense argument with two prison officers when on remand for a violent offence. The death was investigated by the police and the papers were ultimately sent to the CPS. At a coroner's inquest the evidence indicated that the death had resulted from the manner in which the deceased's head had been held by an officer during the incident and the jury returned a verdict of unlawful killing. A specialist senior caseworker at the CPS undertook a detailed examination of all the available evidence including that produced at the inquest and in his review note he recorded his investigations, his conclusion and the reasoning on which they were based. Although the CPS caseworker referred to the weaknesses and inconsistencies of the prison officers' evidence, he rejected alternative potential charges and considered that in respect of 'unlawful act manslaughter' it was only the fatal force to the deceased's neck which should be characterised as excessive. Consequently, the only potential defendant was the officer identified as holding the deceased's head. He concluded that there was a *prima facie* case but no realistic prospect of the prosecution being able to establish that excessive force had been used deliberately as opposed to an attempt to effect a proper restraint that had been frustrated by the struggle with the deceased. When he communicated his decision not to prosecute, the caseworker stated that there was insufficient evidence to justify any criminal prosecution. Moreover, he was not satisfied that the available evidence would provide a realistic prospect of convicting either of the officers of an offence arising from the death. Having unsuccessfully requested full reasons for that decision, the applicant sought judicial review to challenge the lawfulness of the decision and, in so doing, the caseworker's review note was served on him. The Divisional Court of Queen's Bench held that there was no absolute obligation imposed on the DPP to give reasons for a decision not to prosecute. However, the court stated that the right to life was the most fundamental of all the rights under the European Convention on Human Rights and Fundamental Freedoms and it allowed limited scope for derogation. The court took the view that the death of a person in the state's custody resulting from violence inflicted by its agents necessarily aroused concern. Consequently it ruled that the DPP would be expected to give reasons for such a decision where an inquest jury had returned a verdict of unlawful killing implicating an identifiable person. Accordingly, the court quashed the DPP's decision.

32   The decision to prosecute

Having made the decision to prosecute, the Crown Prosecutor should select those charges that reflect the seriousness of the offending, give the court adequate sentencing powers and enable the case to be presented in a clear and uncomplicated fashion. However, a Crown Prosecutor need not proceed with the most serious charge available where there is a choice and should not continue with more charges than is necessary. Nor should he/she go ahead with a more serious charge in order to encourage the accused to plead guilty to a less serious one. According to para. 9.1, Crown Prosecutors should accept a plea arrangement put forward by the defendant (or his legal adviser) only if they think that the court would be able to pass a sentence that matches the gravity of the offending, especially where there are aggravating features. Paragraph 9.1 stipulates that Crown Prosecutors must never accept a guilty plea just because it is convenient and para. 9.2 states that particular care must be observed when considering pleas that would enable the defendant to avoid a mandatory minimum sentence.

33   Consent for a prosecution

It is necessary to obtain the consent from either the Attorney General or the DPP as a precondition for the prosecution of certain types of offences. The Attorney General's consent is required where issues of public policy, national security and relations with foreign countries may affect the decision to prosecute. Examples of such offences include those under the Official Secrets Act 1911, offences stirring up racial hatred contrary to the Public Order Act 1986 and the Law Reform (Year and a Day) Act 1996 for the prosecution of a homicide where the victim dies after three years have elapsed from the actual event finally causing death or if the accused has already been convicted for the lesser offence that caused the death. The consent of the DPP is required for a diverse range of offences under the Theft Act 1968, the Criminal Law Act 1967, the Sexual Offences Act 1956, the Suicide Act 1961, the Public Order Act 1986 and the War Crimes Act 1991. However, the consent of the DPP may be given to a Crown Prosecutor under the Prosecution of Offences Act 1985 s. 1(7), who must consider the propriety or otherwise of an offence before proceedings are commenced.

34   Immunity from prosecution

Before commencing any proceedings, the CPS must always consider whether an offender has personal immunity from prosecution. Children under 10 years of age are irrebuttably presumed to be incapable of committing a crime. For those children between the ages of 10 and 13, the prosecutor must consider whether the evidence is strong enough to rebut the presumption that the child is incapable of forming the necessary criminal intent (*mens rea*). In addition, foreign sovereigns or heads of state, their families and servants all have immunity under the State Immunity Act 1978 s. 20, as do diplomats, members of staff of diplomatic missions and their families under the Diplomatic Privileges Act 1964.

35 Other prosecuting agencies

The police and the CPS are not the only agencies that are involved in criminal prosecutions. There are a number of other prosecuting authorities including local councils, trading standards officers, Inland Revenue, HM Customs and Excise, the DHSS, the Post Office, RSPCA and the Health and Safety Executive. In addition, victims and their relatives may bring private prosecutions although in some instances they may need official permission as explained. The Financial Services Authority has statutory powers to summon persons suspected of committing certain offences (such as 'insider trading') before a tribunal which may impose fines if the person or persons are found guilty.

36 Jurisdiction of the criminal courts

In general, English and Welsh courts normally decline to accept jurisdiction over offences that were committed outside their territorial jurisdiction. Nevertheless, there are some important exceptions to this general rule. The Criminal Justice (Terrorism and Conspiracy) Act 1998 ss. 5–8 confer on English and Welsh courts the jurisdiction to try conspiracies to commit offences abroad if the qualifying conditions are met. The Criminal Justice Act 1993 Part I confers jurisdiction on English and Welsh courts in respect of certain offences of fraud and dishonesty (and the inchoate offences linked with them) provided that any of the relevant events occurred in England and Wales. Widespread disgust over the phenomenon known as 'sex tourism' led to the enactment of the Sexual Offences (Conspiracy and Incitement) Act 1996 which confers jurisdiction on British courts in respect of certain acts of incitement to commit sexual acts against children abroad. All offences committed in British territorial waters are triable by the British courts and under the Merchant Shipping Act 1995 s. 282, a crime committed ashore or afloat by a person who was employed as a master or seaman of a British ship is triable in Britain regardless of where it is committed. The Civil Aviation Act 1982 makes offences committed on British-controlled aircraft in flight elsewhere than over the UK, triable in Britain.

37 Anti-terrorism, Crime and Security Act 2001

Foreign nationals who are reasonably suspected by the Secretary of State for the Home Department of being international terrorists can be detained indefinitely under the provisions of ss. 21–23 without being charged with any offence, if they are certified as such. The Secretary of State must also believe that their presence in the UK is a risk to national security. However, there is provision for an appeal against certification in s. 25 and provision for bail in s. 24 but, in both cases, the application has to be made to the Special Immigration Appeals Commission. According to s. 29, ss. 21–23 automatically expire at the end of 15 months from the date of the Royal Assent but they can be renewed annually by statutory instrument passed under the affirmative resolution procedure. Although on 16 December 2004 the House of Lords declared ss. 21–23 to be incompatible with the Convention rights contained in the Human Rights Act 1998 Schedule 1, in *A (FC) and others (FC) (Appellants)* v *Secretary of State for the Home Department (Respondent)*, this, of itself, does not invalidate the statutory provisions.

■ Summary

This first chapter on the criminal justice system has focused mainly on police powers under the Police and Criminal Evidence Act 1984, which have been extended by the enactment of the Criminal Justice Act 2003. Although such powers are essential if the police are to be pro-active in combating crime and maintaining order, it is important to understand the limits of these powers. These limitations have been set out in some detail. Considerable space has been devoted to the arresting, detention, questioning and charging of suspects but, throughout, emphasis has been placed on the 'rights' of suspects whilst in police detention. For this reason excerpts from the new PACE Codes of Practice have been incorporated into the text as appropriate. Not everyone who is arrested and who admits guilt of a relatively minor offence is charged and subsequently prosecuted and so some space has been allocated to the alternatives to charging suspects, particularly the new conditional cautioning scheme introduced by the Criminal Justice Act 2003. The enhanced role of the Crown Prosecution Service has been considered in relation to the decision to charge and the formulation of the charge(s) although the decision whether or not to prosecute (with the exception of minor road traffic offences) has resided with the CPS since the coming into effect of the Prosecution of Offences Act 1985. It has been noted that there are a number of prosecuting authorities apart from the CPS, that some prosecutions require special consent and that certain persons have immunity from prosecution.

PROGRESS TEST

For suggested answers to the tests below, go to the companion website at
www.pearsoned.co.uk/wheeler

1 Under PACE 1984 s. 1, what is the main proviso that governs the
   power that police have to stop and search?
2 What limitations are imposed on a search that is conducted under
   s. 1?
3 What conditions must be met to justify police entering and searching
   premises under PACE 1984 s. 17?
4 If a police officer asks a person to accompany him/her to a police
   station to assist with an investigation, would it be necessary to caution
   that person if it was subsequently decided to arrest him/her at the
   police station, assuming he/she came willingly?
5 What does the phrase 'lay an information' mean and is there a time
   limit after which no action can be taken in respect of an information?
6 What are the three types of offence that, if committed, enable a constable to arrest without a warrant?
7 What powers of arrest does a constable have under the Public Order
   Act 1986, if any?
8 What powers of arrest are conferred by PACE 1984 on persons who
   are not police officers, if any?
9 What is the normal time limit for detention without charge and what
   limitations are imposed on extending this limit?
10 Who is responsible for deciding whether to charge a suspect and what
   the charge(s) will be?
11 What alternatives, if any, are there to charging a suspect?
12 What is the procedure for charging a suspect?
13 When would a decision not to prosecute be justified and would it still
   be subject to judicial review?
14 What is meant by 'immunity from prosecution' and who, if anyone,
   has it?
15 What jurisdiction, if any, do the English and Welsh courts have to try
   a person for a crime committed abroad?

FURTHER READING

■ Books

Cownie, F., A. Bradney and M. Burton (2003) *The English Legal System in Context* (Oxford: Oxford University Press, chapters 12–14).

Murphy, P. (ed.) (2005) *Blackstone's Criminal Practice* (Oxford: Oxford University Press).

Sprack, J. (2004) *A Practical Approach to Criminal Procedure* (Oxford: Oxford University Press).

■ Articles

Dennis, I. (2002) 'Silence in the police station: the marginalisation of s. 34', *Criminal Law Review* January, pp. 25–38.

Hucklesbury, A. (2004) 'Not necessarily a trip to the police station: the introduction of street bail', *Criminal Law Review* October, pp. 803–813.

Ormerod, D. and A. Roberts (2003) 'The Police Reform Act 2002', *Criminal Law Review* February, pp. 141–164.

USEFUL WEBSITES

The Metropolitan Police website can be located at www.met.police.uk and the Home Office website can be located at www.homeoffice.gov.uk/rds.

Useful information of the Crown Prosecution Service can be obtained from www.cps.gov.uk.

11 Criminal justice system 2

1 Introduction

Almost all criminal cases begin in magistrates' courts, even if they do not end there. The *Criminal Statistics for England and Wales* for 2003 (a not untypical year) indicate that magistrates' courts dealt with some 1.925 million cases. A minority of cases go to the Crown Court and, to appreciate why this should be so, it is necessary to understand the way in which criminal offences are categorised. This chapter therefore begins with the classification of criminal offences before dealing with summary trial procedure for adults. After that, the matter of remand and the related matter of bail will be considered. It will then be appropriate to describe trial on indictment for adults. The chapter concludes with an overview of sentencing and an outline of the system of appeals.

2 Classification of offences

Criminal Offences are normally classified according to their mode of trial. The Criminal Law Act 1977 s. 14 states that there are three types of offence, namely:

1 summary offences,
2 indictable only offences (serious offences triable only at the Crown Court), and
3 offences that are triable either way, that is summarily or on indictment.

Summary offences are classified as such by the statutes that define them but, in addition, a number of offences which, before the enactment of the Criminal Law Act 1977, were not classified as summary offences are now classed as such. These offences are generally regarded as the least serious and, with few exceptions, are always tried in a magistrates' court. Most motoring offences are summary offences but also included in this category are offences such as minor theft, common assault and threatening behaviour. The jurisdiction of a magistrates' court to try summary offences in its criminal justice area is set out in the Magistrates' Courts Act 1980 s. 2. According to the *Criminal Statistics for England and Wales* for 2003, approximately 73 per cent of all the cases tried in magistrates' courts were summary offences. The midway category between summary and indictable offences is the 'either way' category which accounts for the remainder of the cases tried in magistrates' courts. A number of offences come within this category such as assaults resulting in injury, theft and other offences of dishonesty, and burglary. If a person is charged with criminal damage, the Magistrates' Courts Act 1980 s. 22 applies. In general, if the damage to the property does not exceed £5,000 the magistrates are obliged to try the offence summarily. If it exceeds this sum, then they must determine the mode of trial in the usual way.

3 The initial appearance

As indicated in the previous chapter, an accused person appears before a magistrates' court either because:

(i) He/she was arrested without warrant and charged at a police station having then been bailed to appear at court on a specified day; or

(ii) as in (i) above, except that instead of being bailed from a police station he/she was held in police custody prior to being brought to court; or

(iii) he/she is responding to a summons issued by a magistrates' court following the laying of an information before a justices' clerk to answer the allegation contained in the information; or

(iv) under the Criminal Justice Act 2003 s. 29 public prosecutors (who may not lay an information to obtain a summons) have issued a written charge with a 'requisition' addressed to the accused requiring him/her to appear before a magistrates' court to answer the charge; or

(v) the magistrates have issued a warrant at the behest of the police (or other public prosecutor) for the arrest of the accused so that he/she can be brought before the court.

In (v) above, the warrant may be 'backed for bail' so that the accused is first arrested and then released on bail on condition that he/she attend court on the date specified as well as comply with any 'extra' bail conditions imposed. If the accused wishes to plead guilty to a minor offence and magistrates take the view that they do not need a pre-sentence report prior to passing sentence, they can dispose of the case then and there. It should be noted that a number of persons charged with lesser motoring offences often do not wish to attend court simply to plead guilty. Where the accused does not wish to contest the charge and also does not wish to attend court in order to plead guilty, he/she may plead guilty by post under the provision of the Magistrates' Courts Act 1980 s. 12 as amended. Statutory instrument SI 1999 No. 1149 (L.12) contains the procedure for doing so. This procedure applies to proceedings by way of summons in an adult magistrates' court for motoring offences. If, however, the sentence would result in the accused having 12 or more points endorsed on his/her licence, a court appearance will be necessary if there is to be a disqualification from driving. Ultimately, offering the option of pleading by post is at the discretion of the prosecution and, if permitted, the CPS will inform the clerk of the court that the summons has been served. The defendant must then notify the clerk in writing if he/she desires to plead guilty without attending the court. However, the majority of cases cannot be disposed of that quickly. The Magistrates' Courts Act 1980 ss. 5, 10 and 18 confer on magistrates a general discretion to adjourn a case at any stage. An accused person intending to plead 'not guilty' will often seek an adjournment from the court. He/she will do so in order to have time to consult a solicitor, to apply for legal aid through the Legal Services Commission and to have some time to prepare a defence. The Crown Prosecution Service (CPS) may also need time to prepare for a trial and/or to ensure that the necessary witnesses are available.

4   Remanding the accused

If the offence is a summary one and the magistrates' court grants an adjournment before trial, the court has discretion to adjourn *without* remanding the accused. If the offence is triable either way and the accused has not been remanded previously and appears in answer to a summons, the court also has discretion not to remand when adjourning. A remand only occurs where the court adjourns the case and either bails the accused for the duration of the adjournment or commits him/her to custody to be brought before the court on the adjournment date. Where the accused is remanded, the adjournment date must be fixed straightaway because this is the date to which the accused is remanded. There is no discretion to adjourn without a remand in respect of:

(a)   offences triable only on indictment, and
(b)   offences triable either way where the prosecution was commenced by way of charge.

Here the magistrates *must* remand the accused by either granting him/her bail or remanding him/her in custody. The difference between adjourning without remand and adjourning with a remand but granting bail is that, in the former, no adverse consequences follow from the accused failing to appear on the adjournment date except that it is likely that the offence will be proved in his/her absence. In the latter instance, the accused is under a legal obligation to appear and will commit an offence in the event that he/she fails to do so without reasonable cause. It is only in the least serious cases that magistrates adjourn without remanding the accused. The decision of the Divisional Court in *R* v *Nottingham Justices ex p. Davies* [1981] received statutory confirmation in the Bail Act 1976 Schedule 1 para. 11A. The result is that the defence is allowed a maximum of two argued bail applications before magistrates unless there has been a change in the circumstances of the accused.

According to the Magistrates' Courts Act 1980 s. 128(6) the maximum period that a magistrates' court can remand in custody is eight days although this is subject to certain exceptions and, in specified circumstances, the accused can be remanded in custody for up to three weeks. A remand on bail can exceed eight days. Where the accused is unable to appear or be brought before the courts at the end of the remand period because he/she is ill or has had an accident, the magistrates can remand him/her in his/her absence to a convenient date. Where an accused person is brought before a magistrates' court after an earlier remand, the court can remand him/her again. If the court remands an accused following a conviction in order to have reports prepared on him/her, the period of the remand must not exceed three weeks in custody or four weeks on bail. Under the new s. 128A an accused may be remanded in custody for up to 28 days if he/she is already serving a custodial sentence for some other offence. The Crime and Disorder Act 1998 s. 57 makes it possible for pre-trial hearings involving persons remanded in custody to be conducted over a live TV link between the prison and the court. Although magistrates' courts are not compelled to use this facility where it exists they must give reasons for not making use of it.

5   Right to bail

The Bail Act 1976 confers a right to bail except in specified circumstances. Thus an accused person may be granted bail unconditionally in which case he/she is only obliged to surrender to custody at the specified time and place in the bail notice. However, a person may be refused bail in the circumstances set out in Schedule 1 Part II paras 2–6. The usual grounds that are relied upon when bail is refused are:

(a)   there is a risk that further offences will be committed, or
(b)   there is a risk of non-attendance at trial, or
(c)   there is a risk of interference with witnesses.

In so far as it is necessary to reduce these risks, a court may impose conditions on the granting of bail such as:

(a)   residence at a home address or bail hostel, and/or
(b)   reporting to a particular police station on specific dates and at specified times, or
(c)   prohibitions on the contact with witnesses, or visiting certain places.

In addition to the above, occasionally a deposit of security or the guarantee of sureties may be required to guarantee attendance at court on pain of paying the forfeiture of a specific sum of money. Nevertheless, the presumption in favour of bail prevails and the Criminal Justice Act 2003 s. 13 has amended para. 3 of Part II of Schedule 1 to the Bail Act 1976 to give effect to the recommendations of the Law Commission to ensure compliance with the Convention rights embodied in the Human Rights

Act 1998. The amendment refers to persons that have been arrested but have been granted bail, and then have been arrested for failure to answer to bail. Bail may only be refused by the court if it is satisfied that there are substantial reasons for believing that, if granted bail, the accused would:

• fail to surrender to custody, or
• commit an offence whilst on bail, or
• interfere with witnesses, or
• otherwise obstruct the course of justice.

However, the Criminal Justice Act 2003 s. 14 does require a court to refuse bail to an adult accused who was on bail at the time he/she committed the alleged offence unless the court is satisfied that there is no significant risk that he/she would commit an offence if released on bail. As regards persons under the age of 18 who commit offences whilst on bail, particular weight can be attached to the fact of further offending when a court is deciding whether they would be likely to re-offend if granted bail. The Criminal Justice Act 2003 s. 15(1) requires a court to refuse bail to an adult who fails without reasonable cause to surrender to custody on the date specified in the bail notice unless it is satisfied that there is no significant risk that he/she would fail to do so again if granted bail. Similar considerations apply to persons under the age of 18 as set out in subsection (2). A new right of appeal has been created by the Criminal Justice Act 2003 s. 16 whereby an accused can appeal against the imposition of certain bail conditions imposed by magistrates to the granting of bail.

If no application for bail is made and the accused has been held in custody, the court will tend to assume that there are sufficient reasons for remanding the accused in custody although there is a limit to the time that an accused can be remanded in custody. The CPS can oppose an application for bail but reasons must be given to the court. These could include the seriousness of the charge, that the accused's previous record makes it likely that he/she will receive a custodial sentence if convicted and/or that he/she is appearing before the courts on other charges and the present offence was committed whilst on bail. The advocate representing the defendant may then attempt to counter the objections put forward by the CPS. Having heard the arguments for and against and the evidence, if any, the court will announce its decision, giving reasons.

In most cases, an accused person who has been refused bail by a magistrates' court can make a further application to the Crown Court. If magistrates do grant bail, the prosecution can appeal against this decision to the Crown Court where the accused has been charged with any imprisonable offence. For a more detailed treatment of the law relating to bail applications, see *A Practical Approach to Criminal Procedure*, Chapter 6.

SUMMARY TRIAL FOR ADULTS

It should be noted at the outset that the trial of the accused (irrespective of whether it be summary or on indictment) cannot proceed without pre-trial disclosure of information. The prosecution has a statutory obligation under the Criminal Procedure and Investigations Act 1996, as amended by the Criminal Justice Act 2003, of disclosure to the defence. In addition, the Guidelines on Disclosure of Information in Criminal Proceedings issued by the Attorney General's Office are also to be observed. The aim of the Act is to ensure a fair trial and there are two aspects to the statutory obligation, namely:

(a) a duty to notify the defence of the evidence upon which the prosecution intend to rely; and

(b) a duty to make available to the defence any relevant material upon which they do not intend to rely.

The accused is now required to set out the nature of his/her defence including any particular defences on which he/she intends to rely as well as indicating any point(s) of law that will be raised.

6 Conduct of a summary trial

Even though the accused is charged with a summary offence it may be necessary to have a pre-trial review to ensure that both prosecution and defence are prepared. The trial itself commences after the magistrates (or district judge) are seated and the accused enters the dock. The layout of a modern magistrates' court can be seen in Figure 11.1. The court clerk, having asked the accused to confirm his/her name, date of birth and address from the dock, reads out the charge(s) and may ask whether the accused understands the charge(s). An interpreter may stand in the dock next to the accused, if his command of English is poor. The accused is then asked by the court clerk to plead in relation to a written charge known as 'the information'. It is a well-established convention that the charge sheet completed at the police station and transmitted to the court is regarded as 'the information'. As with a count on an indictment, an information may allege only one offence. There may, however, be more than one information to which the accused is asked to plead. One may allege a more serious offence and the other a lesser offence. The only pleas that can be entered in response to the information are 'guilty' or 'not guilty'. Even if the accused pleaded 'not guilty' at his/her initial appearance, he/she may subsequently change his/her plea to 'guilty'. If the accused pleads 'guilty' (as the majority do), the court will usually convict him/her without hearing the prosecution evidence. However, the court will hear a brief summary of the facts from the prosecution advocate. At the end of this summary the prosecution will give details of any relevant previous convictions and ask for an award of costs and forfeiture of a vehicle or drugs, if appropriate, as

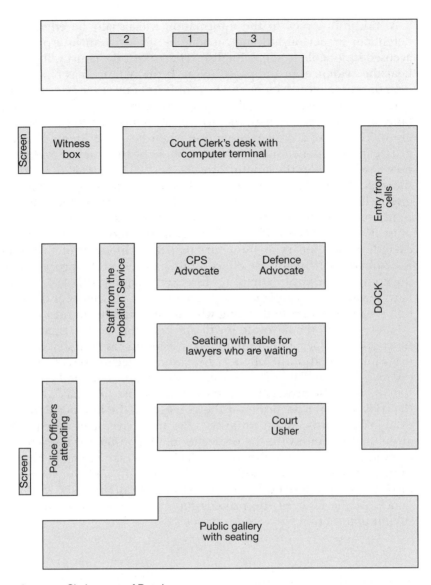

1   Chairperson of Bench
2 and 3   Other magistrates

Figure 11.1 **Layout of magistrates' court with 'live' video link**

permitted by the Powers of the Criminal Courts (Sentencing) Act 2000. The court will hear a plea in mitigation from the defence if the accused is legally represented and the defence may ask for an adjournment for the bench to consider a pre-sentence report and alternatives to custody. The magistrates may retire to confer. They may then adjourn the case before sentencing so that a pre-sentence report on the offender can be prepared, enabling the court to take into account all relevant matters before making the decision on sentence.

A 'not guilty' plea to the information will usually be entered by the defendant in person although it may be given by an interpreter if the accused is not able to speak English. Thereafter, the court will proceed to hear the evidence for the prosecution. If the defence has objected to an item of prosecution evidence (e.g. a confession or other evidence which it is alleged was obtained illegally) the magistrates must consider its admissibility as a preliminary issue before the evidence for the prosecution is given. They have a limited discretion when dealing with an objection to prosecution evidence since they must abide by the rules of evidence. It is now possible under the Criminal Justice Act 2003 s. 101(1) for evidence of the defendant's bad character (including previous convictions) to be given where it is considered relevant to the offence with which he/she currently stands charged. However, s. 101(3) makes it clear that the court must not admit such evidence if, on an application by the defendant to exclude it, it appears to the court that the admission of this evidence would have such an adverse effect on the fairness of the proceedings that the court ought not to admit it. Moreover, under s. 101(4) a court must have regard to the age of the evidence of bad character that the prosecution seek to produce in deciding whether it would be unjust to allow it.

At the outset, the advocate for the prosecution has the right to make a short opening speech outlining the prosecution case but in a trial of relatively minor road traffic offences he/she may decide to dispense with an opening address. The defence will normally have obtained copies of the statements of the prosecution witnesses and a case summary in advance of the trial. Thus the advocate for the defence will be in a position to cross-examine the prosecution witnesses after they have been called and have given their testimony for the prosecution. Oral testimony is given on oath or by affirmation where the witness declines to take the oath. Young children give their evidence without taking an oath and the statements of those witnesses whose evidence is not disputed can simply be read into evidence. At the close of the prosecution case, the defence advocate may submit that there is 'no case to answer'.

7   A submission of 'no case'

The test to be applied by magistrates when such a submission is made is to be found in Practice Direction (Submission of No Case) [1962] 1 WLR 227 which states that the submission may be properly made and upheld when:

(a)   no evidence has been produced to prove an essential element in the alleged offence, or

(b)   the evidence adduced by the prosecution has been so discredited as a result of cross-examination or is so manifestly unreliable that no reasonable tribunal could safely convict upon it.

Where the submission is made, the clerk, in guiding the court on matters of law, should draw the attention of the magistrates to the Practice

Direction. If the magistrates do decide to uphold the submission, the accused is discharged – otherwise the trial will continue.

8 The defence

According to the Magistrates' Courts Rules 1981 r. 13 paras (2)–(6) the defence advocate is entitled to call evidence and make a speech after calling all the evidence for the defence. If the defence advocate calls evidence, the prosecution may call evidence to rebut that evidence. The accused may give evidence on his/her own behalf but cannot be compelled to do so and the prosecution may cross-examine an accused who does give evidence. Although the prosecution advocate has no right to make a closing speech, he/she will normally be permitted to address the court on any point of law raised in the speech for the defence. If the prosecution is permitted to make a second speech, the defence advocate must be permitted to make a closing speech thereby giving the defence the final word.

An accused who is unrepresented on his/her arrival at court can avail himself/herself of the services of the 'duty solicitor' but the latter cannot act as an advocate for him/her. The court clerk may be able to help persons accused of relatively minor Road Traffic Act offences (driving without insurance and/or without a valid licence) who do not qualify for legal aid under the usual criteria. The clerk may give advice on the presentation of the case for the defence but the clerk should not permit himself/herself to become an 'advocate' for the accused because his/her primary responsibility is to the court and for its efficient management. At the conclusion of the evidence for the prosecution, the accused may address the court in person irrespective of whether he/she subsequently calls evidence.

9 The verdict

Lay magistrates will usually retire to consider their verdict but they do so without the court clerk although the clerk may be called upon subsequently to assist with the drafting of the statement of reasons for their decision. The result of the magistrates' deliberations need not be unanimous but they may never return a verdict of guilty of a lesser charge where there is only one information. Thus they must either convict or acquit the accused of the offence charged in the information. However, under the Road Traffic Offenders Act 1988 s. 24, magistrates may return an alternative verdict and thus acquit on the offence charged but convict of another lesser offence. Where the verdict is 'guilty', the magistrates will then sentence the offender but may adjourn the case for a pre-sentence report and/or a medical report. If there is an adjournment for reports prior to sentencing following a summary conviction, the defendant must be remanded either on bail or in custody. District judges of magistrates' courts tend to deliver their verdict at the conclusion of the case for the defence. Since the coming into operation of the Human Rights Act 1998, both magistrates and district judges must give reasons for their decisions.

EITHER WAY OFFENCES

10 Summary trial or trial on indictment?

The court cannot proceed to determine the mode of trial unless the defence has been given advance information about the prosecution case or has waived its right to this advance information (but this is unlikely in practice). The Magistrates' Courts (Advance Information) Rules 1985 (SI 1985 No. 601) r. 5 requires that the prosecution provide copies of all written statements as to the facts and a summary of the facts and matters the prosecution intends to produce as evidence in the proceedings. The Criminal Justice Act 2003 s. 41 has amended the Magistrates' Courts Act 1980 in respect of the allocation of offences triable 'either way' and for the sending of cases to the Crown Court that need to be tried on indictment. On appearing in court the charge(s) will be read out to the accused. He/she will be asked whether or not he/she wishes to *indicate* a plea, that is, to say whether he/she will plead 'guilty or 'Not guilty'. He/she can choose not to do this, and give no indication and ask for an adjournment. This procedure, known as 'plea before venue', can now take place before one magistrate sitting alone in court (albeit assisted by the court clerk). Although this lone magistrate can take a 'guilty plea', he/she may not conduct a contested trial nor may he/she impose a sentence on the offender. According to the new s. 19 inserted into the Magistrates' Courts Act 1980, the matters to be attended to by magistrates *before* deciding whether the offence would be more suitable for summary trial or trial on indictment are as follows:

(a) the prosecution is to be given an opportunity to inform the court of the accused's previous convictions (if any), and

(b) the prosecution and the accused are to have an opportunity to make representations as to whether summary trial or trial on indictment would be more suitable.

Then, in making the actual decision under s.19, the court is required to consider:

(a) whether the sentence which a magistrates' court would have power to impose for the offence would be adequate, and

(b) any representations made by the prosecution or accused regarding this matter, together with the guidelines issued under the Criminal Justice Act 2003 s. 170 by the Sentencing Guidelines Council.

Where a magistrates' court decides that the case is suitable for summary trial, it must follow the procedure set out in the new s. 20(2) and explain to the accused in ordinary language:

(a) that it appears to the court that a summary trial is more suitable;
(b) that he/she can consent to be tried summarily, or, if he/she wishes, be tried on indictment at the Crown Court;
(c) that if he/she is tried summarily and convicted of a 'specified offence' (serious violent offence or sexual offence) he/she may be committed to the Crown Court under the Powers of the Criminal Courts (Sentencing) Act 2000 s. 3A.

In making his/her decision, the accused is likely to be influenced to some degree by the knowledge that once the magistrates have accepted jurisdiction it is generally no longer possible to be committed for sentence to the Crown Court (except as indicated in (c) above). Consequently, the accused cannot receive a sentence that is beyond the magistrates' sentencing powers. Nevertheless, rates of acquittal on 'not guilty pleas' are significantly higher in jury trials, and some defendants may feel they will receive a fairer hearing before a jury than before magistrates. Ultimately, the accused is free to choose – summary trial or trial on indictment. According to the White Paper *Justice for All*, in 2000 (a not untypical year) 87 per cent of either way cases were tried by magistrates, with 13 per cent going to the Crown Court – 9 per cent because the magistrates declined jurisdiction and 4 per cent because the accused elected for trial by jury. With the increase in sentencing powers of magistrates' courts introduced by the Criminal Justice Act 2003, it is likely that magistrates will accept jurisdiction in a greater number of these cases in future.

If the accused is actively considering the option of a summary trial, he/she (usually through his/her advocate) may request an indication from the magistrates whether, if he/she pleads 'guilty', the sentence would be custodial or not. A magistrates' court has discretion whether to give such an indication to an accused who asks for one. If an indication is given, the accused will be given the opportunity to reconsider his/her original *indication* as to his/her plea. Should the accused then decide to plead 'guilty', a magistrates' court will then proceed to sentence. It should be noted that a custodial sentence will only be available if such a sentence was indicated when an 'indication of sentence' was sought or where the offence is a 'specified offence' as defined in the Criminal Justice Act 2003. If the accused pleads 'not guilty', the trial proceeds as a summary trial.

11 Committal proceedings – preliminary matters

Where a person accused of an either way offence opts for trial on indictment at the Crown Court, a magistrates' court will institute committal proceedings, its jurisdiction to do so being conferred by the Magistrates' Courts Act 1980 s. 2(3). Committal proceedings will also be instituted if, after due consideration, a magistrates' court has decided that trial on indictment would be more suitable than summary trial. Where the court decides in favour of trial on indictment, it is obliged by the Magistrates' Courts Act 1980 s. 21 to inform the accused of that decision. It should be noted that committal proceedings are never conducted in respect of 'indictable only' offences by virtue of the Crime and Disorder Act 1998 s. 51. The accused is sent directly to the Crown Court after a brief appearance and preliminary hearing at a magistrates' court at which he/she will either be remanded in custody or remanded on bail. If there is a remand on bail the accused will be reminded that he/she will be committing an offence if he/she does not attend the Crown Court on the date specified in the bail notice.

12   Committal proceedings – the procedure

Although a lone lay magistrate may conduct committal proceedings under the Magistrates' Courts Act 1980 s. 4(1), it is more usual for committal proceedings to be conducted by a bench of three magistrates. They inquire into the information as 'examining justices' in exercise of their jurisdiction under s. 2 to decide whether to commit for trial. In doing so, they follow the Magistrates' Courts Rules 1981 and decide on the basis of the test laid down in the Magistrates' Courts Act 1980 s. 6. Shortly after entering the dock, the accused will have been informed of the charge(s) and it is for the court to decide whether to conduct a committal hearing with consideration of the evidence or one without any consideration of the evidence. It will adopt the former approach where it is aware that the accused has no legal representative acting for him/her in the case or that the accused's legal representative has requested the court to consider a submission that there is insufficient evidence to put the accused on trial by jury.

According to the Magistrates' Courts Rules 1981 r. 7 the prosecution advocate will outline the case for the prosecution and explain any relevant points of law that require explanation before presenting the evidence, all of which is documentary. Rather than present the documentary evidence in the form of witness statements in full, the court may consent to the evidence being summarised, after which it may view any original exhibits. Although no evidence can be called for the defence at this stage, the accused (normally through his/her advocate) can make a submission of 'no case to answer'. If such a submission is made, the prosecutor is entitled to respond and the court must then make its decision whether to commit the accused for trial or not. According to the Magistrates' Courts Act 1980 s. 6(1), magistrates must commit if they are of the opinion that there is sufficient evidence to put the accused on trial by jury for any indictable offence. If this test cannot be satisfied, they must discharge the accused unless he/she is in custody for some other matter. It should be noted that a discharge at the committal stage does not amount to an 'acquittal' and it would be possible for the person concerned to be prosecuted in future on the same charge(s). The Magistrates' Courts Act 1980 s. 6(2) makes it possible for magistrates to commit the accused for trial at the Crown Court without any consideration of the evidence provided certain conditions are satisfied. The necessary conditions are as follows:

(a) all the evidence before the court must consist of written statements tendered under s. 5A(3);

(b) the accused must have a solicitor acting for him in the case although he need not necessarily be present in court; and

(c) the barrister/solicitor acting for the accused must not have requested the justices to consider a submission that the statements disclose insufficient evidence to put the accused on trial by jury for the offence(s).

If there are two or more accused, each must have a solicitor acting for him/her and a submission for any of them of 'insufficient evidence' will preclude a committal without consideration of the evidence. If the committal is to be conducted without consideration of the evidence, the clerk to the court will ask the barrister/solicitor appearing for the defence whether he agrees to a s. 6(2) committal and the advocate for the CPS whether the Crown is ready for a trial. If the replies are affirmative, the clerk will indicate a date for the initial appearance at the Crown Court. Where there is an application for bail this must be dealt with. If bail is refused, the magistrates must indicate why it is being refused and will remand the accused in custody until trial. Otherwise the accused will be remanded on bail to appear at the Crown Court on the date indicated. If conditions are attached to bail, these will be read out in court and reasons given for the conditions imposed.

TRIAL ON INDICTMENT OF AN ADULT

13 Pre-trial disclosure of information

According to the Criminal Procedure and Investigations Act 1996 s. 3, as amended by the Criminal Justice Act 2003, the prosecution must:

> ... disclose to the accused any prosecution material which has not previously been disclosed to the accused and which might reasonably be considered capable of undermining the case for the prosecution against the accused, or of assisting his/her case. Where material consists of information which has been recorded in any form, the prosecution discharges its obligation of disclosure for the purpose of the section either:
>
> **(a)** by securing that a copy is made of it and that the copy is given to the accused, or
>
> **(b)** if in the prosecutor's opinion that is not practicable or not desirable, by allowing the accused to inspect it at a reasonable time and a reasonable

place or by taking steps to secure that he is allowed to do so and a copy may be in such form as the prosecutor thinks fit and need not be in the same form as that in which the information has already been recorded.

Following disclosure by the prosecution, the court may then make an order for defence disclosure either of its own motion or on the application of any party so that a detailed written defence statement is available to the court, the prosecution and any co-accused. The accused is now required to set out the nature of his/her defence (including any particular defences on which he/she intends to rely) and indicate any point of law that he/she wishes to pursue. If the accused intends to rely on an alibi defence the details of alibi witnesses must now include details of an alibi witness's date of birth as well as the name and address of the alibi. In addition, the defence statement must indicate any facts on which the accused takes issue with the prosecution (together with the reasons for taking issue) and matters relating to the admissibility of evidence and abuse of process issues. If necessary an updated defence statement should be provided immediately prior to trial but, if there is nothing to add to the earlier statement, he/she may give a statement to that effect. It should be noted that a defence statement served on behalf of the accused by his/her solicitor is deemed to have been given on the authority of the accused unless the contrary is proved. A new s. 6C has been inserted into the Criminal Procedure and Investigations Act 1996 which imposes a requirement on the accused to serve, before trial, a notice giving details of any witness (name, address and date of birth) he/she intends to call to give evidence. If an address is not known, the accused must provide any information that might assist in identifying or finding the witness. An amended notice must be submitted if the accused subsequently decides to call a witness who is not included in the notice or decides not to call someone who is on the list. A new s. 6D imposes a new requirement on the accused, namely the obligation to serve before trial a notice for each expert witness, giving the name and address, but if this information has been provided under s. 6C it is not necessary to replicate it. The prosecution is now under a continuing duty under the new s. 7A to disclose unused material until such time as the accused is either acquitted or convicted and must keep under review whether there is any material that meets the new disclosure test set out in s. 3. Moreover, should the accused have reasonable cause to believe that there is prosecution material that should have been disclosed but has not been, he/she may apply to the court for an order of disclosure.

14 Evidence of the defendant's bad character

As indicated previously, the Criminal Justice Act 2003 s. 101(1) makes it possible for evidence of the defendant's bad character to be admissible in criminal proceedings if, but only if:

(a) all parties to the proceedings agree to the evidence being admissible,

(b) the evidence is adduced by the defendant himself or is given in answer to a question asked by him in cross-examination and intended to elicit it,

(c) it is important explanatory evidence,

(d) it is relevant to an important matter in issue between the defendant and the prosecution,

(e) it has substantial probative value in relation to an important matter in issue between the defendant and a co-defendant,

(f) it is evidence to correct a false impression given by the defendant, or

(g) the defendant has made an attack on another person's character.

Sections 102 to 106 contain provisions supplementing subsection (1) in which the terminology used therein is further defined. Nevertheless, it is clear from subsection (3) that the court must not admit evidence under subsection (1)(d) or (g) if, on an application by the defendant to exclude it, it appears to the court that the admission of the evidence would have such an adverse effect on the fairness of the proceedings that the court ought not to admit it. Moreover, subsection (4) provides that on an application to exclude evidence under subsection (3) the court must have regard, in particular, to the length of time between the matters to which that evidence relates and the matters which form the subject matter of the offence charged.

15   Plea bargaining prior to trial

It is by no means unusual for the prosecution and defence to reach agreement outside court prior to the trial. The essence of such an agreement is likely to be that if the accused pleads guilty to some of the counts on the indictment or if he/she pleads guilty to a lesser offence, as permitted by the Criminal Law Act 1967 s. 6, the Crown will not seek to prove him/her guilty as charged in the indictment. Where the accused has agreed to plead guilty to some of the counts but not guilty to other counts, the prosecution will adopt one of two courses of action. Either, the prosecution will offer no evidence on the latter counts in which case a formal verdict of 'not guilty' will be entered on the judge's order or the prosecution will ask the judge to leave these latter counts on the file, marked 'not to be proceeded with' without the permission of the court or Court of Appeal. Leaving those counts on the file to which the accused has pleaded 'not guilty' avoids the need for an expensive trial and also avoids actually acquitting the accused in respect of those counts. Ultimately, it is for the prosecution to decide what pleas are acceptable although the views of the trial judge will frequently be sought. If the judge disapproves, the prosecution will undoubtedly wish to reconsider its position. This reconsideration will take place in the knowledge that the judge may decline to proceed with the case unless and until the prosecution consults with the DPP on whether he/she should proceed in the light of the judge's comments. If a plea of 'guilty' to a lesser offence is acceptable, no evidence will be presented by the prosecution on the more serious charge and the defendant will stand acquitted of this offence; the court will proceed to sentencing him/her for the lesser offence once he/she enters a guilty plea.

16   Meetings between advocates and judge

Subject to the judge's agreement, the advocates for the parties may see the judge privately in his/her room before (or during) the trial on a matter relating to the case. The most usual reasons for such a meeting are to obtain guidance about the appropriate pleas and the likely sentence. However, it is possible that the advocate for the defence may wish to see the judge to discuss other relevant matters that, in the interests of justice, should not be dealt with in open court. Since such meetings can give rise to misunderstandings and may occasionally be open to abuse, the Court of Appeal in *R* v *Turner* [1970] laid down certain guidelines for such private meetings. Although the Court of Appeal confirmed that there must be freedom of access between the defence advocate and the judge, any discussion that takes place must be between the judge and both advocates (prosecution and defence). Moreover, the advocate for the defence should only ask to see the judge privately when he/she considers that this is really necessary. For his/her part, the judge should not indicate in private that he/she would be likely to impose one sentence following a 'guilty' plea but that on conviction following a not guilty plea he/she would impose a more severe sentence. Were this to happen, this could put the accused under pressure to plead guilty and effectively deprive him/her of his/her essential freedom of choice over the pleas to be entered to the count(s) on the indictment. By way of exception to this rule, a judge may indicate that irrespective of whether the accused pleads guilty or not guilty the sentence will, or will not, take a particular form. If it is made clear to the accused that he/she will not face a custodial sentence, this may encourage him/her to plead guilty and avoid the expense of a jury trial. If the judge does give an indication of the sentence that he/she will impose, he/she cannot later change his/her mind and seek to impose a different sentence.

17   The indictment

An indictment is a document containing the charges against the accused which always follows a standard layout. The word 'indictment' always appears as a heading. Since most prosecutions on indictment are stated to be in the person of the Crown, this is signified by the letter *R* (denoting the person of the monarch using the Latin *Regina*) followed by the letter *v* (in lower case) after which the name or names of the accused appear. An example might be as follows: *R* v *Algernon Fortescue Green and Ernest*

Claude Pink. The person or persons who are named at the beginning of the indictment are named again in that part of the document known as the 'presentment', in which it is stated that they 'are charged as follows'. The 'count' or 'counts' then appear. These are the offences alleged against the accused but each count can only allege one offence. A 'count' comprises the statement of the offence followed by the basic details including the date on which the offence is alleged to have been committed. An indictment may contain two or more counts against the accused. The Administration of Justice (Miscellaneous Provisions) Act 1933 s. 2(1) states that an indictment must be signed by a proper officer of the Crown Court, who shall only sign it if he/she is satisfied that the requirements of s. 2(2) of the Act have been complied with. This subsection enacts that no bill of indictment may be preferred unless the accused has been committed for trial or a notice of transfer has been given to the relevant magistrates' court or a High Court judge has directed or consented to the preferment of a voluntary bill of indictment or the Court of Appeal has ordered a retrial. The ultimate responsibility for the drafting of the indictment resides with the prosecution, who are required to ensure that it is in proper form prior to the arraignment of the accused. As well as being able to indict the accused for those offences for which he/she has been committed for trial and other indictable offences disclosed by the evidence, the drafter of the indictment can, under the Criminal Justice Act 1988 s. 40(1) include counts for certain summary offences. Summary offences such as common assault, driving whilst disqualified and taking a motor vehicle without the owner's consent may be based on the same facts as those for an offence for which the accused has been committed for trial for an indictable offence. If this should be so, then the CPS may, at its discretion, include as a count on the indictment, a summary offence. For a more detailed treatment of the counts that can be included on an indictment, see *Blackstone's Criminal Practice* Section D9. Specimen counts for all common indictable offences are to be found in Parts B and C.

18   Preparing for a plea and directions hearing

The Criminal Procedure and Investigations Act 1996 ss. 39 and 40 aim to promote the efficient conduct of trials on indictment. These sections consolidate and supplement the rules for Plea and Directions Hearings (hereafter PDH) that were set out in Practice Direction: Crown Court (Plea and Directions Hearings) [1995] 1 WLR 1318. According to para. 2 the 'purpose of the PDH will be to ensure that all necessary steps have been taken in preparation for trial and to provide sufficient information for a trial date to be arranged. It is expected that the advocate briefed to appear in the case will appear at the PDH wherever practicable.' The Practice Direction applies to all cases except serious fraud. A PDH is usually fixed for 28 days from committal but, for cases that are sent to the

Crown Court under the Crime and Disorder Act 1998 s. 51, the date is fixed eight days after the case is sent by the magistrates. If the defendant intends to plead 'guilty' to all or part of the indictment, the defence advocate must notify the probation service, the prosecution and the court as soon as this is known. Prior to the commencement of a PDH a detailed questionnaire, as set out in the Practice Direction para. 10(a)–(r), has to be completed (as far as possible with the agreement of the advocates for both sides) and sent to the court. The defence must supply the court and prosecution with a full list of the prosecution witnesses they require to attend the trial, at least 14 days before the PDH where the defendant intends to plead 'not guilty' to some or all of the counts on the indictment. For all class 1 offences and for lengthy and complex cases, the prosecution should prepare a case summary for use by the judge at the PDH. In addition, the Practice Direction requires that the prosecution should scrutinise all class 2 offences to decide whether a case summary should also be provided for the judge at the PDH.

19   The plea and directions hearing

The PDH itself will be held in open court and can be conducted by a judge who will not be the eventual trial judge. It is normal for the arraignment of the defendant to take place at the PDH and it is therefore essential that the defendant is present so that the arraignment can take place. If the defendant is absent, the judge will adjourn the proceedings and will issue a bench warrant for his/her arrest under the Bail Act 1976 s. 7 unless the reason for absence is illness. If the defendant has been remanded in custody, he/she will be brought to court for the arraignment. The procedure commences with the clerk reading out the counts on the indictment to the defendant, asking him/her whether he/she pleads 'guilty' or 'not guilty'. Should there be a number of counts on the indictment, a plea must be taken on each one separately as soon as it is read out in court. If it is known that the accused intends to plead 'guilty' to one of two alternative counts, that count should be put to him/her first, irrespective of whether it is first on the indictment. Where there is a joint indictment against several accused, it is usual to arraign them together and separate pleas must be obtained from each of those named in a joint count. Where an accused, who is not suffering from a mental or physical disability, remains wilfully silent on arraignment or fails to give a direct answer to the charge, the court will enter a plea of 'not guilty' on his/her behalf.

If the defendant pleads 'guilty', the Practice Direction para. 9 states that the judge should proceed to sentencing whenever possible. If two persons are charged in a single indictment but one pleads 'guilty' whilst the other pleads 'not guilty', it is usual for the judge to adjourn the case of the person who has pleaded 'guilty'. He/she will be either remanded in custody or on bail until the conclusion of the trial of his/her co-accused.

If, however, the judge considers that he/she has enough information available on the accused who has pleaded 'guilty', the judge may sentence him/her straightaway following the 'guilty' plea.

Where the defendant pleads 'not guilty' (or where part or alternative pleas have not been accepted) the prosecution and defence must inform the court of the matters set out in the Practice Direction para.10 (a)–(r) as contained in the completed questionnaire that has been filed. These relate to matters such as the issues in the case, the number of witnesses, details of any alibi defence and points of law that it is anticipated will arise at the trial. The advocate for the defence should have warned the prosecution of any evidence to which the defence intends to object being called. This is usually, but by no means always, disputed confessions evidence. At the PDH the judge can make rulings on questions such as the admissibility of such evidence or on questions of law relating to the case. Although he/she may do so of his/her own motion, such rulings are usually made on the application of the advocates for the parties. Once such a ruling is made, it has binding effect but it may subsequently be varied or discharged if it is in the interests of justice to do so. It should be noted that the Criminal Justice Act 2003 s. 62 gives the prosecution a right of appeal against such evidentiary rulings. The Act has modified the law of evidence on the admissibility of hearsay in ss. 114–117 so that a far wider range of such evidence is now admissible than previously.

20   Trial on indictment without a jury

The Criminal Justice Act 2003 s. 43 has made it possible for trial on indictment for serious and complex fraud at the Crown Court to be conducted without a jury. An application must be made by the prosecution well in advance. The judge to whom the application is made must be satisfied that the length or complexity (or both) of the trial is likely to make it so onerous for the jury that the interests of justice require serious consideration to be given to conducting the trial without a jury. In the process of arriving at his/her decision, the judge is required to consider whether anything can be done to make the trial less complex and lengthy by using a preparatory hearing procedure. The Criminal Procedure and Investigations Act 1996 ss. 28–38 allow for preparatory hearings in long and complex cases. The Criminal Procedure and Investigations Act 1996 (Preparatory Hearings) Rules 1997 (SI 1997 No. 1052) set out deadlines for both defence and prosecution to apply for a preparatory hearing and establish the procedure for determining any such application. If a preparatory hearing has been convened in a serious fraud case, the defence may be ordered to supply a written statement setting out the nature of the defence with an indication of the principal matters on which it is proposed to take issue with the prosecution. There is no obligation, however, to disclose the names of the witnesses that they will be calling. If the judge is satisfied with the application made under s. 43, he/she has discretion to order that the trial should be conducted without a jury. Such an order requires the approval of the Lord Chief Justice or a judge nominated by him. In addition, the Criminal Justice Act 2003 s. 44 provides for trial on indictment without a jury where there is a 'real and present danger' of jury tampering. In this context, jury tampering is understood to mean actual or attempted harm or intimidation or bribery of a jury or any of its members. If there is a 'real and present danger' the prosecution can make an application for the trial to be conducted without a jury. If necessary, a preparatory hearing can be ordered to consider whether there should be a non-jury trial. Where a court orders a trial to be conducted without a jury, the trial proceeds in the usual way except that the trial judge will perform the function that would have been discharged by the jury. There is a safeguard provision in that, once a decision has been made, either the prosecution or the defence can appeal to the Court of Appeal against the determination made by a court at a preparatory hearing that the trial should be without a jury.

21 Empanelling the jury

If the accused pleads 'not guilty' to some or all of the counts on the indictment, a jury panel (comprising 20 or more potential jurors) will be brought into court by the usher. The names of the jury panel are selected at random from the electoral roll by computer and are contained on cards that are given to the clerk of the court. The clerk calls the names of the first 12 persons, who enter the jury box as their names are called. They take the oath individually or may elect to affirm that they will faithfully try the defendant and give a true verdict on the evidence presented. Just before each juror takes the oath or affirms, he/she can be objected to by the prosecution or defence under the provisions of the Juries Act 1974 s. 12(1)(b). Both prosecution and defence are able to challenge as many jurors as they wish provided they have good cause because certain classes of person are either disqualified or ineligible for jury service but this right is rarely used nowadays. In addition, the prosecution (but not the defence) can ask any juror to 'stand by' without being required to give a reason to the judge. Once 12 jurors have been sworn (or have affirmed), the trial commences. Once the trial is underway, the judge has discretion to discharge up to three jurors whilst allowing the trial to continue, with the remaining jurors giving their verdict at the end. A plea of 'not guilty' requires that the prosecution (usually the CPS) satisfies the jury beyond a reasonable doubt that the accused has committed the *actus reus* of the offence (or aided, abetted, counselled or procured its commission). The *actus reus* is the criminal act and, in addition to establishing this, the prosecution must normally establish beyond a reasonable doubt that the accused has the necessary 'intent' or state of mind required for the commission of the particular criminal act at the time, which is known as *mens rea*. There are, however, some offences of strict liability where there is no need for the prosecution to prove *mens rea*. Most of these offences are statutory and many arise in the context of the regulatory framework for the sale of food and drink. In addition, the prosecution is released from the obligation to prove each element of the offence (*actus reus* and *mens rea*) if the defence has made a formal admission under the Criminal Justice Act 1967 s. 10 or where a particular fact is either presumed or 'judicially noticed'.

22   Conduct of the trial

The prosecution must be legally represented and the prosecution advocate puts the case for the Crown. Although a trial on indictment is an adversarial affair, the advocate for the prosecution should not strive for a conviction, come what may. Instead, he/she should regard himself/herself as a 'minister of justice' whose principal task is to assist the court with the administration of justice. The accused will usually be legally represented and the advocate for the defence is entitled to use all his/her legal skills to obtain an acquittal. Thus he/she is not obliged to point out any flaw in the indictment or errors that would adversely affect the prosecution case which could easily be rectified. Nevertheless, he/she must not deceive or mislead the court. The judge's task is to remain above the fray and ensure that the necessary conditions prevail whereby the respective advocates can fulfil their duties fairly and properly. If the judge intervenes excessively and shows partiality towards the prosecution, the accused would be unlikely to receive a fair trial and the Court of Appeal would almost certainly quash a resulting conviction. However, a judge can intervene to prevent unnecessary repetition, to exclude irrelevant matter and to prevent the oppression of witnesses by either advocate. Although it is the jury who decide all issues of fact and the ultimate guilt or innocence of the accused, the judge determines all issues of law as they arise in the course of the trial.

23   The prosecution case

Once the clerk of the court has placed the accused in the jury's charge, the prosecution advocate will present an overview of the case for the Crown to the members of the jury. He/she will normally specify the charges against the accused and then explain any relevant points of law with which they are unlikely to be familiar. He/she must be careful to indicate that what is said in relation to points of law is intended only as a guide because it is for the judge to decide and rule on matters of law. The advocate will also inform the members of the jury that the prosecution must prove their case and that they, the jury, must be sure of the defendant's guilt. It must be made clear to them that if they are unsure whether the accused is guilty, they must acquit. Having done this, the prosecution advocate proceeds to summarise the evidence that he/she intends to call and, on the basis of the documentary evidence tendered at the committal proceedings, he/she will tell the jury the principal facts that he/she anticipates the prosecution witnesses will prove. In addition, he/she will attempt to show how the items of evidence link together to demonstrate beyond a reasonable doubt that the accused committed the offence(s) charged. Where the advocate for the defence has informed the prosecution that he/she intends to object to certain pieces of evidence, then that evidence must not be included in the prosecution's opening address to the jury unless the objection has been overruled at the PDH. The advocate for the prosecution will then call the witnesses whose names are said to appear on the reverse of the indictment, who will give oral testimony for the Crown.

24 Evidence and admissibility

The reader should refer to *Blackstone's Criminal Practice* for a detailed treatment of the law of evidence because a book of this size cannot cover this very important subject in any depth. Certain aspects of the law of evidence are mentioned because they are essential to an understanding of trial procedure.

Irrespective of whether they are appearing for the prosecution or defence, witnesses appearing in person should normally give their evidence orally in open court so that the jury can not only hear but can see the persons concerned and thereby decide from their general demeanour and body language how credible they are. As a result of the Criminal Justice Act 2003 s. 51 the court may now authorise witnesses (other than the accused/defendant) to give evidence through a live video link in certain criminal proceedings and, although the term 'live link' will normally mean a closed circuit television link, it could apply to new technology delivering the same capabilities. Where evidence is given by video link, the Criminal Justice Act 2003 s. 54 permits the judge to give direction to the jury, if necessary, to ensure that they give the same weight to evidence given through a live link as oral testimony given in court. The Criminal Procedure and Investigations Act 1996 Schedule 2 enables the prosecution to read in evidence undisputed statements tendered at the committal stage and the Magistrates' Courts Act 1980 s. 97A has an identical provision in relation to depositions tendered in evidence at the committal stage. Although the defence can object within 14 days of committal to the reading of a statement, under para. 1(4) of Schedule 2 the trial judge may overrule this objection if he/she considers it to be in the interests of justice to do so. Under the Children and Young Persons Act 1933 s. 42 a deposition taken out of court from a child or young person who was the victim of certain sexual or violent offences is admissible in evidence in a trial on indictment. The court must be satisfied on the basis of medical evidence that attendance before the court would involve serious danger to his/her life or health and the deposition is only admissible if the accused was given notice of the intention to take it. In addition he/she must be in a position to cross-examine the child or young person. When children give evidence, it is usually via a video link in the court building and their evidence in chief may be given by playing a video recording of their initial interview by the police.

The admissibility of written statements other than in committal proceedings is provided for by the Criminal Justice Act 1967 s. 9. If a statement is to be admissible it must be signed and contain a declaration that it is true to the best of the knowledge and belief of its maker. Thus, properly attested statements can be read to the jury as evidence so that there is no need to call a witness in person provided these statements are uncontroversial. Nevertheless, such statements are only admissible if there is no objection from either side but, even then, the trial judge could require the maker of the statement to attend court. Where a witness is too ill to attend court or is outside the UK and is unable to return, the Criminal Justice Act 1988 s. 23 provides that a statement in a document shall be admissible in evidence of any fact which the maker could give as direct oral testimony. This section also extends to deathbed declarations and confessions. The provisions of s. 23 are, however, subject to s. 25 which enables the trial judge to exclude such evidence.

As indicated above, the judge may have ruled on the admissibility of evidence to which the defence has objected at the PDH but it may not have been possible to resolve all issues of admissibility at the PDH stage. Once the prosecution has called all the evidence that is not the subject of an outstanding objection by the defence, the defence advocate will usually invite the judge to request that the jury leave the courtroom. After the jury has left, the defence advocate will make his/her objections to the prosecution evidence known to the judge and the prosecution advocate will reply. The judge will then make his/her ruling on admissibility. This procedure is referred to as a trial on the *voir dire* when it relates to admissibility of a confession and where the issue of admissibility cannot be decided without making prior determinations of fact. If the evidence is ruled inadmissible, the jury will not hear it but if it is ruled admissible, it will be called just as soon as the jury returns. The advocate for the defence will wish to cross-examine all those prosecution witnesses who have given oral testimony. Where prosecution witnesses have given evidence by live video link, the Criminal Justice Act 2003 s. 52 makes it clear that any cross-examination is to be by live video link. In cross-examining the defence advocate is free to ask any question provided it is relevant and provided the question will not elicit inadmissible material and non-expert opinion. A defence barrister must also observe the Bar Council's Code of Conduct, especially paras 5.10(e), 5.10(g) and 5.10(h), in cross-examining. Solicitor advocates must observe the corresponding rules in the Law Society's Code for Advocacy.

25   Submission of 'no case to answer'

Once the prosecution evidence has been heard, the prosecution advocate will indicate to the jury that the prosecution case is complete. At that point the advocate for the defence may submit that there is 'no case to answer'. A submission of 'no case to answer' will succeed if there is no evidence to prove an essential element of the offence. If there is some evidence which establishes each essential element of the offence, the case should be left to the jury but the judge does have a residual duty to consider whether the evidence is inherently weak or tenuous. If it is, such that no reasonable jury properly directed could convict on it, the submission of 'no case to answer' should be upheld. Although the question of whether a witness is lying is one for the jury, according to *Blackstone,* there may be exceptional cases where the inconsistencies in that person's evidence or between that person's evidence and other prosecution witnesses are so great that any reasonable tribunal would be forced to the conclusion that the witness is untruthful. Thus, in the absence of other evidence that is capable of founding a case, the judge should withdraw the case from the jury when the members of the jury return to the courtroom. If the submission of 'no case to answer' has been successful, the judge will briefly explain to the jury what has happened in their absence. One of them is asked to stand as foreman. On the judge's direction, he/she formally returns a verdict of 'not guilty' to each count on the indictment and the accused is free to leave the court. If the defence's submission is unsuccessful, the jury are not informed of what transpired in their absence and the case continues with the advocate for the defence presenting the defence case. The submission may have been partly successful in that the judge decided that there is a case to answer on some counts. If so, he/she will inform the jury that he/she will be directing them to return a verdict of 'not guilty' in respect of those counts (on which the submission was successful) and that for the remainder of the trial they should concentrate on the other counts on the indictment.

26   The case for the defence

The advocate for the defence has a right to make an opening speech only if he/she proposes to call evidence other than testimony from the accused. If he/she does intend to call witnesses other than the defendant, the advocate for the defence may give an overview of the defence case in terms of the testimony to be given by the witnesses and he/she may even criticise the evidence given for the prosecution. Although the defence should have given advance notice to the prosecution in the 'defence statement' at the disclosure stage relating to the defence of alibi, a failure to do so does not prevent the accused from relying on this defence. The defence of alibi is now governed by the Criminal Procedure and Investigations Act 1996 and is effectively defined by s. 5(8) which makes it clear that the evidence of alibi must be such that it establishes that the accused was at a place other than the place where the offence was committed. However, the accused must give the name and address of any witness who is believed to be able to give evidence to support the defence of alibi. Nevertheless, the advocate for the defence is required to consult with the accused before deciding to call alibi evidence and failure to do so will amount to a material irregularity which may result in a conviction being quashed on appeal.

The accused is not obliged to give evidence on his/her own behalf but if he/she chooses to do so, he/she is liable to be cross-examined by the advocate for the prosecution. If the accused is to give evidence, he/she will normally be called before any of the other defence witnesses. As a result of the Criminal Justice and Public Order Act 1994 s. 35 it is important that the accused should be advised whether or not to give evidence. If the accused decides not to give evidence he/she must be warned in public by the judge in the presence of the jury. The jury may then draw adverse conclusions from his/her failure to give evidence. Where the accused decides not to go into the witness box, the advocate for the defence should insist that the accused signs a statement on the brief to the effect that (1) he/she decided of his/her own accord not to testify and (2) that he/she made that decision bearing in mind the advice received, regardless of what it was; otherwise this could provide the basis for an appeal against conviction.

Once all the evidence has been given, it is usual for the jury to be escorted from the courtroom and for the judge to indicate his intentions as to summing up. The advocates then have the opportunity to address him/her on any matter which may be important to their closing speeches. When the jury return, the prosecution is able to make a closing speech after which the defence will make a closing speech.

In the comparatively rare event that the accused is not legally represented, the court will seek to assist him/her in conducting his/her defence and will explain his/her right to cross-examine witnesses and to give evidence himself/herself as well as call witnesses in his/her defence. Failure to do so may result in any conviction being quashed. There are, however, certain statutory restrictions on the right of an unrepresented accused to cross-examine witnesses. Unrepresented adult male defendants may not cross-examine children and women when accused of certain sexual offences against them.

27 The judge's summing up

The judge will remind the jury of the judge's role and their role and for this reason the summing up is in two stages. First, there is a direction from the judge on the law and secondly a summary of the evidence. Whilst the jury must accept what the judge says in relation to the law, it is they who are the judges of the facts as presented in evidence and they may disregard anything that the judge may say in relation to the evidence. In every summing up the judge must direct the jury regarding the burden of proof (which resides with the prosecution) and the standard of proof (beyond a reasonable doubt) as well as the elements of the offence or offences (*actus reus* and *mens rea*) on the indictment. If the summing up takes some time and does not finish until late in the day, the jury should not be asked to consider their verdict until the following day.

28   Retirement of jury and verdict

At the end of the judge's summing up, the jury bailiff takes an oath to escort the jury to some 'private and convenient place' where he/she will not 'suffer anybody to speak to them about the trial this day, nor will he/she speak to them without leave of the court except it be to ask them if they are agreed upon their verdict'. The jury must not leave the jury room without the consent of the trial judge but they will be sent home to return the next day if they have not reached a verdict by the late afternoon. During their retirement, the jury are permitted to ask questions of the judge by passing a note to the jury bailiff but the reply must be read out in open court in the presence of the advocates so that they are aware of the question and the answer. Prior to commencing their deliberations the jury will have appointed one of their number to act as foreman. Members of the jury are allowed at least two hours and ten minutes before being told that their verdict need not be unanimous. When they have reached a verdict on which they are all agreed (or a majority verdict where permitted by the Juries Act 1974) they will inform the jury bailiff who will escort them back to the courtroom. The foreman is then asked by the clerk what the jury's verdict is on each count on the indictment. If the jury is unable to agree (even on a majority verdict), the judge will discharge the jurors and the accused may be tried subsequently by a different jury. If the jury find the accused 'not guilty' he/she is, of course, acquitted and is free to leave the court.

SENTENCING

29   Introductory remarks

As proposed in the White Paper *Justice for All*, the Criminal Justice Act 2003 s.167 has created a Sentencing Guidelines Council headed by the Lord Chief Justice whose role it is to set guidelines for sentencing the full range of criminal offences. These guidelines are available for consultation by the public, legal practitioners and judges. The Sentencing Guidelines Council published the final versions of its first guidelines for judges and magistrates, designed to promote consistent and effective sentencing, on

16 December 2004. In addition, there is an independent Sentencing Advisory Panel whose role is to promote consistency in sentencing throughout the courts of England and Wales. Amongst other things, the White Paper drew attention to considerable inconsistency in sentencing by courts in different parts of England and Wales and it is intended that this will be addressed by the Sentencing Advisory Panel. Sentencing is virtually a subject in its own right on which books are published and so what is said in this chapter can only be the merest outline.

30 Purposes of sentencing

The Criminal Justice Act 2003 s. 142(1) enacts that any court dealing with an offender in respect of his/her offence must have regard to the following purposes of sentencing:

(a) the punishment of offenders,
(b) the reduction of crime (including its reduction by deterrence),
(c) the reform and rehabilitation of offenders,
(d) the protection of the public, and
(e) the making of reparation by offenders to persons affected by their offences.

However, s. 142(2) specifies that the above subsection does not apply:

(a) in relation to an offender who is aged under 18 at the time of conviction,
(b) to an offence the sentence for which is fixed by law,
(c) to an offence the sentence for which falls to be imposed under s. 51A of the Firearms Act 1968 or ss. 110(2) and 111 of the Sentencing Act (required custodial sentences) or under ss. 225–228 of the Act (dangerous offenders), or
(d) in relation to the making under the Mental Health Act 1983 Part 3 of a hospital order (with or without a restriction order), an interim hospital order, a hospital direction or a limitation direction.

31 Types of sentence

In almost 75 per cent of all cases where the accused is convicted or pleads 'guilty' to one or more offences, the sentence imposed by the court will be a fine which is either payable as a lump sum or by instalments. There is a limit on the fine that can normally be imposed by a magistrates' court. Currently the amount is £5,000 (a level 5) but this can be exceeded for conviction for certain environmental and fisheries offences. It is likely that the £5,000 limit will be increased before too long because the government has not followed Lord Justice Auld's recommendation to create an intermediate level court between magistrates' courts and the Crown Court.

There is no limit to the fine that can be imposed by the Crown Court and very hefty fines are sometimes levied. Before appearing in court the defendant is obliged to disclose his/her income with supporting documentation as well as his/her expenditure on a pre-printed form so that the court can match the fine to the offender's ability to pay. Where the defendant has refused or failed to provide the necessary information, the court is entitled to assume that he/she is not short of means and fine him/her accordingly, as well as fine for failing to complete the requisite form. Fine officers are tasked with the responsibility of ensuring that fines are paid in accordance with the schedule of payment agreed with the court. The Community Legal Service offers 'fines clinics' to provide support and guidance for those who have accumulated multiple debts which make it difficult for the schedule of repayments to be maintained. For those who can afford to pay but try to avoid payment, a range of powers (from wheel clamping of vehicles prior to their sale, to ordering deductions from pay) have been conferred on fines officers to enable them to recover what is due.

Apart from financial penalties, the White Paper *Justice for All* proposed a new sentencing framework in which the severity of the sentence increases in relation to the gravity of the offending. This has now been implemented in the Criminal Justice Act 2003 Part 12. There are six main categories, as follows:

1 Customised community sentence for persons aged over 16
2 Custody plus
3 Custody minus
4 Intermittent custody
5 Custodial sentences of 12 months and over
6 Indeterminate sentences – for violent/sexual offences.

32 Customised community sentence

The Criminal Justice Act 2003 s. 174 imposes a general obligation on courts to give reasons for and explain in ordinary language the effect of the sentence imposed. The customised community sentence category is intended to provide courts with a menu of options which can be combined to form a single sentence and include the following:

- compulsory unpaid work on projects set up by the probation service;
- an activity requirement as specified in Schedule 2 to the Powers of Criminal Courts (Sentencing) Act 2000 such as receiving help with employment applications;
- attendance on offending behaviour programmes such as anger management;
- a prohibited activity requirement so that the offender is required to refrain from participating in certain activities or from contacting certain persons;

- a curfew order requiring an offender to stay at home during evenings and/or at weekends;
- an exclusion requirement for a maximum of two years requiring an offender to stay away from a specified town centre after dark;
- a residence requirement so that an offender must live only at one or two specified addresses for a defined period;
- drug testing, treatment and abstinence requirements;
- alcohol treatment requirement;
- a mental health treatment requirement;
- intensive community supervision;
- a supervision requirement by a probation officer; and
- an attendance centre requirement for offenders aged under 25 to participate in practical activities and sport at weekends.

Courts are able to make an order for electronic monitoring of compliance with many of these community orders. If an offence does not merit a term of imprisonment of six months or more, magistrates are required to impose one of these community sentences. Under the Criminal Justice Act 2003 s. 178 the Secretary of State is empowered to make an order permitting or requiring a court to review the progress of an offender under a community order. In addition, the Secretary of State can also allow a court to attach or remove a review provision from a community order and regulate the timing of reviews. It is important to note, however, that the Criminal Justice Act 2003 s. 148 enacts that a court must not pass a community sentence on an offender unless it is of the opinion that the offence and one or more offences associated with it was serious enough to warrant such a sentence. It is further provided by s. 150 that the power of a court to make a community order or youth community order is not exercisable in respect of an offence for which the sentence:

(a) is fixed by law,
(b) falls to be imposed under s. 51A(2) of the Firearms Act 1968 (which requires custodial sentence for certain firearms offences),
(c) falls to be imposed under ss 110(2) or 111(2) of the Sentencing Act (there is a requirement to impose custodial sentences for certain repeated offences committed by offenders aged 18 or over), or
(d) falls to be imposed under any of ss 225–228 of the Criminal Justice Act 2003 (there is a requirement to impose custodial sentences for certain offences committed by offenders posing a risk to the public).

33   New forms of custodial sentence

The power of magistrates to sentence to imprisonment for a minimum term of five days is preserved by s. 164(7) but this likely to be limited to cases of fine default and where there is contempt of court. Section 152(2) provides that a court:

... must not pass a custodial sentence unless it is of the opinion that the offence, or combination of the offence and one or more offences associated with it, is so serious that neither a fine alone nor a community sentence can be justified for the offence.

Where magistrates decide to sentence for less than 12 months they must use one of the new forms of short custodial sentence. Custody Plus is served partly in custody and partly in the community. The custody element consists of a minimum of two weeks but a maximum period of three months in custody served in full, followed by a compulsory period of supervision on licence in the community with a maximum overall timescale of 12 months. The licence period must be at least 26 weeks. The community element will be tailored to the needs of the offender as identified in the pre-sentence report and specified in a 'custody plus order' with a view to rehabilitation. The aim is to ensure, as far as possible, that there is a lower risk of re-offending. Where the defendant is convicted of multiple crimes s. 182(7) makes provision for consecutive sentences but limits the term of imprisonment for two or more offences to 15 months with a maximum of 6 months in custody.

Custody Minus is a suspended sentence which enables judges and magistrates to impose a sentence of less than 12 months. However, this sentence is suspended for a period of between six months and two years on condition that the defendant undertakes a demanding programme of activity referred to as 'the supervision period' in the community. The range of options that are available to a court to impose during the period of suspension are the same as those making up the Customised Community Sentence and these will be kept under review. If there is any breach of the conditions, the defendant will be imprisoned. The Criminal Justice Act 2003 s. 189(5) prevents a court from imposing a community sentence alongside a suspended sentence and subsection (6) makes it clear that a suspended sentence is to be regarded as a sentence of imprisonment.

Intermittent Custody is designed to be served in open prisons at weekends by persons who are not dangerous and who are given relatively short sentences. The minimum overall term is 28 weeks, of which a total of 14 days will be served in custody. The maximum is 51 weeks with no more than 13 weeks in custody. During their time in custody the offenders will be obliged to take programmes to address their offending behaviour or make reparations to the community. In this way offenders will be able to continue with their jobs and maintain their family relationships. It is particularly suitable for women offenders who have young children. Whilst not in custody, offenders can be electronically tagged and subjected to curfew. However, it is not available everywhere in England and Wales. The Secretary of State has to make an order when suitable arrangements are available in a particular area. Moreover, a court must consult with the local probation service before making an intermittent custody order.

34   Other custodial sentences

Where offenders are sentenced to custodial sentences of 12 months and over, they will serve part of their sentences in the community provided they are not dangerous offenders. Release for non-dangerous offenders will normally be 'automatic' at the halfway stage of their sentence but there will be supervision until the end of the entire sentence period. Prior to release, the Prison and Probation Service decide on the elements constituting the community element of the sentence. If the offender fails to comply with the conditions of the supervised community element, he/she will be returned to prison to serve the remainder of the sentence.

Life imprisonment for murder has obviously always been an indeterminate sentence even though a court must now specify the amount of time the offender must serve before the Parole Board can consider an application for release on licence. The Criminal Justice Act 2003 Chapter 5 now makes provision for a new extended sentence of imprisonment for 'public protection' which is also an indeterminate sentence for dangerous offenders.

The provisions of Chapter 5 are somewhat complex and it is necessary to understand the terminology used in s. 224 first, which refers to a 'specified offence' and a 'serious offence'. It then refers to a 'relevant offence', a 'specified violent offence' and 'specified sexual offence'. According to s. 224 a specified offence is a 'specified violent offence' or a 'specified sexual offence', the former being located in Part 1 of Schedule 15 to the Act whilst the latter will be found in Part 2. A 'serious offence', on the other hand, is a specified offence which is punishable, in the case of an adult, by imprisonment for life or imprisonment for a determinate period of 10 years or more. Where an adult is convicted of a 'serious offence' and the court is of the opinion that there is a significant risk to members of the public of serious harm occasioned by the commission of further specified offences, the court must impose a sentence of imprisonment for life. This is subject to the provisos that the offence is one for which the offender would be liable to imprisonment for life and the court considers that the seriousness of the offence and one or more offences associated with it justifies a life sentence. In other instances, the court must impose a sentence of imprisonment for public protection which is a sentence of indeterminate term and is subject to Chapter 2 of Part 2 of the Crime (Sentences) Act 1997. In passing such a sentence, a court must decide the part to be served in custody for the purposes of punishment and deterrence. Whether the offender is then released on licence depends on the recommendation of the Parole Board. Section 226 enacts similar provisions in respect of persons under the age of 18 although it is a sentence of detention rather than imprisonment. Persons who are convicted of a 'specified offence' which is *not* a 'serious offence' but is one where a court considers there is a significant risk to members of the public of serious harm, it must impose on the offender an extended term of imprisonment which is equal to the total of the appropriate custodial term (subject to a minimum of 12 months) plus a further period for which the offender is to be subject to a licence if the Parole Board recommends a release. Although it is for a court to decide the duration of the 'extension period', this must not exceed:

(a) five years in the case of a specified violent offence, and
(b) eight years in the case of a specified sexual offence.

There is a further qualification in that the extended sentence must not exceed the maximum term permitted for the offence. Whilst on licence the offender is subject to supervision for public protection.

35 Concurrent and consecutive sentences

Where an offender is convicted of more than one offence on an information or count on the indictment, the court should impose separate sentences in respect of each offence/count. Prison sentences may run concurrently (together from the same point in time) or consecutively but there may be a mix of concurrent and consecutive sentences. The magistrates/judge must therefore decide whether the sentences are to run concurrently or consecutively. In the event of a failure to do so, there is a presumption that the sentences are to run concurrently. The Magistrates' Courts Act 1980 s.133 has been amended by s. 155 of the Criminal Justice Act 2003 so that magistrates have new powers in relation to consecutive custodial sentences but consecutive terms of imprisonment must not exceed 65 weeks in total.

36 Pronouncing sentence

It is a basic principle that an offender should only be sentenced for those crimes for which he/she has pleaded guilty or has been convicted and not for anything else that the court thinks that he/she may have done. There are, nevertheless, three exceptions to this basic principle, where:

(i)   the court is satisfied that the defendant, in committing the primary offence, also committed a secondary offence that is not on the indictment (and which is no more serious than the count on the indictment) but yet constitutes an aggravating feature
(ii) the offender specifically asks for other offences to be taken into consideration by the court; and
(iii) the prosecution case is that the offences on the indictment are merely examples of a continuing course of conduct and this is accepted by the defence.

In relation to (i) above, if the judge is satisfied that the prosecution version of the facts is accurate, then he/she may take into consideration the secondary offence when passing sentence. In *R* v *Boswell* [1984] Lord

Lane CJ, in the course of providing guidelines on sentencing for causing death by reckless driving, stated that an aggravating feature justifying a custodial sentence was where the offender's driving had involved other offences such as driving whilst disqualified or under the influence of drink. The judge may pronounce the sentence immediately but he/she may adjourn briefly to consider his/her decision. The Powers of the Criminal Courts (Sentencing) Act 2000 imposes a number of obligations on courts when passing sentence. Section 79(4) in particular requires that a judge, passing a custodial sentence for offences covered by the Act, must explain to the offender in open court and in ordinary language why he/she is passing a custodial sentence. Under s. 155(1) a sentence imposed by the Crown Court may be varied or rescinded within 28 days but any variation must be made by the judge who originally passed the sentence. A judge would be likely to exercise his/her powers under s. 155(1) in order to correct a technical error in the original sentence or to alter it to the advantage of the offender if he/she considers, on reflection, that he/she has been too severe.

37   Anti-social behaviour orders

Since April 1999 magistrates' courts have had the power to make anti-social behaviour orders to combat behaviour that intimidates neighbours or a community in general. Local authorities and chief police officers, in consultation with each other, are able to apply to a magistrates' court for an ASBO to protect the community from the actions of an individual or group of individuals over the age of nine years who cause harassment, alarm or distress to others. The proceedings are civil (not criminal) and so the case need only be proved according to the rules of civil evidence. Thus hearsay evidence is admissible and the standard of proof is 'the balance of probabilities'. Once an order is made the individual (or individuals) does not get a criminal record but will be prohibited from doing anything specified in the order. The breach of an order is, however, *a criminal offence.* If there is a subsequent prosecution, the breach of an order must be proved beyond a reasonable doubt and on conviction the defendant can receive a prison term of up to five years. As a result a number of young people are now being sentenced to imprisonment for breaching an ASBO whereas the original offence for which the ASBO was imposed was not an offence that attracted a custodial sentence. The Police Reform Act 2002 ss 61–66 update the procedure for obtaining an ASBO whereby:

* an interim ASBO can be granted to enable immediate action to be taken prior to undertaking the formal process;
* ASBOs will attach to the persons concerned and will be effective even if they move to other parts of the country;
* British Transport Police and registered social landlords can apply for ASBOs; and

• county courts can make ASBOs when dealing with applications for injunctions and evictions.

In *R (on the application of McCann)* v *Crown Court at Manchester* and *Clingham* v *Kensington and Chelsea Royal London Borough Council* [2002] the House of Lords ruled that the making of an ASBO was a *civil process* such that a defendant did not have the benefit of special protection under Article 6 of the European Convention on Human Rights.

APPEALS

38 Appeals from magistrates' courts

Less than one per cent of the decisions of a magistrates' court are ever the subject of an appeal but they can be contested in one of three ways:

(i)   by appeal to the Crown Court,
(ii) by appeal to the High Court by way of case stated for the opinion of the High Court, and
(iii) by way of claim for judicial review to the High Court.

The appeal to the Crown Court mentioned in (i) above following a plea of 'not guilty' may be against conviction and/or sentence. In general, a plea of 'guilty' before a magistrates' court bars an appeal against conviction although there are certain exceptions to this rule – see *R* v *Huntingdon Crown Court ex p. Jordan* [1981]. If a 'guilty' plea is entered, an appeal is normally restricted to the sentence handed down by the court. The procedures outlined in (ii) and (iii) above are available to both a convicted accused and an unsuccessful prosecutor (usually the Crown Prosecutor). Moreover, decisions of the Crown Court that do not arise from its jurisdiction over trials on indictment may also be challenged by way of case stated for the opinion of the High Court or by way of a claim for judicial review. In all these instances the jurisdiction of the High Court is exercised by the Divisional Court of Queen's Bench.

39 Appeals to the Crown Court

Appeals to the Crown Court are governed by the Magistrates' Courts Act 1980 ss. 108–110 and the Crown Court Rules 1982 (SI 1982 No.1109). There is a right of appeal to the Crown Court not only against a fine or custodial sentence but also the decision of a magistrates' court to place an offender on probation, to discharge him/her conditionally or unconditionally, to disqualify him/her from driving, to recommend him/her for deportation or to make a confiscation or compensation order. If there is to be an appeal, notice of an appeal must be given to the clerk of the magistrates' court in question in writing and to the prosecution within 21 days of sentence being passed or the offender being otherwise dealt with by magistrates (by being committed for sentence to the Crown Court). The notice must clearly state whether the appeal is against conviction or sentence or both but the grounds of the appeal need not be given. Permission to appeal is not required and the Crown Court has discretion to extend the time for giving notice of the appeal. If a convicted person gives notice of appeal where the magistrates have passed an immediate custodial sentence, the magistrates may grant bail under the Magistrates' Courts Act 1980 s. 113(1) subject to him/her appearing at the Crown Court at the time fixed for the hearing of the appeal. An application for bail can also be made to the Crown Court under the Supreme Court Act 1981 s. 81(1)(b) where magistrates have refused to grant bail.

The appeal will normally be listed for hearing by a circuit judge or recorder who must usually sit with two magistrates who were not concerned with the original case. An appeal against conviction will take the form of a rehearing of the case and the advocate for the prosecution will make an opening speech and call evidence. Previously unheard evidence may be called. Thereafter, the advocate for the appellant can make a submission of 'no case to answer'. If this should fail, the advocate will then call the evidence for the defence, after which the advocate will make a closing speech. The court will announce its decision after this. If the appeal is against sentence only, the advocate for the prosecution simply outlines the facts and previous evidence together with any report compiled on the defendant for the court. The role of the advocate for the defence is largely confined to presenting a plea in mitigation. It is then for the Crown Court to decide how the appellant should be sentenced and the court will give reasons for its decision. If it takes the view that the appropriate sentence is at variance with the one imposed by the magistrates, then the appeal will be allowed and the sentence of the Crown Court will be substituted but the Crown Court can remit the case back to the magistrates having given its 'opinion' for its disposal.

The Supreme Court Act 1981 s. 48 confers wide powers on the Crown Court when disposing of an appeal in that it may confirm, reverse or vary any part of the decision appealed against. It may increase the sentence imposed by the magistrates' court even in a case where the appeal is simply against a conviction, as well as impose a separate penalty for an offence where the magistrates had decided not to impose a penalty. However, the Crown Court must not pass a sentence which exceeds that which the magistrates had the power to pass. It may also remit the case to the magistrates with its opinion on how it should be disposed of, particularly where it considers a 'guilty' plea to be equivocal. In addition, it may make whatever order in relation to costs it considers just. For example, in the event of a successful appeal, it may order that the costs of the defence in the magistrates' court are paid by the prosecution or paid out of central funds although there are limitations on the power to order costs.

40   Appeal by way of case stated

By means of this procedure the aggrieved party invites the magistrates to state a case for consideration by a Divisional Court of Queen's Bench. The appeal must be on one of the two grounds mentioned in the Magistrates' Courts Act 1980 s. 111(1). Thus, an appeal must be on one or more point(s) of law or relate to jurisdiction and be identified in a document compiled by the clerk of the magistrates' court in consultation with the magistrates whose decision is being contested. An application must be made within 21 days of the day on which the magistrates' court sentenced or otherwise dealt with the appellant. Bail may be granted by magistrates where the appellant has been given an immediate custodial sentence but, if this was refused, an application for bail can be made to a High Court judge in chambers. Usually two High Court judges will sit in a Divisional Court of Queen's Bench to hear the appeal – sometimes three judges will sit, one of whom may be the Lord Chief Justice. In disposing of the appeal, the Divisional Court may reverse, affirm or amend the decision of the magistrates. If the prosecution has appealed, the Divisional Court can remit the case to the magistrates with instructions that they convict and proceed to sentence but it may simply replace the acquittal with a conviction and impose the appropriate penalty. If an application is made to magistrates to state a case for the opinion of a Divisional Court of Queen's Bench, the appellant loses any right that he/she had to appeal to the Crown Court.

An appeal by way of case stated may be used to contest a decision of the Crown Court that does not relate to trial on indictment. Here the appellant has the responsibility for compiling an initial draft case to be put before a judge who presided in the proceedings where the disputed decision was arrived at.

41   Appeal by claim for judicial review

The procedure for instituting a claim for judicial review is set out in Chapter 15. An appeal by way of claim for judicial review relates to jurisdictional disputes. The appellant may argue that the magistrates were in error in attempting to exercise jurisdiction. An appeal by way of judicial review can also be based on the regularity of the decision-making process and its legality. Since magistrates do not have the power to bail a person who is challenging their decision by claim for judicial review, an application for bail has to be made to a judge in chambers. If the claim for judicial review succeeds, the Divisional Court can issue one or more of the prerogative orders described in Chapter 15. The Supreme Court Act 1981 s. 29(3) permits a decision of the Crown Court to be challenged by way of a claim for judicial review provided it is not a decision that relates to a trial on indictment.

42   Appeals to the Court of Appeal (Criminal Division)

If a person has been tried on indictment, convicted and sentenced, any appeal has to be addressed to the Court of Appeal (Criminal Division) irrespective of whether the appeal is against conviction, sentence or both. Numerous types of error can be made in the course of a trial, any one of which may form the basis of an appeal against conviction. These errors may be summarised as follows:

(a)   wrongful admission or exclusion of evidence by the trial judge;
(b)   erroneous exercise of discretion by the trial judge;
(c)   errors made by the advocate for the defence in presenting the case;
(d)   a ruling by the trial judge at the end of the prosecution case that 'there is a case to answer';
(e)   defects in the form or wording of the indictment;
(f)   illogical and inconsistent verdicts given by the jury between separate counts on the indictment;
(g)   excessive intervention on the part of the trial judge; and
(h)   errors and omissions in the summing up by the trial judge.

The Criminal Appeal Act 1968 s. 1 gives a person convicted of an offence a right to appeal against conviction but an appeal is only possible with the permission of the Court of Appeal or if the trial judge grants a certificate that the case is fit for appeal. Where a certificate is granted at the initiative of the trial judge, he/she will draft the question that he/she considers ought to be raised on appeal and will read this to the advocates so that they can comment on it before it is actually certified. If the advocate makes the application for the certificate, the advocate will draft the question and the application will be made in chambers with a shorthand writer in attendance. For a certificate to be granted, there must be a particular basis for appeal on which the convicted person will have a substantial chance of succeeding.

If the trial judge has not granted a certificate that the case is fit for appeal, a prospective appellant needs permission to appeal. The power of the Court of Appeal (Criminal Division) to grant permission to appeal is one that is usually exercised by a single judge reading the papers, including the application for leave, without oral argument or even written representations from the advocates representing the parties. In the event that permission to appeal is refused by this judge, the applicant is entitled to have the application decided by a court subject to the requirement on his/her part to serve notice upon the Registrar of Criminal Appeals. The entire process can be hastened where an appeal has obvious merit because the Registrar can list the application for a hearing by a court. Where the appeal is against conviction, both prosecution and defence will be represented at the hearing and, if the application is granted, the court can proceed immediately to consider the appeal itself.

The Criminal Appeal Act 1968 s. 1 does not distinguish between persons convicted following a 'guilty' plea and those convicted by a jury following a 'not guilty' plea. However, in *R* v *Forde* [1923] Avory J stated:

> A plea of guilty having been recorded, this court can only entertain an appeal against conviction if it appears (1) that the appellant did not appreciate the nature of the charge or did not intend to admit he was guilty of it, or (2) that upon the admitted facts he could not in law have been convicted of the offence charged.

Thus the Court of Appeal (Criminal Division) will only grant permission to appeal, where the applicant has pleaded 'guilty' in the Crown Court, if there are exceptional circumstances. For example, the applicant's confession may be doubted because he/she is of low intelligence.

43   Determination of an appeal against conviction

The Criminal Appeal Act 1968 s. 2(1) as amended provides:

> Subject to the provisions of this Act, the Court of Appeal –
> (a) shall allow an appeal against conviction if they think that the conviction is unsafe; and
> (b) shall dismiss such an appeal in any other case.

The simplification of the wording of s. 2(1) achieved by the enactment of the Criminal Appeal Act 1995 has not changed the effect of the statutory provision. Thus, for a conviction to be safe, it must be lawful. If it should transpire that the trial should never have taken place, the conviction cannot be regarded as safe. Moreover, a conviction can be quashed if it can be shown that it resulted from an abuse of process. In *R* v *Mullen* [2000] the Court of Appeal (Criminal Division) took the view that the conduct of the British authorities in procuring the deportation to England of the appellant was so unworthy and shameful that it amounted to an affront to the public conscience for the prosecution to succeed. In *Condron* v *UK* (the facts of which were set out in Chapter 10) the European Court of Human Rights stressed the necessity for the Court of Appeal to focus on the fairness of the trial rather than the safety of the conviction when deciding whether to uphold an appeal from the Crown Court. The applicants contended before the European Court of Human Rights that their right to a fair trial under Article 6 had been violated when the 'no comment' interview was not excluded by the trial judge. The European Court of Human Rights took the view that there had been a violation of Article 6. Furthermore the Court rejected the Court of Appeal's conclusion that the exercise of the right to silence on the part of the applicants did not play a significant part in the jury's decision to convict. In the course of its judgment the Court stated:

> The question whether or not the rights of the defence guaranteed to an accused under Article 6 of the Convention were secured in any given case

cannot be assimilated to a finding that his conviction was safe in the absence of any enquiry into the issue of fairness.

Since the Court of Appeal is required by the Human Rights Act 1998 s. 2(1) to take into account the jurisprudence of the European Court of Human Rights in determining a question that has arisen in connection with a Convention right, it should interpret the Criminal Appeal Act 1968 s. 2(1) in such a way as to embrace the notion that there should be no incompatibility between the Criminal Appeal Act 1968 s. 2(1)(a) and the Human Rights Act 1998 s. 3(1).

The Court of Appeal (Criminal Division) can decide the outcome of an appeal by majority of its members but, because of the necessity of certainty in criminal proceedings, only one judgment is given. The Supreme Court Act 1981 s. 59 allows a departure from this general practice if the presiding judge states that in his opinion the question is one of law on which separate judgments should be pronounced. If the appeal is successful, there will be one of two possible outcomes. The first is that the conviction is quashed and the Crown Court is instructed to substitute a verdict of acquittal for the conviction. If such is the case, a successful appellant cannot normally be retried for the offence for which the appeal was brought nor for any other offence for which he/she could have been convicted by way of an alternative verdict. Nevertheless, a successful appeal does not rule out altogether the possibility of a trial for a different offence based on the same facts and evidence. The other possible outcome of a successful appeal is that the original conviction is quashed and a retrial is ordered. The Criminal Appeal Act 1968 s. 7(1) provides:

> Where the Court of Appeal allow an appeal against conviction and do so only by reason of evidence received or available to be received by them under s. 23 of this Act and it appears to the court that the interests of justice require, they may order the appellant to be retried.

However, the retrial may not be for any offence other than the one for which the successful appeal was brought. The Court of Appeal (Criminal Division) relies on its powers under the Criminal Appeal Act 1968 in most criminal appeals. In addition, and quite independent of statute, the Court of Appeal has inherited a power from the Court of Crown Cases Reserved to quash a conviction and issue a writ of *venire de novo*, the effect of which is to order a retrial.

44   Appeal against sentence

The Criminal Appeal Act 1968 s. 9(1) gives a person convicted on indictment the right to appeal to the Court of Appeal (Criminal Division) against any sentence passed on him/her for the offence that is not fixed by law. The Criminal Appeal Act 1968 s. 10 deals with the right to appeal when the offender was sentenced in the Crown Court following a summary conviction. He/she may only appeal if:

(a)   he/she is sentenced to six months or more imprisonment;

(b)   the sentence is one that the magistrates had no power to pass; or

(c)   the court in dealing with him/her for the offence:

    (i)   recommends that he/she be deported,

    (ii)   disqualifies him/her from driving,

    (iii) makes an order under the Powers of the Criminal Courts (Sentencing) Act 2000,

    (iv)   makes an order under the Football Spectators Act 1989, or

    (v)   orders his/her return to prison.

In an appeal against sentence, it is unusual for the prosecution to be represented.

45   Appeal to the House of Lords

The Criminal Appeal Act 1968 ss. 33 and 34 provide that either the prosecution or the defence can appeal to the House of Lords from a decision of the Court of Appeal (Criminal Division) but the appeal is subject to:

(a)   the Court of Appeal (Criminal Division) certifying that its decision which is being appealed against involves a point of law of general public importance; and

(b)   either the Court of Appeal or the House of Lords giving permission to appeal because the point of law is one that should be considered by the House.

An application for permission to appeal to the House of Lords should be made to the Court of Appeal either orally immediately after it has delivered its decision or it should be made within 14 days of the decision at the latest. Notice of the application must be served on the Registrar in the requisite format. In hearing an appeal, the House of Lords may exercise any powers of the Court of Appeal (Criminal Division) or it may remit the case to it.

46   An application to the European Court of Human Rights

If a person considers that the national courts have failed to protect a right contained in the European Convention on Human Rights and Fundamental Freedoms, then he/she can petition the European Court of Human Rights in Strasbourg. The Court must consider the preliminary issue of 'admissibility' and in the region of nine out of ten applications are rejected on this basis. Article 35 of the Convention states that an application is inadmissible if:

(a)   it is anonymous;

(b)   it concerns a matter that the Court has adjudicated upon;

(c)   it deals with a right not contained in the Convention;

(d) the national remedies have not been exhausted;

(e) it was not made within six months of the date of the decision complained of;

(f) the applicant was not a 'victim' as required by Article 34;

(g) it is an abuse of the right of petition; or

(h) it is manifestly ill-founded on its merits.

A committee of three judges can decide that the application is inadmissible, acting under Article 28, and there is no appeal from this decision. If the application surmounts this first hurdle, the Court will attempt a 'friendly settlement' between the parties which may involve payment of compensation and/or a change in the law on which the complaint is founded. The procedure before the Court is mainly written in that affidavits and other documents are filed at the Court. If there is no settlement, there will be a short oral hearing before a chamber comprising seven judges which may award a payment as 'just satisfaction' if it finds that there has been a violation. Quite often, however, the Court will direct that the finding of a violation of the Convention should be 'sufficient satisfaction' for the applicant. The judgment of the Court is by majority and dissenting judgments are quite common. The UK government, as a signatory to the Convention, is committed to implementing the judgments of the Court, which may entail amending the offending legislation and amending the decision that caused the violation.

47 Criminal Cases Review Commission

The Criminal Cases Review Commission was established by the Criminal Appeal Act 1995 as an independent body comprising 14 Commissioners appointed by the Queen on the recommendation of the Prime Minister. Its statutory remit is to investigate and process alleged miscarriages of justice in England, Wales and Northern Ireland. It is able to investigate convictions following trial on indictment, referrals regarding sentences imposed and it may even investigate convictions by magistrates. The Forensic Science Service is often called upon to assist the Commission with its investigative work. References will only be made to either the Court of Appeal or Crown Court if it considers that there is a real possibility that the conviction, verdict, finding or sentence would not be upheld if the reference were to be made. Where the Commission decides to refer a case that was originally dealt with in the Crown Court, it will be treated as an appeal under the Criminal Appeal Act 1968 which will be referred to the Court of Appeal. Cases that were originally dealt with in a magistrates' court will be referred to the Crown Court. Details concerning recent references made by the Commission can be found on its website and the Annual Report describes its working methods. It is likely that the Commission will be reviewing a number of cases where parents have been convicted of inflicting serious harm on their children now that it has been discovered that 'brittle bone disease' (Osteogenesis Imperfecta) among infants and small children has gone undiagnosed in many instances.

48 Retrial for serious offences

The Criminal Justice Act 2003 is a landmark in the history of criminal justice in that it creates an exception to the normal rule against double jeopardy. For those offences that carry a maximum sentence of life imprisonment (listed in Schedule 5 to the Act) and which have a serious impact on the victim(s) or on society generally, it will be possible to retry a person who was acquitted either on indictment or subsequent appeal. The Crown Prosecution Service is able to make an application under s. 76 to the Court of Appeal (Criminal Division) for an order that quashes the person's acquittal and orders him/her to be retried for the offence. Such applications require the written consent of the Director of Public Prosecutions, who must also consider whether it is in the public interest to proceed. There must be new and compelling evidence, as required by s. 78, on which the Court of Appeal (Criminal Division) can base its decision. Evidence will be new under s. 78 if it was not produced at the original trial and it will be compelling if the Court of Appeal (Criminal Division) considers it to be reliable and substantial so that it is highly probative of the case against the person previously acquitted. It is expressly provided in s. 81 that the Court of Appeal's decision can be taken on appeal on a point of law to the House of Lords.

49 Assets Recovery Agency

The Proceeds of Crime Act 2002 represents an attempt by government to deprive convicted criminals of their 'ill gotten' gains and, in Part 7, to combat more effectively the persistent problem of money laundering. An Assets Recovery Agency has been created which, according to s. 2(1), functions in the way 'best calculated to contribute to the reduction of crime'. Law enforcement officers can search and seize money anywhere in the country if they suspect that it represents the proceeds of crime. Confiscation orders can be made following a conviction. Although confiscation orders are nothing new, their application and scope have been significantly extended by the Act. Under s. 6, two preliminary conditions need to be satisfied before the court can make a confiscation order:

(a) there has been a conviction and the defendant is in the Crown Court; and

(b) the prosecution or the court has decided that a confiscation order should be considered.

A new committal procedure has been created under s. 70 whereby magistrates must commit a defendant to the Crown Court if requested by the

CPS following a conviction. Even if the prosecutor in the magistrates' court does not ask for the case to be committed to the Crown Court for a confiscation hearing, if the case is committed to the Crown Court for sentencing, the prosecutor (or Crown Court) could still decide to hold a confiscation hearing. Having dealt with these preliminary matters, the court must decide whether the defendant has a 'criminal life-style' as specified in s. 75. If it does so determine, it must then decide whether he/she has benefited from his/her criminal conduct and the value of the benefit. The court then determines the actual amount to confiscate. If it cannot be said that the defendant has a criminal life-style, the court can only consider the defendant's benefit from the offence(s) of which he/she stands convicted. The Act also contains in Part 5 a separate scheme for civil recovery of the proceeds of crime. The procedure is set in motion when the Agency makes an application to the High Court for a civil recovery order in respect of property anywhere in the world obtained through unlawful conduct. There is no need for a prior conviction before such an application can be made. Magistrates also have *civil jurisdiction* under s. 240 to order forfeiture of cash if they are satisfied that it has been obtained through unlawful conduct or is intended to be used in unlawful conduct.

■ Summary

This chapter commenced with the classification of criminal offences as a basis for examining the two modes of trial. Prior to any trial, a court must usually deal with the issues of remand and bail and so there has been a consideration of these matters. Since most trials in magistrates' courts are heard before a panel of magistrates, the focus has been on this type of summary trial, although some trials do take place before a district judge. Now that the sentencing powers of magistrates have been extended, even more 'either way' offences should be routinely tried in magistrates' courts but the accused will still be able to opt for jury trial at the Crown Court. As has been seen, trial on indictment is the mode of trial for all serious criminal offences and the Criminal Justice Act 2003 has introduced some important changes. Arguably the most important is the prospect of allowing evidence of bad character; there is also the possibility of dispensing with jury trial altogether, but this will only happen in the most extraordinary circumstances. The abolition of the 'double jeopardy' principle by the Act will result in the occasional retrial for a very serious offence. Some space has been devoted to the new sentencing framework introduced under the Criminal Justice Act 2003 in which the severity of the sentence is supposed to increase in relation to the gravity of the offending. It was noted that the Act has created a Sentencing Guidelines Council headed by the Lord Chief Justice, whose role is to set guidelines for sentencing for the full range of criminal offences. Anyone wishing to monitor the embedding of the new sentencing framework will want to refer to the Council's website from time to time. Having set out the route for appeals from magistrates' courts and from the Crown Court, the role of the Criminal Cases Review Commission was considered because it is vital to have an institutionalised mechanism for dealing with miscarriages of justice. It was thought appropriate to mention the establishment of the Assets Recovery Agency under the Proceeds of Crime Act 2002, which represents a determined effort on the part of government to ensure that, as far as possible, criminals do not benefit financially from crime.

WWW   PROGRESS TEST

For suggested answers to the tests below, go to the companion website at www.pearsoned.co.uk/wheeler

1   How does the Criminal Law Act 1977 s. 14 classify criminal offences?
2   What is meant by 'remanding' the accused and when are magistrates required to remand the accused?
3   If magistrates refuse bail under the Bail Act 1976, how might such a refusal be justified?
4   On what basis does the Criminal Justice Act 2003 s. 14 require a magistrates' court to refuse bail?
5   In what circumstances would the defence advocate make a submission of 'no case to answer' in a summary trial?
6   In a summary trial, must the magistrates reach a unanimous verdict in order to convict the accused?
7   How has the Criminal Justice Act 2003 s. 41 amended the Magistrates' Courts Act 1980 in respect of the allocation of offences triable 'either way' and for the sending of cases to the Crown Court that need to be tried on indictment?
8   What is the purpose of a plea and directions hearing in a trial on indictment?
9   What is meant by the 'burden of proof' and 'standard of proof' in a criminal trial?
10 The Criminal Justice Act 2003 s. 101(1) makes it possible for evidence of the defendant's bad character to be admissible under certain conditions. What are these?
11 What is the purpose of the judge's summing up in a trial on indictment?
12 Is it possible for the accused to be convicted in a trial on indictment by majority verdict or must it be unanimous?
13 What are the two possible outcomes of a successful appeal from the Crown Court to the Court of Appeal (Criminal Division)?
14 Custody Plus, Custody Minus and Intermittent Custody are important elements of the new sentencing framework. How will each of these operate in practice?
15 What is the role of the Criminal Cases Review Commission in the criminal justice system? What is the role of the Assets Recovery Agency?

FURTHER READING

■ Books

Cownie, F., A. Bradney and M. Burton (2003) *The English Legal System in Context* (Oxford: Oxford University Press, chapters 12–14).

Murphy, P. (ed.) (2005) *Blackstone's Criminal Practice* (Oxford: Oxford University Press).

Sprack, J. (2004) *A Practical Approach to Criminal Procedure* (Oxford: Oxford University Press).

■ Articles

Birch, D. and D. Birch (2004) 'The evolution of the discretionary exclusion of evidence', *Criminal Law Review* October, pp. 767–788.

Burton, M. (2002) 'Reviewing Crown Prosecution Service decisions not to prosecute', *Criminal Law Review* May, p. 371.

Cape, E. (2002) 'Incompetent police station advice and the exclusion of evidence', *Criminal Law Review* June, p. 471.

Dennis, I. (2004) 'Prosecution appeals and retrials for serious offences', *Criminal Law Review* August, pp. 619–638.

Von Hirch, A. and J. Roberts (2004) 'Legislating sentencing principles, the provisions of the Criminal Justice Act 2003 relating to sentencing purposes and the role of previous convictions', *Criminal Law Review* August, pp. 639–652.

Redmayne, M. (2004) 'Criminal Justice Act 2003: disclosure and its discontents', *Criminal Law Review* June, pp. 441–462.

USEFUL WEBSITES

Reference should be made to the website of the Sentencing Guidelines Council for information on the new sentencing framework at www.sentencing-guidelines.gov.uk/about/sgc.

The web address of the Criminal Cases Review Commission can be accessed at www.ccrc.gov.uk.

The web address of the Assets Recovery Agency is: www.assetsrecovery.gov.uk.

To read about the information technology system that is used to support the day-to-day operations of the criminal justice system, visit the Court Service website at www.courtservice.gov.uk.

12 Dispute resolution 1: Alternatives to litigation

1 Introduction

Disputes can be resolved through litigation by the application of rules of law to the facts as agreed and/or established at a trial. Litigation, however, may not always be the best method of dispute resolution. This is because it usually involves delay, considerable cost and is adversarial to some extent even in the new climate of civil litigation engendered by the Woolf reforms. At the conclusion of the litigation process there will normally be a clear 'winner' and a clear 'loser' and this may serve to further embitter the relationship between the parties which may have taken many years to foster. For this reason litigation is often the worst possible means of resolving a business dispute because of the damage done to a long-standing commercial relationship. A costly civil trial may even fail to resolve the matter to the total satisfaction of the 'winning' party, especially if the remedy sought has not been obtained because it is discretionary or if all the costs cannot be recovered from the other side. Indeed, a victory may prove hollow in that the amount, if any, recovered may be dwarfed by the costs of the action. Even if damages are awarded to the winning side, it may be necessary to commence another set of legal proceedings to enforce the judgment if the losing side does not pay up immediately.

Firms and companies can always resolve any disputes that arise on a purely informal basis by means of a compromise with the other side by making concessions with a view to preserving business relationships. They may do this themselves or they may seek to involve neutral outsiders as 'facilitators' and formalise the process to a degree but without adopting the very high degree of formality that attends legal proceedings. This may be done through a process that has become known as alternative dispute resolution, or ADR for short. The simplest forms of ADR to understand are mediation and conciliation. Some important providers of ADR include arbitration within the ambit of ADR since it is an alternative to litigation in the courts. Others would exclude arbitration on the basis that it is a legal process, the outcome of which is binding. As will be seen in Chapter 13, the prevailing ethos pervading the Civil Procedure Rules is that litigation should be avoided if possible and the parties are actively encouraged to consider ADR instead. Parties to a dispute have always been able to refer their dispute to arbitration which is a far older and more formal means of dispute resolution than either mediation or conciliation. Although arbitration is conducted outside the court system, it is, nevertheless, an 'imposed' solution; but it is less formal than litigation in the courts and it is also conducted in private. In this chapter, attention will focus, first on mediation and then on conciliation before moving on to consider other forms of ADR. Arbitration has been singled out for separate treatment at the end of the chapter.

2 Mediation

Mediation is defined by the Chartered Institute of Arbitrators, which offers a variety of dispute resolution services, as:

> ... a private and structured form of negotiation assisted by a third party that is initially non-binding. If a settlement is reached the mediator can draw up an agreement that can then become a legally binding contract.

As indicated above, mediations are conducted in private at a time and place to suit the parties. A hotel meeting room would be a suitable venue but the Chartered Institute of Arbitrators offers extensive modern facilities to those wishing to have a dispute resolved through mediation. The person appointed as mediator should be properly trained and there are currently a number of training schemes in the UK including one offered by the Chartered Institute of Arbitrators. Both sides are more likely to be open with and repose trust in a mediator who is properly qualified and experienced. In many instances it may be desirable to appoint someone who is legally qualified as a mediator, particularly if an agreement is to be drawn up subsequently that will take effect as a binding contract.

When the parties come to a mediation they should ideally sit opposite each other at a rectangular table with the mediator sitting at the head of the table. The mediator will normally have read all the relevant papers beforehand and will usually commence by explaining how the process will be conducted. If required by the mediator, each side (or their legal representatives) will then explain what is in dispute and state their aspirations for the outcome of the process. In order to facilitate the discussion it is then usually necessary for the mediator to separate the parties and place them in rooms near the main meeting room. Thereafter, the mediator will act as a go-between to explore the possibility of a solution that is acceptable to both sides. These individual meetings with the parties are known as caucuses. The mediator must treat what is said by each side as confidential. He/she must not try to impose his/her views on the parties and confidential information can only be disclosed to the other side if consent has been given. Information given to the mediator is not given under oath or affirmation and there is no scope for cross-examination given the nature of the process. Once it seems to the mediator that the gap between the parties is narrowing, he/she may then attempt to bring about another joint session with a view to achieving an agreement. If a settlement is agreed it will be because the parties themselves wish to resolve their dispute as amicably as possible. If an agreement has been reached that is embodied in the form of a contract it will be binding on the parties; but, unless an agreement incorporates what in contract law is known as 'consideration', it will not be legally binding on the parties. If a settlement is achieved it is not limited to the normal remedies available from a court and may include the provision of replacement goods or the provision of additional services free of charge. Should the process prove to be inconclusive, the mediator will not act as a witness in any subsequent arbitration or litigation. All discussions in the course of the mediation are 'without prejudice' which means that, should the process fail to achieve an outcome, the parties are then free to consider arbitration or litigation. Mediation is not always successful. It is unlikely to be successful where the dispute centres on one or more issues of law rather than facts or where precedent (or legislation) favours one of the parties. Where it is successful, it will usually have resulted in the repairing of a business relationship that would otherwise have irretrievably broken down. An article in the *Financial Times* of 28 October 1997 reported a survey conducted by the Royal Institute of Chartered Surveyors in which almost 70 per cent of the UK's leading property lawyers favoured mediation as an alternative to litigation for resolving property or construction disputes. Although mediation offers the prospect of a speedy settlement it is not a 'free service' because the mediator will expect to be paid. A relatively straightforward mediation could cost between £1,500 and £2,000. Moreover, if companies are in dispute they may have briefed lawyers to represent them in the mediation and the lawyers, too, will have to be paid.

It is government policy to promote mediation over court-based dispute resolution. The Department for Constitutional Affairs in conjunction with the Civil Mediation Council has launched the National Mediation Helpline (available weekdays from 8 a.m. to 6.30 p.m.) to provide information and advice on mediation as well as put parties in contact with available mediators. The European Commission is behind an initiative to merge the ECC/EEJ-Net service to provide advice to users of the single market and European internet shoppers that can be accessed at www.euroconsumer.org.uk where problems have been encountered with defective products. Where mediation or some other form of ADR is appropriate and possible it will assist in referring a dispute to an ADR body in its role as a clearing house.

3 Conciliation

Mediators can adopt one of two distinct approaches – a facilitative approach which has already been described above or an evaluative approach which is sometimes referred to as conciliation. Some of the groups promoting ADR do not distinguish between mediation and conciliation. The Centre for Effective Dispute Resolution (CEDR) and the

Chartered Institute of Arbitrators, on the other hand, do make a distinction. Whilst CEDR views conciliation as an informal attempt to achieve an agreed settlement between the parties, the Chartered Institute of Arbitrators defines it as:

> ... a process whereby a conciliator investigates the facts of the case, attempts to reconcile the opposing contentions of the parties and prompts them to formulate their own proposals for settlement of the case by indicating the strong and weak points of their arguments and the possible consequences of failure to settle. The conciliator will not usually make a recommendation of his/her own for settlement of the dispute, however he/she acts as a catalyst for settlement by the parties themselves.

On the other hand, the Institution of Civil Engineers have a slightly different view of the process. Their Conciliation Procedure 1999 is an important ADR scheme; the preface to the scheme states:

> The main difference between conciliation and adjudication or Arbitration is that the outcome of conciliation is not imposed and only becomes binding with the consent of each party. Conciliation therefore allows the parties to the dispute the freedom to explore ways of settling the dispute with the assistance of an independent impartial person – the Conciliator.

The Institution of Civil Engineers Conciliation Procedure allows for the appointment of a conciliator by the President of the Institution and on taking up his/her appointment the conciliator issues instructions regarding the date and place for the conciliation meeting. Each side then informs the conciliator of the name of its representative. The representative must have full authority to act on behalf of the party in question. According to para. 4.5:

> The Conciliator may:
> **(a)** issue such further instructions as he considers to be appropriate;
> **(b)** meet and question the Parties and their representatives, together or separately;
> **(c)** investigate the facts and circumstances of the dispute;
> **(d)** visit the site;
> **(e)** request the production of documents or the attendance of people whom he considers could assist in any way.

Paragraph 4.6 states:

> The Conciliator may conduct the proceedings in any way that he/she wishes, and with the prior agreement of the Parties obtain legal or technical advice, the cost of which shall be met by the Parties, in accordance with Paragraph 5.4, or as may be agreed by the Parties and the Conciliator.

If an agreement cannot be arrived at, the conciliator will make a recommendation. Under the Institution of Civil Engineers contracts, a recommendation is a distinct stage in the dispute resolution process. Paragraph 5.1 goes on to state:

> The Conciliator shall advise all Parties accordingly and prepare his recommendation forthwith:

(a) if, in the opinion of the Conciliator, it is unlikely that the Parties will achieve an agreed settlement to their disputes; or

(b) if any Party fails to respond to an instruction by the Conciliator, or

(c) upon the request of any Party.

The nature of a recommendation in this context is specified in para. 5.2 as follows:

> The Conciliator's Recommendation shall state his solution to the dispute which has been referred for Conciliation. The Recommendation shall not disclose any information which any Party has provided in confidence. It shall be based on his opinion as to how the Parties can best dispose of the dispute between them and need not necessarily be based on any principles of the Contract, law or equity.

The conciliator is not required to give reasons for his/her recommendation. It is simply his/her opinion of how the dispute might be resolved in the most practical way. Nevertheless, should he/she choose to do so, his/her reasons will be issued as a separate document, within seven days of giving the recommendation.

Thus, a person acting as a conciliator can be more pro-active in exploring a basis for a settlement and may suggest ideas that have not occurred to the parties. If requested by the parties, he/she may sometimes offer a non-binding legal opinion if this is likely to assist with a settlement. Such a non-binding legal opinion may progress discussions that have become stalled. It may focus on a single issue or the likely outcome of the case were it to be litigated. If the conciliator is likely to be called upon to give a legal opinion he/she must be legally qualified. The International Chamber of Commerce devised a set of Rules of Conciliation in 1988 that are still in force for the resolution of international business disputes. Article 2 of the Rules of Conciliation specifies that:

> The party requesting conciliation shall apply to the Secretariat of the International Court of Arbitration of the International Chamber of Commerce setting out succinctly the purpose of the request and accompanying it with the fee required to open the file as set out in the Appendix hereto.

According to Article 3 the Secretariat informs the other party as soon as possible of the request and that party then has 15 days in which to inform the Secretariat of its willingness, or otherwise, to participate in a conciliation. If the parties are willing to attempt a conciliation, the Secretary General of the International Court of Arbitration will appoint a conciliator who will then inform the parties of his/her appointment in order to arrange a meeting with them. Article 7 states:

> The Conciliation shall come to an end:
>
> (a) Upon the parties signing an agreement. The parties shall be bound by such agreement. The agreement shall remain confidential unless and to the extent that its execution or application require disclosure.
>
> (b) Upon the production by the conciliator of a report recording that the

attempt to conciliate has not been successful. Such report shall not contain reasons.

(c) Upon notification to the conciliator by one or more parties at any time during the conciliation process of an intention to no longer pursue the conciliation process.

Article 8 then goes on to state that:

Upon termination of the conciliation, the conciliator shall provide the Secretariat of the International Court of Arbitration with the settlement agreement signed by the parties or with his report of lack of success or with a notice from one or more parties of the intention to pursue the conciliation process.

The Chartered Institute of Arbitrators has devised a Consumer Dispute Resolution Scheme in consultation with the Office of Fair Trading and the National Consumer Council. The scheme does not extend to claims for physical injury, illness and nervous shock and different trade associations set different financial ceilings for the monetary amounts of claims by consumers. It applies to claims made by private consumers of goods and services. It operates in two stages: first there is a conciliation process which is controlled by the Institute, and if conciliation fails there is provision for arbitration. According to para. 2.1 of the 2000 Edition:

Where a written complaint by a consumer to a supplier has been rejected or where there has been no reply or where the parties have not been able to settle their dispute within four weeks of the date of the written complaint that matter can be referred to conciliation.

The process begins after both sides have signed and submitted the Institute's application form together with the appropriate fee and the President or a Vice President of the Institute has appointed a conciliator. According to para. 3.1:

The Conciliation procedure will be at the discretion of the Conciliator. However, each party will be requested to submit case statements and all relevant supporting evidence. These will be reviewed by the Conciliator who may ask the parties for clarification of their cases either in writing or at a meeting.

Paragraph 3.2 then goes on to state:

The Conciliator will provide the parties with a report which, together with the Conciliator's suggestions for a settlement, will form the basis of a possible agreement. If accepted by the parties the Conciliator will incorporate the settlement terms in a written agreement to be signed by both parties.

It is clear from para. 3.3 that if the parties do not settle within six weeks of the conciliator's appointment, the dispute may be referred to arbitration and the documents submitted to the conciliator will be passed on to the arbitrator with the conciliator's report. However, unless the parties request it, the conciliator cannot act as arbitrator nor must he/she divulge to the arbitrator information given to him/her in confidence. Moreover, the conciliator must not act as an advocate, adviser or witness for any party in the course of the arbitration.

4   Other forms of ADR

Mediation and conciliation often do, but need not, focus on clearly defined points of law. If a point of law or the interpretation of the wording of a contract lies at the heart of a dispute, the parties involved may apply to bodies like ACI for an 'early neutral evaluation'. This will often entail a QC giving an indication of the likely outcome of the dispute were it to be litigated. The person appointed as the 'neutral' will issue his/her non-binding written opinion at the end of the process with a view to encouraging the parties to settle. As long ago as 1990, the Chartered Institute of Arbitrators devised guidelines for a supervised settlement procedure. Under these guidelines most business disputes can be submitted to a panel comprising one or more senior executives from both sides who will be assisted by a neutral chairperson who need not be a lawyer. This procedure is sometimes referred to as a 'mini trial' but this is a misnomer because the normal rules of procedure and evidence do not apply and, as stated above, the chairperson need not be legally qualified. The process aims at the achievement of a workable compromise rather than a legal solution as such. The opening paragraph of the explanatory notes to the guidelines states:

> Most bona fide disputes between reputable parties are capable of settlement in a manner that is business orientated, thus avoiding or at least curtailing legal expenditure, the loss of executive time and the deterioration of a valuable business relationship.
>
> Such a settlement can be facilitated by the use of a structured procedure which ensures that authorised management representatives are presented with the facts, viewed from both sides, and can then enter into negotiations under the guidance of a neutral adviser experienced in conciliation, mediation and arbitration techniques.
>
> This procedure can be invoked at an early stage when there is goodwill and a history of good relationships or after litigation or arbitration has been initiated.

Included with the guidelines is a draft agreement for the signature of those wishing to embark on a supervised settlement procedure. A compromise agreement must normally be concluded within 60 days of the date of the agreement unless the parties agree to an extension of time. All statements and documents produced are treated 'without prejudice' and are therefore inadmissible in any subsequent legal proceedings if the process should prove to be inconclusive.

5   Lawyers and ADR

Since the first edition of this text, it is clear that mediation and conciliation have gained ground as methods of dispute resolution. The evidence
for this is provided by the large number of barristers' chambers and solicitors' practices that now offer their services as mediators via their websites.
An increasing number of barristers and solicitors are qualifying as mediators each year as they perceive this as an important source of income. One
set of chambers boasts 10 QCs with special expertise in medical law who
will act as mediators.

6   Arbitration

Arbitration has long been a popular method of dispute resolution in
spheres such as construction, reinsurance and shipping but it is also used
in other types of dispute. Although arbitration occurs outside the normal
court structure, the arbitrator's decision (or 'award' as it is technically
known) can be enforced through the courts if necessary, as stipulated in
the Arbitration Act 1950 s. 26. It is therefore legally binding on the parties.
All the detailed rules governing arbitrations are set out in the Arbitration
Acts 1950 and 1996 but some can be modified by agreement between the
parties. There are a number of significant advantages to be gained from
trying to resolve a dispute through arbitration as opposed to litigation.
These are as follows:

1 There is a greater degree of flexibility in the procedure in arbitration as
   compared with litigation in that the rules of evidence need not be so
   strictly applied in an arbitration and the entire matter can be decided
   on the basis of written submissions if the parties agree to this.
2 The parties are at liberty to decide upon the location, together with the
   date and time of proceedings, whereas in litigation the parties only have
   limited opportunities to request that the case be heard at a court in a
   particular locality.
3 A person with the appropriate technical qualifications can be appointed
   by the parties where a dispute arises in a particular trade or business and
   it involves technical issues so that the arbitrator(s) can bring his/her (or
   their) specialist knowledge to bear when arriving at a resolution of the
   dispute.
4 The parties will avoid the attention of the press and media because the
   proceedings will be conducted behind closed doors.
5 There can be a saving of time and therefore expenses although the
   parties themselves must bear the cost of the arbitration proceedings
   (but there will undoubtedly be a saving of court fees and lawyers' fees if
   the parties are not legally represented).
6 The decision of the arbitrator may be given more quickly than the judgment of a court which may be reserved for weeks or even months.

In relation to 5 above, if the parties decide upon a full-scale hearing and on being represented by lawyers, the cost may be as high as litigation in the courts and may therefore confer no financial advantage whatever. Savings are likely, however, if the dispute is a technical one and the arbitrator is a technical expert who can dispose of the matter without the need for lawyers and expert witnesses. Very often the parties will agree that the issue can be decided upon on the basis of the documentation that they submit to the arbitrator and this will be likely to result in considerable savings of time and money. Even if lawyers are involved, they may be able to narrow the area of dispute as well as shorten the preparation time and time taken up with the hearing. Arbitration will not be an appropriate method of dispute resolution in all cases. For example, if the case involves a completely novel set of facts for which there is no existing precedent or relevant statute law, arbitration will be inappropriate. On the other hand, if a dispute simply requires an authoritative interpretation of a statutory provision, this can be obtained from a court as specified by the Arbitration Act 1996 s. 45.

Many contracts nowadays contain arbitration clauses. For example, the Royal Institute of British Architects has a standard form contract for minor building works which contains such a clause. Even if there is no arbitration clause in a contract there is nothing to prevent the parties from submitting their dispute for resolution by arbitration. The agreement to do so must itself be in writing as required by the Arbitration Act 1950 s. 32 and should contain a provision governing the appointment of the arbitrator. The Limitation Act 1980 s. 13 applies to arbitration proceedings and so it is important that they should commence within the limitation period. At the outset the parties may agree on the powers that will be exercisable by the arbitral tribunal (a single arbitrator or a panel of arbitrators). Where one party is a UK national and the other is a foreign national it would be common practice to provide in the contract for a panel of three arbitrators to be appointed. One would be appointed by each side (usually in consultation with the advocate appointed) and a third person would be appointed as an 'umpire' to guarantee at least a majority decision of 2:1 in the event that unanimity was not possible. The Chartered Institute of Arbitrators (whose president is often a judge from the Court of Appeal) can provide a list of suitable persons from among its 7,500 members to act as competent arbitrators in virtually any dispute. An arbitrator need not be a barrister or solicitor but parties in dispute often nominate lawyers to act as arbitrators. In high-value commercial contracts (those involving the hire of ships and aircraft or large-scale civil engineering projects) it would not be uncommon to find a term in the contract requiring the parties to submit all disputes to arbitration before resorting to litigation. The Arbitration Act 1996 s. 9(1) provides:

> A party to an arbitration agreement against whom legal proceedings are brought (whether by way of claim or counterclaim) in respect of a matter which under the agreement is to be referred to arbitration may (upon giving notice to the other parties to the proceedings) apply to the court in

which the proceedings have been brought to stay (suspend) the proceedings so far as they concern that matter.

Section 9(4) further provides that:

> On an application under this section the court shall grant a stay unless satisfied that the arbitration agreement is null and void, inoperative, or incapable of being performed.

The party making the application must demonstrate that the legal proceedings brought against him/her deal with a dispute that can be referred to arbitration under the arbitration clause or agreement. The Arbitration Act 1996 s. 1(a) and (b) state that:

(a)   the object of arbitration is to obtain the fair resolution of disputes by an impartial tribunal without unnecessary delay or expense;
(b)   the parties should be free to agree how their disputes are resolved, subject only to such safeguards as are necessary in the public interest;

so the parties and/or their legal representatives must identify their priorities. If it is important that the dispute is resolved quickly it must be decided whether full pleadings are really necessary or whether an opening statement of case with skeleton arguments will suffice. Similarly, opening and closing submission can be given in writing. Where time is of the essence, s. 33(b) requires that the arbitrator:

> adopt procedures suitable to the circumstances of the particular case, avoiding unnecessary delay or expense, so as to provide a fair means for the resolution of the matters falling to be determined.

If the arbitrator fails to deal with matters quickly, the parties, acting together, are at liberty under s. 23 to terminate his/her appointment or any one party may apply to the court under s. 24 to remove the arbitrator. Unlike mediation and conciliation, the Arbitration Act 1996 normally requires the arbitral tribunal to apply the relevant law to the facts as agreed by the parties and/or established at the arbitration hearing. Thus the role of an arbitral tribunal is similar to that of a judge in a civil trial but the arbitrator can be a little more inquisitorial than a judge. According to s. 46(1) the arbitral tribunal must decide the dispute:

(a)   in accordance with the law chosen by the parties as applicable to the substance of the dispute, or
(b)   if the parties agree, in accordance with such other considerations as are agreed by them to be determined by the tribunal.

Apart from the ability of an arbitral tribunal to award damages it may grant other remedies under the Act. The Arbitration Act 1996 s. 48(5) specifies that a tribunal has the same powers as a court to:

(a)   order a party to do or refrain from doing anything;
(b)   order specific performance of a contract other than one relating to land;
(c)   order rectification, setting aside or cancellation of a deed or other document.

7 Arbitration schemes

As was noted above, the Chartered Institute of Arbitrators has assisted the Office of Fair Trading in the setting up of a wide range of Consumer Arbitration Schemes and there are now over 50 of these schemes in operation sponsored by various trade associations. The arbitration itself will be administered by the Chartered Institute of Arbitrators and can take up to 14 weeks as indicated below:

1 week	The Institute sends out a claim form to the applicant and the arbitrator.
4 weeks	The applicant's claim must be received by the Institute which will copy it to the respondent.
3 weeks	The defence and any counterclaim is submitted to the Institute by the respondent and a copy will be forwarded to the claimant from the Institute.
2 weeks	Any reply to the defence must be submitted to the Institute and a copy will be forwarded to the respondent from the Institute.
1 week	All documents are to be sent to the arbitrator.
3 weeks	The arbitrator gives his/her decision (known as an 'award').

The claimant pays only a modest registration fee and legal representation is not strictly necessary. The trade body pays the CIA's fee and the arbitrator's fee. The arbitration is usually conducted on the basis of written argument and evidence but if either party requests it, or if the arbitrator considers it appropriate, a meeting can be held between the parties and the arbitrator. The arbitrator can use such a meeting to ask questions in order to clarify the matters in dispute. The Institute will send a copy of the award to each party and to the organisation acting as a sponsoring body for the scheme. If the award entails the payment of money it must normally be paid within 21 days of the posting of the award. Such schemes are intended to be a real alternative to litigation but they cannot operate to exclude the right of consumers to take legal action in the courts.

Arbitration a Commercial Initiative (ACI) operates from Gray's Inn, London and offers a variety of arbitration schemes to industry and commerce. Disputes can be transferred between the various ACI schemes when appropriate. These schemes are

1 fixed fee arbitration
2 standard arbitration
3 fast track arbitration.

Fixed fee arbitration is designed for parties who are able to cooperate with a view to obtaining a speedy resolution of their dispute. Those cases that are not suitable for fixed fee arbitration are conducted under the rules for standard arbitration whilst fast track arbitration will be appropriate when there is urgency and ACI is able to provide arbitrators who will hear a dispute as soon as the parties are ready to be heard. In addition,

ACI also offers individually designed arbitration schemes where firms and companies have similar recurring disputes and wish to have them resolved by a neutral body.

The International Chamber of Commerce offers an arbitration service for the resolution of business disputes through the International Court of Arbitration whose Secretariat is based in Paris, although it operates in and through the major international financial centres, including London. It is not, however, attached to the ordinary English court system. Indeed, the court is truly international in that its members are drawn from some 60 countries. This body ensures that the Rules of Arbitration of the ICC are properly applied and provides a highly supervised form of arbitration in that it:

- ascertains whether there is an agreement to arbitrate;
- decides on the number of arbitrators;
- appoints the arbitrators;
- decides challenges to the appointment of arbitrators;
- ensures that the arbitration is conducted according to the ICC Rules;
- decides the location for the arbitration if the parties cannot agree;
- fixes and extends time limits;
- decides the fees and expenses of the arbitrator(s); and
- scrutinises the award.

The members of the International Court of Arbitration do not adjudicate on the issues submitted to the ICC because this is the province of the arbitrator(s) appointed. Instead, the court supervises the arbitration process from the initial request to the making of the final award. The staff of the Secretariat receive copies of all pleadings and other communications exchanged between the parties. Under the ICC Rules, the court must approve all awards to ensure that they conform to its high standards so that they are unlikely to be annulled in national courts thereafter.

8   Appeals from an arbitrator's award generally

According to the Arbitration Act 1996 s. 68(1) an application can be made to the High Court where there is a 'serious irregularity' in respect of the tribunal's conduct of the proceedings or in the award itself. Any application is made under the Civil Procedure Rules PD49G on notice to the other party/parties and to the tribunal. The appeal must be brought within 28 days of the award. The phrase 'serious irregularity' is defined in s. 68(2) as follows:

(a)   failure by the tribunal to comply with s. 33 which is the requirement to observe the normal standards of procedural fairness sometimes known as the principles of natural justice;

(b)   the tribunal exceeding its powers other than by exceeding its substantive jurisdiction;

(c)   failure by the tribunal to conduct the proceedings in accordance with the procedure agreed by the parties;

(d) failure by the tribunal to deal with all the issues that were put to it;

(e) any arbitral or other institution or person vested by the parties with powers in relation to the proceedings or the award exceeding its powers;

(f) uncertainty or ambiguity as to the effect of the award;

(g) the award being obtained by fraud or the award or the way in which it was procured being contrary to public policy;

(h) failure to comply with the requirements as to the form of the award; or

(i) any irregularity in the conduct of the proceedings or in the award which is admitted by the tribunal or by any arbitral or other institution or person vested by the parties with powers in relation to the proceedings or the award.

In the event that there should be any serious irregularity affecting the tribunal proceedings or the award, the court may, under s. 68(3):

(a) remit the award wholly or in part to the arbitral tribunal for reconsideration; or

(b) set the award aside wholly or in part; or

(c) declare the award to be of no effect, wholly or in part.

Any matters that do not come within s. 68(2), as specified above, may not be challenged under that section. An appeal on a point of law is possible under the Arbitration Act 1996 s. 69 which states:

> Unless otherwise agreed by the parties, a party to arbitral proceedings may (upon notice to the other parties and to the tribunal) appeal to the court on a question of law arising out of an award made in the proceedings.

A question of law is defined by s. 82(1) as meaning a question of the law of England and Wales or Northern Ireland as appropriate. Consequently, if the parties have chosen to conduct the proceedings under foreign law, no appeal is possible. The tribunal's findings on questions of fact are conclusive and final and, if there is to be an appeal on a question of law, it must arise from the award. Even then s. 69(2) provides that an appeal can only be brought:

(a) with the agreement of the other party/parties, or

(b) with the permission of the court.

Moreover s. 70(2) provides that such an appeal may not be brought unless the applicant has exhausted recourse under s. 57 which empowers the tribunal to correct its award and make an additional award. According to s. 69(3) the court must be satisfied:

(a) that the determination of the question will substantially affect the rights of one or more of the parties;

(b) that the question is one which the tribunal was asked to determine;

(c) that on the basis of the finding of fact in the award –
   (i) the decision of the tribunal on the question is obviously wrong, or
   (ii) the question is one of general public importance and the decision of the tribunal is at least open to serious doubt; and

(d) that, despite the agreement of the parties to resolve the matter by arbitration, it is just and proper in all the circumstances for the court to determine the question.

The content of an application and the procedure for making an appeal are set out in s. 69(4)–(6). On hearing the appeal the court may, under s. 69(7):

(a) confirm the award;
(b) vary the award;
(c) send the award back to the arbitral tribunal, wholly or in part, for reconsideration in the light of the court's determination; or
(d) set aside the award wholly or in part.

It should be noted that the parties are free under s. 69 to agree beforehand that there will be no right of appeal whatever.

Summary

At the end of a successful mediation or conciliation process there is a sense in which the parties 'own' the solution that has been arrived at through discussion and negotiation in private. There is no 'loser' but, as has been stated, not all attempts at mediation and conciliation succeed. It seems that mediation has yet to become the dispute resolution method of choice in some areas such as personal accident claims. Although arbitration has much to commend it, at the conclusion of the process the party who has 'lost' may harbour resentment because it is an imposed solution. Moreover, the arbitrator's award can be enforced through legal process, if necessary. All this may have negative consequences for a business relationship that has taken many years to develop. Arbitration does, however, offer the prospect of finality and for this reason has long been a popular method of resolving commercial disputes where mediation has been tried but failed to produce a solution.

WWW PROGRESS TEST

For suggested answers to the tests below, go to the companion website at www.pearsoned.co.uk/wheeler

1 Why might the management of a business be reluctant to take a dispute to court?
2 What do you understand by the term 'mediation' and does it differ from 'conciliation'? In general, are both suitable for resolving business disputes?
3 Do lawyers favour mediation and conciliation as methods of dispute resolution?

4 How does arbitration differ from mediation and conciliation?
5 Is arbitration really an alternative to litigation? If so, why; if not, why not?
6 What advantages do you see for a business in submitting a dispute to arbitration?
7 Are there any disadvantages?
8 Is it more likely that the parties will preserve a cordial business relationship by referring a dispute to arbitration rather than by resorting to litigation?
9 In arbitration, how is natural justice ensured?
10 On what grounds is it possible to appeal from an arbitrator's award? Can an appeal be precluded from the outset?

FURTHER READING

Doyle, M. (2000) *Advising on ADR* (London: Advice Services Alliance).
Newman, P. (1999) *Alternative Dispute Resolution* (Welwyn Garden City: CLT Professional Publishing).
Stone, M. (1998) *Representing Clients in Mediation* (Oxford: Oxford University Press).
Tweeddale, A. and K. Tweeddale (1999) *A Practical Approach to Arbitration* (Oxford: Oxford University Press).

USEFUL WEBSITES

The website of the Chartered Institute of Arbitrators is www.arbitrators.org and the Centre for Dispute Resolution has a website at www.cedr.co.uk.
The reader will find the website of the ADR Group at www.adrgroup.co.uk and the International Chamber of Commerce at www.iccwbo.org. Details of the ICC ADR scheme can also be found on this website.
The website of the ACI – (Arbitration a Commercial Initiative) can be found at www.aci-arb.com.
The national mediation helpline can be accessed via the following address: www.nationalmediationhelpline.com.

13 Dispute resolution 2: Civil litigation

1 Introduction

It is an observable fact that disputes of various types arise in every area of human activity. In the business world, many firms and companies do their very best to avoid disputes. They do so by taking care over the drafting of contracts and by attempting, at the outset, to provide for as many eventualities as possible in their contractual documentation. For example, in a building contract the main contractor might wish to exclude liability altogether for delays that are completely beyond his/her control (e.g. a strike at one of the ports where materials must be imported). Alternatively, the main contractor may seek to limit the amount of compensation payable for delay, caused by a particular event, to a fixed sum by agreement with the other party to the contract. This chapter deals with the resolution of disputes in the civil courts and begins by explaining the rationale for the Civil Procedure Rules. A hypothetical scenario will be introduced that will serve as a basis for the subsequent examination of the civil litigation process and the rules of procedure. There then follows an outline of the system for civil appeals.

2 The quiet revolution

On 26 April 1999 a quiet revolution occurred in the procedure for conducting civil litigation in England and Wales. The sweeping changes ushered in were a response to the findings of an inquiry undertaken by Lord Woolf. In 1994, he had been commissioned by Lord Mackay of Clashfern (who was then Lord Chancellor) to conduct a review of the rules and procedures of the civil courts. His report, entitled *Access to Justice*, condemned the existing system as being too slow and too expensive. Its rules were too complex, the costs involved were too uncertain and, as a result, justice was inaccessible for many people.

The Civil Procedure Act 1997 paved the way for the Civil Procedure Rules 1998 (hereafter CPR) which came into operation on 26 April when most of the old rules were revoked. These rules have been supplemented by a number of Practice Directions. Together, they comprise a set of civil procedural rules that aim to create a climate of openness for the parties involved in litigation. However, it was not possible to devise new rules for all legal procedures in time, so it was necessary to incorporate some of the old rules of procedure into the new CPR and they were re-enacted in Schedules 1 and 2 of the CPR.

3 Pre-action protocols

The new climate of openness in civil litigation has been underpinned by the introduction of pre-action protocols. Prior to issuing proceedings, the claimant must write to the defendant informing him/her of the claim. A claim should not be commenced until three months have elapsed following the issue of this letter. There are a number of protocols in final form, namely:

the personal injury protocol
the clinical negligence protocol
the construction and engineering protocol
the defamation protocol
the family law protocol.

The construction and engineering protocol has been devised to include professional negligence claims against architects, engineers and quantity surveyors. It is now clear that in cases not covered by a specific protocol, the courts will expect the parties to act reasonably in exchanging information and documents relevant to the claim and to avoid the necessity for legal proceedings. Although no sanctions are specified for non-compliance, the courts have wide discretion when making orders for costs and awarding interest and, as a result, the court may order that:

(a) a party at fault must pay all or part of the costs of the proceedings to date;
(b) a party at fault pay costs on an indemnity basis;
(c) where the party at fault is the claimant, interest on any damages awarded may be denied; or
(d) where the party at fault is the defendant he/she may be required to pay additional interest on damages awarded against him/her.

The parties are encouraged to exchange full information at an early stage about the potential legal claim with a view to encouraging them to avoid unnecessary litigation by achieving a settlement. It is also intended that they should support the efficient management of proceedings where litigation cannot be avoided. The *Civil Justice Reform Evaluation 2001*, published by the Lord Chancellor's Department, reported that a survey was conducted by the Association of Personal Injury Lawyers of its members, according to which 33 per cent of personal injury cases had been settled without the need for litigation. Of course, there are likely to be many instances of failure to comply with the appropriate protocol but the CPR enables the court to take non-compliance into account when making orders for costs. If the court takes the view that non-compliance has resulted in the commencement of proceedings unnecessarily or has led to additional costs being incurred, it has the power to order that the party at fault must pay the costs involved wholly or in part. The *Civil Justice Reform Evaluation* indicated that there has been a fall in the number of claims issued following the introduction of the CPR.

4 Issue and service of proceedings

Apart from certain types of case (such as insolvency proceedings, non-contentious (uncontested) probate, proceedings under the Mental Health Act 1983 and family proceedings) there is no distinction between the procedure that obtains in the High Court and that which applies in the county courts. A common process applies to commencement of most claims (apart from Admiralty claims, claims in the Commercial Court and applications for judicial review) in that the same claim form is used. It is Form N1 which can be obtained free of charge from any county court office together with a set of guidance notes to assist with completion. However, forms N394, N396 and N397 are used for county court applications under the Landlord and Tenant Acts 1927 and 1954. The claimant will be provided with three copies of the blank form N1 (see Figure 13.1). The form N208 is used where there is no dispute over the essential facts of a case or if the claim requires an authoritative interpretation of a document or where the claimant seeks a declaratory judgment. A claim for less than £15,000 cannot normally be issued from the High Court in London and personal injury claims must normally exceed £50,000 to be issued from the High Court. Nevertheless, cases involving complex issues of law and fact may exceptionally be commenced in the High Court below these limits.

As can be seen on pages 270–271, the N1 claim form must state on its face the name of the claimant and the claimant's address. The defendant's name and address (or place of business) must also appear. Brief details of the claim and its monetary value must be given (unless a remedy other than financial compensation is being sought). On the reverse of the form, the claimant should provide more detailed particulars of the claim that is being made. However, if he/she does not complete this section, these 'particulars of claim' must then be submitted to the defendant within 14 days after service of the claim form on the defendant. If the particulars are served separately on the defendant, a copy of the particulars of claim must be filed with the court within seven days of their service (on the defendant), together with a certificate of service. In any event, the particulars of claim must be a precise statement of the facts on which the claimant relies and must state the remedy or remedies sought. The court now has the power, of its own motion and without conducting a hearing, to strike all or part of a statement of case on form N1 on the basis that no reasonable ground for bringing the claim is disclosed. The court can also,

Claim Form

In the

for court use only

Claim No.

Issue date

Claimant

SEAL

Defendant(s)

Brief details of claim

Value

Defendant's name and address

	£
Amount claimed	
Court fee	
Solicitor's costs	
Total amount	

The court office at

is open between 10 am and 4 pm Monday to Friday. When corresponding with the court, please address forms or letters to the Court Manager and quote the claim number.

N1 Claim form (CPR Part 7) (01.02)

Printed on behalf of The Court Service

Figure 13.1 N1 Claim Form – front
Source: © Crown copyright

	Claim No.	

Does, or will, your claim include any issues under the Human Rights Act 1998? ☐ Yes ☐ No

Particulars of Claim (attached)(to follow)

Statement of Truth
*(I believe)(The Claimant believes) that the facts stated in these particulars of claim are true.
* I am duly authorised by the claimant to sign this statement

Full name _____

Name of claimant's solicitor's firm _____

signed _____ position or office held_____

*(Claimant)(Litigation friend)(Claimant's solicitor)   (if signing on behalf of firm or company)

*delete as appropriate

Claimant's or claimant's solicitor's address to which documents or payments should be sent if different from overleaf including (if appropriate) details of DX, fax or e-mail.

Figure 13.2 **N1 Claim Form – back**

of its own motion, give a summary judgment *against a claimant* if it is considered that the claimant has no real prospect of success with the claim. If the claimant wishes to recover interest on a sum of money claimed, this must be detailed. The claimant must sign a statement on Form N1 to the effect that he/she believes that the facts alleged are true. A false declaration would amount to a contempt of court which, in this context, is a criminal offence. If the claimant has entered into a conditional fee agreement, notice, using form N251, must also be filed at the court offices. Copies of form N1 will be numbered and sealed with the court seal by the court staff upon payment of the appropriate fee and one copy of the claim form will be posted to the defendant by the court office with a 'response pack'. Under the CPR, the proceedings are officially commenced when the claim form is issued by the court and it must be served on the defendant within four months (or six months if it is to be served out of the court's jurisdiction). Once the initial proceedings have been served they can only be amended with permission of the court. The 'response pack' includes an admission form, a defence form and an acknowledgement of service form.

It is interesting to note that county court forms are being made available online as part of a new pilot initiative from mid-January 2005. Nine county courts across England and Wales will take part in the six-month pilot which, if successful, might be rolled out across the entire country. The county courts chosen are Basildon, Birmingham, Bournemouth, Coventry, Dartford, Leicester, Llangefni, Norwich and Preston. Claimants will be able to complete forms online either from the comfort of their own homes or at certain locations where they can receive advice and help with the completion of forms, such as the offices of the Citizens' Advice Bureaux. Court fees can also be paid online using a debit or credit card.

5   Responding to the particulars of claim

On receiving the N1 form, the defendant has a number of options which can be conveniently summarised as follows:

(a)   admit liability and make an offer to pay;
(b)   file a defence to the whole or part of the claim within 14 days of service of the particulars of claim;
(c)   file an acknowledgement of service within 14 days of service of the particulars of claim *and then file a defence* within 28 days of service of the particulars of claim.

If the defendant does nothing, 'judgment by default' can be entered against him/her for the figure stated on the claim form but, if the defendant has applied for a summary judgment under Part 24 of the CPR, a default judgment cannot be entered in favour of the claimant until that application has been disposed of. Also, judgment by default cannot be entered if the proceedings were commenced using form N208. If no precise sum is specified on the claim form and judgment by default is to be entered for the claimant, the judge can award an appropriate sum without the need to convene an 'assessment hearing'. In many instances a defendant will admit the claim and make an offer to pay but a defendant who wishes to defend the claim must file a defence. A defendant who has not acknowledged service may not participate in the hearing of the claim without permission of the court even though he/she may attend the hearing. According to the CPR r. 16.5(1) the defence must state which of the allegations contained in the particulars of claim he/she denies or which he/she is unable to admit or deny but requires the claimant to prove. Moreover, he/she must indicate those allegations which he/she admits. If the defendant denies an allegation he/she must state his/her reasons for doing so and state his/her own version of events if it is different from the claimant's. A bare denial of the claimant's allegations contained in form N1 or an incoherent defence is liable to be 'struck out' on the court's own initiative so the defendant will not help his/her cause by resorting to delaying tactics. If the defendant disputes the value of the claim stated in form N1 he/she must state why he/she disputes it, giving his/her own value of the claim. Where the defence relates to a personal injury claim and the claimant has attached a medical report pertaining to his/her injuries, Practice Direction 16 para. 13.1 requires that the defence should state whether the defendant:

(a)   concurs with the medical report,
(b)   disputes it (and if so, giving reasons why), or
(c)   neither agrees nor disputes it but has no knowledge of the details comprising the report.

Where a medical report has been obtained by the defendant which is to form part of his/her defence, this must be attached to the defence form. Of course, if both parties have complied with the pre-action protocol for personal injury, the medical report will have been agreed and it is unlikely that the defendant will have procured his/her own report.

Under the CPR it is possible for a defendant to raise a counterclaim by which he/she asserts that it is really him/her that has a claim against the claimant. If the defendant does raise a counterclaim, the original claimant must file a defence to the counterclaim. Where a defence is filed with or without a counterclaim it must be accompanied by a statement of truth, as must any counterclaim. If the statement of truth is to be signed by the legal adviser rather than the client, the latter should give an assurance to the former in respect of the details of the case to be verified. Moreover, a legal adviser should not sign the statement of truth unless he/she is specifically authorised to do so; nor should he/she sign without having explained the consequences of a false declaration to the client. If a legal adviser should fail to observe these precautions he/she might be open to an allegation of professional misconduct.

6 The scenario

Suppose that nine months ago David, the managing director of Modern Builders Ltd, was contacted by a firm of local architects who asked him to submit an estimate for a house extension that had been designed by the firm. The house is a detached property standing in half an acre of ground just outside Guildford, Surrey.

The house had been bequeathed to Alice on the death of her father in a road accident. She had recently returned from Hong Kong where she had given up her practice as a dentist so that she could look after her mother who had been seriously injured in the same accident. Alice's mother was undergoing a protracted course of treatment at Stoke Mandeville Hospital for her spinal injuries. In the meantime, Alice had decided to have the house modified so that her mother could live on the ground floor when she was finally discharged from hospital.

The contract to build the extension was awarded to Modern Builders Ltd because the company had submitted the most competitive tender for the work. The contract was for £30,000 but it allowed for stage payments to be made as work progressed and was inspected and 'passed' by the firm of architects. Work was to start on 1 March with completion set by 30 September. It was estimated that Alice's mother would be discharged from hospital in early October.

Although Modern Builders had a number of similar contracts underway at this time, work did commence on schedule but it became clear by the end of June that all the work would not be complete by the end of September as had been agreed. Although Alice protested to David that the work must be completed by the agreed date, he replied that he had been obliged to divert some of his workmen to deal with 'emergencies' and that there had been a very high rate of absenteeism due to illness. At this point, Alice offered to pay Modern Builders Ltd an additional £8,000 at completion if David would agree to engage additional workers and hire extra equipment so that the extension would be completed by the end of September. David agreed and promised that all the work, including decorating, would be finished by 30 September.

On 1 October Alice wrote to the company stating that, although the extension had been completed, there were aspects of the work with which she was dissatisfied. In the same letter she refused to pay the additional £8,000 and stated that she was withholding £4,500 of the original £30,000 to cover the cost of, what she regarded as, necessary rectification work. David considers that all the work has been satisfactorily completed and that the company is entitled to all the money that is being withheld.

If the parties adopt entrenched positions it will only be possible to resolve the dispute by resorting to litigation. This would ultimately entail presenting the material facts to a judge whose role would be to apply the relevant law and give judgment for one of the parties to the dispute. However, under the CPR the parties are actively encouraged to achieve a settlement before proceedings are even commenced.

The company (Modern Builders Ltd) would be the claimant for £12,500 and Alice, as defendant, would have to consider her options. She could admit liability in full in respect of the company's claim. She might take the view that she is in the right and decide to defend the action by completing and filing a defence to the effect that she is not legally obliged to make the payment of £8,000. In addition, she might counterclaim under CPR r. 20.4(1) regarding the £4,500 stating that she has the right to retain this sum to cover the cost of what she considers to be rectification work. If so, she must file her counterclaim with the court and pay the appropriate fee. The counterclaim should normally form a single document in which the counterclaim follows the defence. Were Alice to ignore the sealed copy of the claim form that is served on her, judgment would be entered against her *by default* on the application of the claimant. If Alice were to file a defence, the company would not be obliged to file a 'reply' but it could. A reply is simply a response to any of the issues raised in the defence and, if a counterclaim is raised by the defendant, the claimant may wish to file a reply and a defence to the counterclaim. Failure to file a reply would not operate to the company's detriment because it is not deemed to have admitted the matters raised in a defence filed by Alice. The various documents referred to above constitute the statement of case.

Under Part 18 of the CPR and Practice Direction 18, any party to the proceedings can obtain from the other party:

(a) further clarification of any matter in dispute regarding the proceedings, and/or

(b) further information relating to any matter in dispute.

This may be done by directing a request to the other party in accordance with Practice Direction 18 without involving the court. It is only if the party does not respond, or if the response is inadequate, that an application can be made for an order under CPR r. 18.1 requiring disclosure.

7 Agreed settlements – Part 36 offers and payments

The CPR encourages the parties to settle their dispute even before the commencement of legal proceedings and certainly long before the actual trial takes place. There is an incentive for them to do so by way of saving of costs. Part 36 of the CPR is quite complex. At the outset it is important to distinguish between a pre-action offer which is not a Part 36 offer and a pre-action offer that comes within the ambit of the CPR Part 36. Whilst both are mentioned in Part 36 of the CPR, a formal Part 36 offer has more serious potential cost consequences for a defendant than an ordinary pre-action offer to settle. A pre-action offer to settle may be made by either side to the dispute and, if it complies with the requirements set out in r. 36.10, the court will take it into consideration together with the surrounding circumstances when making any order as to costs in any subsequent proceedings. The circumstances referred to include whether the person making the offer (offeror) has complied with a relevant pre-action protocol or, in the absence of a protocol, whether the offeree was given sufficient information to assess whether to accept the offer. It is quite possible that, if the offeror ignored a relevant protocol, the court may refuse to allow him/her any cost benefit. The offer may consist of a proposal to settle for a specified sum or for some other remedy. It must be clear to the offeree that the offer is indeed a Part 36 offer. Thus, to comply with the requirements of r. 36.5, it has to be in writing and be signed stating:

(a) whether it relates to all or part of the claim being made;
(b) whether it takes account of any counterclaim that has been made;
(c) whether it is inclusive of interest and giving details of interest to be paid.

According to r. 36.10(2)(a) the offer must also be expressed to be open for 21 days after it has been made but, thereafter, it will lapse. The party who would be the claimant, if proceedings were to be initiated, should normally consider making a pre-action offer 21 days before commencing proceedings in virtually every case. He/she should do so with a view to putting financial pressure on the party who would be the defendant to resolve the dispute. If the defendant is held liable for more than what was contained in the claimant's offer (or judgment against the defendant is more advantageous to the claimant), r. 36.21 will apply. This means that the court may order interest on the entire or any part of any sum awarded to the claimant from the date on which the defendant could have accepted the offer. Interest will not, however, be due on the interest already payable. In addition, the court may order that the defendant must pay the claimant's costs from the latest date on which he/she could have accepted the offer. The court does, however, have the discretion not to make such an order if it considers that it would be unjust. In considering whether it would be unjust, it will take into account all the circumstances of the case including:

(a) the terms of the Part 36 offer;
(b) the stage in the proceedings an offer (or payment) was made;
(c) the information available to the parties at the time; and
(d) the conduct of the parties in relation to the giving or refusing to give information for the purpose of evaluating the offer (or payment).

If the claimant has not made a pre-action offer to settle, the defendant should take the initiative as soon as he/she can evaluate the substance of the claim being brought against him/her. Such an offer should include an offer to pay the costs of the claimant (offeree) for 21 days after the offer was made. These costs could be considerable and could include the costs of reviewing documents, compiling witness statements, expert evidence, together with draft particulars of claim. If the claimant decides to accept an offer from the defendant relating to every aspect of claim made he/she will be entitled to recover his/her costs up to the date of the notification of acceptance. A realistic Part 36 offer from the defendant should focus the claimant's mind on the advisability of resolving the dispute as early as possible. If the claimant declines the offer, then fails to obtain a more advantageous judgment in court, he/she could be held liable for the costs the defendant incurred after the latest date on which the pre-action offer could have been accepted. The permission of the court is not required for a pre-action settlement and, if accepted, the case will be closed.

If proceedings, as described above, are started after a pre-action offer that complies with CPR r. 36.10 has been made, that offer cannot be accepted without the court's permission. Where the defendant in a money claim makes a pre-commencement offer but proceedings are then commenced, a defendant seeking to avail himself/herself of the costs advantage must make a payment into court. This must be done within 14 days of the service of the claim form. Moreover, the amount of the payment must not be less than the sum offered before the proceedings began. Thus, in the scenario above, Alice could make a payment into court as indicated but it must equal or exceed the amount offered before proceedings were commenced. The payment, however, cannot be accepted by the claimant without the court's consent.

A new Part 36 offer can be made any time after proceedings have been commenced because the parties have not settled. A defendant's Part 36 offer or payment made 21 days or more before the start of the trial may be accepted by the claimant without the necessity of obtaining the court's permission if the claimant gave the defendant notice of acceptance in writing no later than 21 days following the offer or the making of the payment. In the event that the defendant should make a Part 36 offer or payment less than 21 days before the trial, or if the claimant does not accept it within the 21-day period, the claimant may still accept without the necessity of obtaining the court's consent provided both reach agreement on the liability for costs. If a claimant accepts a defendant's Part 36 offer or payment that does not require the approval of the court, the defendant, as offeror, must pay the claimant's costs up to the date of serving notice of acceptance of the offer. If the defendant accepts a Part 36 offer made by the claimant that does not require the approval of the court, the defendant, as offeree, must pay the claimant's costs up to the date of the serving of the notice of acceptance. The incentive for the claimant to settle resides in the fact that if he/she should be awarded less at the end of the trial than the amount offered by the defendant, the court will not usually allow him/her to recover costs incurred after the date on which the offer could have been accepted. If the claimant makes an offer to the defendant to settle for *less* than the amount claimed, but the defendant decides to decline the offer, and then the claimant is awarded *more* at the trial, the defendant will be penalised in costs and by the interest that is payable in respect of the claim.

Part 36 offers do not apply to the small claims track but this does not operate to bar a party from making an offer or a payment in such a case; however, the consequences set out in Part 36 will not apply in a small claim. The fact that a Part 36 offer has been made will not be communicated to the trial judge until the issues of liability and the amount of damages payable (if any) have been determined, except where:

(a) the defence of tender before claim has been raised;

(b) the proceedings have been stayed under r. 36.15 after acceptance of a Part 36 offer (or payment); or

(c) the issue of liability has been decided before any assessment of the money claimed and the fact that there has or has not been a Part 36 payment could be relevant to the question of costs on the issue of liability.

The essence of (a) above is that before a claimant starts proceedings the defendant unconditionally offers him/her the amount due or, if no specified sum is claimed, an amount sufficient to satisfy the claim.

8 *Huck* v *Robson* [2002] 3 All ER 263

The Court of Appeal's decision clarifies further the operation of Part 36 pre-action offers to settle. In this case the claimant, Huck, had sustained personal injuries as a result of a collision between her car and the defendant's car. Huck alleged that she had pulled over on a narrow lane to allow the defendant to pass and that at the time of the collision her car was stationary. For his part, the defendant alleged that both cars were moving at the time of the collision. On 18 September Huck made an offer under CPR r. 36.10 to settle her claim on the basis that she would accept a 5 per cent reduction on the amount of her claim for damages. This offer was repeated on 6 October 2000 in a letter from the claimant's solicitors headed 'Part 36 Offer'. It stated:

> We refer to the above matter and are instructed to put forward our client's proposal in respect of liability only.
> We confirm that our client will accept a 95/5 per cent split on liability.
> This proposal will remain open for a period of 21 days after which it can only be accepted with leave of the court or with the consent of all other parties.

The defendant rejected the offer on 15 October 2000. Legal proceedings were commenced on 7 November 2000 and a county court hearing to determine the issue of liability took place on 27 July 2001. The judge decided that the defendant Robson was 100 per cent to blame for the harm suffered by the claimant and that costs should be awarded against him on the standard (rather than indemnity) basis on the grounds that the claimant's pre-action offer had been derisory. The claimant then appealed against the costs ruling on the grounds that she had been awarded more (100 per cent) than her pre-action offer (95 per cent) and accordingly was entitled to the costs advantages set out in Part 36. The Court of Appeal ruled that the matter had to be determined on the true meaning and effect of r. 36.10 and in particular the words 'the court will take that offer into account'. The purpose and effect of r. 36.10 is to

enable a party to make an offer which complies with Part 36 before proceedings are commenced and has all the consequences of a Part 36 offer.
Thus, r. 36.10 clearly enables a court to take a pre-action offer to settle
made in accordance with r. 36.10 together with the remainder of Part 36
into account when deciding the matter of costs to be recovered. The
Court of Appeal then went on to consider the application of r. 36.21
which deals with the costs consequences (indemnity costs and higher
interest) where a claimant is awarded more than his/her Part 36 offer. In
this case the court considered the r. 36.21 factors which a judge should
use to assess whether or not it would be unjust to apply the cost consequences. These factors are:

(i)   the terms of any Part 36 offer;
(ii)   the stage in the proceedings when any Part 36 offer is made;
(iii) the information available to the parties at the time when the
       offer/payment into court is made;
(iv)   the conduct of the parties with regard to the giving or refusal to give
       information for the purpose of enabling the offer/payment to be
       evaluated.

The Court of Appeal held that:

- Although it was not mandatory for a judge expressly to identify the four
  factors above, it would be prudent for him/her to do so.
- The trial judge had erred in his judgment that the 'illusory' apportionment of liability at 95/5 contained in the offer was relevant. The
  relevant factors were whether the defendant chooses to accept such an
  offer and (if he/she does not and the claimant is awarded more) if
  there is anything unjust in awarding indemnity costs and higher
  interest.
- The court was not required to measure the offer against the likely
  apportionment of liability at a trial because offers are not based on the
  court's likely apportionment of liability but reflect the reality that
  claimants prefer the relative certainty rather than face the ordeal of a
  trial.
- Where such an offer was merely a tactic to secure the benefit of CPR
  Part 36 (e.g. an offer to settle for 99.9 per cent of the claim) a judge
  would be entitled to exercise his/her discretion and refuse indemnity
  costs. This could not, however, be said of the claimant's offer in this
  case.
- Rule 36.21 requires a court to take justice into account in the individual
  case.

Accordingly, the claimant was entitled to indemnity costs and higher rate
interest. It is clear that a Part 36 offer need not be drafted to reflect what
a court may award at trial and does not have to be one that would be
unreasonable for the defendant to refuse as long as it affords the defendant a real opportunity for a settlement.

9 Allocation of the case

Although a claimant has an element of choice over which court to use when commencing proceedings (High Court or county court) this may not be the court that ultimately hears the case. This is because every defended claim has to be allocated to one of the three tracks – small claims, fast track or multi track – by a procedural judge. Although there are several factors to be considered when allocating a case to a 'track' (the nature of the remedy sought, the number of parties involved, the complexity of the facts, law or evidence, the amount of oral testimony to be given and the views and circumstances of the parties), in practice it is normally the amount of the claim that will be the deciding factor. Usually cases involving amounts up to £5,000 will be allocated to the 'small claims track' in the county courts. The CPR r. 26.6(1) provides that the following claims will normally be allocated to the small claims track:

(a) those with a financial value of no more than £5,000;
(b) personal injury cases where the damages claimed do not exceed £5,000 in total and where general damages do not exceed £1,000; and
(c) breach of covenant to repair cases where both the cost of repair and the value of any other claim for damages do not exceed £1,000.

Cases involving amounts over £5,000 up to £15,000 will be placed on the 'fast track' and will be heard in a county court where both district and circuit judges have jurisdiction. The fast track is also appropriate for non-monetary claims comprising applications for injunctions, declarations and claims for specific performance that are unsuitable for the small claims track but which are too straightforward for the multi track. For those cases involving a fixed sum, these will be transferred to the county court that has jurisdiction for the area where the defendant lives or carries on business. Most of those cases involving more than £15,000 are allocated to the so-called 'multi track' whereby they are transferred to a trial centre. These are the venues for multi track trials and a proportion of fast track trials and are the county courts for the geographical areas of England and Wales. If, however, a case simply entails the assessment of damages because liability has been admitted, then it may or may not be allocated to a track.

A procedural judge makes the first case management decision by deciding which is the most appropriate court to hear the case. In the Royal Courts of Justice (High Court) the procedural judges are High Court Masters, whereas in the civil trial centres they are circuit judges or district judges. If a claim, which is for a specified sum and is against an ordinary person, is defended, it will automatically be transferred to the defendant's home court by the court that received the defence. Thus, when Alice filed her defence, the case would have been transferred to Guildford County Court. In other cases, transfers are governed by the CPR Part 30. The criteria for deciding whether to transfer is set out in the High

Court and County Court Jurisdiction Order 1991 (SI 1991 No. 724). In order to assist the court with the allocation process, each party is normally required to complete and file an allocation questionnaire using form N150 soon after the defence is filed (see Appendix 3). It is always the court where the proceedings were commenced that has the responsibility for serving the allocation questionnaires. The recently revamped questionnaire asks each side (or their legal representative):

(a) whether they would like proceedings to be stayed (suspended) for a month in order to achieve a settlement by means other than litigation,

(b) if there is some reason why the claims should be heard at a particular court,

(c) whether a pre-action protocol (if appropriate) has been complied with or whether the party has exchanged information and/or documents with the other side to assist in settling the claim.

In the case management information section (part (d)) each party is required to state what amount of the claim is in dispute, whether application has been made for summary judgment and what expert witnesses and other witnesses are to be called. In the guidance notes, the parties are reminded to include themselves as witnesses of fact if they will be giving evidence. Each party is then asked which is the most suitable track for the claim, and thereafter:

(e) how long the trial is expected to last,

(f) whether a list of directions have been attached and if they have been agreed with the other side, and

(g) what costs have been incurred to date and what are the estimated overall costs. (This is addressed to solicitors and is completed for fast track and multi track claims only.)

In relation to (a) above, if both parties consent to a 'stay', the court will expect them to use the time in a genuine effort to resolve the dispute without the necessity of a court hearing. The allocation questionnaire will specify the date by which it must be filed and on receipt the court will be able to decide the most appropriate venue and the most appropriate track. It will also assist the court in deciding on the nature of any appropriate directions and whether a case management conference will be required in the event that the case is to be allocated to the multi track. Allocation questionnaires are not usually used in specialist cases that are automatically allocated to the multi track, such as cases involving applications under the Companies Act 1985 and claims allocated to the Technology and Construction Court. These courts have their own procedures for dealing with case management. If one of the parties fails to file an allocation questionnaire, the court may give any direction it deems appropriate but, if it takes the view that it does not have sufficient information at its disposal, it will list the case for an allocation hearing. The claimant is obliged to pay a fee (currently £200 in the High Court and £100 in the County Court) on filing his/her allocation questionnaire unless the claim is for a sum of money of not more than £1,000. Under the CPR r. 3.7, the claim will be struck out automatically if the allocation fee is not paid after the court has served a warning notice using form N173.

10 Directions

Once the court has decided which track to allocate the case to, it sends an allocation notice to the parties with copies of their allocation question-naires. This allocation notice gives directions and the reasons for the judge's allocation decision. The form of directions that the court makes at the allocation stage is dependent on the track that the case is allocated to and the particular circumstances of the case. In cases that are allocated to the small claims track, the court will make standard directions contained in Practice Direction 27. These basic standard directions require the parties to serve copies of documents on each other and provide copies for filing with the court. The original documents must be brought to the hearing. For cases allocated to the fast track or multi track, it will consider making directions covering the disclosure of documents, the exchange of witness statements, disclosure of experts' reports and narrowing the scope of the expert evidence as well as listing the claim for trial. Under the CPR r. 26.6(5) cases will not normally be assigned to the fast track unless oral expert evidence at trial can be limited to two separate fields of expertise and each party is limited to one expert for each area of expertise. For cases allocated to the multi track, the court will consider if a case manage-ment conference is necessary and whether a pre-trial review is required. Under the CPR r. 32.1 the court has the power to give directions limiting the issues in which it wishes to be addressed and on the evidence that may be produced at trial on these issues. However, this power will normally be exercised only in accordance with the overriding objective of the CPR, namely that cases must be dealt with justly and fairly.

In fast track cases, the court will normally order disclosure of docu-ments at the allocation stage and the order will be limited to what is known as standard disclosure. This requires a party to disclose only:

(a) the documents on which he/she relies; and
(b) the documents which:
    (i) adversely affect his own case,
    (ii) adversely affect the other party's case; or
    (iii) support the other party's case; and
(c) the documents that he/she is required to disclose by a relevant Practice Direction.

In a multi track case, an order for disclosure will usually be made by the court at a case management conference. However, if the case does not merit a case management conference, disclosure will be dealt with by the court as part of the case management directions given at the allocation stage. Each side will normally give disclosure by making a list using the form N265 and by serving it on the other side. Once a document has been disclosed in this way, each side can then make arrangements to inspect and copy any document which the other side possesses, provided it is still within their control. Inspection of a particular document can be refused if one of the parties asserts that it is a privileged communication, but this can be contested.

11 The small claims procedure

Under the CPR r. 27.4(1)(d) the court may fix a date for a preliminary hearing although the CPR r. 27.6 states that a preliminary hearing of a small claim may only be convened in one of three situations:

(a) if the court considers that special directions are necessary under r. 27.4 to ensure a fair hearing;
(b) where one of the parties has no real prospect of success, to facilitate disposal of the claim;
(c) so that the court can strike out the whole or part of a statement of case that discloses no reasonable basis for bringing or defending a claim.

At the end of the preliminary hearing the court will set a date for the final hearing and inform the parties, giving them any further directions necessary. The hearing itself is normally conducted in public before a district judge (unless a hearing in private is justified by the Convention rights enshrined in the Human Rights Act 1998) who may require that all or part of the proceedings shall be tape-recorded. Nevertheless, the proceedings are likely to be relatively informal and the strict rules of evidence are not applied. The district judge will have read the papers beforehand and may adopt any method of proceeding which he/she considers fair and he/she may even adopt an inquisitorial approach, questioning witnesses before even the parties themselves can do so. Expert evidence can only be given with the court's consent and the court may also limit cross-examination to a fixed time or to a particular subject. Alternatively, the court can, with the consent of the parties, dispose of the case without a hearing at all. The judge must give reasons for his/her decision. This can be done at a subsequent hearing or orally at the hearing but subsequently confirmed in writing.

A hearing may be conducted in the absence of one of the parties because either party may now give notice at least seven days prior to the hearing that he/she does not propose to attend, requesting that the court deal with the case in his/her absence on the basis of documents submitted. A party not present at the hearing nor represented and who has neither given notice of non-attendance nor consented to disposal without a hearing is able to apply for the judgment to be set aside and the case re-heard. The appropriate application must be made no later than 14 days after notice of judgment was served on him/her. However, the application will only be successful if he/she can satisfy the court:

(a) that he/she had a good reason for not attending (or being represented) or for not giving notice of non-attendance; and

(b) that he/she has a reasonable prospect of success at the hearing.

A party may not make such an application where the court dealt with the claim without a hearing, with the consent of the parties. The court can grant the same final remedies under the small claims procedure that can be granted in cases on the fast track or the multi track. There is, nevertheless, a limit imposed by the CPR r. 27.14 and Practice Direction 27 para. 7 on the costs that can be recovered under the small claims procedure.

A party who is dissatisfied with the outcome of the case can appeal from the decision of a district judge to a circuit judge by serving notice of appeal using form N161 but only on grounds of a serious irregularity affecting the proceedings or a mistake of law. This must usually be done within 14 days of the original decision. Particulars of the grounds of appeal must be given in the notice and, on hearing the appeal, the court can make any order it considers appropriate.

12 The listing questionnaire

For cases allocated to the fast track or multi track, a listing questionnaire will be sent out to the parties either at the allocation stage with the case management directions given or, at the very latest, shortly before the hearing date. If it was sent with the directions given at the allocation stage this document has to be returned (usually within 14 days) by the parties. If neither party returns the listing questionnaire then the court will usually make an order to the effect that, if they are not filed within three days from the service of the order, the claim and any counterclaim will be struck out. If only one party is at fault, the court will give listing directions based on the questionnaire that *is* received. The listing questionnaire asks:

(a) whether all previous directions given by the court have been complied with and whether any further directions are required to prepare the case for trial;

(b) whether the court has already given permission to use written expert evidence and whether permission has been granted for oral testimony from experts to be given at the trial;

(c) for information concerning the availability of other witnesses and whether interpreters will be required;

(d) whether a solicitor/barrister will be presenting the case;

(e) for an estimate of the length of time the trial will take and the number of pages of evidence to be included in the trial bundle.

13   Trials on the fast track

The dispute between Modern Builders Ltd and Alice would be allocated to the fast track. Further directions may be given at the listing stage when the parties have filed their listing questionnaires. Under the CPR r. 28.6(1) the court will:

(a)   set the date for the trial or confirm one already given,
(b)   give any additional directions deemed necessary and, if appropriate, set a trial timetable, and
(c)   detail any further steps that need to be taken prior to a trial of the action.

Fast track trials are supposed to conform to a strict timetable of 30 weeks between the allocation of the case and the trial of the action. The underlying assumption is that the solicitors acting for the parties will have sufficient time to undertake the necessary preparatory work for the trial. Thus claimants need to ensure that their cases are already well prepared even before they issue proceedings lest they fall behind schedule once the very strict timetable starts to apply. Defendants, too, will find themselves under pressure although compliance with a relevant pre-action protocol should ensure that they are well prepared. Normally trials are limited to a single day (five hours) but, if a trial is not finished on the day for which it is listed, the judge will normally sit on the next court day to complete it. As indicated previously, trials must usually be conducted in public (unless a hearing in private is justified by the Convention rights enshrined in the Human Rights Act 1998). Hearings in private may be justified on the grounds of morals, public order, national security, where the interests of juveniles are involved, for the protection of private life or in instances where a public hearing would prejudice the interests of justice. Although the entire rationale of the fast track procedure is to have a swift resolution of the dispute, the judge will bear in mind that under Article 6(1) of Schedule 1 to the Human Rights Act 1998 the parties have a right to a fair trial. This means that each must be given an equal opportunity to present his/her case. Time will nevertheless be saved because expert witnesses will normally give their evidence in writing – indeed, jointly instructed experts are becoming established practice. The judge will have read the papers, which must have been submitted in a properly indexed and paginated trial bundle beforehand. A case summary not exceeding 250 words may also have been prepared by the procedural judge. Thus the trial judge may decide to dispense with opening addresses by the advocates representing the parties. Witness statements will normally stand as 'evidence in chief' and the extent of cross-examination is likely to be limited by the judge. At the end of the trial the judge will deliver his judgment and summarily assess costs. In order to assist the trial judge in assessing the costs, the parties are required to file signed statements of their costs using form N260 at least 24 hours before the trial. Should they fail to do so without reasonable excuse, this will be taken into account in deciding the costs order relating to the claim, the trial and any subsequent assessment hearing that might be necessary as a result of the failure. The trial judge has the responsibility for ensuring that the costs claimed are not disproportionate or otherwise unreasonable. Since the costs of the trial are fixed in relation to the amount claimed, with no discretion permitted, it is likely that all but the most junior members of the Bar will not find it financially worthwhile to appear as advocates and so solicitors are more likely to do most fast track advocacy.

14 Multi track trials

The multi track is intended for a very wide range of cases. These include relatively straightforward cases, such as contractual disputes where the amount claimed exceeds the financial limit for fast track trials, to the most difficult cases that involve complex issues of law and fact with amounts at stake that could run into millions of pounds. All Part 8 claims (those commenced using form N208) are allocated to the multi track as are those raising points of law of great public importance. Of course, the straightforward cases involving amounts just over the limit for fast track trials will be the subject of standard case management directions but really complex cases will be subject to more active case management by way of case conferences and pre-trial reviews. If a case involves less than £50,000 it will usually be heard at a civil trial centre but, if it exceeds that amount, it will normally be heard at the Royal Courts of Justice. At a case management conference the agenda is effectively set by Practice Direction 29. A judge can ask probing questions in relation to a party's case with a view to narrowing the issues to be tried so that minor ones are eliminated by agreement with the parties. At the conclusion of a pre-trial review, the court must draw up a trial timetable if one has not been set earlier. Rule 1.4(2) of the CPR requires courts, as part of the process of active case management, to encourage and facilitate the use of alternative dispute resolution (ADR) where appropriate (see Chapter 12). Moreover, r. 26.4 allows the court to 'stay' proceedings to permit the use of ADR, either where the parties themselves request it or where the court of its own initiative considers it to be appropriate because both sides seem prepared to reach an agreed settlement. In *Dunnett* v *Railtrack (in administration)* [2002] because Railtrack refused to participate in a mediation the Court of Appeal ruled that it could not recover its costs even though it was the successful party. Nevertheless, a refusal to mediate in some instances may be completely justified and in *Société Internationale de Telecommunications Aeronautiques* v *Wyatt Co (UK) Ltd* [2002] it was held that, where this was the case, the party concerned would not suffer a costs penalty. The Court of Appeal in *Halsey* v *Milton Keynes NHS Trust; Steel* v *Joy and another* [2004] provided guidance on what will constitute unreasonable refusal to mediate but at the same time it refused to impose a costs sanction on the successful party for a refusal to participate in mediation.

15 Conduct of the trial

According to the CPR r. 39.2(1) trials must be conducted in public but r. 39.2(3) states that hearings may be conducted in private under certain circumstances. Practice Direction 39 gives a list of the proceedings that will be conducted in private. Most civil trials at first instance take place before a judge sitting alone but there is a statutory right to a jury trial for certain tort actions. The County Courts Act 1984 s. 66 and the Supreme Court Act 1981 s. 69 allow for jury trial in actions in the torts of deceit, defamation, malicious prosecution and false imprisonment unless the court takes the view that the trial requires prolonged examination of documents, scientific or local investigation that cannot be conveniently carried out with a jury. If there is to be a jury trial, High Court juries have 12 members and county court juries have 8 members. As previously stated, the CPR require judges sitting at first instance to assert greater control over the preparation and conduct of hearings. The judge will have read the relevant documents comprising the trial bundle beforehand, as well as the skeleton arguments submitted by the advocate. The barrister/solicitor representing the claimant may be allowed to make a short opening speech setting out the background to the case but immediately afterwards he/she must call the witnesses that are appearing for the claimant, who are duly sworn or make an affirmation. Since every witness statement will now stand as 'evidence in chief', witnesses can be cross-examined without delay by the advocate for the defendant to expose any inconsistencies or gaps in the evidence given. The court may, however, allow a witness to amplify the content of a witness statement under the CPR r. 32.5 and give evidence in relation to new matters that have arisen since the witness statement was served on the other side. Nevertheless, the judge may limit cross-examination if he/she considers that it is achieving no useful purpose. Witnesses may also be asked questions by the judge who may wish to clarify certain points. When the advocate for the claimant has called all the witnesses for his/her client, he/she makes his/her submissions on the relevant law to the judge. In doing so, he/she will cite all relevant case law precedents and legislation but not in detail. Although he/she is required to cite all the relevant law, even though this may lend some support to the defendant's case, he/she is at liberty to interpret it to the claimant's advantage and to attempt to persuade the judge that this body of law really advances and supports the claimant's case.

The advocate for the defence will then call the witnesses for his/her client, who are duly sworn or affirmed and then cross-examined by the advocate for the claimant. Once the advocate for the defendant has called all the witnesses for the defence and has cited all the evidence for the defence, he/she will cite all the relevant law, but not in detail, in support of the defendant's case to the judge. If the defendant's advocate elects not to cite evidence at the trial, the advocate for the claimant will make a closing speech and the advocate for the defendant will follow this with a statement of the defendant's case.

16 Delivering judgment

At the end of the trial, the judge must give a reasoned judgment stating the conclusions he/she has reached on any factual issues in dispute. If the evidence given is conflicting, he/she must state which version of the facts is the most likely to be accurate and therefore on which he/she will rely. In giving his/her judgment, the judge will recite the material (key) facts of the case as established in evidence and state how the relevant law (statute and/or precedent) is to be applied to those facts. The end result must be that judgment is given in favour of one party and the other party loses. A copy of the judgment is normally completed by the court and sealed so that it can be served on the parties. The costs of the action (including the claimant's costs) are, for the most part, borne by the losing party but, as has been seen, this is not an invariable rule.

17 Remedies

A court may make both interim remedies and final remedies at the conclusion of the trial. The interim remedies that may be granted are set out in r. 25.1 and include interim injunctions and interim declarations. The most usual final remedy given by a court will entail the payment of money to settle a debt or settle some other unpaid, ascertained sum. (If the court were to give judgment for Modern Builders Ltd against Alice it might order her to pay the entire £12,500.) Alternatively, the claimant may simply have asked for an award of damages in the claim form to be settled by the court but, if there has been an infringement of a legal right that has not resulted in any real loss, the court will only award nominal damages. Compensatory damages can be divided into pecuniary and non-pecuniary damages. The former compensates the claimant for measurable financial loss, caused by the defendant's wrongdoing. Non-pecuniary (or general) damages are awarded in recognition of the suffering that the wrongdoing has caused the defendant. The amount awarded as non-pecuniary damages will be assessed according to what the court considers appropriate in the particular case, but it will take into account what has been awarded in similar cases. In tort claims, the amount awarded is that which will restore the claimant (in so far as it is possible to do so) to the position he/she would have been in had the wrongful act not been committed. In a claim for breach of contract, the damages sought can be awarded on two different bases:

(a) to restore the claimant to the position he/she would have been in had the contract been performed properly; or

(b) to compensate for expenditure rendered futile by the breach of contract.

The claimant can choose on which basis to claim. Sometimes a court may award aggravated damages (as defined in the CPR Glossary) for the defendant's objectionable behaviour but a claim for such damages must be made separately in the particulars of claim. Very occasionally a court may award exemplary damages (as defined in the CPR Glossary). These must also be claimed separately in the particulars of claim, and are awarded to show the court's disapproval of the defendant's behaviour. Orders for the payment of a debt and damages are the basic common law remedies but sometimes a court can give a declaratory judgment defining the parties' rights, without granting any other remedy. Damages are not always the most appropriate remedy and the court may award one of the equitable remedies discussed in Appendix 1, if requested by the claimant. These remedies are injunction, specific performance, rectification and rescission. Various other remedies are available in special proceedings: for example, in insolvency proceedings, bankruptcy orders and winding-up orders for companies can be obtained, as can company director disqualification orders.

18 Enforcement of judgments

Obtaining a judgment from the court involving the payment of money by the losing party is one thing; enforcing it, if he/she is reluctant to pay, is quite another matter. Judgments requiring the payment of money may be enforced by warrant of execution but in only one case in three are the bailiffs able to recover anything that can be sold. Sometimes this may be due to the fact that they are unable to gain access to premises – as the law currently stands they must be invited onto the premises unless they find an open door. Garnishee proceedings (where a claim can be made on a person's bank account) may be a possibility, but the claimant would need to have very precise details relating to the defendant's bank account. There must also be cleared funds on the account. Another possibility exists in the form of a bankruptcy notice (or an order to wind up a company) but that will entail additional expense. Where the judgment has been given against a private individual there is the possibility of an attachment of earnings by the court. This is usually done through the county court. The Attachment of Earnings Act 1971 s. 6(1) provides that:

> An attachment of earnings order shall be directed to a person who appears to the court to have the debtor in his employment and shall operate as an instruction to that person –

> **(a)** to make periodic deductions from the debtor's earnings ... and
> **(b)** at such times as the order may require, or as the court may allow, to pay the amounts deducted to the collecting officer of the court, as specified in the order.

Once the money has been paid over by the employer to the court, the court will then pay it to the party that has sought to enforce the judgment.

19 Appeals

The system for civil appeals can be conveniently summarised as follows:

1 An appeal from the decision of a district judge may be made to a circuit judge of the county court provided notice of appeal is filed within 14 days of the date of the decision and permission to appeal is obtained.

2 An appeal from a preliminary decision of a High Court Master or a district judge may be made to a High Court judge.

3 An appeal from the decision of a circuit judge in the county court should be made to the High Court within 14 days of the date of the decision and permission to appeal is required either from the lower court or the appeal court.

4 A final decision in a multi track case or in specialist proceedings must be appealed to the Court of Appeal within 14 days of the date of the decision and permission to appeal is required either from the lower court or from the appeal court.

5 An appeal from the decision of a High Court judge must be made to the Court of Appeal within 14 days of the date of the original decision and it is necessary to obtain permission to appeal either from the lower court or from the appeal court.

6 Decisions of the Court of Appeal can be appealed to the House of Lords within one month of the order being made or within three months if permission to appeal is granted by the Court of Appeal itself.

According to CPR r. 52.3(6) permission to appeal will be given only where:

(a) the court takes the view that the appeal would have a real prospect of success; or

(b) there is some compelling reason why the appeal should be heard.

CPR r. 52.11(10) states that every appeal will be limited to a review of the decision of the lower court unless:

(a) a Practice Direction requires otherwise for a particular category of appeal; or

(b) the appeal court takes the view that in the particular circumstances it would be in the interests of justice to hold a re-hearing.

The appeal court will only permit an appeal to go ahead if the decision of the lower court was wrong or unjust because of a serious procedural or other irregularity in the proceedings. It will not make original findings of fact. Indeed, a finding of fact of a lower court can only be overturned if there was no evidence to support it or if the finding of fact goes against the weight of the evidence. According to the earlier ruling in *Ladd* v *Marshall* [1954] fresh evidence can only be admitted on appeal if:

(a) the evidence could not have been obtained with reasonable diligence for the hearing in the lower court;

(b) it would probably have an important influence on the outcome; and

(c) it is apparently credible.

Even in the era of the CPR the appeal court will be unwilling to allow fresh evidence to be introduced at the appeal stage unless there are special reasons. Under the CPR r. 52.10(2) the appeal court has the power to:

(a) affirm, set aside or vary any order or judgment made or given by a lower court;

(b) refer any claim or issue for determination by the lower court;

(c) order a new trial;

(d) make orders for the payment of interest; and

(e) make a costs order.

In some circumstances an appeal may occasionally be made directly from the High Court to the House of Lords thereby 'leapfrogging' the Court of Appeal. This is only likely to happen when the Court of Appeal is bound by one of its existing precedents and an advocate for one of the parties considers that the House of Lords may be willing to overrule the Court of Appeal. There is also a possibility of an appeal to the European Court of Human Rights at Strasbourg if it can be shown that one of the parties did not receive a fair hearing either at first instance or on appeal. On the other hand, a complaint to the European Court of Human Rights under the Convention can only be made if the complainant has exhausted his/her rights under national law. There is also a time limit of six months after which complaints will not be entertained.

Summary

As indicated in the previous chapter, disputes of various types arise on a daily basis but most can be satisfactorily resolved without recourse to litigation in the civil courts. If one or both parties take entrenched positions and refuse to compromise or to submit the dispute to arbitration, then litigation may be the only way to resolve the issue or issues. It has been noted, however, that the introduction of the various pre-action protocols has significantly reduced the number of civil claims being brought before the courts in recent years. The central concern of this chapter has been to chart the procedure involved in bringing a claim, focusing initially on the county courts because this is where the majority of civil claims are heard and disposed of. It was noted that the CPR encourage openness and that there is an inbuilt incentive to settle claims long before the scheduling of the hearing of a dispute through the mechanism of Part 36 offers and payments. The allocation process was examined whereby cases are assigned to one of three 'tracks' depending on their complexity but more often because of the amount of the claim. An outline description of the trial process was given, in which it was seen that most civil cases are heard by a single judge sitting without a jury who adjudicates on issues of fact and applies the relevant law.

Finally, it was noted that appeals from county courts and the High Court go to the Civil Division of the Court of Appeal, although an appeal can sometimes go directly from the High Court to the House of Lords.

WWW PROGRESS TEST

For suggested answers to the tests below, go to the companion website at www.pearsoned.co.uk/wheeler

1   What criticisms did Lord Woolf make of the old civil justice system in his report entitled *Access to Justice?*
2   What function is the pre-action protocol intended to serve?
3   Are there any sanctions that may be imposed on litigants who fail to observe the requirements of a pre-action protocol?
4   How does a claimant normally set about commencing legal proceedings against someone? To which courts may the relevant form(s) be taken?
5   On receipt of the claim, what options are open to the defendant?
6   What is a Part 36 offer?
7   Why might a claimant make a pre-action Part 36 offer?
8   What is the function of the allocation questionnaire and what questions does it ask?
9   What are the 'tracks' to which a case may be allocated and what is/are normally the determining factor(s)?
10   What is the function of the listing questionnaire?
11   What are the main objectives in allocating a case to the fast track?
12   What types of case will be allocated to the so-called 'multi track' and can a judge suspend proceedings to refer the dispute to some form of ADR?

FURTHER READING

■ **Books**

Grainger, I. and M. Fealy (2000) *The Civil Procedure Rules in Action* (London: Cavendish Publishing).

Plant, C. et al (eds.) (2004) *Blackstone's Civil Practice* (Oxford: Oxford University Press).

Rose, W., His Honour Judge (2002) *Pleadings Without Tears* (Oxford: Oxford University Press).

Sime, S. (2004) *A Practical Approach to Civil Procedure* (Oxford: Oxford University Press).

Slapper, G. and D. Kelly (2004) *The English Legal System* (London: Cavendish Publishing, chapter 7).

■ **Articles**

Harrison, R. (2004) 'First principles and witness statements', *New Law Journal* Vol. 151 No. 6982.

Lightman, His Honour, Mr Justice (2004) 'Litigation: the last resort', *New Law Journal* Vol. 154 No. 7114.

Pliener, D. (2000) 'At last, clarity for mediation', *New Law Journal* Vol. 154 No. 7132.

USEFUL WEBSITE

The Court Service website at www.courtservice.gov.uk is a useful source of up-to-date information and the actual forms used in civil litigation can be downloaded from this site.

Dispute resolution 3: The role of tribunals

1 Introduction

There are a very large number of tribunals of various types in England and Wales whose status is perceived as being lower than that of the ordinary civil courts. These tribunals may:

(a) hear complaints against and/or adjudicate in disputes with a government department; or

(b) hear appeals against decisions taken by public officials; or

(c) hear cases to resolve disputes between employer and employee concerning alleged infringements of statutory employment rights; or

(d) deal with matters of discipline within a profession, trade union or trade association.

The tribunals that deal with matters referred to in (a) and (b) above are usually referred to as 'administrative tribunals' because the sphere within which they operate is that of 'public administration'. A few of these tribunals predate the creation of the welfare state post Second World War and the assumption by government of responsibility for the overall management of the national economy. However, it is these two occurrences that have necessitated additional avenues for the airing of grievances arising from mistakes and illegalities as the activity of the state has come to impinge on the lives of citizens and businesses to a greater extent. Consequently, the number of administrative tribunals has grown steadily since the 1950s. There are now in the region of 100 different types, although some are much busier than others. It is interesting to note that another five such tribunals were created in 2004 alone. Now that civil servants and those working in agencies of the state are required to have regard to the Convention rights of those whom their decisions are likely to affect, there is scope for challenges under the Human Rights Act 1998 to administrative tribunals. The official review of administrative tribunals by Sir Andrew Leggatt in 2001 covered just 70 of these tribunals. Tribunals that adjudicate between employers and employees in disputes over statutory employment rights have been known as employment tribunals since August 1998. For political reasons, the UK never set up a system of 'labour courts' that exist in other European countries and so the employment tribunal is something of a compromise. Tribunals dealing with those matters referred to in (d) above are normally referred to as 'domestic tribunals', for the want of a better nomenclature. The term is a convenient 'hold all' for a wide variety of tribunals that are neither concerned with public administration nor with statutory employment rights. Some of them have been created by statute but many more owe their origin to the terms of some form of contract of membership. The aim of this chapter is to examine the role of these very different categories of tribunal. The government published a White Paper entitled *Transforming Public Services: Complaints, Redress and Tribunals* in July 2004, having had some time to consider the Leggatt Report. It intends to create a unified tribunal system, along the lines suggested by Sir Andrew Leggatt, incorporating both administrative tribunals and employment tribunals. It is therefore necessary to deal with this important development.

2   Administrative tribunals

The 100 or so administrative tribunals, virtually all of which have been created by statute, deal with over 1m cases annually. This is far more than the ordinary civil courts and the case loads of some may even increase as a result of the coming into operation of the Freedom of Information Act 2000 in January 2005. The 'defendant' is always the state or some state agency. For this reason these tribunals can properly be regarded as the lynchpin of the system of administrative law and justice that obtains in England and Wales. The wide variety of subject matter coming within the ambit of this system of administrative law and justice can be readily appreciated by scanning the names of some of the more important tribunals. They include:

The Asylum Support Adjudicators
Criminal Injuries Compensation Appeals Panel
Information Tribunal
Lands Tribunal for England and Wales
Mental Health Tribunal for England and Wales
Social Security and Child Support Commissions
Special Commissioners of Income Tax
Special Immigration Appeals Commission
Special Educational Needs and Disability Tribunal
VAT and Duties Tribunal.

The composition of these tribunals varies in terms of the number of persons (and their qualifications) who sit to hear a case and determine its outcome. The Lands Tribunal must be presided over by a senior barrister (usually a QC) or a High Court judge and, despite its name, is actually a court of law rather than an administrative tribunal. Its rules of procedure are set out in a statutory instrument. Other tribunals are presided over by a chairperson who is normally legally qualified (either as a barrister or solicitor) and the remainder of the adjudication panel will be made up of non-lawyers who have specialist knowledge and experience in the subject matter on which the tribunal is called upon to adjudicate. Consequently, these tribunals rarely need to call expert witnesses. The non-lawyer members normally 'vote' with the chairperson to decide the outcome of a claim and the tribunal as a whole should produce a reasoned decision at the end of its deliberations. Until now most administrative tribunals have devised their own rules of procedure. In general, the procedure is supposed to be less formal than that which obtains in the civil courts and for this reason it was assumed for a long time that persons appearing before tribunals would not normally require legal representation. There was a widespread belief that tribunal support staff would be able to provide all the help needed by complainants. In fact, many people lack the organisational skills to present their case in the best possible light in a stressful situation. The Community Legal Service does now provide assistance known as 'legal help' which covers advice and assistance short of representation. Persons are, therefore, able to obtain advice on the merits of a case and assistance with form filling from the Citizens' Advice Bureaux and law centres. Legal aid is now available to appellants in certain appeal proceedings and in certain proceedings before the Special Commissioners of Income Tax and VAT and Duties Tribunal. It is interesting to note that the Department for Constitutional Affairs commissioned MORI to conduct some research among users of administrative tribunals in 2001. The results indicated a very high level of satisfaction (89 per cent) with the courtesy shown by tribunal members and (79 per cent) with the willingness of the tribunal to ensure that the user had an adequate opportunity to contribute to the hearing. According to the White Paper, the shortcomings of the existing arrangements are not the failures of individual tribunals but rather failures attributable to the lack of a coherent system.

Until recently most administrative tribunals were sponsored by the government departments that had the lead responsibility for the branch of law on which the tribunals were adjudicating. They often appointed members of the panel and they paid their fees and expenses. Sir Andrew Leggatt highlighted this as an issue in his Report and stated that responsibility for tribunals and their administration should not be the responsibility of those departments whose decisions the tribunals were supposed to be reviewing. He doubted the term 'system' could be applied to the arrangements existing in 2001 which, in his Report, he described as incoherent and inefficient. He stated that most tribunals covered by his review had been developed to meet the needs and conveniences of the sponsoring departments themselves (and other bodies) rather than the needs of users. The government's own proposals, set out in its White Paper, do not accord exactly with the recommendations of Sir Andrew. It is likely that the government's proposals will be implemented in 2005 because in the Queen's speech in November 2004 it was indicated that legislation reforming the structure of tribunals would be presented to Parliament in the forthcoming session.

3 A Courts and Tribunals Bill

In Chapter 12 of the White Paper it is projected that by June 2005 the new Bill should be ready and that by December 2005 it should have received the Royal Assent. This will be tracked on the companion website. Since there is no text of a Bill to refer to at the time of writing, it has been assumed that the new legislation will mirror the proposals set out in the White Paper, which differ somewhat from those advocated by Sir Andrew Leggatt. The government has, nevertheless, opted for the 'one system, one service model'. At the core of the new system is a tribunal service which brings within its structure the 10 largest administrative tribunals which collectively hear more than 90 per cent of the cases brought each year. Responsibility for five of these was already within the Department for Constitutional Affairs and responsibility for the other five is to be transferred from other government departments shortly. Between 2006 and 2008 responsibility for a number of other important tribunals will transfer from their existing sponsoring department to the Department for Constitutional Affairs so that they too will be integrated into the unified system. These tribunals include the Special Educational Needs and Disability Tribunal for England, the Appeals Service (which currently hears appeals from only a few tribunals), the Criminal Injuries Compensation Appeals Panel and the Mental Health Review Tribunal for England. The Investigatory Powers Tribunal will not be included within the new unified structure, even though it has an adjudicatory function, because its powers are primarily investigatory. The Employment Tribunals Service is scheduled to transfer in 2006, if all goes to plan, but it will retain its identity within the new structure because of the special nature of the claims that are brought before employment tribunals and the fact that they are, for the most part, dealing with claims by private parties against private parties. As tribunals transfer, the responsibility for making their rules of procedure will transfer to the Secretary of State for Constitutional Affairs, with the notable exception of employment tribunals. The Secretary of State for Trade and Industry will continue to have responsibility for the rules of procedure of employment tribunals. For the others, it is intended that there should be a procedure committee that will bring the process of making tribunal rules more into line with the procedure that obtains in the civil courts.

Although tribunals will continue to have panel members who are non-lawyers, the legislation will create a single judicial office for those legally qualified who are appointed to preside over first-tier tribunals; they will be known as 'tribunal judges'. Not only will they have a judicial role, it is also intended that they should have the power to act as mediators so that they will be able to offer mediated settlements where appropriate. Those persons appointed to hear appeals from first-tier tribunals will be known as 'appellate tribunal judges'. As at present, all new posts will be advertised and there will be open competition for appointments, with the involvement of the Judicial Appointment Commission. New appointments in the first instance are likely to be part-time and fee paid before a person is eligible for appointment to a full-time salaried position. The new tribunal service will be presided over by a Senior President of Tribunals, who is to have the same rank as a judge of the Court of Appeal and will be appointed by the Lord Chief Justice.

A key feature of the new system is to be a coherent appeal system. Appeals from first instance tribunals will go to a new appeal tribunal rather than to the ordinary courts (as some do at present). The major exception is that appeals from employment tribunals will continue to go to the Employment Appeal Tribunal, which, despite its name, is effectively a part of the High Court. All claimants must obtain permission to appeal from a first-tier tribunal to a second-tier appeal tribunal and it will also be necessary to obtain permission to appeal from a second-tier tribunal to the Court of Appeal. In view of this, it is intended that the only scope for judicial review in future will be a refusal by the first-tier or second-tier to grant permission to appeal.

4   An Administrative Justice Council

The existing Council on Tribunals is to be revamped to become an Administrative Justice Council which will focus particularly on the needs of the users of tribunals. In the past it has functioned as a part-time body comprising 15 persons appointed by the Lord Chancellor and Lord Advocate for Scotland that meets on a monthly basis. Under the Tribunals and Inquiries Act 1992 it was limited to reviewing the constitutions and working of administrative tribunals. Although it has a full-time secretariat, it has no executive powers and has operated mainly as an advisory and consultative body. Sir Andrew Leggat envisaged a more pro-active remit for the Council and the government seems to have accepted the recommendations contained in his Report. According to the White Paper, it is to play a key role in supporting the creation of the new dispute resolution system and to continue its collaboration with the Judicial Studies Board in the interests of developing the tribunal service. The White Paper states that it is to continue to promote effective judicial training, performance management and appraisal for tribunal members in accordance with the JSB's framework of standards. It is intended that, whilst retaining its supervisory role, the Council should evolve into an advisory body for the entire administrative justice sector whereas previously not all administrative tribunals came within the ambit of its responsibilities.

5   Benefits to users

In the White Paper, the government seems anxious to state that there will be significant advantages to users of the new tribunal service apart from the efficiency gains through the more coordinated use of information technology. A more active case management that will be instituted is intended to dispense with unnecessary adjournments and late postponement of hearings. It is also proposed that, by bringing together the ten largest administrative tribunals initially, the Department for Constitutional Affairs will be able to provide users with a network of hearing centres with a better geographic spread. In addition, it is intended to improve the general standard of accommodation for tribunals, with better support facilities including better disabled access.

6 Employment tribunals

Although employment tribunals were originally created as 'industrial tribunals' in 1964 and were initially a form of administrative tribunal, they soon took on a very different identity as a venue for the hearing of alleged infringements of statutory employment rights. As the number of statutory employment rights burgeoned through the 1980s and 1990s (largely as a result of EU social policy developments), these tribunals became increasingly important and are now probably better known among the general public than any other type of tribunal as the outcome of cases is often reported in the print and broadcast media. The Employment Tribunal Service (ETS) exists to provide the necessary administrative support to persons bringing claims to employment tribunals as well as appeals to the Employment Appeal Tribunal. It operates currently from 34 permanent offices across Great Britain and it arranges hearings (where these are necessary) at a large number of locations to meet the needs of the many tribunal users. The chairperson of an employment tribunal is appointed by the Lord Chancellor/Secretary of State for Constitutional Affairs and must be legally qualified either as a solicitor or barrister with over seven years' experience. Some chairpersons are full-time appointees but most act on a part-time basis. The country is divided into regions and each region is supervised by a regional chairperson who is responsible for the tribunals in his/her area to a national President who has the rank of a circuit judge. Apart from the tribunal chairperson, every tribunal panel includes two non-lawyers. These are appointed by the Secretary of State for Trade and Industry from two separate lists. One list includes persons who can be said to represent the employers' interests generally, whilst the other list comprises persons (usually trade unionists) who can be said to represent employees' interests. The non-lawyer members of the tribunal panel can 'outvote' the chairperson in arriving at the outcome of the hearing. Most employment tribunal hearings are open to the public. The parties are usually responsible for their own costs, including the costs of being legally represented, which can be considerable if they do not have legal costs insurance or, in the case of employees, support from a trade union. However, tribunals are now able to make 'preparation time orders' toward costs incurred for preparatory work directly related to the proceedings (although not for time spent at the hearing) in certain circumstances.

A new set of procedural rules – the Employment Tribunal (Constitution and Rules of Procedure) Regulations 2004 (SI 2004 No. 1861) came into operation from 1 October 2004. The time limit for bringing a claim for unfair dismissal has been extended from three months to six months in most instances. Once a claim has been sent by the ETS, the employer has 28 days to respond but, if the claim is uncontested by the employer, the tribunal will be able to issue a default judgment. Employment tribunals are no longer required to issue written reasons for their decisions so that, where the judgment is given orally, a written judgment will not be issued unless the parties request one either at the hearing or within 14 days of the judgment. The new procedural rules aim to bring employment tribunal practice more into line with the Civil Procedure Rules for civil litigation.

Employment tribunals now deal with almost 70 different types of employment claim, although some claims may cover more than one aspect

Table 14.1 **Employment tribunal statistics 2003–2004**

Nature of claim	
Unfair dismissal	37,644
Unauthorised deduction of wages	20,853
Breach of contract	8,195
Sex discrimination	14,284
Breach of Working Time Directive	11,218
Redundancy compensation	4,210
Disability discrimination	2,764
Redundancy – failure to inform or consult	4,159
Equal pay	3,217
Racial discrimination	2,830
Written statement of terms and conditions	566
Written statement of reasons for dismissal	123
Unfair dismissal on transfer of undertaking	791
Itemised pay statement	262
Transfer of undertaking – failure to inform and consult	489
Unfair dismissal – pregnancy	413
Infringement of Part Time Workers Regulations	439
National minimum wage	252
Others	2,333
Total	**115,042**

Source: © Crown copyright

of employment law. The Annual Report for 2003/04 of the Employment Tribunal Service makes very interesting reading. The main categories, together with the number of claims for 2003/04, are set out in Table 14.1.

The figures in Table 14.1 are compiled on the basis of what the ETS staff recognised as the principal type of claim when it first received the claim form, IT1. A claim could be amended prior to the hearing so that its nature changes. It is clear that unfair dismissal is the largest single category but this has always been so. Nevertheless, this could change from October 2004 when the provisions of the Employment Act 2002 come into operation. This Act has brought in new statutory dismissal and disciplinary procedures which employers must follow, otherwise a dismissal will be automatically unfair. The new statutory grievance procedures are backed up by a requirement for employees to raise grievances in writing with their employer *before* applying to a tribunal. In this way it is hoped to reduce the total number of applications to the Employment Tribunal Service in respect of unfair dismissal, but this remains to be seen. Not all tribunal applications necessarily result in a tribunal hearing because, as soon as the application is made to the Employment Tribunal Service, the Advisory, Conciliation and Arbitration Service (ACAS) becomes involved and tries to reach a conciliated settlement between the parties. It is said that ACAS is successful in about 40 per cent of cases. Of the 37,901 unfair dismissal claims disposed of in 2003/04, a total of 16,700 were conciliated through ACAS and a further 10,225 were subsequently withdrawn. If fact, less than 25 per cent of the total proceeded to a full tribunal hearing because a significant number were settled by the parties beforehand. Although large compensation awards make good newspaper headlines, with the maximum award in 2003/04 being £113,117, the average award was far less at £7,275, with the median award even lower at £3,375.

The claims for sex and racial discrimination have shown no significant tendency to diminish in recent years and, if equal pay is combined with sex discrimination, the number of claims actually went up in 2003/04. Approximately 24 per cent of sex discrimination claims were conciliated through ACAS in 2003/04, with a further 45 per cent withdrawn. Less than 10 per cent proceeded to a tribunal hearing, with around 23 per cent settled prior to a hearing. Only 3 per cent of claims were successful at a hearing and the compensation awarded was modest. Although there was a very large award of £504,433, the average award was £12,971 but the median award was lower at £5,425. Claims for racial discrimination showed a slightly different pattern. Of the total number of claims dealt with in 2003/04, 39 per cent were conciliated through ACAS, with a further 31 per cent withdrawn. A much lower percentage were settled just prior to a hearing (6 per cent) but only 4 per cent were successful at a hearing. Compensation awards were higher than for sex discrimination, with the maximum award at £635,150. However, the average award was £26,660 and the median was £8,410.

For some time employment tribunals (unlike administrative tribunals) have been able to make an award of costs up to £10,000 against either of the parties. Claims brought by employees which are considered to be frivolous or vexatious may be disposed of with a costs sanction. On the other hand, if the tribunal considers that the employer has behaved unreasonably or refused to reinstate an employee, a cost order can be made against the employer. In 2003/04 such orders were made only in about 1 per cent of cases; but a total of 332 cost orders were made against claimants, whereas 644 were made against employers. Employment tribunals undoubtedly fulfil an essential role but sometimes their decision-making is at fault and so it is essential for there to be an appeal process for both employees and employers.

7 Appeals from employment tribunals

Appeals from the decisions of employment tribunals go straight to the Employment Appeal Tribunal, which was originally brought into being by the Employment Protection Act 1975 but is now governed by the Industrial Tribunals Act 1996. The EAT is situated in central London but appeals are also heard in Cardiff and Edinburgh. It has the status of a division of the High Court (notwithstanding its title) because it is presided over by a High Court judge and is a superior court of record. Unless the original tribunal decision was made by the chairman sitting alone, the presiding judge in the EAT will sit with two lay persons who can outvote him/her in deciding the appeal. Appeals are restricted to points of law so as to limit the number of possible appeals and therefore an appellant must be able to show that the tribunal went wrong in law. Guidance was given by the Court of Appeal in *British Telecommunications Plc* v *Sheridan* [1990] on what is considered to amount to a point of law. In *Post Office* v *Lewis* [1997] the Court of Appeal made it clear that, where a decision of an employment tribunal was neither perverse nor affected by an error of law, it was not permissible for the Employment Appeal Tribunal to interfere on the basis that the tribunal had failed to refer in its decision to the main part of the claimant's defence. The claimant was dismissed by his employer when 59 items of mail destined for a block of flats were found in a post box in Tooting, South West London. Since these items of mail had already been through the sorting process they should not have been in the post box and, since the applicant was the only postman on that round on that day, he was dismissed following an internal inquiry. The tribunal had found that the decision to dismiss was unfair due to insufficient investigation but it concluded that, even if the Post Office had investigated the matter more thoroughly, it would still have dismissed the claimant and acted fairly in doing so. It also found, on the balance of probability, that he had wilfully delayed delivery of the mail and ruled that his conduct was blameworthy so that it would not be just and equitable to make any award of compensation or, for that matter, award reinstatement. The Employment Appeal Tribunal allowed an appeal by Lewis because the tribunal's decision did not deal with the 'main plank' of Lewis's defence. In giving the judgment of the Court of Appeal, Henry LJ stated that the employment tribunal had not found it necessary to resolve the 'main plank' issue because of the weight the tribunal gave to another matter. He emphasised that the weight that should be given to evidence was a matter for the original tribunal (the tribunal of fact) and the EAT should not have interfered with the tribunal's decision. Even though two or more employment tribunals reach different conclusions on the same facts does not mean that one or other has made an error of law, particularly where the conclusions relate to questions of 'reasonableness'. In 2003/04 there were 840 appeals disposed of at a full hearing of the EAT but, of these, only 419 were successful in overturning the decision of the tribunal that originally heard the case. A total of 421 appeals were dismissed at a full hearing in 2003/04. A further appeal on a point of law from the decision of the EAT to the Court of Appeal is possible with the permission of that court. Very occasionally there can be a further appeal on a point of law to the House of Lords but, again, only with the permission of the House of Lords.

8 Domestic tribunals

Within this category are found a wide range of tribunals ranging from disciplinary and grievance committees at the workplace to the disciplinary committees established by professional associations such as the Institute of Actuaries, Institute of Chartered Accountants and Chartered Association of Certified Accountants. The disciplinary bodies for the legal profession were considered in Chapter 2. Universities and trade unions, too, have disciplinary bodies which decide whether a member should be disciplined if an allegation of an infringement of the rules is established. When actions amounting to gross misconduct are substantiated, the member may be expelled, although, in the case of trade unions, there are now restrictions on the right to expel a member contained in the Trade Union and Labour Relations (Consolidation) Act 1992. The jurisdiction of such organisations over their members usually arises out of the 'contract of membership' which is deemed to exist between the organisation (if it is a legal entity) and the individual members or between the person concerned and his/her fellow members if the organisation is not a legal entity. Certain tribunals that have been set up to deal with misconduct by members of the medical and healthcare professions have been established by statute. For example, the Professional Conduct Committee of the General Medical Council was established by the Medical Act 1978. It exercises a disciplinary function over doctors and receives in the region of 4,000 complaints annually. It may suspend or remove a doctor's name altogether from the Medical Register for 'serious professional misconduct' although not all complaints necessarily amount to serious professional misconduct. In recent years, it has been heavily criticised for being too lenient. This was particularly true of its treatment of Dr Harold Shipman, the General Practitioner from Greater Manchester, who was subsequently convicted of the murders of over 200 of his elderly patients. There have been other cases since where the PCC has been criticised for its leniency. In response to media criticism and heightened public concern, it introduced changes to its system of complaint handling in November 2004. In her final report published in December 2004, the then High Court Judge, Dame Janet Smith, who was appointed to conduct an inquiry into the Shipman affair, indicated that these latest reforms do not go far enough. It is possible that the government may now intervene to put in place a more rigorous regime for dealing with misconduct by medical practitioners if the GMC fails to deal with doctors' misconduct more effectively. Disciplinary tribunals have also been created by separate Acts of Parliament for dentists and opticians.

9 Procedural fairness

Since the majority of domestic tribunals are not presided over by a judge, nor for that matter by a person who is legally qualified (except those dealing with the legal profession), it is essential that the proceedings are conducted fairly. Otherwise, the courts can and do intervene to ensure that a minimum degree of procedural fairness is observed. This is often referred to as applying the 'principles of natural justice'. There are two basic principles: the first is that the person making the decision should be independent and unbiased. This is sometimes expressed in the maxim 'no person should be a judge in his/her own cause'. The second principle is that both sides must be given a proper hearing and this is particularly important with regard to someone accused of wrongdoing who must be allowed to explain his/her conduct. In addition, the tribunal should give reasons for the decision it has reached at the end of the proceedings to demonstrate that its decision is not irrational. The observance of these principles will normally ensure minimum standards of procedural propriety. The same high standards obtaining in an ordinary court are not expected of a domestic tribunal, but the proceedings must be conducted as fairly as possible and a decision can be challenged in the courts if it is blatantly unfair. There is now an automatic right of appeal to the High Court from the decisions of those tribunals dealing with complaints against doctors, dentists and opticians but those against vets still go to the Judicial Committee of the Privy Council.

Domestic tribunals are not supervised by means of the prerogative orders which are explained in Chapter 15. Nevertheless, their decisions may be reviewed by the High Court where an injustice has been done. This was established in *Lee* v *Showmen's Guild* [1952] where Frank Lee owned and operated a fairground ride which he called *Noah's Ark*. He was a member of the guild, which was a registered trade union and, under its rules, no member should apply for the use of a site at a fairground which another member had occupied for two years previously if that other member wished to use the position again. Moreover, rule 14a enabled the committee to impose a fine on a member, who was then deemed to have forfeited his membership within a month if he did not pay the fine that was imposed. Rule 15c provided that no guild member should engage in 'unfair competition' with regard to the taking of a position at a fairground. However, rule 26 stated that all members of the guild should have the option at the termination of the Second World War (1939–45) of taking up their pre-war positions at all fairs. From 1934 to 1943 one William Shaw occupied the no. 2 site at the Bradford Summer Fair but in 1945 and 1946 this position was occupied by Frank Lee. Although no fair was held in 1947, Shaw applied to the guild committee to have the option of taking up the no. 2 site and the committee, acting under rule 26, granted him the right to take up his pre-war position at the Bradford fair. Notwithstanding this decision, it seems that Frank Lee occupied the no. 2 site in 1949 and Shaw complained to the guild's committee, who fined Lee £100 and ordered him to give up the position to Shaw. When Lee failed to pay the fine, the committee decided that he was no longer a member of the guild. This decision operated to deprive Lee of his livelihood because he could not work on any fairgrounds controlled by the guild. He successfully challenged the decision of the guild's committee in the High Court and there was a subsequent appeal to the Court of Appeal by the guild. The judges of the Court of Appeal decided that they had jurisdiction to examine any decision of the committee which involved a question of law and this would extend to the interpretation of the committee's rules; and it upheld Frank Lee's claim. It decided that the committee had misinterpreted its rule 15c and its decision to expel him was, in the circumstances, beyond its powers and therefore devoid of legal effect.

In *Bonsor* v *Musicians' Union* [1955] the appellant joined the respondent union because he was a professional musician and it was very difficult for him to obtain paid work without union membership. Although he had been a member for many years, during 1948 he omitted to pay his weekly union subscriptions and, by the end of June 1949, he had accumulated 52 weeks' arrears. The branch secretary of the union expelled him from the union at the end of June under rule 27(7) of the rule book. Bonsor asked to be reinstated so that he could obtain paid work but the branch secretary refused to reinstate him unless he actually paid all his outstanding subscriptions together with fines. He offered to pay the amount in question from his first week's earnings but the branch secretary refused. As a result, Bonsor was unable to obtain work as a professional musician (except with the very few non-union bands) and applied to the High Court claiming:

(a) a declaration that his actual expulsion from the union in November 1949 was null and void;
(b) a declaration that he was entitled to be reinstated as a member of the union;
(c) an injunction restraining the union and its officers from acting on the assumption that he was not a union member;
(d) damages from the union for breach of contract; and
(e) other unspecified relief.

In the High Court, Bonsor abandoned claims (b) and (d), although he reserved the latter claim for argument in the event of a subsequent appeal. The High Court held that a proper interpretation of rule 27(7) meant that only a branch committee could expel a member. Thus the apparent exercise of the power in the rules by a branch secretary was *ultra vires* and devoid of legal effect. It therefore granted the declaration requested in (a) and the injunction sought in (c) but the claim for damages was dismissed. The union appealed to the Court of Appeal and Bonsor cross-appealed over the rejection of the claim for damages for breach of contract. Bonsor then appealed to the House of Lords on the issue of whether damages could be awarded against the union arising from the branch secretary exceeding his powers and expelling him. Having conducted an extensive review of the case law, the House of Lords held by majority that the union could be liable in damages for breach of contract with one of its members. Thus, not only may the courts review the decision-making process to ensure that a rule book or similar constitutional document has been interpreted and applied properly, they may also award damages to compensate individual members of an organisation who suffer loss as a result of officials abusing their powers.

■ Summary

In the same way in which magistrates' courts are central to the criminal justice system, administrative tribunals are the lynchpin of the system of administrative law and justice that obtains in England and Wales as they deal with more cases annually than the ordinary courts. The government's proposals to streamline the existing network of tribunals is to be welcomed in so far as it does manage to make it more efficient and 'user friendly' through the creation of a unified system. The Employment Tribunal Service is already a highly efficient service (although there are regional variations) and so it will be interesting to see whether it becomes even more so when it is transferred into this new unified system. Conferring the title of tribunal judge on those chairing adjudicating panels may blur the distinction between tribunals and the ordinary courts at the lower level but this may turn out to be a positive development. Very little can be said about the various non-statutory domestic tribunals by way of summary except that they evidently fulfil a valuable role within the different organisations of which they are part. Their supervision can safely be left to the ordinary courts if they fail to observe the principles of natural justice. It is possible that, once the new unified tribunal system has had time to become firmly established, some of the statutory disciplinary tribunals may be transferred into it.

PROGRESS TEST

For suggested answers to the tests below, go to the companion website at www.pearsoned.co.uk/wheeler

1 What differences are there between a domestic tribunal, on the one hand, and an administrative tribunal on the other?
2 What is the basis of the authority and jurisdiction of a domestic tribunal?
3 What do you understand by the phrase 'procedural fairness'?
4 Is it more likely that a domestic tribunal might depart from the principles of procedural fairness? If so, why? If not, why not?
5 Who is to be responsible for appointing the chairpersons of administrative tribunals?
6 Do administrative tribunals really differ from the ordinary civil courts?
7 Are administrative tribunals really quicker and cheaper than the ordinary courts?
8 How important will the Council on Tribunals become in the new unified system?
9 If you were dismissed by your manager for refusing to work overtime in order to cover for an absent colleague who was sick, how would you go about obtaining legal redress assuming that you had worked for your former employer for one year? You may also assume that working overtime was voluntary.
10 How and by what means does the High Court exercise supervisory jurisdiction over non-statutory domestic tribunals?

FURTHER READING

■ Books

Parpworth, N. (2001) *Constitutional and Administrative Law* (Oxford: Oxford University Press, chapter 15).
Smith, I.T. and G.H. Thomas (2003) *Industrial Law,* (Oxford: Oxford University Press, chapter 8).
Ward, R. (2005) *English Legal System* (Oxford: Oxford University Press, chapter 9).

USEFUL WEBSITES

The website of the Council on Tribunals can be accessed on www.council-on-tribunals.gov.uk.
The Employment Tribunal Service can be accessed on the website www.employmenttribunals.gov.uk from which a great deal of useful information is available on how to bring claims.

Judgments of the Employment Appeal Tribunal can be accessed on www.employmentappeals.gov.uk. It is likely that there will soon be a website for the new unified tribunal service and details will be given on the companion website in due course.

Information on the Lands Tribunal can be accessed on the following website: www.landstribunals.gov.uk.

15 Dispute resolution 4: Judicial review

1 Introduction

Judicial review is a process whereby the superior courts examine official acts, alleged omissions, decisions and orders of those persons and institutions under a legal duty to perform public functions. Viewed in this way, it may be said that judicial review is concerned with the maintenance of the rule of law in a democratic society by ensuring that government, national and local, does not exceed its powers and exercises those that it has when under a common law or statutory duty to act.

Both national and local government are held accountable to the governed through the mechanism of periodic elections. Another control over government is the rather ill-defined constitutional principle of 'ministerial responsibility', by which ministers are politically accountable to Parliament such that they can be embarrassed into resigning for their political mistakes following a vote of 'no confidence' in the House of Commons. Constituency MPs hold regular 'surgeries' for their constituents and have long been accustomed to pursuing grievances on their behalf relating to the conduct of government departments, local authorities and certain public officials. In addition, there are now well-established ombudsman schemes to deal with complaints of maladministration against both national and local government. Within this framework of accountability the superior courts, through the process of judicial review, protect individuals and groups against the abuse of official power. The process of judicial review has evolved over centuries. It has been closely tied to the development of the remedies that the superior courts devised to supervise the decisions and acts of inferior courts and administrative bodies (these are discussed fully in **14**). The jurisdiction of the courts in judicial review is supervisory rather than appellate in that they oversee the exercise of discretionary powers, as was made clear in *Associated Provincial Picture Houses Ltd* v *Wednesbury Corporation* [1948].

This chapter begins by examining the form of the action before proceeding to consider the established bases for judicial review. Some space is then devoted to an explanation of the modern procedural aspects under the Civil Procedure Rules and the available remedies.

2 Form of the action

Prior to 1977, when the Rules of the Supreme Court were revised, persons seeking to challenge the acts and decisions of governmental bodies and public officials had some degree of choice. They had the option to proceed on a public law basis when seeking a public law remedy in the form of one of the prerogative orders (discussed in **14**). Alternatively, they could pursue an ordinary civil action for a declaratory judgment and/or an injunction. Public law actions have always proceeded on the basis that the individual litigant is, in theory, acting on behalf of the monarch in seeking to ascertain whether there has been an infringement of the law. The action used to be styled *R* v *Secretary of State for . . . ex parte* followed by the name of the litigant. Latin is being rooted out of the law and its administration so the action is now styled as *R (on the application of . . .* v *Secretary of State for . . .* An ordinary civil action has long taken a form with the applicant's name (now the claimant's name) appearing first, followed by the name of the defendant; for example, *Ridge* v *Baldwin.* There were a number of procedural advantages in taking the ordinary civil action route, not least of which was that the time allowed for the commencement of proceedings was far more generous than for the public law action which was time-barred after six months.

The new procedural rules cured the procedural disadvantages associated with the public law action but still seemed to leave open the possibility of a choice for litigants. This was retained when the rules were put on a statutory basis in the Supreme Court Act 1981 s. 31. However, no doubt motivated by a desire to prevent abuse of the ordinary civil law process, the House of Lords in *O'Reilly* v *Mackman* [1983] sought to curtail this choice. The case arose as a result of a riot that took place at Hull Prison but the action was not begun until three years after the decision of the board of visitors to punish certain of the participants by reducing their remission. Under the new rules governing claims for judicial review, any claim to challenge the decision of the board of visitors would have to have been brought within three months; so a public law action was time-barred. In refusing to permit a challenge in an ordinary civil law action, Lord Diplock, giving the judgment of the House of Lords, said:

> it would in my view as a general rule be contrary to public policy, and as such an abuse of the process of the court, to permit a person seeking to establish that a decision of a public authority infringed rights to which he was entitled to protection under public law to proceed by way of an ordinary action and by this means to evade the provisions of Order 53 for the protection of such authorities . . .

Within months of delivering its judgment in *O'Reilly* v *Mackman,* the appeal in *Cocks* v *Thanet County Council* [1983] came before the House of Lords. The claimant applied to the council for permanent housing for himself and his family in September 1981 under the Housing (Homeless Persons) Act 1977 whilst living with a friend. He then commenced proceedings against the council in the county court in January 1982 for a declaration that the council was in breach of its obligation to provide permanent housing for himself and his family under the Act. A High Court judge ruled that he could proceed with his claim in the county court but the council then appealed directly to the House of Lords arguing that, amongst other matters, the court could only consider the claim by way of an application for judicial review. The House of Lords applied its ruling in *O'Reilly* v *Mackman* and held that the claimant could only proceed by way of judicial review. Although the House of Lords indicated that challenges to governmental decisions should normally proceed by way of a public law action for judicial review, it made it clear at the time, and has done since, that its guidance is not to be applied in a rigid fashion especially where it might result in a denial of justice. In *Wandsworth Corporation* v *Winder* [1985], the council tried to argue that the defendant could not raise a public law issue as a defence in a civil action. It had let a flat to the defendant under Part V of the Housing Act 1957 on a weekly tenancy at a rent of £12.06. Under a newly incorporated schedule to this statute, the council was obliged to review its rents and increase them from time to time. In 1981 the council resolved to increase its rents, and in March it served notice on the defendant that the rent of his flat would be increased to £16.56 weekly. He objected to this increase and continued to pay the former amount so that arrears gradually accumulated. In the following year the council passed a further resolution to increase its rents and it served notice on the defendant in March 1982 to the effect that his rent would rise to £18.53. He again refused to pay any increase and the council began legal proceedings for possession of the flat and recovery of the arrears of rent. In his defence, Winder claimed that he was not liable to pay the arrears because the resolutions passed by the council were *ultra vires* and therefore void. The council applied to have this defence struck out as an abuse of process of the court and at first instance this was done on the basis that the conduct of a local authority should be challenged by way of an application for judicial review. The Court of Appeal allowed the defendant's subsequent appeal but the council then appealed to the House of Lords. Their Lordships held that it was a paramount principle that a private citizen's recourse to the courts to determine his rights could not be excluded except by very clear words in a statute. Moreover, there was nothing in the Supreme Court Act 1981 s. 31 or in the Rules of the Supreme Court that could be interpreted as abolishing the citizen's right to challenge a decision of a local authority in the course of defending an action.

The right to raise a point of public law is not limited to instances where a person is a defendant in an action, as was demonstrated in *Roy* v *Kensington and Chelsea and Westminster FPC* [1992]. Dr Roy was a general practitioner in the area administered by the Family Practitioner Committee (FPC), which had reduced his practice allowance as it was legally entitled to do if it was satisfied that he was not devoting a substantial amount of his time to his NHS practice. The statement of fees and allowances made by the Secretary of State under regulation 24 of a statutory instrument, required that all FPCs make payments to NHS general practitioners, providing for basic and supplementary practice allowances. Although Dr Roy was abroad for between one-third and one-half of each year, he did arrange cover for his NHS patients by securing the services of a locum doctor, and so he sought to challenge the FPC's decision and assert that he was indeed devoting a substantial amount of his time to general practice. He therefore commenced an ordinary civil action for breach of contract against the FPC in the High Court. The court struck out certain parts of his statement of claim on the basis that it was an abuse of the process of the court because the issues involved matters of public law that should have been pursued by way of an application for judicial review. However, the Court of Appeal allowed Dr Roy's appeal; but the FPC then appealed to the House of Lords, which availed itself of the opportunity to conduct an exhaustive review of the relevant case law. In giving the leading judgment, Lord Lowry stated that the rule in *O'Reilly* v *Mackman* was subject to many exceptions based on the nature of the claim and on the undesirability of erecting procedural barriers. At the close of his judgment he said:

> it seems to me that unless the procedure adopted by the . . . party is ill-suited to dispose of the question at issue, there is much to be said in favour of the proposition that a court having jurisdiction ought to let a case be heard rather than entertain a debate concerning the form of the proceedings.

Accordingly, the House of Lords unanimously dismissed the appeal brought by the FPC.

In *Boddington* v *British Transport Police* [1999] the House of Lords made it clear that, in principle, a public law defence can be raised in criminal proceedings to ensure that a conviction is not based on an invalid legal instrument. It is important to note that the decisions of private bodies that do not derive their powers from statute cannot normally be challenged in a claim for judicial review, as is illustrated by the ruling in *R* v *Disciplinary Committee of the Jockey Club ex p. Aga Khan* [1993]. However, in *R* v *Panel on Takeovers and Mergers ex p. Datafin* [1987] the Court of Appeal permitted an application by way of judicial review because of the special functions exercised by the Panel in the City of London.

3 Exclusion of judicial review

In the past, successive governments have steered statutes through Parliament that contained express provisions which seemed to exclude any scope for judicial review of administrative action. These provisions have come to be known as 'ouster of jurisdiction' clauses since they appear to remove official acts and decisions from judicial scrutiny. In *Anisminic Ltd* v *Foreign Compensation Commission* [1969] the House of Lords devised an ingenious way of circumventing such clauses. The Commission was established to administer claims under the Foreign Compensation Act 1950 in respect of assets owned by UK nationals that had been confiscated by foreign governments. The company owned property in Egypt that was confiscated by that government and it made a claim for compensation to the Commission which declined to accept the claim. Not surprisingly, the company sought to challenge the Commission's decision. The Foreign Compensation Act 1950 s. 4(4) contained the following provision:

> The determination by the Commission of any application made to them under this Act shall not be called in question in any court of law.

The House of Lords held that the Commission's decision was not a determination but rather a 'purported determination' and, since the above provision made no reference to purported determinations, their Lordships were not precluded from inquiring whether or not any order or decision of the Commission was a legal nullity.

4   The bases for judicial review

In the case of *Council for Civil Service Unions* v *Minister for the Civil Service* [1985] Lord Diplock set out the modern basis for judicial review in terms of 'illegality', 'procedural impropriety' and 'irrationality'. More recently, the Human Rights Act 1998 has added a new dimension to judicial review proceedings in that it requires courts to take a more interventionist approach where Convention rights are involved. In the exposition that follows, these general headings will be used to expound the basic principles pertaining to judicial review. However, the first three should not be thought of as being self-contained because, in practice, there is sometimes a degree of overlap between them. For example, a decision-making body (or an official) that unlawfully fetters its discretion may have its decision reviewed on the grounds of illegality or procedural impropriety.

5   Illegality

At common law, a decision may be illegal if it infringes a basic right. For example, in *Raymond* v *Honey* [1983] the Home Secretary had power to make rules for the regulation and management of prisons under the Prison Act 1952 s. 47. Raymond, a prison governor, was under the impression that the Prison Rules 1964 rr. 33 and 37A empowered him to prevent mail being sent by prisoners in certain circumstances and he prevented some of Honey's mail being sent to his solicitors. Honey was advised to initiate contempt of court proceedings against the governor, which Lord Russell in *R* v *Gray* [1900] defined as:

> Any act done which is calculated to obstruct or interfere with the due course of justice or the lawful process of the courts.

The governor's action came within this definition but his defence was that he had been authorised to intercept prisoners' mail under the prison regulations. This then focused attention on whether the Home Secretary was empowered under the Prison Act 1952 s. 47 to make regulations granting the governor such powers. The House of Lords took the view that it did not and ruled accordingly. In the course of his judgment, Lord Wilberforce said:

> [U]nder English law, a convicted prisoner, in spite of his imprisonment, retains all civil rights which are not taken away expressly or by necessary implication ... There is nothing in the Prison Act 1952 that confers power to make regulations which would deny, or interfere with, the right of the respondent, as a prisoner, to have unimpeded access to a court. Section 47 ... is quite insufficient to authorise hindrance or interference with so basic a right.

An administrative act or decision is illegal if it goes beyond the scope of the authority that has made the act or decision possible. It will also be illegal if it contravenes that authority in any way or if the person acting or deciding pursues an objective other than the one for which the power to act or decide was conferred. In the sphere of administrative law there are a number of instances where an Act of Parliament confers a discretionary power on a government minister, a public body or an official, and the courts have long taken the view that the exercise of this discretion must be according to the law. This principle was clearly established in the land-mark, if somewhat controversial, judgment of the House of Lords in *Padfield* v *Minister of Agriculture, Fisheries and Food* [1968]. A milk marketing scheme had been introduced by Act of Parliament that required milk pro-ducers to sell all their output to regional Milk Marketing Boards. The various boards included both consumers' and producers' representatives. Subsequent legislation in the form of the Agricultural Marketing Act 1958 made provision for two separate bodies to hear complaints about the oper-ation of the scheme. Most complaints were to be referred to a consumers' committee, but s. 19(3) provided that:

> A committee of investigation shall ... (b) be charged with the duty, if the Minister in any case so directs, of considering and reporting to the Minister on ... any ... complaint made to the Minister as to the operation of any scheme which, in the opinion of the Minister, could not be considered by a Consumers' Committee.

The minister had refused to exercise his discretion to empanel a com-mittee to investigate complaints made by the south-eastern producers that the majority of the board had fixed prices in a way that was particularly unfavourable to them. They therefore applied for a court order that would require the minister to do so. The House of Lords held that the minister's discretion was not unfettered (unlimited) and that the reason that he had given for his refusal showed that he had gone beyond his powers not only by taking into account factors that were irrelevant from a legal standpoint but also by using his powers in a way that was calculated to frustrate the policy behind the Act as interpreted by their Lordships. On this basis, the House of Lords considered that it was entitled to inter-vene and declare the minister's decision illegal. Although their Lordships made a mandatory order requiring the minister to empanel a committee, the minister subsequently declined to follow the committee's advice – he was legally entitled to do this. For the milk producers who brought the action it was a hollow victory.

Even where an Act of Parliament confers an unfettered discretion on a minister, the courts may still assert their right to review a ministerial decision because Lord Upjohn said in *Padfield* v *Minister of Agriculture, Fisheries and Food*:

> [T]he use of that adjective [unfettered], even in an Act of Parliament, can do nothing to unfetter the control which the judiciary have over the executive, namely, that in exercising their powers the latter must act lawfully and that is a matter to be determined by looking at the Act and its scope and object in conferring a discretion upon the Minister rather than by the use of adjectives.

Nevertheless, the courts will decline to review decisions involving matters of economic and social policy that involve difficult choices between competing priorities because they recognise that this is not their sphere. Such decisions are matters requiring the exercise of political judgement.

Statute law is not the only source of the UK government's legal authority. The government also possesses a number of common law powers which lawyers refer to as 'prerogative powers', that is, powers exercised under the royal prerogative. These prerogative powers were largely defined at the time of the 1688 revolutionary settlement and, although the monarch does still have some prerogative powers that she is able to exercise, most of these are exercised by Her Majesty's government. In *Council for Civil Service Unions* v *Minister for the Civil Service* [1985], the House of Lords held that most prerogative powers are now subject to judicial review. Such a review occurred in *R* v *Secretary of State for the Home Department ex p. Bentley* [1994], the applicant being the sister of Derek Bentley. Derek Bentley and Christopher Craig were convicted in 1952 of murdering a police officer but the jury had recommended mercy. The prosecution had argued that both were engaged in a joint criminal endeavour. Although Craig had fired the fatal shot, this had occurred after Bentley, who had been arrested, uttered the ambiguous sentence 'Let him have it, Chris'. Since Bentley was aged 19 at the time, he was sentenced to death, whereas Craig, who was aged 16, was ordered to be detained at Her Majesty's pleasure. After the trial, the judge wrote to the Home Secretary stating that he could find no mitigating circumstances in Bentley's case. In spite of a campaign and the advice of the senior civil servants to the contrary, the Home Secretary declined to reprieve Bentley who was then executed. Following a long campaign for a posthumous pardon by the applicant, the case was reviewed by a later Home Secretary. He concluded in October 1992 that there were no grounds for recommending a free pardon on the basis that he could not substitute his judgement for that of the Home Secretary at the time. In addition, he stated that it had been a long-established policy of successive Home Secretaries that a free pardon in relation to a conviction for an indictable offence should be granted only if moral as well as technical innocence of the convicted person could be established, which was not possible in the particular case. On considering the substantive application for judicial review, the Divisional Court held that decisions taken under the royal prerogative were susceptible to judicial review if their nature and subject matter were amenable and in so far as the challenge did not require the court to review questions of policy. Moreover, even though the formulation of the criteria for the exercise of the royal prerogative of mercy, by the grant of a free pardon, was probably not justiciable, failure by the Home Secretary to recognise that the prerogative of mercy could be exercised otherwise than by way of a free pardon was subject to judicial review. The court took the view that the Home Secretary had not given sufficient consideration to the possibility of granting a form of pardon suitable to the circumstances of the case and that he should consider the matter afresh.

The subsequent case *R* v *Secretary of State for the Home Department ex p. Fire Brigades Union* [1995] centred on a scheme for compensating victims of crime. The Criminal Injuries Compensation Scheme had originally been introduced under the Crown's prerogative in 1964 but was then to be placed on a statutory basis under the Criminal Justice Act 1988 ss 108–117 and Schedules 6 and 7. The aim was to provide compensation to victims on a case by case basis, applying the compensatory principles of the law of tort. According to the Criminal Justice Act 1988 s. 171(1) the statutory scheme was to come into force 'on such day as the Secretary of State may ... appoint'. In fact, the Secretary of State did not make a commencement order and in 1993 he indicated that the statutory provisions would not be brought into operation but that the non-statutory scheme would be replaced by a non-statutory tariff scheme. This meant that awards to victims would be made on an *ex gratia* basis by reference to a tariff fixed according to particular categories of injury. In July 1994 the House of Commons in the Appropriation Act 1994 approved supply estimates which included funding for the Home Office to operate the revised scheme. In an application for judicial review, the union representing persons liable to suffer injury as victims of violent crime sought two declarations: (a) that the Secretary of State by failing or refusing to bring the statutory scheme into operation had acted unlawfully and in breach of his duty under the 1988 Act; and (b) that by implementing the non-statutory tariff scheme he had acted unlawfully in breach of a duty under the Act and accordingly had abused his prerogative powers.

The Divisional Court dismissed the application but the Court of Appeal allowed the appeal in part by granting the second declaration. The Secretary of State then appealed to the House of Lords. By majority the House of Lords dismissed the appeal by the Secretary of State and a cross-appeal by the union. In relation to the second declaration, their Lordships held that the Criminal Justice Act 1988 s. 171(1) imposed a continuing obligation on the Secretary of State to consider whether to bring the statutory scheme into operation. They also took the view that he could not lawfully bind himself not to exercise the discretion conferred on him and that the non-statutory tariff scheme was inconsistent with the statutory scheme. Thus the decision of the Secretary of State not to bring ss 108–117 into operation but to introduce the non-statutory tariff scheme was unlawful. However, in dismissing the union's cross-appeal their Lordships indicated that the 1988 Act did not impose a legally enforceable duty on the Secretary of State to bring ss 108–117 into operation at any particular time.

Where a power has been granted for one purpose but is exercised for another, the courts will normally take the view that the power has not been validly exercised. This principle was established initially in relation to the exercise of powers of compulsory purchase but it has since been developed to the point that it is now a fundamental principle of administrative law of general application. It was applied in *Hazell* v *Hammersmith & Fulham LBC* [1992]. In this case the local authority had power to borrow money under the Local Government Act 1972 on both a long-term and a short-term basis. It exercised these powers to finance certain capital projects. However, from 1987 to 1989, it entered into a number of interest rate swap contracts with banks. The swap market enables a borrower to raise funds in the market to which the borrower has best access but then to make interest and capital repayments in its preferred form of currency. From April 1987 to February 1989 the local authority did this mainly with a view to boosting its income because, if it swapped from a fixed interest rate to a variable rate, it stood to make considerable financial gains if interest rates went down – but if they rose, it stood to make serious losses. If it swapped from a variable rate to fixed rate the opposite result would obtain. In July 1988, the district auditor challenged the validity of these interest rate swap transactions on the basis that they amounted to speculative trading for profit because the authority had made no attempt to match its actual debts and investments with any of the transactions. The auditor applied, under the Local Government Finance Act 1982, for a declaration that the items appearing in the local authority's capital market fund account for 1987 and 1988 were contrary to law and for an order for rectification of the accounts. The case eventually reached the House of Lords, which ruled that the local authority had no power to enter into the interest rate swap transactions with a view to increasing its financial resources because such transactions were inconsistent with its borrowing powers in the Local Government Act 1972.

In *R* v *Secretary of State for Foreign Affairs ex p. World Development Movement Ltd* [1995] the Foreign Secretary was empowered under the Overseas Development and Cooperation Act 1980 s. 1(1):

> for the purpose of promoting the development or maintaining the economy of a country ... outside the UK, or the welfare of its people, to furnish any person or body with assistance whether financial, technical or of any other nature.

The Malaysian government had identified the Pergau River as an appropriate site for a hydroelectric power station. A consortium that included GEC and Balfour Beatty informed the Department of Trade and Industry that it would be seeking financial assistance under the 'aid and trade provision' in the Act, and in November 1988 it submitted a formal application that gave its indicative costs for the project amounting to £315 m to the Overseas Development Administration (ODA). Then, in January 1989, it produced a firm contract proposal for £316 m with a UK content of £195 m. Following the report of an appraisal mission that was sent to Malaysia by the ODA, the UK government made an oral offer of £68.25 m for the project conditional upon a full economic appraisal. A subsequent appraisal mission reported that, at the consortium's price of £316 m, the economic viability of the project was marginal. In March 1989 the consortium informed the ODA that its budget estimate had been revised upwards from £316 m to £397 m and the ODA minuted that the project was no longer marginal but uneconomic. Nevertheless, the UK government gave the Malaysian government written notice of an offer of assistance based on the original estimate of £316 m with an indication that it would be willing to discuss the possibility of further financial assistance. By early 1990 the ODA completed yet another economic appraisal which concluded that, at £397 m, the project would be a 'very bad buy' and a burden on Malaysian consumers. In spite of advice from the ODA that the project was an abuse of the aid programme and was not a sound development project, the Foreign Secretary approved the financial support under the 'aid and trade provision' in the legislation, on the basis that a contrary decision would affect the credibility of the UK abroad. The World Development Movement (WDM), which functions as a non-partisan pressure group dedicated to improving the quantity and quality of British aid to developing countries, sought an assurance from the Foreign Secretary that no further funds for the project would be provided. When he refused to give such an assurance, the WDM applied for judicial review of his decision to grant financing under the 'aid and trade provision' and his decision to refuse to withhold outstanding payments. The Foreign Secretary argued that s. 1(1) did not limit aid to projects that were viable in narrow economic terms but allowed aid to be granted which served wider political and economic considerations such as the promotion of regional stability and good government. The Divisional Court held that the Foreign Secretary was fully justified under the legislation, when making decisions of whether to grant assistance, to take account of political and economic considerations and to consider the impact on the UK's credibility of the withdrawal of an offer already made. However, it ruled that on the evidence no development purpose under the Act existed. Accordingly, the Foreign Secretary's decision was unlawful.

Even though an Act of Parliament may confer a discretionary power without expressly referring to a particular purpose, this will not prevent the courts from insisting that the discretionary power is exercised in accordance with what they regard as the implied purpose of the legislation. If the exercise of a discretionary power has been influenced by a consideration that ought not to have been taken into account, the courts will usually rule that the power has not been validly exercised where these extraneous considerations have influenced the decision.

In *R* v *Liverpool University ex p. Caesar-Cordon* [1991] the University of Liverpool Conservative Association applied for and was granted provisional approval by the university to hold a meeting to be addressed by a South African diplomat in November 1988. Having consulted with the local police, the university then withdrew its approval because it was not reasonably practicable to make adequate arrangements for the maintenance of good order at the meeting and in the adjacent residential area. The Association appealed to the university vice-chancellor, who rejected the appeal, but the Association then sought permission for a meeting in January 1989 to be addressed by two South African diplomats. Permission was granted provided that entry would be restricted to staff and students of the university and that, whilst the Association could issue invitations to its own members, there would be no other publicity apart from notices within the university on the day of the meeting. Attendance was to be limited by the size of the venue and admission was to be on proof of identity. On the day of the meeting, the university revoked its permission because of fear of public disorder outside the university precincts. The chairman of the Association applied for judicial review requesting a declaration that the university had acted contrary to the Education (No. 2) Act 1986 s. 43 by failing to take such steps as were reasonably practicable to ensure freedom of speech. The Divisional Court held that, in the performance of its duty to ensure freedom of speech, the university was not acting beyond its powers by restricting publicity and admission; however, it was not entitled to take into account threats of public disorder outside the university precincts.

Under the general heading of illegality, particular difficulties arise in relation to the delegation of discretionary powers. There is a general principle that a discretionary power should be exercised only by the body or official to whom it has been entrusted unless there is an express power to delegate it to another. The case *Ellis* v *Dubowski* [1921] involved an appeal by a local authority inspector following the refusal of the local magistrates to convict the respondents for an infringement of the Cinematograph Act 1909. County councils were empowered under the Act to impose conditions on the granting of licences to operate cinemas. A licence was granted to the respondents on the basis that no film was to be shown which was likely to be injurious to morality or to encourage or incite crime or to lead to disorder. In addition, the respondents were prohibited under the terms of their licence from showing a film that had not been certified for public exhibition by the British Board of Film Censors (BBFC), a body which then had no statutory or constitutional authority. The respondents had failed to comply with this latter requirement but argued that the county council had no authority to delegate its powers under the Cinematograph Act 1909 other than in accordance with s. 5, which permitted delegation to a council committee or to local magistrates. In essence, their case was that the condition in the licence was *ultra vires* and void in so far as the council had delegated its powers to the BBFC. Lawrence CJ ruled that this condition in the licence was unlawful on the basis that 'The condition sets up an authority whose *ipse dixit* is to control the exhibition of films. The effect is to transfer a power which belongs to the County Council ...'. Later in his judgment he stated: 'a condition putting the matter into the hands of a third person or body not possessed of statutory or constitutional authority is *ultra vires* the committee'.

More recently, in *R* v *DPP ex p. Association of First Division Civil Servants,* (1988), the delegation of a power to review prosecutions in order to decide whether there was sufficient evidence to proceed was held to be illegal because the Act of Parliament conferring the power on the Director of Public Prosecutions envisaged that it would be delegated only to a member of the Crown Prosecution Service, who would be a lawyer. Nevertheless, the courts have recognised that special considerations arise where a statutory power is conferred on a Secretary of State but is exercised by a senior departmental official. Under what has become known as the *Carltona* principle, formulated by Lord Greene MR in *Carltona Ltd* v *Commissioners of Works* [1943], the courts have accepted that powers entrusted to senior ministers can normally be exercised by senior officials of the department acting under the authority of the Secretary of State. However, the *Carltona* principle can be expressly excluded by the wording of the legislation. For example, the Immigration Act 1971 ss 13(5), 14(3) and 15(4) all refer to action by the minister 'and not by a person acting under his authority'.

As was stated in Chapter 8, all public authorities are now required by the Human Rights Act 1998 s. 6 to act in accordance with the Convention rights as set out in Schedule 1 to the Act. The case of *R* v *North and East Devon Health Authority ex p. Coughlan (Secretary of State and another intervening)* [2000] (to be considered below) illustrates how a Convention right can arise in relation to decisions made by agencies of the NHS. Should public authorities fail to act in accordance with the Convention rights, their decisions can be reviewed by the courts on the basis of illegality because they will either have contravened or have exceeded the provisions of the statute. Although the Act has great constitutional importance it has to be remembered that the European Convention on Human Rights and Fundamental Freedoms has not been incorporated into UK law in the same way as has the EC Treaty. Moreover, the European Court of Human Rights has not devised a doctrine of direct effect. Thus the scheme of the Human Rights Act 1998 requires that legislation should be interpreted and applied in a way that is compatible with the Convention rights set out in Schedule 1. If, because of the very precise wording of the statute, this is not possible, the courts are limited to the making of a declaration of incompatibility. They are not at liberty to suspend the operation of an Act of Parliament where one (or more) provision conflicts with rights contained in Schedule 1. The courts will nevertheless be required to review their previous case law. For example, in the case *Brind and others* v *Secretary of State for the Home Department* [1991] the House of Lords held that there was no presumption that the courts would review the exercise of an administrative discretion on the basis that the discretion had to be exercised in accordance with the Convention. In the light of the Human Rights Act, however, a similar case today may have a different outcome; the House of Lords would have to review its previous decision and take into account the principle of proportionality. In *Raymond* v *Honey* [1983] the House of Lords upheld the rights of a prisoner on common law principles but today it is likely that the judgment in a similar case would be based on the relevant Convention right in the Schedule.

As was stated in Chapter 7, certain provisions of the EC Treaty have direct effect in the legal systems of member states. Individuals and private corporations (as well as foreign nationals) may have recourse to these Treaty provisions and challenge governmental decisions in the courts of England and Wales. For example, Article 87(1) of the EC Treaty states:

> Save as otherwise provided in this Treaty, any aid granted by a Member State or through State resources in any form whatsoever which distorts or threatens to distort competition by favouring certain undertakings or the production of certain goods shall, in so far as it affects trade between Member States, be incompatible with the common market.

The European Court of Justice has declared that Article 87(1) has direct effect and if a UK company is to receive illegal state aid (aid that has not been approved by the European Commission) a competitor may make an application to the courts to have the payment of the aid suspended pending an investigation by the Commission.

As has been stated, directives can have vertical direct effect provided the criteria are satisfied, and where this occurs they can form the basis for challenging official decisions. In *R* v *Secretary of State for the Home Department ex p. Dannenberg* [1984] the applicant was a German national who entered the UK in 1981 and in 1982 was given a resident's permit for five years. On 29 April 1983 he appeared before Mid Sussex Magistrates' Court charged with a number of offences to which he pleaded guilty. The magistrates had before them a copy of a notice that had been given to the applicant pursuant to the Immigration Act 1971 s. 6(2) to the effect that they should recommend him for deportation. Having sentenced the applicant, the magistrates made a recommendation under s. 6(1) of the Act for deportation. Following the recommendation, the applicant was ordered to be detained until the Secretary of State could consider the recommendation. In due course the Secretary of State was able to do so and he made an order for deportation under s. 5(1) of the Act. Neither the magistrates nor the Secretary of State gave reasons for the recommendation or the deportation order. Although the Civil Division of the Court of Appeal held that the refusal of the Divisional Court to quash the recommendation was a judgment in a criminal matter and no appeal could be addressed to the Civil Division concerning it, the Court of Appeal still allowed the appeal. It did so on the basis that the deportation order did not contain any information relating to the grounds on which it was made, nor did the magistrates' recommendation. This was an infringement of Articles 6 and 9 of Directive 64/221/EEC. Accordingly the deportation order was invalid and was therefore quashed.

Parliamentary legislation may also be challenged for illegality by way of judicial review where it conflicts with EU law, and it will be recalled from

Chapters 5 and 7 that a successful challenge to the legality of the Merchant Shipping Act 1988 Part II and the regulations created thereunder was made in *R* v *Secretary of State for Transport ex p. Factortame Ltd.*

6 Procedural fairness in general

Whilst illegality focuses mainly on the need to ensure that decisions are made within the scope of the powers that have been delegated and that the powers themselves have been properly exercised, procedural fairness focuses on the decision-making process. First, the courts require that decision-makers should not be biased or in any way prejudiced, otherwise there is a real likelihood that their judgments will be flawed as proper consideration will not have been given to the representations put forward by those most concerned. Secondly, individuals and groups should have the opportunity, in so far as this is practicable, to make representations and thereby influence the outcome of the decision-making process. Thus, under the heading of procedural fairness, the courts impose a duty on those acting in an official capacity to act fairly. Accordingly, they will examine the consultation process, if any, with a view to determining whether it is adequate and whether it contributes towards the administration process rather than hindering it. In so doing the judges are motivated to ensure the quality and rationality of the decision-making process. The requirement of procedural fairness has generated a vast amount of case law and some of the more significant cases are considered in 7 and 8.

7 Procedural fairness: the rule against bias

If administrative decisions are to be intrinsically fair it is essential that the decision-maker is not biased or prejudiced. Bias or prejudice on the part of the decision-maker is likely to have the result that a proper consideration of the arguments put forward by interested parties is precluded. Bias may arise because of a financial or proprietary interest but other factors too give rise to actual bias. In practice, the rule against bias is concerned with the risk of bias just as much as the fact of actual bias to ensure that justice is not only done, but is also seen to be done. Although an administrative decision must be invalidated if actual bias on the part of the decision-maker is established, the same result will obtain if there appears to have been a real danger of bias, as was stated by the House of Lords in *R* v *Gough* [1993]. This was not an application for judicial review as such but an appeal to the House of Lords against conviction, albeit on the flimsiest grounds. The appellant and his brother were charged on indictment with conspiracy to rob, but his brother was discharged on the application of the prosecution. However, in the course of the trial, the brother was referred to by name and a photograph of him and the appellant was shown to the jury and a statement containing the brother's address was read to the jury. At the conclusion of the trial the brother caused a disturbance in the courtroom and one of the jurors recognised him as her next-door neighbour. The brother then informed the defence of the connection. Soon afterwards the juror was interviewed by the police and she swore an affidavit to the effect that she was unaware of the connection until after the jury had delivered its verdict. The Criminal Division of the Court of Appeal had ruled that the correct test was whether the appellant had a fair trial. Since it concluded that he had, it dismissed the appeal. The basis of the appeal to the House of Lords was that the presence of the brother's neighbour on the jury was a serious irregularity. In giving the leading judgment of the House of Lords, dismissing the appeal, Lord Gough stated that the test for bias to be applied by courts and administrative tribunals should be stated in terms of whether there was a real danger rather than just a real likelihood of bias.

In the later case of *R* v *West London Coroner ex p. Dallagho and another* [1994] the Court of Appeal seems to have applied this guidance strictly. The applicants were mothers of two of the victims of the *Marchioness* tragedy. In 1989 the vessel had been chartered for a night-time pleasure cruise on the River Thames with a discotheque and licensed bar. The *Marchioness* collided with the dredger *Bowbelle* near Southwark Bridge and the *Marchioness* sank very quickly. Of the passengers and crew, who numbered 131, there were only 80 survivors. Most of those who died were between the ages of 18 and 30. All the 51 bodies recovered were taken to the Westminster mortuary which was within the jurisdiction of HM Coroner for Inner West London. Inquests into these deaths were opened and adjourned in the weeks immediately following the disaster. In February 1990 the coroner indicated that he would commence the inquest hearings on 23 April, taking them in two parts: part one dealing with forensic and identification evidence relating to who had died, when and from what cause; part two dealing with eye witnesses and technical evidence on how the deceased met their deaths.

When the hearings began on 23 April, relatives of seven of the deceased, including the applicant, objected to this two-stage inquest so that the coroner heard only 44 part one inquests and soon afterward the inquests were adjourned pending criminal proceedings. Following a misunderstanding, Mrs Lockwood-Croft, a bereaved mother, was denied sight of her son's body by persons claiming to be, but who were not, acting on the coroner's instructions. On her subsequent request for an exhumation order because she was having nightmares that the interred body was not that of her son, the coroner expressed his belief to the appropriate authorities that she had been deeply psychologically affected in her grief and was not acting rationally and that other relatives were mentally unwell. By late June 1992 all the criminal proceedings had concluded and the coroner had to decide whether to resume the inquest under the provisions of the Coroners Act 1988 s. 16(3), the relevant text of which is: 'After the conclusion of the relevant criminal proceedings ... the coroner may ... resume the adjourned inquest if in his opinion there is sufficient cause to do so.'

On 22 July 1992 the coroner announced his decision not to resume the adjourned inquests and he decided in late 1992 not to grant the exhumation order to Mrs Lockwood-Croft. She and the first applicant joined forces to challenge the coroner's decision not to proceed with the inquests on the grounds that he had shown apparent bias towards them by the comments that he made about their mental condition. The Court of Appeal quashed the coroner's decision and the matter was remitted to another coroner in a different district for a fresh decision. Referring to the decision of the House of Lords in *R* v *Gough*, Simon Brown LJ in the Court of Appeal stated the following propositions:

1 Any court seized of a challenge on the ground of apparent bias must ascertain the relevant circumstances and consider all the evidence for itself so as to reach its own conclusion on the facts.
2 It necessarily follows that the factual position may appear quite differently as between the time when the challenge is launched and the time when it comes to be decided by the court. What may appear at the leave (permission) stage to be a strong case of 'justice [not] manifestly be[ing] seen to be done', may, following the court's investigation, nevertheless fail. Or, of course (although perhaps less probably), the case may have become stronger.
3 In reaching its conclusion the court 'personifies the reasonable man'.
4 The question on which the court must reach its own factual conclusion is this: is there a real danger of injustice having occurred as a result of bias? By real is meant not without substance. A real danger clearly involves more than a minimal risk, less than a probability. One could, I think, as well speak of a real risk or a real possibility.
5 Injustice will have occurred as a result of bias if 'the decision maker unfairly regarded with disfavour the case of a party to the issue under consideration by him'. I take unfairly regarded with disfavour to mean 'was predisposed or prejudiced against one party's case for reasons unconnected with the merits of the issue'.
6 A decision-maker may have unfairly regarded with disfavour one party's case whether consciously or unconsciously. Where, as here, the applicants expressly disavow any suggestion of actual bias, it seems to me that the court must necessarily be asking itself whether there is a real danger that the decision-maker was unconsciously biased.
7 It will be seen, therefore, that by the time that legal challenge comes to be resolved, the court is no longer concerned strictly with the appearance of bias but rather with establishing the possibility that there was actual although unconscious bias.

The rule against bias must not be taken to absurd lengths, as necessity may sometimes dictate that a person who is not completely neutral and totally objective makes an official decision. Moreover, in matters of policy, public officials may have previously indicated their position on a particular issue but this does not necessarily preclude them from giving proper consideration to representations before a decision is made.

8   Procedural fairness: the duty to act fairly

Particular Acts of Parliament may set out a consultation procedure, and where this is the case the procedure must be followed otherwise there will be scope for a successful challenge of the decision in the courts. In other circumstances the court may infer that a fair hearing is required because of the need to safeguard some right or interest. In *Ridge* v *Baldwin* [1964] the House of Lords reasserted the principle that public bodies must observe certain standards of procedural fairness in their decision-making. The appellant was appointed chief constable of Brighton in 1956. The appointment was made subject to the Police Act 1919 and the regulations made under it. On 25 October 1957, he was arrested and charged, with others, of conspiracy to obstruct the course of justice and three days later he was suspended from duty by the local Watch Committee (the fore-runner of the modern Police Authority). He was subsequently acquitted of the charges against him by a jury on 28 February 1958, but Donovan J, on passing sentence on his co-accused, said that the facts disclosed in the course of the trial:

> establish that neither of you had that professional and moral leadership which both of you should have had and were entitled to expect from the Chief Constable of Brighton ...

After his acquittal, the appellant applied to be reinstated, but on 7 March 1958 the Watch Committee met and decided that he had been negligent in the performance of his duties as chief constable. The committee also decided to dismiss him from office in the apparent exercise of its powers under the Municipal Corporations Act 1882 s. 191(4). Under that subsection it could dismiss him if he was negligent in the discharge of his duty or otherwise unsuitable to hold office. Whilst no specific charge was formulated against him, either at that meeting or at another on 15 March, when the committee was addressed by the appellant's solicitor, the committee in arriving at its decision considered his own statements in evidence and the observations of Donovan J above. The appellant then addressed an appeal to the Home Secretary who decided that there was sufficient material on which the committee could, in purporting to exercise its power under s. 191(4), dismiss him. The appellant then brought an action against members of the committee for a declaration that his dismissal was illegal, *ultra vires* and void. He also claimed arrears of remuneration and damages. The House of Lords held that the decision of the committee to dismiss him was null and void and that, notwithstanding the fact that the decision of the Home Secretary was final and binding on the parties under the Police Appeals Act 1927, that decision could not give validity to the decision of the committee. The appellant was not an employee of the committee and the latter could dismiss him only on the grounds set out in s. 191(4), that is for neglect of duty (as opposed to breach of contract). Three of the five Law Lords held that the committee had not observed the principles of natural justice by informing him of the charge against him and giving him an opportunity to be heard.

Public administration abounds with instances where administrative decision-making must be preceded by a formal consultation process. For example, planning legislation requires public participation in the drafting of development plans. It also provides for appeals to be made against the refusal of planning applications or against any conditions that might be attached to such applications. Even in the absence of a statutory require-ment to consult, the courts will often, in the interests of procedural fairness, presume that an opportunity is to be afforded for consultation or at least a chance to make representations where an individual's or entity's common law or statutory rights are at stake. In *R* v *Liverpool Corporation ex p. Liverpool Taxi Fleet Operators' Association* [1972] the corporation had power under the Town Police Clauses Act 1847 to 'license ... such number of hackney coaches or carriages ... as they think fit' in its area. In exercise of this power it limited the number to 300. Then, in 1970 and 1971 when many private minicabs were operating for hire in the streets, the applicants who represented the interests of the 300 existing licence-holders were assured by the town clerk that they would be consulted if any change in the number of licences was contemplated. In 1971, a special subcommittee of the corporation recommended increases for 1972 and 1973 and no restriction in numbers thereafter, but it heard the applicants' case against its proposals. At a public meeting of the full corporation on 4 August 1971, the committee chairman gave a public undertaking that the numbers would not be increased above 300 until provision controlling minicabs had been enacted by Parliament and had come into force. This undertaking was confirmed orally by the chairman and then by letter dated 11 August 1971 from the town clerk. However, in November 1971 the subcommittee decided to increase the number of licences for 1972, and on 22 December the corporation confirmed this resolution. An appli-cation for judicial review to the Divisional Court was declined but the Court of Appeal allowed an appeal and granted the relief sought on the basis that the corporation had not acted fairly by failing to fulfil the terms of the assurance it had given.

More recently, in *R* v *Secretary of State for Health ex p. United States Tobacco International Inc.* [1992] an American company had received financial support to establish a factory in the UK to manufacture oral snuff from tobacco. Subsequently, having inquired into its possible detrimental effects, the Secretary of State for Health made regulations banning the product but without affording the company an opportunity to challenge the evidence. Although it was held that the company, prior to the ban, had no legitimate expectation of a continuation of the government's original policy, the negative impact of a ban on the company's business interests required a fair hearing. The fact that no opportunity had been provided rendered the regulations in question void and they were quashed by order of the court.

The principle of legitimate expectation seems to have become estab-lished in administrative law with the case of *Schmidt* v *Secretary of State for Home Affairs* [1969]. A legitimate expectation of consultation may arise as a result of the past conduct of the decision-maker, and this was recognised in the case of *Council for the Civil Service Unions* v *Minister for the Civil Service* [1985]. Although the House of Lords ultimately decided against the civil service unions on the basis of a risk to national security certified by a government minister, it confirmed that the principle of legitimate expectation existed in administrative law. Indeed, Lord Fraser said that a legitimate expectation could arise 'either from an express promise given on behalf of a public authority or from the existence of a regular practice which the claimant can reasonably expect to continue'.

Although the protection of legitimate expectations is an important aspect of procedural fairness, it should not mean that officials are prevented from ever changing their policies and practices. If they were, they would be falling foul of another requirement of procedural fairness in that they would be fettering their discretion for the future. If there is to be a change to a long-standing policy, some form of notice should be given with an opportunity afforded for comment and for objections to be raised by those affected.

Apart from those instances where the form of hearing is prescribed by statute, the degree of consultation deemed appropriate will vary depending on the nature of the decision and the context. In *R* v *Secretary of State for the Home Department ex p. Doody* [1994], Lord Mustill said:

> The principles of fairness are not to be applied by rote identically in every situation. What fairness demands is dependent on the context of the decision, and this is to be taken into account in all aspects. An essential factor of the context is the statute that creates the discretion, as regards both its language and the shape of the legal and administrative system within which the decision is taken. Whilst the statute is an essential factor, it is not the only feature and the courts will supplement the statutory code or, if the statute is silent, imply a code.

In general it may be said that a party who is likely to be directly affected by a proposed administrative act or decision should be given adequate notice of what is proposed so that he/she may be in a position to make representations and/or appear at any official inquiry. Such notice should afford him/her the time to prepare his/her case or responses to allegations that are to be made. Where the words 'hearing' or 'an opportunity to be heard' are used in a statute they will normally require that an oral hearing is conducted; interested parties may be entitled to call witnesses to support their case and they may also be legally represented (unless there is a statutory provision to the contrary). Where witnesses are called there must normally be provision for cross-examination unless this serves no useful purpose. In *Bushell* v *Secretary of State for the Environment* [1981] the Secretary of State published two draft schemes for the construction of motorways and access roads under the Highways Act 1959 s. 11. As a result of objections to the scheme, a public local inquiry was held, but at the time the Highways (Inquiries Procedure) Rules 1976 were not in force although the Secretary of State had announced his willingness to comply with similar rules. In the course of the inquiry, counsel for the Department of the Environment indicated that a departmental publication known as the Red Book had been used as the basis for assessing future traffic growth and was the foundation for the Department's case for the new motorways. The applicant and other objectors who sought to challenge the Department's case wished to cross-examine the witnesses that gave evidence for the Department, to test the accuracy of the traffic predictions contained in the Red Book. The inspector presiding over the inquiry ruled that he would not permit these witnesses to be cross-examined as to the need for the motorways or on the reliability of the Red Book. He did, nevertheless, permit the objectors to call their own evidence questioning the need for the motorway scheme. In drafting his report, he recommended that the scheme go ahead. However, following the closure of the inquiry but before the inspector made his report, the Department of the Environment issued new design and flow standards that demonstrated that the existing roads in the area could take much more traffic than had been previously estimated. Although this revised method of predicting traffic growth indicated a slower rate of growth than had been predicted by the Red Book, the Secretary of State refused the objectors' request for the inquiry to be reopened so that this new information could be considered. He did indicate that such representations as they wished to make regarding the need for new motorways against the background of the new estimates could always be considered by him as part of the ongoing consideration of any part of the Department's proposals. He assured them that if the new information led him to disagree with the inspector's recommendation they would be given an opportunity to comment on it. Nevertheless, he went on to state that he had fully taken into account the general changes relating to design flow standards and traffic forecasts that had taken place since the inquiry and that he was satisfied that they did not materially affect the evidence on which the inspector had made his recommendations. He then went on to approve the scheme. The applicants then applied under the Highways Act 1959 Schedule 2 for his decision to be quashed on a number of grounds. These included that the inspector had been wrong in law to disallow cross-examination of the Department's witnesses on the Red Book and that since the inquiry the Secretary of State had taken account of undisclosed information which affected the fundamental issue, namely whether the motorways were needed. On the basis of this new information, it was argued, the inspector might have reached a different set of conclusions. Initially the application was dismissed by the Divisional Court but the Court of Appeal, by majority, allowed the appeal. The Secretary of State then appealed to the House of Lords and their Lordships allowed the appeal. They did so on the basis that, in the absence of statutory rules as to the conduct of the inquiry, the Act required only that the procedure had to be fair to all parties concerned. Moreover, the issue of whether the procedure, particularly the lack of cross-examination, was fair depended on the subject matter and the practical realities. Their Lordships took the view that the inspector's refusal to allow cross-examination as to the reliability of the Red Book was not a breach of natural justice and that the Secretary of State had not been bound to communicate the new departmental advice received after the close of the inquiry.

In many instances the decision-maker is merely placed under a duty to consult. However, this is still interpreted by the courts as requiring the decision-maker to afford those affected an opportunity to make representations or comments upon proposals that have been previously announced. Even in the absence of a duty to consult, the courts will often impose such a duty.

In *Chief Constable of North Wales* v *Evans* [1982] the applicant, Evans, was a probationary member of the North Wales Constabulary and until January 1978 he received good progress reports. On 31 January a report was conveyed to the divisional chief superintendent that contained a number of spurious allegations relating to his private life. It also transpired that when he had been given police accommodation in the form of a council house he asked whether it would be in order for him to keep his four dogs there and was informed that this would be acceptable provided nobody complained. In the autumn of 1978, the council informed him that he would have to get rid of the dogs and he indicated that he would try to find alternative homes for them. In a memorandum to the chief constable, the deputy chief constable who had interviewed Evans concerning the dogs expressed his view that people who flouted the terms of their tenancy agreements were unsuitable to be in the police service. The chief constable interviewed the applicant briefly on 8 November and informed him that he had made a mistake in accepting him and gave him the opportunity of resigning as an alternative to being dismissed. Despite his resignation, he subsequently applied for judicial review of the chief constable's decision. Woolf J in the Divisional Court held that the chief constable was bound to act fairly in exercising his discretion and the Court of Appeal largely upheld this ruling. When the chief constable appealed to the House of Lords, their Lordships applied their earlier ruling in *Ridge* v *Baldwin*. They took the view that the chief constable's discretion under the Police Regulations 1971 was not absolute but qualified and that he had not dealt with the applicant fairly because he had not put the adverse factors upon which he had acted to the applicant before deciding to dispense with his services.

With regard to legitimate expectations, mention was made of the requirement of a public decision-making body (or official) entrusted with discretionary power not to fetter its discretion. If it does so, its decision may be reviewed on the grounds of both illegality and procedural impropriety. The decision will be illegal if the decision-maker fails to utilise the discretion that has been conferred and instead imposes restrictions on himself/herself. There will be an infringement of procedural propriety if the persons affected are not permitted to influence the use of that discretion. In *R* v *Herrod ex p. Leeds County Council* [1976] local authorities had passed resolutions under the amended Betting and Gaming and Lotteries Act 1963 Schedule 6 para. 3, stating that permits would not be granted or renewed under s. 49 of the Act for the provision of amusements with prizes on specified premises. As a result, applications for the grant or renewal of a permit for prize bingo on the premises in question were refused by the local authorities in line with the resolutions that had been passed. Appeals had been allowed by the Crown Court on the basis that, under para. 4 of Schedule 6, the resolutions could not take effect because the premises were to be used wholly or mainly for a 'pleasure fair' consisting wholly or mainly of amusements. The Divisional Court quashed the ruling of the Crown Court but, in a subsequent appeal, the Court of Appeal held that the local authorities were not at liberty to pass a resolution that resulted in a 'blanket refusal' and that they had to consider each application on its merits.

This does not mean that a public decision-making body cannot formulate a policy in the interests of efficient administration but it does mean that such a policy must normally allow for exceptional cases. Moreover, it must afford interested individuals the opportunity to persuade the decision-maker to amend or deviate from a policy or rule in appropriate cases. The rationale for the rule against the fettering of discretion is, therefore, to ensure that there is some degree of responsiveness on the part of the decision-maker so that justice may be done in individual cases. In *R* v *Law Society ex p. Reigate Projects* [1993] the applicants had engaged a solicitor to act for them in the acquisition of a set of premises for future development. They paid over to him £250,000 but the solicitor used only £25,000 of this sum for a deposit on the property and he stole the remainder. He subsequently committed suicide and it emerged that he had defrauded many of his clients and that his practice was really in ruins. The initial £25,000 that had been paid to the vendors was forfeit and, in an attempt to rescue the development project, the applicants faced both an increased purchase price and increased development costs. Therefore, they applied for compensation totalling £981,991 from the compensation fund operated by the Law Society under the Solicitors Act 1974 s. 36. The Law Society awarded them £315,672, comprising £225,000 (the balance of the purchase price of the premises), £4,380 (costs) and £86,292 (money previously deposited with the solicitor by the applicants).

The applicants were informed that the balance of their claim was regarded by the adjudication committee as consequential loss and therefore beyond the scope of the compensation fund. When the applicants commenced their application for judicial review of the decision, the committee reconsidered the application for compensation. The applicants were subsequently informed that under the policy guidelines for the administration of the fund it was not usual practice to award compensation for consequential loss and that there were no special reasons in the applicants' case to justify a departure from the policy. On hearing the application for judicial review the Divisional Court decided that the Law Society was entitled to have a policy for the administration of the fund provided it was made known, was reasonable and did not unwarrantably fetter its discretion. The court took the view that the Solicitors Act 1974 s. 36(2)(a) provided for the payment of compensation mainly for the loss resulting from a solicitor's dishonesty of clients' money entrusted to him/her and that the Law Society's policy guidelines were not improper and did not impose an unwarranted fetter on its discretion. Since there had been no flaw in the way in which the decision had been arrived at or in the reasons provided, the decision could not be invalidated.

Although there is no general rule requiring the decision-maker to give reasons for an administrative decision, there are a number of recognised exceptions. The Tribunals and Inquiries Act 1971 s. 12 imposes an obligation on a large number of statutory tribunals and ministers notifying official decisions following the holding of a statutory inquiry, to supply reasons for a decision upon request. Where reasons are necessary they must be intelligible and meet the substance of the arguments put forward in order to avoid the impression that the decision was based on extraneous considerations rather than on matters raised at the hearing.

In other circumstances, fairness may require that reasons for an administrative decision are given. In *R v Civil Service Board ex p. Cunningham* [1991] the applicant was, until February 1988, the physical education officer at one of HM detention centres. He was dismissed from the prison service following an alleged attack on a prisoner. Although the alleged incident was investigated by the police, the applicant was not prosecuted. At the time of his dismissal he was 45 years of age and had worked for the prison service for 23 years. The applicant first appealed to the Civil Service Appeal Board which, in November 1988, ruled that his dismissal had been unfair and recommended that he be reinstated. As it was entitled to, the Home Office refused to accept the recommendation of the Board and so the Board assessed compensation for unfair dismissal at £6,500. The applicant had been in receipt of full pay until January 1989 but thereafter the only payment he received from the Home Office was £6,500. Had he been an ordinary employee as opposed to a civil servant, he would have received between £14,240 and £16,374 in similar circumstances. The Board declined to give reasons for its award of compensation beyond its assertion that it employed simple and informal procedures. The applicant was granted judicial review of the Board's decision on the basis that it was irrational and there had been a failure to observe the principles of natural justice. The judge granted the application on the failure to give reasons alone and this was upheld on appeal by the Court of Appeal.

In *R v Secretary of State for the Home Department ex p. Fayed* [1997] the Court of Appeal, by majority, steered its way around a statutory provision that appeared to exclude review by the courts to require some reasons to be given for a decision. The applicants were two brothers, Mohammed and Ali, both of whom were born in Egypt. The first brother had lived in the UK since 1964 and was granted leave to remain indefinitely. At the time of this litigation, he was married to a citizen of Finland and had dependent children who were British citizens. The second brother had come to live in the UK in the late 1960s and in 1977 was granted indefinite leave to remain. At the time he was married to a British citizen and his children were British citizens. They both had substantial business interests in the UK and were residents for tax purposes. On 29 January 1993, the second brother submitted an application for naturalisation as a

British citizen under the British Nationality Act 1981 and the first brother made a similar application soon afterwards. The application forms requested limited information, but on 23 February 1995, in separate letters, both brothers were informed that 'after careful consideration your application has been refused'. No reasons were assigned and so the brothers made applications to the Home Office asking for reasons for the refusals but these were declined. Although permission for a judicial review was granted, Judge J dismissed the applications on the basis that the British Nationality Act 1981 s. 44(2) did not require the Secretary of State for the Home Department to give reasons for the granting or refusal of any application involving the exercise of his discretion. Thus, according to the ruling of Judge J the failure to give the brothers an opportunity to deal with factors that might be adverse to their applications was not unlawful. However, the Court of Appeal allowed the subsequent appeal. Lord Woolf MR accepted that the Secretary of State was not required under s. 44(2) to give reasons for refusing an application for British citizenship where the decision involved the use of his discretion, but he ruled that he was required to exercise his discretion reasonably and was not relieved of the obligation to be fair in arriving at his decision. Furthermore, until the areas of concern were identified which caused the Secretary of State to doubt that the applicants were of good character (so that they would be in a position to make further representations) justice had not been seen to be done.

9 Irrationality or unreasonableness

The assertion of irrationality requires the courts to consider whether the decision-maker who acts under a discretionary power has improperly exercised that power, and so the applicant must surmount a high threshold of proof. This is because a claim of irrationality or unreasonableness takes the courts very close to the line beyond which it would be examining the merits of the decision. In *Council of the Civil Service Unions* v *Minister for the Civil Service* [1985], Lord Diplock described irrationality in terms of a decision which is so outrageous in its defiance of logic or accepted moral standards that no sensible person who had applied his mind to the question to be decided could have arrived at it.

Although this formulation is by no means perfect because it hints at a degree of mental incapacity, it does convey the notion of an abuse of power on the part of the decision-maker. It is necessary to establish such an abuse of power in judicial review proceedings.

The courts assume that certain principles apply to the exercise of all powers, even where a decision-maker is invested with a wide discretion. They take the view that the discretion is to be exercised according to these principles unless an Act of Parliament clearly indicates to the contrary. The governing principle is the rule of law. This encompasses the principle of legal certainty and the principle of equality. The essence of legal certainty is that legitimate expectations in the substantive sense (as distinct from the procedural sense) are to be upheld. An example of this can be seen in the case *R* v *North and East Devon Health Authority ex p. Coughlan (Secretary of State for Health and another intervening)* [2000]. The applicant was a patient at an NHS hospital for the chronically sick and disabled that was administered by the Exeter Health Authority, the predecessor of the appellant health authority. In 1993, the applicant and seven other similarly disabled patients were moved with their agreement to Mardon House, a purpose-built NHS facility, after receiving assurances from Exeter Health Authority that they could live there for as long as they wished. However, five years later the health authority decided to close Mardon House and to transfer responsibility for the applicant's care to a local authority social services department. In arriving at its decision, the health authority relied on a policy statement in which it had classified the type of nursing care required by the applicant as standard nursing care. The classification was apparently based on NHS policy guidance which distinguished between general nursing care (to be provided by local authorities as a social service for which the patient paid according to means) and specialist nursing services which were to be provided free by the NHS. When the applicant applied for judicial review of the decision to close Mardon House, the judge ruled that the health authority was bound by the assurances given previously by the Exeter Health Authority.

In his ruling the judge held that both general and specialist nursing care were the sole responsibility of the health authorities and therefore granted the application and quashed the decision of the Exeter Health Authority. The health authority appealed and the Secretary of State for Health intervened because he was concerned by the judge's decision that both general and specialist nursing care were the sole responsibility of the NHS. The Court of Appeal therefore had to consider the duties of the Secretary of State under the National Health Act 1977 ss 1 and 3 in respect of the provision of health services and a local authority's powers under the National Assistance Act 1948 s. 21 to provide accommodation for persons who were in need of care and attention.

The Court of Appeal held that although the Secretary of State was entitled to exclude some nursing care from the nursing services provided by the NHS, the health authority's criteria of eligibility were flawed. In addition, the court ruled that the disabilities of the applicant and her fellow patients went far beyond the scope of local authority services and that the error made by the health authority called into question the closure decision. The assurances given by the health authority had induced a legitimate expectation of a substantive benefit; the negation of it would be so unfair as to amount to an abuse of power. It is also interesting to note that the Court of Appeal stated that, in revoking its promise, the health authority had infringed the applicant's rights under Article 8 of the European Convention on Human Rights and Fundamental Freedoms to respect for her home.

Not every statement by a public official will give rise to a legitimate expectation that will be upheld by the courts, especially where it has been given on the basis of misleading information provided by or on behalf of the applicant. In *R v Inland Revenue Commissioners ex p. Matrix Securities Ltd* [1994] the applicant sought a declaration that the Inland Revenue Commissioners were not entitled to revoke a clearance that had been given at a local level after the Court of Appeal had refused to grant such a declaration. The applicant's solicitor had given information that was inaccurate and misleading to a tax inspector. On the basis of the information received, the inspector gave an assurance, on which the applicant sought to rely regarding the acceptability to the Revenue of a certain tax avoidance scheme. The House of Lords held that the Revenue was entitled to withdraw the clearance that it had given.

The principle of equality embraces formal equality and substantive equality. The former simply requires that public officials apply the law in an even-handed way. Thus persons similarly situated will be treated equally. Substantive equality is concerned more with non-discrimination and is closely associated with the notion of equality as a general principle of EU law. An example of formal equality arose in *R v Port Talbot B.C. and others ex p. Jones* [1988], where a local councillor applied to the council for a house. The Divisional Court held that the preferential allocation of a council house to a councillor with a view to putting her in a better position to contest a local election in her own ward was an abuse of power because it was unfair to others on the housing list. It is also an example of a decision based on irrelevant considerations. The courts have also declared invalid instances of substantive inequality. In *James v Eastleigh Borough Council* [1990] the House of Lords held that the adoption by a local authority of the statutory pensionable ages (then 65 for men and 60 for women) as the qualification for free admission to a leisure centre was a breach of the statutory prohibition against sex discrimination.

It is essential that administrative decisions should not be tainted with impropriety of any kind. In *Victoria Square Property Co. Ltd v Southwark LBC* [1978] the owners of a house let the house to a tenant under an agreement pursuant to the Housing Act 1957. The local authority was not satisfied that it was suitable for human habitation and served a notice on the owners requiring an extensive schedule of repairs and renovations to bring it up to the required standard. The owners appealed against the notice contending that the house could not be rendered fit for human habitation at reasonable expense. A county court judge allowed the appeal and quashed the notice. The local authority then decided to compulsorily purchase the property and execute the necessary work. It therefore made a compulsory purchase order but then realised that it had not obtained an express finding from the county court judge that the house was not capable of being rendered fit for human habitation at reasonable expense. This was an essential precondition to accompany the compulsory purchase order. When the judge refused to make such an order, the local authority realised that the minister could not confirm the compulsory purchase order and so it attempted to achieve its aim by another route. It served notice on the owners specifying a time and place when it would consider the condition of the property and any offer that the owners might wish to submit in connection with the work. The owners did not submit a notice of intention to execute work but offered a formal undertaking not to let the house until the local authority was satisfied that it had been rendered fit for human habitation. The local authority refused to accept this undertaking and served notice on the owners to purchase the property. The owners appealed and the judge found:

(a) the intention of the local authority on acquiring the house was to re-house the existing tenant and render it fit for human habitation for a period of more than 30 years by carrying out not only the work specified in its notice but also extra work to bring it up to an even higher standard;

(b) that its reasons for wishing to acquire the house were to avoid the loss of residential accommodation and to ensure that it was occupied by a person on its waiting list; and

(c) that the owners would suffer a financial loss if the local authority compulsorily purchased the house.

The judge ruled that the local authority had no statutory power to acquire the house to increase its existing stock of housing. The local authority then appealed to the Court of Appeal which held that, although it could acquire property under the Housing Act 1957 s. 17(2) prior to demolition where its condition fell short of the standard set for human habitation, the subsection could not be stretched to cover an acquisition made with the intention of restoring the property for long-term occupation.

If inadequate weight has been attached to an important and relevant consideration by a decision-maker, the courts will be prepared to declare the administrative decision to be invalid, as can be illustrated by the case of *Glamorgan C.C.* v *Rafferty* [1987]. Under the Caravan Sites Act 1968 s. 6(1) the council was obliged to exercise its powers to provide adequate accommodation for gypsies residing in or regularly resorting to its area. However, for more than 10 years the council had ignored its statutory duty to provide adequate accommodation for the gypsies in its area. On 16 September 1985, it resolved to commence proceedings to evict a number of gypsy families who were trespassing on a site in Neath owned by the council. On 2 October, a High Court judge made an order that enabled the council to recover possession of the site. A writ of possession was issued in November 1985 but was not served because a local solicitor interceded on behalf of the gypsy families. In December 1985 the order for possession was set aside by another High Court judge who directed that the council's claim for possession should proceed by way of a trial in the High Court on the basis that the council was in breach of its statutory duty to provide adequate accommodation. At this time, one of the gypsies had applied for judicial review of the council's decision of 16 September 1985. The council then appealed against the order and the judgment given in judicial review proceedings. The Court of Appeal held that the council had not given adequate weight to the breach of its statutory duty and the consequences before proceeding to evict the gypsies. It therefore confirmed that the council's decision to evict should be quashed.

Taking into account irrelevant considerations will tend to bring about the same result, as was illustrated by the decision in *R v Secretary of State for the Home Department ex p. Venables* [1997]. Venables and Thompson murdered a young child when they were both aged 10. The trial judge imposed the mandatory sentence provided by the Children and Young Persons Act 1933 s. 53(1) of detention during Her Majesty's pleasure. In his report to the Home Secretary, the trial judge recommended that the penal element of their sentence should be set at eight years. The Lord Chief Justice subsequently advised the Home Secretary that the penal element should be increased to 10 years. Having received this advice the Home Secretary, acting pursuant to his discretion under the Criminal Justice Act 1991 s. 35 and a policy statement of 27 July 1993, deliberated over the penal element of the sentence and ultimately decided that it should be increased to 15 years. In a letter announcing his decision, he stated that he had taken account of the widespread public concern about the case which was evidenced by petitions and other correspondence that he had received. At the time there was an intense media campaign in the popular press urging that the applicants should be detained for life. In an application for judicial review by the boys, the Divisional Court quashed the decision of the Home Secretary, who then appealed to the Court of Appeal but without success. The House of Lords then heard a final appeal from the Home Secretary and a cross-appeal from the boys in relation to the imposition of the penal element. In a long and detailed judgment their Lordships held, among other things, that the Home Secretary ought not to have taken account of the public protests in fixing the penal element of the sentence. Accordingly, he had misdirected himself in giving weight to irrelevant considerations which influenced his decision to the detriment of the applicants.

If there is no evidence for a finding on which an administrative decision depends or where the evidence cannot be regarded as supporting a finding of fact, there will be a basis for impugning the decision. Official decisions may be invalidated by the courts on grounds of irrationality or unreasonableness if they are unduly oppressive because they subject an individual to excessive hardship. In *R v Hillingdon LBC ex p. Royco Homes Ltd* [1974] the applicants were granted outline planning permission for the construction of seven blocks of three-storey flats within the borough subject to certain conditions. Conditions 4 and 5 required that the dwellings built should be occupied by persons on the local authority's housing list for a guaranteed period of 10 years. This effectively required the company to assume, at its own expense, part of the local authority's housing obligations as a housing authority. The Divisional Court took the view that these conditions were quite unreasonable and the grant of planning permission embodying them was quashed.

In general, even though it is pleaded more often than the other grounds for judicial review, it is more difficult for an applicant to challenge an official act or decision on the basis of irrationality alone.

10 Human Rights Act 1998

Section 3 of the Human Rights Act 1998 requires a court to interpret the relevant provisions of an Act of Parliament in so far as it is possible to do so, in a way that is compatible with the Convention rights embedded in Schedule 1. This may sometimes entail giving the words a narrower meaning than the usual meaning. When considering the range of possible meanings, guidance may be provided by the Strasbourg jurisprudence, which s. 2(1) requires a court to consider. As was seen in Chapter 8, if a compatible interpretation is not possible, then a court must make a declaration of incompatibility under s. 4 but it cannot disregard the language of the statutory provisions. Where certain individual human rights are at stake in judicial review proceedings, the principle of proportionality comes to the fore.

11 Proportionality

Both the European Court of Justice and the European Court of Human Rights recognise proportionality as a general principle of law. The balancing test requires a balancing of the ends to be achieved by an official decision and the means adopted to achieve them. An application of this balancing test has already been considered in Chapter 7 in EU law in Case 114/76 *Bela-Muhle Josef Bergmann KG* v *Grows-Farm GmbH & Co. KG* [1977]. In that case the ECJ ruled that a regulation which imposed a disproportionate burden on farmers who were required to purchase milk powder was null and void. Where the courts in England and Wales apply directly effective EU law embodied in a Treaty provision or in a regulation, the general principle of proportionality may be invoked to challenge official action in appropriate cases on the basis that the action has been disproportionate.

The concept of proportionality has been raised in a number of judicial review cases where the Human Rights Act 1998 has been pleaded. In *R (on the application of Alconbury Developments Ltd)* v *Secretary of State for the Environment* [2001], where Article 6 was raised unsuccessfully, Lord Slynn stated:

> ... even without reference to the Human Rights Act, the time has come to recognise that this principle (of proportionality) is part of English administrative law, not only when judges are dealing with Community acts but also when dealing with acts subject to domestic law.

As was noted in Chapter 8, some of the Convention rights are absolute in the sense that they are not subject to qualification (see Articles 3, 4, 7 and 12). Articles 2 and 5 are subject to strict limitations. The other rights are qualified in some way. In a case involving the infringement of an unqualified right, there is no scope for a balance to be struck. It is merely a question of whether the action/decision is required by Act of Parliament.

If the answer is negative, there can be reconsideration of the merits of the decision because a public authority is not supposed to act in contravention of unqualified rights. This approach is supported by Lord Hoffmann's speech in *Secretary of State for the Home Department* v *Rehman* [2001]. If the action/decision has resulted in the infringement of a qualified right, it is appropriate for the courts to apply the test of proportionality to ascertain whether the correct balance has been struck. The balance is between the demands of the general interests of the community and the requirements of the protection of the individual's human rights. This will not, however, extend to a complete re-hearing of the merits of the decision. In *R (on the application of Farrakhan)* v *Secretary of State for the Home Department* [2002] the Secretary of State made an order under rules and regulations drafted under powers granted by the Immigration Act 1971 refusing entry into the UK of an American citizen who is the leader of a sect known as the Nation of Islam. The decision was justified on the basis that his visit would threaten community relations and public order as Farrakhan had used extreme, inflammatory language about Jews. The challenge was based on Article 10(1) but freedom of speech is subject to such restrictions as are necessary in a democratic society for the prevention of public disorder, among other considerations. The Court of Appeal ruled that the Secretary of State's decision had struck a proportionate balance between the freedom in Article 10(1) and the prevention of public disorder. This case may be contrasted with that of *International Transport Roth GmbH* v *Secretary of State for the Home Department* [2002]. The Court of Appeal by majority held that a fixed scheme of penalties created under the Immigration and Asylum Act 1999 for lorry drivers bringing illegal immigrants into the UK was incompatible with Article 6 and the scale and inflexibility of the penalty infringed an individual's property rights under Protocol 1, Article 1 and was disproportionate in relation to the objectives sought to be achieved.

12   Procedure: making an application

The Lord Chancellor appointed a committee under the chairmanship of Sir Jeffery Bowman with instructions to undertake a review of the operation of the procedure for the Crown Office list at the High Court in relation to applications for judicial review. The committee reported in March 2000 and new rules of procedure were laid before Parliament on 2 August which came into effect on 2 October 2000. The Crown Office list has since become the Administrative Court list. Unfortunately, the new rules do not implement all the recommendations of the Bowman Report. Applications for judicial review are now referred to as 'claims for judicial review' and are governed by the Civil Procedure Rules Part 8 as modified by a new Part 54 and supplemented by Practice Direction 54. A claimant in judicial review proceedings is expected to give prior warning of a claim to the party who would be the defendant unless it is an urgent matter.

There is a pre-action protocol with a standard format letter in Annexe A. According to paras 10 and 11, this should contain:

(a) the date and details of the decision, act or omission being challenged;
(b) a clear summary of the facts;
(c) details of any relevant information that the claimant is seeking; and
(d) details of any interested parties known to the claimant.

The defendant too is required to display a considerable degree of openness when dealing with the claimant and should normally use the standard format letter in Annexe B. If the claimant does not communicate by letter with the defendant prior to the commencement of proceedings where it was appropriate to do so, the defendant is likely to raise this omission if the case is resolved without a hearing when costs are considered. Moreover, failure to communicate by letter might result in a 'wasted costs' order being made against the lawyer acting for the claimant. A claimant must still obtain permission from the Administrative Court to proceed by submitting:

(a) a claim form (N461),
(b) written evidence in support of the claim,
(c) a copy of any order that the claimant wishes to have quashed,
(d) an approved copy of the reasons for reaching the decision where the claim relates to a decision of an inferior court or tribunal,
(e) copies of any documents on which the claimant intends to rely,
(f) copies of any relevant statutory material, and
(g) a list of essential documents for advance reading by the court.

If the claimant seeks to raise an issue under the Human Rights Act 1998 or seeks a remedy under that legislation, the claim form must include the information required by Practice Direction 16 para. 16 (statements of case).

There is a general requirement that all claims for judicial review are made promptly. This means that an application must normally be made within three months of the date when the basis for the application arose. All pending applications are placed on the Administrative Court list and are usually considered by a single judge from a specially nominated group of High Court judges, of whom there are currently 25. The requirement that the claimant must first obtain permission operates as a filtering device in that spurious and frivolous applications can be eliminated. All claimants are required to display the utmost good faith because the permission to proceed will be revoked if there has been any misrepresentation or concealment of material facts. The first hurdle that the claimant must surmount is to show that he/she has the required 'standing' which is sometimes referred to as *locus standi*. The Supreme Court Act 1981 s. 31(3) provides that a claimant who has sufficient interest in the matter to which the application relates should be accorded standing. In the *Inland Revenue Commissioners* v *National Federation of Self Employed and Small Businesses* [1982] the majority of the House of Lords took the view that standing should no longer be seen as a preliminary issue or a threshold issue. The Federation wanted to challenge the validity of a tax amnesty granted to casual workers who had worked in newspaper production in Fleet Street. Their Lordships indicated that any applicant who approaches the court with what appears to be a convincing legal argument to the effect that a national or local governmental body has committed an illegal act should expect to be granted permission even if he/she had only a remote personal interest in the matter. On the facts of this particular case, the House of Lords unanimously decided that the Federation did not have standing in the case because their Lordships considered that the Inland Revenue Commissioners (IRC) were within the ambit of their statutory discretion and that in any event the relationship between the IRC and individual taxpayers was confidential.

In the past, the courts have not always shown themselves to be sympathetic to actions initiated by interest groups. In *R v Secretary of State for the Environment ex p. Rose Theatre Trust* [1990] property developers were granted planning permission to erect an office block on a site where, in the course of preliminary work, the remains of the old Rose Theatre were discovered. Two of Shakespeare's plays were premiered there and it was the venue for most of Marlowe's plays. A group of distinguished archaeologists and thespians formed a company to campaign for the preservation of the archaeological remains and the company applied to the Secretary of State to have the site included in the schedule of monuments maintained by him under the Ancient Monuments and Archaeological Areas Act 1979 s. 1(1). Although the Secretary of State agreed that the archaeological remains were of national importance, he declined to schedule the site as requested, not least because it was being preserved and protected voluntarily. In giving his judgment, Schieman J denied that the company had 'sufficient interest' to be accorded the necessary standing. Since then the courts have been more sympathetic to applications for judicial review brought by interest groups. As has been seen, an application by an interest group was allowed to proceed in *R v Secretary of State for Foreign Affairs ex p. World Development Movement Ltd.*

The usual ground for refusal of an application is that the claimant has not taken a more appropriate route to pursue his/her grievance. For example, the 'case stated procedure' is the most suitable method for appealing from an administrative decision of magistrates. In addition, the Administrative Court imposes a more stringent test when considering applications for judicial review in relation to decisions on immigration, homelessness and child protection. It is aware that allowing challenges to these types of decision by way of judicial review is detrimental to good public administration. The application takes the form of a full statement that identifies the applicant and sets out the relief sought. It is necessary to set out the facts and the legal grounds for challenge supported by precedent and statute law. According to Practice Direction 54 the question of permission will usually be considered without an oral hearing. If the initial application is refused, this refusal can be challenged before the Court of Appeal under the Supreme Court Act 1981 ss 16 and 18 but it is necessary for the applicant to obtain permission to do so from the Court of Appeal or from the Administrative Court. If the Court of Appeal should refuse the application there cannot be a further appeal to the House of Lords. (See *R* v *Secretary of State for Trade and Industry ex p. Eastway* [2001].) Even if permission to proceed is granted, the respondent may apply to have the permission revoked on the grounds that the application discloses no arguable case or because there has not been full and frank disclosure of all the material facts and relevant law. All such applications are examined carefully because they tend to be regarded unfavourably.

Once permission has been granted, the substantive application is commenced by serving the order granting permission on the defendant and on all persons directly affected who filed an acknowledgement of service. Any of those persons who wish to contest the claim (or support it on additional grounds) must do so within 35 days following service of the permission file. They must serve the detailed grounds for contesting (or supporting) together with their written evidence. It should be noted that permission to proceed with a judicial review is permission to proceed on specified grounds only since the claimant will not be permitted to rely on other grounds without the consent of the court. The full hearing of the claim will often be heard before a single High Court judge or, where the Administrative Court Office requires, before the Administrative Court comprising two High Court judges. In very important cases, the court may comprise three High Court judges. Criminal matters are always referred to a Divisional Court. In general, the parties are not cross-examined although the court does have the discretion to order cross-examination where there is a conflict of evidence or where the applicant alleges that a precondition to the making of a decision did not exist. If the facts are agreed, the court will be concerned only with the inferences that can be drawn from them and the legal consequences that follow.

13 Appeals

There can be an appeal from a decision of the Administrative Court. The rules relating to appeals differ depending on whether the matter is civil or criminal. In a criminal matter an appeal can be made to the House of Lords where the provisions of the Administration of Justice Act 1960 s. 1 are satisfied. These are as follows:

(a) the Administrative Court certifies that a point of law of general public importance is involved; and

(b) either the Administrative Court or House of Lords gives permission.

In civil matters, permission is required to appeal to the Court of Appeal except in proceedings arising from a decision made pursuant to the Immigration Act 1971, the British Nationality Act 1981, the Asylum and Immigration Appeals Act 1993 or any other decision relating to nationality or immigration. Unless permission to appeal has been granted, a valid notice of appeal cannot be served.

14   Remedies

The powers of the superior courts to grant remedies are contained in the Supreme Court Act 1981 s. 31. Even before the hearing of the substantive claim, a claimant may ask the court to grant an interim remedy. This could take one of two forms:

(a)   an interim injunction to preserve the *status quo* prior to the conclusion of the full hearing or a stay of proceedings to prevent the public body (or official) from continuing with its disputed conduct when the remedy sought is one or more of the prerogative orders; or

(b)   an interim declaration to prevent some imminent danger to himself or his property.

These interim remedies will be granted only at the discretion of the court. If the applicant is successful at the conclusion of the substantive hearing, the court will consider the remedy or remedies sought in the claim. It is usual for an applicant to ask for one or more of the prerogative orders, but he/she may have asked for an injunction in final form and/ or a declaration. In its 1994 report *Administrative Law: Judicial review and statutory appeals*, the Law Commission recommended that the prerogative orders should be renamed, and this finally occurred in the year 2000. They are now known as mandatory orders, quashing orders and prohibiting orders. A court may grant these individually or in combination but they are always granted at the discretion of the court.

If, prior to submitting a claim for judicial review, the applicant requested a public body (or official) to perform a duty imposed by law, the court can make a mandatory order requiring that the duty be performed. A mandatory order is also appropriate to require a tribunal to 'state a case' and give reasons for its decision where this is required by statute. Applicants often apply for a quashing order and a prohibiting order at the same time. The quashing order operates to nullify the decision that has been impugned and the prohibiting order operates to prevent the body in question from exceeding its jurisdiction.

In many ways, injunctions and declaratory judgments are more flexible forms of relief and can be granted in those situations where the prerogative orders are available if the court considers it just and convenient. The jurisdiction of the High Court to grant injunctions in judicial review cases is to be found in the Supreme Court Act 1981 s. 31(2). The court may do so taking into account:

(a)   the nature of the matters in respect of which relief may be granted by prerogative orders;

(b)   the nature of the persons and bodies against whom the relief may be granted by such orders; and

(c)   the other circumstances of the case.

Injunctions, whether interim or in final form, may be either mandatory, requiring an act to be done, or prohibitory, requiring the addressee to refrain from acting in a certain way. In final form they may be granted for a fixed period with permission granted to apply for an extension. Alternatively, they may be granted for an indefinite period with provision for subsequent termination.

A declaration at the conclusion of the substantive hearing is simply a formal statement by the court of the legal position and of the respective rights of the parties. It does not contain any order that can be enforced against the respondent.

15   Liability in tort

In general, public officials and bodies that fail to act in accordance with the principles considered in this chapter when exercising their discretion do not commit a tort such that they would be liable at common law to pay damages. Moreover, the careless performance of a statutory duty does not in itself give rise to any cause of action unless there is a right of action for breach of statutory duty or a situation exists where a common law duty of care arises in the tort of negligence. In relation to negligence claims at common law, many of the powers and duties conferred on departments of national and local government involve a substantial policy component and for this reason it is difficult for the courts to establish whether a duty of care arises in the first place and, if it does, the standard of care required. The High Court does, nevertheless, have power under the Supreme Court Act 1981 s. 31(4) to award damages in judicial review proceedings where appropriate, but it will usually deal with the public law issues first. If the applicant's claim is successful, the claim for damages will be considered at a separate hearing. Such claims are often for financial loss only (referred to in legal parlance as economic loss) and the courts are usually reluctant to award damages for economic loss unless there is a contractual relationship. Whether there is a cause of action capable of giving rise to a claim for damages very much depends on the facts of the particular case.

A public official or public body could incur liability in the tort of 'misfeasance in public office' where the official or public body acts/decides or refrains from acting/ deciding but is activated by malice towards the applicant. Alternatively it may arise if the actor/decision-maker knows that his/her act or omission or decision is unlawful and the result is that the applicant is deprived of a benefit or suffers loss. Thus, if a decision-maker takes account of irrelevant matters he/she could be liable in damages for the tort of misfeasance in public office provided that it can be established that the act was done maliciously or he/she knew that he/she was acting unlawfully. Apart from the personal liability of the individual, the public authority may be liable (through the doctrine of vicarious liability) for officials who commit the tort. There have been few successful claims and magistrates and those exercising judicial functions normally have immunity from actions in tort.

Some statutes (for example, the Highways Act 1980) specifically create a right of action for breach of statutory duty for which damages can be claimed. In the absence of a clear, express statutory provision the courts are reduced to drawing an inference whether it was intended that there should be a right of action. This is made all the more difficult by the fact that most statutory duties in the area of public administration are owed not to individuals but to the public at large. In such cases the courts are unlikely to conclude that there is a private right of action. Procedural impropriety does not automatically give rise to the tort of breach of statutory duty or misfeasance in public office. A statement of a public official might create a legitimate expectation and thereby give rise to a claim in damages for negligent misstatement but only if the statement transpires to be untrue and was given in response to a specific request. Excessive delay by a public body in making a decision may occasionally give rise to a claim in the tort of negligence but it will be essential for the court to be able to infer a duty of care from the facts of the case.

Where, in a claim for judicial review, the court is prepared to allow a claim for compensation on the basis of a right of action in tort, damages will be assessed to place the applicant as nearly as possible in the position he/she would have been in had the tort not been committed.

■ Summary

Judicial review of ministerial and administrative action is vital in a state where the rule of law is paramount. As indicated, judicial review covers a wide area and it is a topic on which substantial books, rather than a single chapter, have been written. Apart from dealing with the procedural aspects, which are important, an attempt has been made to give a brief account of the long-established bases on which the courts have been asked to review the legality (or otherwise) of ministerial and administrative decision-making. These are: illegality, procedural impropriety and irrationality. The Human Rights Act 1998 has added a new dimension to the evaluation of ministerial and official action and a significant number of cases have been brought in recent years based on the Act. In some of these, the principle of proportionality has come to the fore as a basis for evaluating claims that allege an infringement of those Convention rights that are qualified in some way.

WWW PROGRESS TEST

For suggested answers to the tests below, go to the companion website at www.pearsoned.co.uk/wheeler

1 What is the purpose of judicial review of administrative action?
2 Have the exceptions to the rule in *O'Reilly* v *Mackman* effectively destroyed the rule?

3 In what circumstances may an official act or decision be challenged on the grounds of illegality?

4 In what circumstances will the courts accept that there must be delegation of the exercise of a discretionary power?

5 What do you understand by the 'rule against bias'?

6 In relation to procedural fairness, when may the courts infer that a fair hearing is necessary?

7 In what circumstances may a public body or official be required to give reasons for an act or decision?

8 When may an official act or decision be challenged in the courts on the basis that it is irrational or unreasonable?

9 How is the principle of 'proportionality' relevant in a claim for judicial review based on alleged infringement of a Convention right?

10 What is meant by 'standing' in the context of a claim for judicial review, and what test is applied?

11 What are the prerogative orders? Are these remedies available as of right?

12 What are the conditions of liability for the tort of misfeasance in public office and what remedy, if any, is available?

FURTHER READING

■ Books

Craig, P. (2003) *Administrative Law* (London: Sweet & Maxwell).

Loveland, I. (2004) *Constitutional Law, Administrative Law and Human Rights* (Oxford: Oxford University Press).

Parpworth, N. (2001) *Constitutional and Administrative Law* (Oxford: Oxford University Press, chapters 12–14).

Wade, H.W.R. and C.F. Forysth (2000) *Administrative Law* (Oxford: Oxford University Press).

Woolf, Lord, Jowell, J. and A.P. Le Sueur (2005) *Principles of Judicial Review* (London: Sweet & Maxwell).

■ Articles

Cornford, T. and M. Sunkin (2001) 'The Bowman Report, access and the recent reforms of judicial review procedure', *Public Law* Spring.

Fordham, M. (2001) 'Judicial review: the new rules', *Public Law* Spring.

Irvine, Lord (2003) 'The Impact of the Human Rights Act: Parliament, the Courts and Executive', *Public Law* Summer, pp. 308–325.

Leigh, I. (2002) 'Taking Rights Proportionately: Judicial Review, The Human Rights Act and Strasbourg', *Public Law* Summer, pp. 265–287.

USEFUL WEBSITE

The Department of Constitutional Affairs is a very useful source of information on judicial review and copies of the pre-action protocol can be downloaded from the website www.dca.gov.uk.

16 Law reform and the Law Commission

1 Introduction

To the modern mind, law is self-evidently a social phenomenon. Clearly law is a prerequisite for an organised society even though an organised society need not necessarily be a civilised society in which there is justice for all. Law as a social phenomenon obviously has many aspects. A system of criminal law and a criminal justice system is essential in any civilised society, at the very least, to prevent a decline into a vendetta culture or mob rule. The rule of law is also a bulwark against tyranny. On a more positive note, law not only facilitates social, political and economic organisation in a developed society, it is also capable of being used to resolve disputes, to control the abuse of power and to uphold political, social and economic rights. As society becomes ever more sophisticated, as people and organisations seek to benefit from the latest discoveries in science and technology, the law and legal system must continually adapt as these forces impact on the way in which people live and choose to organise their lives. This modern conception of law is so different from that held by the ancient Greeks, who viewed law as a moral and creative power which did not alter with changing circumstances. The modern conception of law, therefore, is that it serves the needs of a changing society and is accordingly a 'work in progress' rather than a finished product. It is appropriate, therefore, that this final chapter should focus on law reform. In order to contextualise law reform, two periods of history have been singled out for consideration: 1786–1875 because this links up with the historical development of the law and its administration discussed in Appendix 1; the main focus of this chapter will be on the period since the Second World War during which the process of law reform was permanently institutionalised in the UK for the first time.

1786–1875

The period of industrialisation at almost breakneck speed from 1786 to 1875 was one of unprecedented upheaval in the long history of the nation, in which, for the most part, change had been gradual. In 1750 the economy was still largely agricultural and the combined population of England and Wales hovered steadily around the 6 m mark. The law and its administration had developed to meet the demands of a mainly agricultural economy in which land was the major source of wealth. At this time, the manufacturing sector was comparatively small and was largely craft-based. Overseas trade was also on a relatively minor scale by the standard of the late nineteenth century. However, by 1811 the population of England and Wales had more than doubled and, by the time of the 1851 official census, it had reached 18 m. Although the factory system of production was well established by the end of the eighteenth century, it continued to extend itself into newer industries during the remainder of the nineteenth. The drift of population from the countryside to the new industrial towns was well under way by the first decade in the nineteenth century and was set to continue apace for the remainder of the century. Overseas trade almost doubled between 1750 and 1800, from £22 m to £42 m. London, with its banking, insurance and control over shipping, became the hub of the UK's vast colonial empire which grew throughout the nineteenth century. This massive transformation in national life generated irresistible pressure for a thorough going reform of all the institutions of the state. The House of Commons was reformed in 1832 after a campaign of popular agitation to make it more representative of the newer centres of population. The new manufacturing 'middle class' were represented in Parliament for the first time through the redistribution of seats in the House of Commons as male members of the new industrial middle class were given the vote. The long ascendancy of the House of Lords' chamber at Westminster could now be challenged as further reforms of the franchise were to follow, as were reforms in local government and in the civil service. The important reforms of the law and its administration by means of legislation enacted by the Westminster Parliament from 1850 to 1875 are outlined in Appendix 1.

■ The post-Second World War era

A second period of accelerating social and economic change has occurred since 1945. Prior to 1939, the UK was a great imperial power and the Westminster Parliament legislated not only for the UK but also for its extensive colonial empire. After 1945, most of the former colonies gradually gained their independence, although a few small former colonies (such as Bermuda) continue to this day to be linked to the UK as 'dependent territories'. Since 1945, the UK has become a 'welfare state' and government has become ever more involved in the active management of the economy and in the development of the nation's human capital. Government spending now accounts for approximately 42 per cent of GNP. As indicated in Chapter 5, there were important constitutional changes towards the end of the twentieth century, with more to come. The major political parties have long since accepted the political philosophy of 'pluralism' as the UK has become a multi-ethnic and multi-cultural society. Such rapid change has subjected existing institutions to great stresses and strains. The law and legal system have struggled to keep pace with the accelerating rate of change. In the first decade of the third millennium, it would seem that the future of the UK is closely bound up with the future of the European Union in which it is just one of 25 member states, and it is not even the largest economy. Until the mid-1960s the approach of successive governments to the pressing need for law reform was not at all systematic. The nineteenth-century practice of setting up Royal Commissions to investigate and report on urgent problems of the day was continued into the twentieth century. Although a systemic solution was needed, government produced two initiatives, in that two part-time committees were then established to deal with the more technical aspects of the civil and criminal law that were considered to be in great need of reform. This chapter considers the contribution to law reform of both Royal Commissions and the two part-time agencies mentioned, before moving on to consider the role and work of the Law Commission which has since supplanted these two part-time bodies.

2 Royal Commissions

A Royal Commission functions as an independent advisory committee to the government of the day. It is a well-established inquiry technique still used by government to investigate urgent problems that emerge from time to time, although it is not the only one. Its mode of operation was completely revamped in the 1830s with the emergence of new techniques of inquiry that are simply now referred to as 'social science methodology'. The term 'Royal' derives from the fact that the Commission is established by Royal Warrant addressed to the Commissioners themselves. It is a convenient piece of make-believe that the appointments appear to be made by the Queen, but the reality is that they are made by the government of the day and confirmed by the Queen. Examples of significant Royal Commissions in the twentieth century include: the Royal Commission chaired by Lord Beeching, which resulted in the Courts Act 1971 (establishing the Crown Court); and the Royal Commission on Criminal Procedure 1980, which resulted in the enactment of the Police and Criminal Evidence Act 1984 and the establishment of the Crown Prosecution Service. The Royal Commission chaired by Sir Henry Benson on the provision of legal services proved to be something of a disappointment in that it did not result in a radical change in the existing working practices of the legal profession. In 1991 the Philips Royal Commission on criminal justice was established to consider reforms to the criminal law arising from certain highly publicised miscarriages of justice, such as those of the 'Guildford four', the 'Birmingham six' and the Judith Ward case. At the time there was widespread concern over certain high-profile convictions on the basis of so-called 'confessions'. The Commission's recommendations found expression in the Criminal Justice Act 1993.

Although a Royal Commission can call upon the resources and expertise of a wide range of people in public life and from the learned professions to collect evidence and produce an authoritative report, there is no guarantee that the government of the day will heed the recommendations contained therein and it is certainly not obliged to do so. Once the Commission has reported, it is disbanded and its personnel revert to their former activities and occupations. Therefore, by its nature, it is not a very suitable means for dealing with the need for comprehensive ongoing law reform. Despite its limitations, the Royal Commission is still likely to be used by governments in the twenty-first century, if only for political reasons, to demonstrate that 'something is being done' about a particularly urgent problem.

3 The Law Reform Committee

The Law Reform Committee was originally established in 1934 by the then Lord Chancellor, Lord Sankey, as the Law Revision Committee. It was revived in 1952 by Lord Simonds and renamed the Law Reform Committee. The Committee comprised six judges, three professors of law, two QCs and two solicitors. Its secretariat was provided by the Lord Chancellor's Department but it had no research facilities of its own, which was a very serious handicap. Its terms of reference were to consider, having regard especially to judicial decisions, what changes were desirable in such legal doctrines as the Lord Chancellor may from time to time refer to the Committee. Its ability to put forward proposals for changes to the civil law was therefore very much restricted to proposals received from the Lord Chancellor. Since all members of the Committee had other full-time occupations and responsibilities, the Committee functioned only on a part-time basis and therefore its contribution to the agenda of law reform was on a very small scale. It is now defunct. However, some of its reports led to new legislation, namely the Law Reform (Frustrated Contracts) Act 1943 and the Occupiers' Liability Act 1957. Nothing was ever done about its *Sixth Report on the Statute of Frauds and the Doctrine of Consideration* (1937) until the Law Commission re-examined the issue of third party rights in the late 1990s, nor its *Twelfth Report on Transfer of Title to Chattels* (1966) among others.

4 The Criminal Law Revision Committee

The Criminal Law Revision Committee was established in 1959 by the then Home Secretary, Mr R.A. Butler, and was the equivalent, in the sphere of criminal law, of the Law Reform Committee. It, too, functioned as a part-time body that met at the request of the Home Secretary – on average, 10 times a year. In its time it did produce a number of controversial reports, some of which resulted in new statute law such as the Theft Act 1968 and later the Theft Act 1978, but the Committee is now defunct.

5   The Law Commission

The landmark event in the development of a systematic approach to law reform was undoubtedly the creation of the Law Commissions in 1965. Traditionally, particular government departments have always assumed responsibility for certain branches of the law. For example, the Department of Trade and Industry has long considered itself to be responsible for company and commercial law. The Home Office has considered itself responsible for criminal law and for aspects of the criminal justice system. However, these huge government departments were usually too preoccupied with new government legislative initiatives and had little time to devote to reform of the existing law. The case for a permanent, full-time statutory law reform body was made convincingly in a book entitled *Law Reform NOW*, edited by Gerald Gardiner QC and Andrew Martin, which appeared in 1963. In retrospect, the 1960s was an era during which there was a widespread desire for a break with the past and a desire for innovation. The book was largely a response to what the authors perceived as inaction on the part of government to the pressing need for law reform. The proposal put forward by Gerald Gardiner QC and Andrew Martin was inspired by the work of the New York Law Revision Commission which had been established in the 1930s and which was doing important work. In 1964, Gerald Gardiner became Lord Chancellor in Harold Wilson's first Labour government and it is reported that he agreed to accept the post only on condition that the incoming government would establish a Law Commission for the UK. In due course the government published a White Paper entitled *Proposals for English and Scottish Law Commissions* which subsequently resulted in the enactment of the Law Commissions Act 1965.

6   The statutory remit of the Law Commission

The Law Commissions Act 1965 s. 3(1) states:

> It shall be the duty of each of the Commissions to take and keep under review all the law with which they are respectively concerned with a view to its systematic development and reform, including in particular the codification of such law, the elimination of anomalies, the repeal of obsolete and unnecessary enactments, the reduction of the number of separate enactments and generally the simplification and modernisation of the law, and for that purpose
> (a) to receive and consider any proposals for the reform of the law which may be made or referred to them;
> (b) to prepare and submit to the Minister from time to time programmes for the examination of different branches of the law with a view to reform, including recommendations as to the agency (whether the Commission or another body) by which any such examination should be carried out;

(c) to undertake, pursuant to any such recommendations approved by the Minister, the examination of particular branches of the law and the formulation, by means of draft Bills or otherwise, of proposals for reform therein;

(d) to prepare from time to time at the request of the Minister comprehensive programmes of consolidation and statute law revision, and to undertake the preparation of draft Bills pursuant to any such programme approved by the Minister;

(e) to provide advice and information to government departments and other authorities or bodies concerned at the instance of the Government with proposals for the reform or amendment of any branch of the law;

(f) to obtain such information as to the legal systems of other countries as appears to the Commissioners likely to facilitate the performance of any of their functions.

The Commission has the statutory right to put forward proposals for law reform which it does in the form of programmes. However, these proposals must be approved beforehand. Thus, the government of the day can effectively exercise a veto on any proposal, although it has done so on only a few occasions since 1965. To date, the Lord Chancellor has laid eight of its programmes for law reform before Parliament, in 1965, 1968, 1973, 1989 (two programmes), 1995, 1999 and 2001. The inclusion of an item in a programme does not guarantee that the reform proposals can be successfully carried through and, in any event, the programmes have not been slavishly adhered to in the past by the Commissioners. The published programmes have really been declarations of intent.

7 Personnel of the Law Commission

Each Law Commission (one for Scotland and one for England and Wales) consists of five Commissioners who are appointed by the Lord Chancellor for a period of five years initially. The chair has always been a High Court judge and there is usually one barrister and one solicitor together with two university academics. The personnel of the Law Commission for England and Wales currently comprises:

Sir Roger Toulson – Chairman
Judge Alan Wilkie QC
Stuart Bridge
Professor Hugh Beale
Professor Martin Partington

The chief executive, formerly known as the Secretary, is Steve Humphries. Professor Beale was re-appointed in November 2004, at the end of his five-year term, until June 2007 to see through to completion a number of projects in which he has been closely involved. The work of the Commissioners is supported by lawyers brought in from private practice, the public service and from academia, having been recruited through an interview process following public advertisement. Personnel are also seconded from the office of Parliamentary Counsel to assist with the drafting of Bills including the consolidation of existing legislation. In addition, it has been the practice of the Law Commission to recruit 12 or so highly qualified graduates for a year, every year. They work as full-time research assistants in the areas of common law, company and commercial law, criminal law, property and trust law, and statute law revision. Although employment has been offered initially for a year, there is the possibility of an extension to a maximum of two years.

Following the review conducted by John Halliday CB, the Department of Constitutional Affairs has published a consultation document which floats the idea of the Chairperson being someone other than a High Court Judge and the appointment of additional part-time Commissioners. The outcome of this consultation will be referred to on the companion website to this textbook in due course.

8 Methods of working

At any particular point in time the Commission is likely to be engaged on between 20 and 30 law reform projects. A project normally commences with a study of the particular area of law in order to identify defects and anomalies. The Commission then consults extensively by issuing one of its consultation papers (working papers) which describes the present law and its shortcomings and sets out possible reforms. According to the Seventh Programme, its initial proposals are based on:

> ... thorough and thoughtful research and analysis of case law, legislation, academic and other writing, law reports and other relevant sources of information both in the United Kingdom and overseas. Its preliminary research seeks to establish the existing legal position here and, if appropriate, in comparable jurisdictions. It highlights the current shortcomings and considers ways in which other jurisdictions have tried to overcome them and ways in which commentators have suggested overcoming them. Most usually we look to the law of other jurisdictions and we often gain considerable assistance from the reports of their Law Commissions.

The consultation process itself covers a wide range of people and groups. It includes the legal and other professions, members of special-interest groups, business people, consumer groups, central and local government and even the public at large. Its consultation documents are available on the Internet and it is making use of its website to elicit opinions from interested members of the public via e-mail. Where a Commission proposal is likely to have significant social or economic repercussions, the Commission may use empirical research of a social scientific nature to underpin its work. For example, during 1999, research was commissioned in the areas of non-financial loss in personal injury cases which subsequently formed the basis of the Commission's report. It was this report that led to the landmark ruling by the Court of Appeal in *Heil* v *Rankin*

[2000] that has resulted in an increase in the level of awards. The Law Commission also maintains links with university departments engaged in socio-legal research.

At the end of the consultation stage, the Law Commission prepares a report for the Lord Chancellor which sets out its final conclusions and recommendations. At the end of this report there will usually be a draft Bill that can be introduced into Parliament if the Commission is proposing a change in the law. The subsequent fate of the Bill is largely in the hands of the government of the day. Its chances of being enacted depend on whether the government accepts the recommendations contained in the report. Although the Bill can be introduced in the House of Lords by the Lord Chancellor, it cannot be put forward for the Royal Assent unless the government is prepared to allow time for its stages in the House of Commons. Although a private member could, in theory, champion a Law Commission Bill, it is not very likely to happen. Generally, private members usually prefer to support measures that are more newsworthy than law reform measures and, in any event, the government would still have to make space in the crowded parliamentary timetable.

9 Quinquennial review

In the past, much was made of the fact that the Law Commission was established as an independent statutory body. By way of contrast, the report on the quinquennial review of the Law Commission carried out by John Halliday describes the Law Commission as a 'non-departmental public body'. The report states that the government requires that all non-departmental public bodies must submit to regular reviews to ensure that their functions meet current requirements. The report, however, provides a very valuable insight into the work of the Law Commission. The terms of reference governing the review were stated as follows:

> To conduct a Review of the Law Commission and the effectiveness of the wider process of law reform to which it contributes (from the setting of priorities for projects to be referred to the Commission to the acceptance and implementation of its recommendations by Government departments).

The review was thorough going in that it scrutinised the following aspects of the Law Commission:

- its organisational structure and possible alternatives;
- its finances, in particular its cost-effectiveness and sources of funding;
- its working methods, including consultation;
- its capacity to analyze the economic and other impacts of its proposals;
- the potential for it to do more to work in partnership with other organisations;
- how its work is regarded by its stakeholders (including Government departments, judiciary, legal profession, academics); and
- the views of the Chair, Commissioners and staff.

The language used in the report, as might be expected, is unashamedly managerial. It states that the ultimate 'customer' for the 'product' or benefits of law reform is the public. It also states that the government is, and should continue to be, the 'primary customer' for the product of the Law Commission's work as the government is responsible for decisions and actions on its proposals. Although the report refers to the independence of the Law Commission in para. 2.13, it takes the view that a close working relationship between government and the Commission does not threaten the Commission's freedom to reach its own conclusions after considering all the available evidence, opinions and arguments. Such a unitary, managerial view is unlikely to command universal assent among those who have followed the work of the Law Commission over the years. Nevertheless, having considered the Law Commission's working methods, the report concluded that:

> A greater focus on the delivery of benefits should be facilitated and/or brought about by:
> - discussing, collectively (where appropriate), the issues and proposals concerning ways of working, and sharing best practice between teams;
> - using periodic sample checks to ensure that best practice is being followed (where appropriate) and is proving useful in delivering benefits;
> - adopting imaginative and flexible methods of consultation, that 'reach out' to target audiences;
> - doing more to ensure that as much information as possible is brought to bear on Regulatory Impact Assessments;
> - ensuring all concerned are clear and confident in handling the Commission's 'after sales' service.

In assessing the performance of the Law Commission over time, performance data is presented in Annex 4. This discloses that between 1985 and 2001 the Law Commission published 91 law reform reports. Paragraphs 7–9 indicate:

> 7. As things stand, law reform projects fall into two categories: programme items and ministerial references. Of the 91 law reform reports published in since 1985, 80 originated from items [identified by the Commission] and 11 originated from ministerial references. Although this shows that the work undertaken by the Commission has traditionally been dominated by items, a comparison of the Seventh and Eighth Programmes of Law Reform suggests that the balance may be shifting: the Seventh Programme comprised of 10 items and 4 references whilst the Eighth includes 5 items and 8 references. This could suggest that the Law Commission is beginning to work more closely with Government on programme setting.
> 8. During the period following the previous quinquennial review (1998 to 2001), 18 law reform reports were published. This is consistent with the number of reports published over previous four-year periods. For example, 20 reports were published between 1994–97 while 17 were published between 1990–93. Similarly, the balance of published reports originating from references and items is not markedly different in the period following the QQR from the overall trend since 1985. (17 reports originated from items and 1 from a reference). This is likely to

change in the near future, now that more of the Commission's projects are references.

9.   Since 1985, 73% of published reports (66 out of 91) have been accompanied by draft legislation. In the period following the last review this figure fell to 61 % (11 out of 18). This drop could be due to the cuts in the number of Parliamentary Counsel on secondment to the Commission at any one time. Alternatively, conscious decisions may have been made not to produce draft legislation with certain reports. However, given the small data sample involved, it would be premature to read these figures as an indicator of a long-term change.

On the matter of implementation, the report contains some interesting data in paras 20–26 as follows:

20   ... The average time taken from the publication to the implementation of a report (between 1985 and 2001) was 3 years and 1 month. (Although when those reports that are currently under consideration or awaiting implementation are finally implemented in, say, a year or two years' time, this average figure will become higher.)

21.   It is also important to acknowledge that there are huge variations between the time taken to implement different reports. For example, the report on Money Transfers (Law Com No 243 – 1996) was published and enacted in the same year. At the other end of the spectrum the report on Polygamous Marriages (Law Com No 146 – 1985) was not implemented until 10 years after its publication.

22.   The time taken between publication and implementation can be broken down into two stages:
      i. time taken from publication to decision by a Government Department to accept/reject the report;
      ii. time taken from decision to implementation.

23.   The analysis in the following section of the paper is based on 14 implemented reports (where the acceptance date is recorded in Hansard) and a further 10 reports that have been accepted, in principle, by Government Departments and which are awaiting implementation.

24.   It took an average of 2 years from the publication of these reports to the time at which the decision was made to accept their recommendations. This varied in individual cases from less than 12 months to 4 years. Of those reports that have been enacted, there was an average lag of 1 year and 7 months between acceptance and implementation.

25.   From this sample, 9 reports were published since the last review. 7 of the 9 reports were accepted within a year of publication, which is a positive message.

26.   However, an assessment of all of the reports currently under consideration paints a bleaker picture. On average the reports were published 4 years and 7 months ago. This raises the question of whether those reports, which have been under consideration for some time, are ever likely to be accepted and implemented.

The report advocates that more extensive use should be made by the Law Commission of the managerial technique of 'project management' and, in its conclusions on implementation, it states in paras 17–18:

7.17 Departments and the Law Commission should keep closely in touch with developing changes in Parliamentary procedure, and Governmental management of the legislative programme, with the aim of exploiting any opportunities that arise.

7.18 The search for new procedural devices to facilitate Parliamentary scrutiny of Law Commission Bills needs to be invigorated. Without new procedures there will be continuing risks of worthwhile law reforms, including codified criminal law, not being implemented, or being implemented only after long delays. A special scrutiny procedure, on the analogy of that created for the Tax Law Rewrite project could perhaps be used to determine which Bills were suitable for the special procedure. The Lord Chancellor's Department should work on identifying and appraising procedural options, in consultation with all interested parties in Government and Parliament. This will require high levels of skill, leadership and application; in order to deliver the project the Department will need to give it a high priority.

It should be noted that since the previous quinquennial review that was carried out in 1997, a Ministerial Review Committee has been established within what is now the Department of Constitutional Affairs. The Halliday report advises that this committee should retain its advisory status. In addition, the report suggests that this Committee could work with the Law Commision by:

• monitoring delivery of the existing programme of work;
• commenting on proposed new programmes;
• monitoring Departmental action on completed reports, and final outcomes.

In all, John Halliday's report contains 42 recommendations. In its 38th Annual Report of June 2004 the Law Commission refers to the quinquennial review but, without identifying specific recommendations, states:

Of the 42 recommendations 16 have been implemented in full. Work is in progress on a further 15 and it is planned to commence later in the year on all the others, bar 3 which it has been agreed are for the longer term.

10   The long view of the Law Commission

Although the Halliday report contains constructive criticisms, there is no doubt that the Law Commission has accomplished a great deal since 1965. In the early years, a good deal of its time was taken up with identifying obsolete and unnecessary statutes relating to a bygone era that should have been repealed, although it did find time for other projects. Since 1965, the Law Commission has been responsible for some important pieces of legislation, including the Unfair Contract Terms Act 1977, the Children Act 1989, the Computer Misuse Act 1990, the Criminal Justice and Public Order Act 1994, the Family Law Act 1996, the Land Registration Act 1997, the Trustee Delegation Act 1999, the Contracts

(Rights of Third Parties) Act 1999, the Trustee Act 2000 and reports dealing with aspects of the criminal law and procedure have been incorporated into the Criminal Justice Act 2003. It seems to have abandoned its early ambitious plans for a complete codification of the law of contract and the law relating to landlord and tenant but it will have made a major contribution to the codification of the criminal law. Not all Law Commission reports have required new legislation. In 1999 a report was commissioned in the areas of non-pecuniary loss in personal injury cases. The Law Commission's subsequent report influenced the landmark ruling of the Court of Appeal in *Heil* v *Rankin* [2000] above that resulted in an increase in the levels of award.

11 The eighth programme and beyond

The eighth programme which appeared in 2001 includes projects carried over from the seventh programme. This was in the nature of a rolling programme. The eighth was intended to cover the period until December 2003 and so a ninth programme can be expected before too long. When it appears, the substance of the programme will be covered on the companion website for this book. The plan of work for the eighth programme, set out in para. 1.8, includes the re-working of the legislation on unfair contract terms which is being overseen by Professor Hugh Beale. In December 2004 the Law Commission published its *Final Report on Compulsory Purchase Procedure*. Since the government has accepted the need for the reform of compulsory purchase of land, new legislation reforming the process may be expected especially if London's Olympic bid is successful. A major project for 2004 will be the codification of the general principles of the criminal law which is essential for a complete codification of the criminal law. It is notable that all targets for 2004/05 come with the disclaimer 'all targets are subject to availability of resources'. The budget has increased in recent years. In 2000 the cost of the Commission was £3.3m but the budget for 2003/04 in the Annual Report was stated to be £5.12m.

Summary

The changes in the economy and national life of the UK have been greater in the last two hundred years than at any period in the nation's history. The law and its administration have struggled at times to keep up with the changing needs of the economy and society. Indeed, there were periods when the law and its administration lagged far behind until Parliament finally intervened to make much needed changes. Prior to the 1960s governments never thought it necessary to permanently institutionalise the process of law reform. Royal Commissions could always be established to investigate and report with recommendations on how to deal with any acutely pressing problem of the time, particularly those dealing with legal administration. The conventional wisdom was that technical problems relating to the rules themselves could be referred to part-time committees of experts who could meet and discuss them. Then, after due deliberation, their reports might be taken up by a government minister, if time permitted. The 1960s was a decade of fundamental reappraisal for the UK. Its role in the world had changed forever and it was necessary to clear away the accretions of the past and embrace the future which would entail modernising parts of its legal fabric. The creation of the Law Commissions in 1965 was a recognition of the need to institutionalise permanently a process of law reform that would ensure that law could evolve more in step with the changing needs of the economy and society on the basis of careful research. Since its inception the Law Commission for England and Wales has done valuable work and will continue to do important work in the future. The recent quinquennial review by John Halliday, although it had many constructive criticisms and recommendations, concluded that there was no reason to disturb the present functions of the Commission, nor its methods of working.

WWW   PROGRESS TEST

For suggested answers to the tests below, go to the companion website at www.pearsoned.co.uk/wheeler

1 Now that virtually all obsolete statutes have been repealed, is there still a need for ongoing law reform? If so, why; if not, why not?
2 What contribution do Royal Commissions make to the process of law reform and what are the advantages and disadvantages of using this type of agency as a means of achieving law reform?
3 How does the Law Commission differ from the other law reform agencies that preceded it and are these differences important?
4 Is the Law Commission truly independent? Does this matter?
5 Are the Commissioners appointed for far too short a period?
6 Are there any problems facing the Law Commission that have to be addressed in the near future?
7 Is there a case for increasing the size of the Law Commission's budget further?
8 Has the Law Commission really made a significant contribution to law reform in England and Wales?

FURTHER READING

■ Books

Zander, M. (2004) *The Law Making Process* (Cambridge: Cambridge University Press, chapter 9).

Zellick, G. (ed.) (1988) *The Law Commission and Law Reform* (London: Sweet & Maxwell).

USEFUL WEBSITES

Useful up-to-date information on the work of the Law Commission can be obtained from its website at www.lawcom.gov.uk and copies of its eighth programme can be downloaded from this source or from www.open.gov.uk/lawcomm.

The quinquennial review of the Law Commission by John Halliday CB published by the Department of Constitutional Affairs is available from its website at www.dca.gov.uk.

Part 4

Appendices

Evolution of the common law and equity

1 Development of common law

Most of the existing precedents, particularly in contract and tort, of contemporary relevance are developments and refinements of much earlier precedents. These precedents were created in the old courts of common law (Court of Exchequer, Court of Common Pleas and Court of King's/Queen's Bench) and subsequently the Court of Chancery. The common law courts developed gradually as offshoots from what legal historians refer to as the *curia regis* (the King's Council). This was both an administrative and a judicial body that was very much centred upon the personage of the medieval kings. Apart from the monarch, the full *curia regis* included the great feudal landowners, important clerics (archbishops and cardinals) and the great officers of state such as the Lord Chancellor. The full *curia regis* was convened infrequently because of its sheer size. A much smaller body, comprising the monarch and important officers of state such as the King's Justiciar (chief justice), Lord Treasurer and Lord Chancellor, conducted most of the business of the Council and moved around the country as the king did. The Court of Exchequer was the first of the common law courts to be established as a separate institution from the *curia regis*. It became permanently located at Westminster. It was followed many years later by the Court of Common Pleas, which started as something of an 'experiment' in the last quarter of the twelfth century and became a permanent institution after the signing of Magna Carta in 1215 by King John, who was the youngest son of Henry II. Henry II (1154–89) had re-established a basic system of criminal justice to end the chaos into which the kingdom had descended during a feudal civil war. He was also responsible for the creation of a system of civil law that was gradually synthesised from royal decrees (assizes) and partly from the rulings of travelling judicial commissioners that he appointed. The Norman and (later) Plantagenet kings (1066–1216) appointed these judicial commissioners to visit the various counties of England and collect taxes, punish wrongdoing and hear disputes mainly involving land or rights associated with land ownership. In addition to applying those laws created by royal decree, they sought to develop a system of civil law that could be applied 'nationwide' by adopting some of the older Saxon laws and by adapting reasonable local customs. The system of law that they synthesised came to be known as 'the common law' because it was intended to be 'common' to the entire kingdom. This medieval criminal and civil law is described in the first legal 'text book' to be written, which is attributed to Sir Ranulf Glanville, chief justicier to King Henry II. It was, however, the foundation of the courts of common law as separate institutions, distinct from the King's Council, in the twelfth and thirteenth centuries that proved to be the catalyst in the subsequent growth of the common law. These courts gradually evolved their own procedural rules. In the early years there was a degree of flexibility in the way in which they operated but this flexibility gradually disappeared as procedure became highly formalised and all important.

Two developments were particularly important in the subsequent growth of the common law. Henry II revived the use of juries in civil cases. Thus the ascertainment of issues of fact became the sole province of a jury of laypersons. The second development was that the presiding judge(s) assumed sole responsibility for deciding issues of legal principle that could not be entrusted to poorly educated laypersons. It was these judges who decided the legal principles that would be applied after the lawyers had pleaded their clients' cases. In time, these judges were creating the early precedents embedded in the case law of the early common law.

The ability to litigate civil claims in the courts of common law depended upon the claimant being able to obtain a writ. Legal historians disagree over whether it was the King's Justiciar in the scriptorium (office) of the Court of Exchequer or the Chancellor in the Chancery Office who was responsible for issuing the originating writs. In the Middle Ages (c. 1100–1350) a writ was quite specific in that there was a special type of writ for every form of recognised claim that could be brought before the common law courts at Westminster. It seems likely that prior to 1258 the King's Justiciar or the Chancellor and his assistants in the Chancery devised new forms of writ as and when the need arose with a view to permitting the litigation of those claims that were thought to have merit. Although it is impossible to be certain, it is unlikely that novel writs would have been drawn up without there being consultation with the King's Council. As a result there came to be a number of specific writs – for example, one for trespass, one for debt (for the recovery of money), another for covenant (breach of an undertaking given in the form of a special document known as a deed), detinue (for the recovery of chattels) and so on. The practice of devising novel writs was stopped in 1258 under the Provisions of Oxford when rebel barons forced King Henry III to agree to the changes they wished to see in the constitutional order (creation of Parliament) and legal system. The ban on the creation of novel writs was partially relaxed in the fourteenth century but, apart from the expansion of the scope of the writ of trespass, there was a general reluctance to create entirely new forms of writ. The judges did not wish to be responsible for a massive increase in the volume of civil litigation with which the courts would be unable to cope.

2   Deficiencies in common law

Although there were a large number of different writs in use by the end of the thirteenth century, there were still many claims that could not be litigated in the common law courts. Some comprised facts that could not be realistically framed within one of the existing writs. For example, it was not possible to litigate a simple breach of an oral contract because it could not be framed within the *writ of covenant*. In those days all agreements of a contractual nature had to be made in the form of a deed to be enforceable at common law. A deed had to be in writing and had to be signed and sealed by the party or parties to be bound. The execution of the deed also had to be witnessed by a third party who could be summoned to court to give testimony if the need arose. Very few defences were allowed to a person being sued who had placed his seal on a document. This in itself could sometimes give rise to injustice. If someone borrowed money and the contract of loan was in the form of a deed, the borrower might sometimes be forced to pay twice in the event that he failed to ensure that the deed was cancelled when he made his repayment. The common law courts would not enforce the arrangement that is today known as a 'trust' whereby land (and other property) was transferred to 'trustees' with instructions that it was to be held for the enjoyment of one or more beneficiaries. The legal title to the land had to be transferred to the trustees and the common law courts would not interfere with their legal rights of ownership. Nor would they allow someone who had mortgaged his land as security for a debt to recover it if he had not paid off the debt with interest by the agreed date. This was often a source of grievance because the value of the land might be worth many times the amount borrowed and this would give the lender a substantial profit if the borrower was not able to repay the debt on the agreed date.

For the above and other reasons, legal historians have described the early common law system as excessively formalised and inflexible. At that time, procedural rules governing the presentation of the case were often as important as what the lawyers refer to as the substantive rules – the actual rules constituting a particular body of law. Of course, this meant that legitimate claims and grievances were lost on mere technical points of procedure. Although an unlawfully dispossessed landowner could recover his land, the only other remedy available in the common law courts took the form 'damages' and this was often an inadequate remedy, especially when an owner of land wanted to prevent a nuisance or an ongoing trespass to his land. The common law defence of 'duress' to the enforcement of a contractual undertaking was limited to actual or threatened physical violence and did not recognise other more subtle forms of pressure which came to be recognised in the development of equity.

3 The development of equity

The defects and deficiencies in the common law system gradually gave rise to a parallel and, for the most part, complementary system of rules and remedies devised in the court of the Lord High Chancellor, the king's chief minister. These rules and remedies became known as 'equity' after the classical Greek notion of fairness as rendered in the Latin *aequitas*. In the fourteenth century, litigants who were unable to obtain justice by pursuing their claims in one of the common law courts would petition the King in Council. They might do this because there was no suitable writ which covered their particular grievance or because they were seeking a remedy other than damages. The medieval kings, who were all Christian, had sworn by their coronation oath to see that justice was done to their subjects and most took this duty very seriously. When the sheer volume of petitions from dissatisfied litigants became so great, the task of hearing them was delegated by the king to his chief minister, the Lord High Chancellor. The first Chancellors were bishops of the medieval church, the most famous being Thomas Becket (who was later canonised as St Thomas following his assassination by four knights of the court of Henry II). These Christian clerics were more concerned with upright behaviour and Christian morality rather than legal niceties. They would deal with these petitions in a far less formal way than the judges who sat in the common law courts and endeavoured to arrive at a fair and just solution on a case by case basis.

Lawsuits in the Chancellor's court were commenced by issuing bills of complaint which, from 1422, were drafted in English, not Latin. The Chancellor could compel the attendance of the defendant by writ of subpoena, in default of which the defendant would face the prospect of a large fine. Witnesses could be summoned in the same way. In comparison with the courts of common law, the process of 'pleading' by which the complainant stated his case was quite informal. There were no formal pleadings as there were in the courts of common law. Evidence could be taken from the parties and from witnesses on oath and the Chancellor could punish those who gave perjured evidence. The fact that there was no jury meant that the Chancellor decided questions of fact as well as the outcome and remedy, if any, to be granted. Prior to 1473 the Chancellor, having heard both sides, would issue a decree in the name of the king in his role as the king's chief minister. The decree would identify the party he deemed to be in the right according to his notions of right reason and good conscience. In the last quarter of the fifteenth century, Chancellors were issuing decrees in their own name instead of in the name of the king but presumably with his approval. It seems reasonable to date the Court of Chancery as a separate court in its own right from this time. The justice dispensed in the Court of Chancery at this time was very much discretionary and no attempt was made until after 1530 to achieve greater consistency of outcomes by rationalising the principles on which it operated and by establishing criteria for the granting of the special remedies available. Nevertheless, the Court of Chancery was used extensively by litigants and eventually became located in the same building, Westminster Hall, as the courts of common law.

Cardinal Wolsey, who was Chancellor from 1515 to 1529, succeeded in alienating the legal profession and judiciary. They objected to his public disdain for legal learning and to his high-handedness in re-opening claims after they had been settled in the common law courts. Henry VIII was reluctant to confer the office of Chancellor on another cleric after Wolsey died and it is likely that he desired to place administration of equity and procedures of the Court of Chancery on a more satisfactory basis and thereby placate the common law judges. He appointed Thomas More, a prominent intellectual who was a trained lawyer and the son of a common law judge, as Chancellor in 1529. Although More was prepared to issue injunctions to prevent persons from exercising their common law rights when he considered this necessary to prevent injustices being done, he was also concerned that equity should be developed as a rational set of principles to operate alongside, and so complement, the existing common law system. Regrettably, More's Chancellorship was of rather short duration because he objected to Henry declaring himself head of the church. His reforming zeal in the Court of Chancery was not shared by all his successors, who were not of the same intellectual calibre. It was only from 1672 that it became a requirement for all subsequent Chancellors to be qualified common lawyers.

4 Common law and equity in conflict

Although equity as a system of rules and remedies had evolved to mitigate the rigidity, harshness and excessive technicality of the common law, tensions and ultimately conflict arose between the two systems towards the end of the Chancellorship of Lord Ellesmere (1596–1617). He encouraged disappointed litigants to pursue claims in the Court of Chancery after judgment had been given in one of the courts of common law. Moreover, he used the injunction as a means of preventing successful litigants from enforcing their common law rights where he considered this was unconscionable. As a result, a large backlog of claims built up in the Court of Chancery. When Sir Edward Coke was appointed Chief Justice of England in 1613 he challenged the Chancellor's (Lord Ellesmere's) right to re-open cases which had been adjudicated in the common law courts and his right to imprison people for not obeying an injunction when they were merely asserting their rights under common law. The imprisonment of successful litigants could be ended by obtaining a writ of *habeas corpus* from the Court of King's Bench, but this rivalry between the two systems became something of a public scandal. Matters came to a head in 1615 and the king, James I, decided to refer this conflict of jurisdictions to a small committee of his advisers presided over by Francis Bacon, a renowned scholar who was also the king's Attorney General. On the basis of the advice received, James I decreed that, whenever there should be a conflict between the principles and rules of equity and common law, equity should prevail over the common law. Thereafter the Court of Chancery and common law courts operated alongside each other in reasonable harmony.

Later Chancellors assumed responsibility for developing the principles of equity and equitable remedies that remain of contemporary relevance. They devised remedies that the beneficiary of a trust could enforce against trustees, such as account and indemnity. Trusts were not officially recognised by the common law courts. The analogy of the trust was then used to establish 'fiduciary duties' for persons such as agents (and, much later, company directors) who were placed in positions whereby others reposed special trust and confidence in them. They would be obliged to observe certain minimum standards of behaviour and failure to do so would result in claims being brought against them in the Court of Chancery. Another innovation of equity was the acknowledgement of a mortgagor's equity of redemption whereby a borrower could recover land given as security for a debt even though the actual date set for repayment had passed. Of course, additional interest would be payable by the borrower until the debt was finally repaid. Other remedies were developed such as the right to disclosure of documents prior to litigation. From 1557 onwards the decisions of the Court of Chancery were reported and subsequently published. Thus, over the centuries, equity gradually became a highly rationalised system of rules and principles in which the system and doctrine of precedent came to play an increasingly important role. Three Lord Chancellors in particular – Lord Nottingham (1673–82), Lord Hardwicke (1736–56) and Lord Eldon (180–27) – were instrumental in this process.

5   Nineteenth-century reforms

By the end of the eighteenth century the legal system that had evolved over many centuries was inadequate to respond to the new demands that would be made upon it arising from the social and economic upheavals to be set in train by the ongoing processes of industrialisation and urbanisation that historians refer to as the Industrial Revolution. The civil justice system was slow, inefficient and expensive. The defining feature of the system was the dual (and not always complementary) systems of common law and equity with their separate courts and procedures. It was often necessary for a litigant to commence two lawsuits simultaneously in respect of the same dispute. One would be commenced in the Court of Chancery for an equitable remedy whilst the other would be commenced in one of the courts of common law in order to claim damages. The reason for this was that before 1858 the Court of Chancery did not have the authority to award damages. In some instances a litigant's preferred remedy might be a decree of specific performance for the breach of a contract for the purchase of land or unique object. If this was refused in the Court of Chancery, it would then be necessary to consider the advisability of a second lawsuit in a court of common law to recover damages. The famous Victorian novelist Charles Dickens mercilessly exposed to a wider public the excessive delays associated with suits in the Court of Chancery in his novel *Bleak House* which revolves around the fictional case of *Jarndyce* v *Jarndyce*. Jeremy Bentham (1752–1832), the English philosopher and prolific writer, was also a barrister. He had long been well aware of the urgent need for reform of the law and legal system. Through his writings he influenced many prominent lawyers, intellectuals and politicians of his day regarding the necessity for a general overhaul of both the criminal and civil justice systems. Although Bentham's writings were highly influential among the intellectual elite of his day, it was really the great economic and social upheavals of the early nineteenth century, together with the needs of expanding commerce, that created the momentum for the reform of existing institutions of government including the law and its administration.

A number of reforms were made possible following the enactment of legislation to reform Parliament in 1832. The most important reform in the civil justice system was the Common Law Procedure Act 1854 which abolished all the old forms of action based on the ancient writs. The Court of Chancery was empowered to decide questions of common law, try issues of fact by jury and award damages where appropriate. The Chancery (Amendment) Act 1858 conferred on the Court of Chancery the discretion to award damages in substitution for, or in addition to, a decree of specific performance to enforce a contract. The courts of common law were permitted to grant injunctions and allow equitable defences to be pleaded. Far-reaching though these reforms were, they did not go far enough to satisfy members of the ruling elite. Thus the entire civil legal system was overhauled between 1873 and 1875 by the Supreme Court of Judicature Acts which abolished the old courts of common law and Court of Chancery. These were replaced by a new Supreme Court of Judicature comprising the High Court of Justice and the Court of Appeal. The Supreme Court of Judicature Act 1873 would have abolished the appellate jurisdiction of the House of Lords but, before the relevant provision came into effect, an incoming Conservative administration enacted the Appellate Jurisdiction Act 1876. This statute conferred on the House of Lords an appellate jurisdiction above that of the Court of Appeal. The administration of the rules of common law and equity were now combined within a single hierarchical court structure (see Figure 3.1 in Chapter 3) and the supremacy of equity was finally put on a statutory basis in the Supreme Court of Judicature Act 1873 s. 25(11) which stated:

> Generally in all matters not herein before particularly mentioned in which there is any conflict or variance between the rules of equity and the rules of common law with reference to the same matter, the rules of equity shall prevail.

This provision has since been re-enacted in the Supreme Court Act 1981 s. 49(1). In addition, the Supreme Court of Judicature Act 1875 Schedule 1 contained a new set of rules for the conduct of civil litigation.

6 Common law and equity – the 'modern' relationship

Equity continues to operate as a discretionary form of justice and equitable remedies are not available merely on demand. The 'maxims of equity' govern the exercise of the court's discretion, the particularly relevant ones being:

(a)   he who comes to equity must come with clean hands;
(b)   he who seeks equity must do equity; and
(c)   delay defeats equity.

The first requires that the claimant must not have behaved harshly or unreasonably towards the other party prior to bringing the action, whereas the second requires that the claimant will accept conscientiously any conditions imposed by the court in relation to the remedy sought as a condition of its being granted. The common law remedy of damages, on the other hand, is available as of right; once the claimant has proved his/her case there is no element of discretion. Common law and equity now operate together as a rationalised, coherent and interrelated system of case law embodied in precedents. This body of case law is still relied upon to resolve a wide variety of disputes that arise nowadays but equity still operates to mitigate the harshness of the common law as is evident from the recent Court of Appeal judgment in *Bank of Credit and Commerce (in liquidation)* v *Ali and others* [2000]. The background to this case was that the House of Lords had previously decided in another case that employees of the bank, which had been managed in a fraudulent manner, should be entitled to 'stigma damages' to compensate them for the difficulty experienced in obtaining alternative employment in the banking and finance sector when the bank collapsed. Approximately one year before the final collapse, in exchange for enhanced redundancy payments, a number of employees had signed a form of release in respect of any claims that they might have against the bank. The appellant contended that signing the release did not prevent him and others (who had also signed) from claiming the 'stigma damages'. Although their claim was rejected by the High Court, the Court of Appeal, exercising its equitable jurisdiction, allowed the appeal on the basis that the release that was signed at the time could not be used as a defence to a claim based on facts known to the bank but not known to, and concealed from, its employees who had signed the release.

7 Equitable remedies in modern litigation

The equitable remedies of injunction, specific performance, rectification and rescission developed in the old Court of Chancery are of importance in modern litigation. A prohibitory injunction is a court order forbidding a person to whom it is addressed from doing some act such as breaking a contract, although it is more usually granted in civil law to prevent someone committing a form of civil wrong known as a 'tort'. A mandatory injunction, on the other hand, requires the person to whom it is addressed to do a certain act such as to remove an impediment to a right of way over land or an obstruction to a right to light associated with the ownership of premises. An injunction is not only granted as a remedy at the end of legal proceedings. It can also be granted on an interim basis if there is a strong likelihood of loss being incurred before the case can be heard in court. This sometimes happens in industrial relations disputes. Injunctions may also take the form of 'freezing orders' to prevent the removal of assets from the jurisdiction of the court and 'search orders' enabling a claimant to enter premises and search for property.

Specific performance takes the form of a court order requiring a person to complete a contract that he/she has made. Decrees of specific performance are usually reserved for contracts for the sale of land but they may be granted where a contract has been made for the sale of some unique object and damages would not be an adequate remedy for the victim of the breach of contract.

Rectification may be sought where a document was executed under seal but it fails to embody accurately the terms of the agreement reached. The error can be corrected by order of the court. It is also possible for a court to order rectification to correct a mistake in a will. In *Wordingham* v *Royal Exchange Trust Co. Ltd* [1992] the court granted a husband rectification of his deceased wife's will under the Administration of Justice Act 1982 s. 20(l)(a) because the solicitor who drew up the will had omitted an essential clause.

Rescission is the formal cancellation of a contract by a court where the plaintiff has been induced to enter into it because of fraud or misrepresentation. Nevertheless, the remedy may be denied if the person requesting it delays in seeking it or if a third party acquires an interest in the subject matter in good faith having paid money to do so. It may also be denied if it is not possible to restore both parties to their former position.

8   Historical development of law reporting

Prior to 1863 law reporting was largely a private, uncoordinated activity although some reports of a very high standard were produced by members of the legal profession and judiciary, particularly those of Chief Justice Coke (pronounced Cook). Those studying the law of contract may need to read the ruling in *Pinnel's* case of 1602. A report of this case was published in a collection by Chief Justice Coke and it is still cited in all the standard student texts on the law of contract. Not all law reporting was of such a high standard and the law reports of Espinasse (1793–1807) are famed for their unreliability. Only in the late eighteenth century were particular barristers appointed to record the decisions of the superior courts, with some editorial assistance from the judiciary, but usually these reports were published under the name of the reporter. Most of these older cases are to be found in one of five collections:

The English Reports
The All England Law Reports Reprint series
The Revised Reports
The Law Journal Reports 1822–1949
The Law Times Reports (Old Series 1843–60) and (New Series 1859–1947).

The learning resource centres of most of the newer universities have the English Reports series and/or the All England Law Reports Reprint series where most of these old cases can be located. The volume numbers of the English Reports run from 1 to 176 and the name of a court and names of the original reports or reporter in smaller print appears on the spine. The entire series of the English Reports is now available on CD-ROMs, and it is possible to access the relevant reports very quickly (especially if the CD-ROMs have been networked) and print off copies for private use.

The All England Law Reports Reprint series is bound in dark blue buckram. This series covers a period from 1558 to 1935 and contains about five thousand cases. From 1843 the cases reprinted in this series are from reports that appeared originally in the Law Times Reports or Times Law Reports. The cases have been selected for reprint because they have been subsequently referred to in the All England Law Reports after 1935 and because they are mentioned in *Halsbury's Laws of England* (a type of legal encyclopaedia).

In 1863 the Council for Law Reporting for England and Wales was established and this body was formally incorporated in 1870 as the Incorporated Council for Law Reporting for England and Wales, whose stated aim remains:

> The preparation and publication in a convenient form, at a moderate price and under gratuitous professional control of Reports of judicial decisions of the superior and appellate courts of England.

The Incorporated Council receives no public funds but functions as a registered charity whose income is derived exclusively from publishing a set of reports that are referred to simply as The Law Reports.

9 The law reports

When the Incorporated Council for Law Reporting for England and Wales began publishing in 1866, it initially produced 11 separate series of reports, each covering a different superior court. These originally had calf leather bindings on the spines, with each volume embossed with the volume number and with the relevant year of Queen Victoria's reign. When the civil court structure was revamped in 1875, the number of separate series was reduced and it was reduced further after 1880.

The reports of appeals heard in the House of Lords and Privy Council respectively were published in separate volumes between 1866 and 1874. Thereafter a series officially entitled Appeal Cases commenced in 1875, which contains reports of appeals to both the House of Lords and Privy Council. The original bindings were in calf leather but it is likely that they will have been rebound since then in a light tan binding. Each of the early volumes covers two years of reports. The official citation given for reports from 1875 to 1890 is such that the year appears enclosed in round brackets followed by the volume number of the report in the series. After that, the abbreviation App Cas appears, followed by the page reference. An example would be the contract law case of *Adam* v *Newbigging* (1888) 13 App Cas 308. Only after 1891 did the year become part of the citation and it therefore appears in square brackets followed by the abbreviation AC and then the page number, for example *Baumwoll Manufacturers* v *Furness* [1893] AC 8.

Equity cases and Chancery Appeal cases appear first in a series dating from 1866 to 1875. Thereafter, the reports of the Chancery Division of the High Court appear as a separate series. The official citation has the year enclosed in round brackets, followed by the volume number of the report in the series. After that, comes the abbreviation Ch D followed by the page number. An example is provided by the contract law case of *Arnison* v *Smith* (1899) 41 Ch D 348. Only after 1891 did the year become part of the citation. It appears in square brackets followed by the abbreviation Ch and the page number, for example *Bonhote* v *Henderson* [1895] 1 Ch 742.

From 1866 to 1875, reports of the cases of the Court of Crown Cases Reserved and the Court of Queen's Bench were each reported in separate series, as were those of the Court of Common Pleas and the Court of Exchequer. These two latter series continued to be published separately until 1880, but after 1875 they were published as the reports of the Common Pleas Division and the Exchequer Division respectively. These may be in their original calf leather spine bindings but they have since been rebound in a material similar to those used for the Appeal Cases. The Incorporated Council has since reissued sets in light green bindings.

The Queen's Bench Division of the High Court was created in 1875. The series bearing this title appeared and for a time incorporated the reports of the Court for Crown Cases Reserved. From 1875 to 1890 the citations that the reader will have been given for the reports of the Queen's Bench Division at this time start with the year enclosed in round brackets followed by the volume number. After the abbreviation QBD comes the page number, for example *Canning* v *Farquhar* (1885) 16 QBD 722. As with the Appeal Cases and those of the Chancery Division, from 1891 the year became part of the citation and so it appears in square brackets thus: *Cullen* v *Knowles* [1898] 2 QB 380. The volumes in this series may be in their original calf leather spine bindings; alternatively they may have since been rebound using material similar to those used for the Appeal Cases but the series title will appear prominently on the spine.

From 1866 to 1875 there was a separate series of reports combining Admiralty with ecclesiastical cases and another series combining reports of probate and divorce cases. After 1875, with the reorganisation of the civil courts, these were all merged as the reports of the newly created Probate, Divorce and Admiralty Division of the High Court. From 1875 the citations for cases reported in this series commence with the year enclosed in round brackets, followed by the volume number. The abbreviation PD for Probate Division is followed by the page number. When the year in which the cases were reported became part of the official citation in 1891 it began to appear in square brackets followed by the abbreviation PD and the page number. Following a further reorganisation in 1972, the Probate, Divorce and Admiralty Division became the Family Division. The former series ended and a new series of Family Law Reports came into being. The citation that will be given for this series will have the year in square brackets, followed by the abbreviation FLR, followed by the page number.

A Practice Direction was issued by Lord Woolf in the Supreme Court of Judicature on 14 January 2002. Since 14 January 2002 a *unique* number has been assigned to all judgments given by the various divisions of the High Court in London: e.g. *Smith* v *Jones* [2002] EWHC 123 (Ch). The abbreviation in round brackets is *not* used when citing the paragraph number of a judgment in court. A similar system of citation is used by both Divisions of the Court of Appeal: e.g. *Arsenal Football Club Plc* v *Reed* [2003] EWCA Civ 696.

2 Human Rights Act 1998

Schedule 1
THE ARTICLES
PART 1
THE CONVENTION
RIGHTS AND FREEDOMS
ARTICLE 1*
ARTICLE 2
RIGHT TO LIFE

1 Everyone's right to life shall be protected by law. No one shall be deprived of his life intentionally save in the execution of a sentence of a court following his conviction of a crime for which this penalty is provided by law.
2 Deprivation of life shall not be regarded as inflicted in contravention of this Article when it results from the use of force which is no more than absolutely necessary:
   (a) in defence of any person from unlawful violence;
   (b) in order to effect a lawful arrest or to prevent the escape of a person lawfully detained;
   (c) in action lawfully taken for the purpose of quelling a riot or insurrection.

ARTICLE 3
PROHIBITION OF TORTURE

No one shall be subjected to torture or to inhuman or degrading treatment or punishment.

ARTICLE 4
PROHIBITION OF SLAVERY AND FORCED LABOUR

1 No one shall be held in slavery or servitude.
2 No one shall be required to perform forced or compulsory labour.
3 For the purpose of this Article the term 'forced or compulsory labour' shall not include:
   (a) any work required to be done in the ordinary course of detention imposed according to the provisions of Article 5 of this Convention or during conditional release from such detention;

*The UK government has complied with Article 1 by securing the enactment of the Human Rights Act 1998.

(b) any service of a military character or, in case of conscientious objectors in countries where they are recognised, service exacted instead of compulsory military service;

(c) any service exacted in case of an emergency or calamity threatening the life or well-being of the community;

(d) any work or service which forms part of normal civic obligations.

ARTICLE 5
RIGHT TO LIBERTY AND SECURITY

1 Everyone has the right to liberty and security of person. No one shall be deprived of his liberty save in the following cases and in accordance with a procedure prescribed by law:

(a) the lawful detention of a person after conviction by a competent court;

(b) the lawful arrest or detention of a person for non-compliance with the lawful order of a court or in order to secure the fulfilment of any obligation prescribed by law;

(c) the lawful arrest or detention of a person effected for the purpose of bringing him before the competent legal authority on reasonable suspicion of having committed an offence or when it is reasonably considered necessary to prevent his committing an offence or fleeing after having done so;

(d) the detention of a minor by lawful order for the purpose of educational supervision or his lawful detention for the purpose of bringing him before the competent legal authority;

(e) the lawful detention of persons for the prevention of the spreading of infectious diseases, of persons of unsound mind, alcoholics or drug addicts or vagrants;

(f) the lawful arrest or detention of a person to prevent his electing an unauthorised entry into the country or of a person against whom action is being taken with a view to deportation or extradition.

2 Everyone who is arrested shall be informed promptly, in a language which he understands, of the reasons for his arrest and of any charge against him.

3 Everyone arrested or detained in accordance with the provisions of paragraph 1 (c) of this Article shall be brought promptly before a judge or other officer authorised by law to exercise judicial power and shall be entitled to trial within a reasonable time or to release pending trial.

Release may be conditioned by guarantees to appear for trial.

4 Everyone who is deprived of his liberty by arrest or detention shall be entitled to take proceedings by which the lawfulness of his detention shall be decided speedily by a court and his release ordered if the detention is not lawful.

5 Everyone who has been the victim of arrest or detention in contravention of the provisions of this Article shall have an enforceable right to compensation.

ARTICLE 6
RIGHT TO A FAIR TRIAL

1 In the determination of his civil rights and obligations or of any criminal charge against him, everyone is entitled to a fair and public hearing within a reasonable time by an independent and impartial tribunal established by law. Judgment shall be pronounced publicly but the press and public may be excluded from all or part of the trial in the interest of morals, public order or national security in a democratic society, where the interests of juveniles or the protection of the private life of the parties so require, or to the extent strictly necessary in the opinion of the court in special circumstances where publicity would prejudice the interests of justice.

2 Everyone charged with a criminal offence shall be presumed innocent until proved guilty according to law.

3 Everyone charged with a criminal offence has the following minimum rights:

(a) to be informed promptly, in a language which he understands and in detail, of the nature and cause of the accusation against him;

(b) to have adequate time and facilities for the preparation of his defence;

(c) to defend himself in person or through legal assistance of his own choosing or, if he has not sufficient means to pay for legal assistance, to be given it free when the interests of justice so require;

(d) to examine or have examined witnesses against him and to obtain the attendance and examination of witnesses on his behalf under the same conditions as witnesses against him;

(e) to have the free assistance of an interpreter if he cannot understand or speak the language used in court.

ARTICLE 7
NO PUNISHMENT WITHOUT LAW

1 No one shall be held guilty of any criminal offence on account of any act or omission which did not constitute a criminal offence under national or international law at the time when it was committed. Nor shall a heavier penalty be imposed than the one that was applicable at the time the criminal offence was committed.

2 This Article shall not prejudice the trial and punishment of any person for any act or omission which, at the time when it was committed, was criminal according to the general principles of law recognised by civilised nations.

ARTICLE 8
RIGHT TO RESPECT FOR PRIVATE AND FAMILY LIFE

1 Everyone has the right to respect for his private and family life, his home and his correspondence.

2 There shall be no interference by a public authority with the exercise of this right except such as is in accordance with the law and is necessary in a democratic society in the interests of national security, public safety or the economic well-being of the country, for the prevention of disorder or crime, for the protection of health or morals, or for the protection of the rights and freedoms of others.

ARTICLE 9
FREEDOM OF THOUGHT, CONSCIENCE AND RELIGION

1 Everyone has the right to freedom of thought, conscience and religion; this right includes freedom to change his religion or belief and freedom either alone or in community with others and in public or private, to manifest his religion or belief, in worship, teaching, practice and observance.

2 Freedom to manifest one's religion or beliefs shall be subject only to such limitations as are prescribed by law and are necessary in a democratic society in the interests of public safety, for the protection of public order, health or morals, or for the protection of the rights and freedoms of others.

ARTICLE 10
FREEDOM OF EXPRESSION

1 Everyone has the right to freedom of expression. This right shall include freedom to hold opinions and to receive and impart information and ideas without interference by public authority and regardless of frontiers. This Article shall not prevent States from requiring the licensing of broadcasting, television or cinema enterprises.

2 The exercise of these freedoms, since it carries with it duties and responsibilities, may be subject to such formalities, conditions, restrictions or penalties as are prescribed by law and are necessary in a democratic society, in the interests of national security, territorial integrity or public safety, for the prevention of disorder or crime, for the protection of health or morals, for the protection of the reputation or rights of others, for preventing the disclosure of information received in confidence, or for maintaining the authority and impartiality of the judiciary.

ARTICLE 11
FREEDOM OF ASSEMBLY AND ASSOCIATION

1 Everyone has the right to freedom of peaceful assembly and to freedom of association with others, including the right to form and to join trade unions for the protection of his interests.

2 No restrictions shall be placed on the exercise of these rights other than such as are prescribed by law and are necessary in a democratic society in the interests of national security or public safety, for the prevention of disorder or crime, for the protection of health or morals or for the protection of the rights and freedoms of others. This Article shall not prevent the imposition of lawful restrictions on the exercise of these rights by members of the armed forces, of the police or of the administration of the State.

ARTICLE 12
RIGHT TO MARRY

Men and women of marriageable age have the right to marry and to found a family, according to the national laws governing the exercise of this right.

ARTICLE 13

[The Act did not include this Article because it provides an effective remedy.]

ARTICLE 14
PROHIBITION OF DISCRIMINATION

The enjoyment of the rights and freedoms set forth in this Convention shall be secured without discrimination on any ground such as sex, race, colour, language, religion, political or other opinion, national or social origin, association with a national minority, property, birth or other status.

ARTICLE 15

[The Act did not include this Article.]

ARTICLE 16
RESTRICTIONS ON POLITICAL ACTIVITY OF ALIENS

Nothing in Articles 10, 11 and 14 shall be regarded as preventing the High Contracting Parties from imposing restrictions on the political activity of aliens.

ARTICLE 17
PROHIBITION OF ABUSE OF RIGHTS

Nothing in this Convention may be interpreted as implying for any State, group or person any right to engage in any activity or perform any act aimed at the destruction of any of the rights and freedoms set forth herein or at their limitation to a greater extent than is provided for in the Convention.

ARTICLE 18
LIMITATION ON USE OF RESTRICTIONS ON RIGHTS

The restrictions permitted under this Convention to the said rights and freedoms shall not be applied for any purpose other than those for which they have been prescribed.

PART II
THE FIRST PROTOCOL
ARTICLE 1
PROTECTION OF PROPERTY

Every natural or legal person is entitled to the peaceful enjoyment of his possessions. No one shall be deprived of his possessions except in the public interest and subject to the conditions provided for by law and by the general principles of international law.

The preceding provisions shall not, however, in any way impair the right of a State to enforce such laws as it deems necessary to control the use of property in accordance with the general interest or to secure the payment of taxes or other contributions or penalties.

ARTICLE 2
RIGHT TO EDUCATION

No person shall be denied the right to education. In the exercise of any functions which it assumes in relation to education and to teaching, the State shall respect the right of parents to ensure such education and teaching in conformity with their own religious and philosophical convictions.

ARTICLE 3
RIGHT TO FREE ELECTIONS

The High Contracting Parties undertake to hold free elections at reasonable intervals by secret ballot, under conditions which will ensure the free expression of the opinion of the people in the choice of the legislature.

PART III
THE SIXTH PROTOCOL
ARTICLE 1
ABOLITION OF THE DEATH PENALTY

The death penalty shall be abolished. No one shall be condemned to such penalty or executed.

ARTICLE 2
DEATH PENALTY IN TIME OF WAR

A State may make provision in its law for the death penalty in respect of acts committed in time of war or of imminent threat of war; such penalty shall be applied only in the instances laid down in the law and in accordance with its provisions. The State shall communicate to the Secretary General of the Council of Europe the relevant provisions of that law.

3

Allocation questionnaire

Allocation questionnaire

To be completed by, or on behalf of,

_____

who is [1ˢᵗ][2ⁿᵈ][3ʳᵈ][   ][Claimant][Defendant]
[Part 20 claimant] in this claim

In the

_____

Claim No.	
Last date for filing with court office	

Please read the notes on page five before completing the questionnaire.

You should note the date by which it must be returned and the name of the court it should be returned to since this may be different from the court where the proceedings were issued.

If you have settled this claim (or if you settle it on a future date) and do not need to have it heard or tried, you must let the court know immediately.

Have you sent a copy of this completed form to the other party(ies)? ☐ Yes ☐ No

A Settlement

Do you wish there to be a one month stay to attempt to settle the claim, either by informal discussion or by alternative dispute resolution? ☐ Yes ☐ No

B Location of trial

Is there any reason why your claim needs to be heard at a particular court? ☐ Yes ☐ No

If Yes, say which court and why?

C Pre-action protocols

If an approved pre-action protocol applies to this claim, complete **Part 1** only. If not, complete **Part 2** only. If you answer 'No' to the question in either Part 1 or 2, please explain the reasons why on a separate sheet and attach it to this questionnaire.

Part 1

please say which protocol

The* _____ protocol applies to this claim.

Have you complied with it? ☐ Yes ☐ No

Part 2

No pre-action protocol applies to this claim.

Have you exchanged information and/or documents (evidence) with the other party in order to assist in settling the claim? ☐ Yes ☐ No

D Case management information

What amount of the claim is in dispute?   £ _____

Applications

Have you made any application(s) in this claim?   ☐ Yes   ☐ No

If Yes, what for?   _____   For hearing on _____
(e.g. summary judgment,
add another party)

Witnesses

So far as you know at this stage, what witnesses of fact do you intend to call at the trial or final hearing including, if appropriate, yourself?

Witness name	Witness to which facts

Experts

Do you wish to use expert evidence at the trial or final hearing?   ☐ Yes   ☐ No

Have you already copied any experts' report(s) to the   ☐ None yet   ☐ Yes   ☐ No
other party(ies)?   obtained

Do you consider the case suitable for a single joint expert in any field?   ☐ Yes   ☐ No

Please list any single joint experts you propose to use and any other experts you wish to rely on. Identify single joint experts with the initials 'SJ' after their name(s).

Expert's name	Field of expertise (eg. orthopaedic surgeon, surveyor, engineer)

Do you want your expert(s) to give evidence orally at the trial or final hearing?   ☐ Yes   ☐ No

If Yes, give the reasons why you think oral evidence is necessary:

continue over ➡

Track

Which track do you consider is most suitable for your claim? Tick one box
☐ small claims track   ☐ fast track   ☐ multi-track

If you have indicated a track which would not be the normal track for the claim, please give brief reasons for your choice

E Trial or final hearing

How long do you estimate the trial or final hearing will take?
_____ days _____ hours _____ minutes

Are there any days when you, an expert or an essential witness will not be able to attend court for the trial or final hearing?   ☐ Yes ☐ No

If Yes, please give details

Name	Dates not available

F Proposed directions *(Parties should agree directions wherever possible)*

Have you attached a list of the directions you think appropriate for the management of the claim?   ☐ Yes ☐ No

If Yes, have they been agreed with the other party(ies)?   ☐ Yes ☐ No

G Costs

*Do **not** complete this section if you have suggested your case is suitable for the small claims track **or** you have suggested one of the other tracks and you do not have a solicitor acting for you.*

What is your estimate of your costs incurred to date?   £

What do you estimate your overall costs are likely to be?   £

In substantial cases these questions should be answered in compliance with CPR Part 43

H   Other information

Have you attached documents to this questionnaire?   ☐ Yes   ☐ No

Have you sent these documents to the other party(ies)?   ☐ Yes   ☐ No

If Yes, when did they receive them?

Do you intend to make any applications in the immediate future?   ☐ Yes   ☐ No

If Yes, what for?

In the space below, set out any other information you consider will help the judge to manage the claim.

Signed   Date

[Counsel][Solicitor][for the][[1ˢᵗ][2ⁿᵈ][3ʳᵈ][   ]
[Claimant][Defendant][Part 20 claimant]

Please enter your firm's name, reference number and full postal address including (if appropriate) details of DX, fax or e-mail

		if applicable
	fax no.	
	DX no.	
Tel. no. Postcode	e-mail	
Your reference no.		

4

Source: © Crown copyright

Index